Middle School Today

Middle School Today

Current Best Practices for Adolescent Learners

Holly Henderson Pinter, PhD

Kim K. Winter, PhD

Kayleigh Kassel, MAEd

ROWMAN & LITTLEFIELD
Lanham • Boulder • New York • London

Rowman & Littlefield
Bloomsbury Publishing Inc, 1385 Broadway, New York, NY 10018, USA.
Bloomsbury Publishing Plc, 50 Bedford Square, London, WC1B 3DP, UK
Bloomsbury Publishing Ireland, 29 Earlsfort Terrace, Dublin 2, D02 AY28, Ireland
www.rowman.com

Copyright © 2025 by Holly Henderson Pinter, Kim K. Winter, and Kayleigh Kassel

All rights reserved. No part of this publication may be: i) reproduced or transmitted in any form, electronic or mechanical, including photocopying, recording or by means of any information storage or retrieval system without prior permission in writing from the publishers; or ii) used or reproduced in any way for the training, development or operation of artificial intelligence (AI) technologies, including generative AI technologies. The rights holders expressly reserve this publication from the text and data mining exception as per Article 4(3) of the Digital Single Market Directive (EU) 2019/790.

British Library Cataloguing in Publication Information available

Library of Congress Cataloging-in-Publication Data
Names: Pinter, Holly Henderson, author. | Winter, Kim K., author. | Kassel, Kayleigh, author.
Title: Middle school today : current best practices for adolescent learners / Holly Henderson Pinter, Kim K. Winter, Kayleigh Kassel.
Description: Lanham, Maryland : Rowman & Littlefield, 2025. | Includes bibliographical references and index.
Identifiers: LCCN 2024041370 (print) | LCCN 2024041371 (ebook) | ISBN 9781538198384 (cloth) | ISBN 9781538198391 (paperback) | ISBN 9781538198407 (ebook)
Subjects: LCSH: Middle school education—United States. | Middle school teaching—United States.
Classification: LCC LB1623.5 .P56 2025 (print) | LCC LB1623.5 (ebook) | DDC 372.2360973—dc23/eng/20241211
LC record available at https://lccn.loc.gov/2024041370
LC ebook record available at https://lccn.loc.gov/2024041371

For product safety related questions contact productsafety@bloomsbury.com.

∞™ The paper used in this publication meets the minimum requirements of American National Standard for Information Sciences—Permanence of Paper for Printed Library Materials, ANSI/NISO Z39.48-1992.

Dedication
To all our students, who have been our best teachers

Contents

Online Resources		xv
Acknowledgments		xvii
1	Introduction to Middle Level Teaching and a Theory of Learning: Setting the Foundation for Middle Level Education	1
	Attributes of an Effective Middle School	2
	A Theory of Learning	3
	Implications for Education	7
	How to Use This Book	10
	Teacher Educators	11
	Teacher Candidates	11
	Practicing Teachers	12
	Meet the Authors	12
	Contributing Authors	14
	Meet the Teachers	15
	Meet the Students	17
	References	19
2	Introduction to Early Adolescent Development	21
	Developmental Issues in Early Adolescence	21
	Promise, Not Problems	22
	The Concept of Development	22
	Individual Differences	22
	Cultural Differences	23
	Domains of Development	23
	Cohort Differences	23
	Physical-Psychological Connections	23

	Developmental Themes in Early Adolescence	24
	Theme 1: Thinking about Possibilities	25
	Possibility Generating	25
	Deductive or Scientific Reasoning	26
	Decision-Making	26
	Theory of Mind	27
	Summary: Possibilities and the Building of Knowledge Bases	27
	Theme 2: Early Adolescents Are Active Explorers	28
	Curiosity: Exploring the Physical and Intellectual Environment	28
	Focused Exploration: Interests	29
	Exploring the Self: Identity Statuses	29
	Exploring the Self: Self-Assessments	30
	Theme 3: Early Adolescents Make Connections	31
	Parents	31
	Peer Influences	33
	Theme 4: Thriving Depends on Adolescent-Environment Fit	34
	Conclusion	36
	References	38
3	**The Physical Self**	**41**
	Defining Adolescence	41
	Physical Development	42
	The Adolescent Brain	47
	Connecting Physical Self to Social Self	48
	Risky Behaviors	48
	Suicide	49
	Anxiety and Depression	50
	Sex	51
	Tobacco and Drugs	52
	Interdependence: Physical, Social, and Cognitive Attributes of Adolescents	55
	Suggested Readings	56
	References	56
4	**The Academic Self**	**59**
	Executive Function	60
	Emotional Outbursts	62
	Susceptibility to Peer Pressure	63
	Lack of Empathy	63
	Self-Regulation and Self-Directed Learning	64
	Developing Academic Identity in the Classroom	66
	Interventions for Executive Functioning and Self-Regulation	68
	Cade and Olivia's Interventions and Toolkits	71
	Suggested Readings and Resources	73
	References	74
5	**The Social Self: Developing Identity**	**75**
	Introduction to Social Identity	75
	Defining Identity	76
	Factors Contributing to Social Identity	77

Identity and Peer Relationships	78
Cultural, Ethnic, and Racial Identity	80
Microaggressions	83
Sexual and Gender Identity	84
Supporting Identity Development in Our Classrooms	89
Resources for Supporting Identity Development	90
Advisory Programs	91
Supporting LGBTQIA+ students	91
Supporting Cultural-, Ethnic-, and Racial-Identity Development	94
Conclusion	95
References	98

6 Creating Inclusive Environments: Supporting Diverse Populations — 99

Setting the Stage for Inclusive Learning Environments	99
Universal Design for Learning	100
Special-Education and Related Services in Middle School	101
Laws Governing Special-Education Services	101
Practices Supporting Effective Specially Designed Instruction in Middle School	103
Co-Teaching	103
Planning for Specially Designed Instruction Implementation	108
Parallel Teaching in Kayleigh's ELA Class	109
Team Teaching in Holly's Math Class	109
Station Teaching in Holly's Math Class	110
Alternative Teaching in Kayleigh's English Language Arts Class	111
One Teach, One Assist in Kayleigh's English Language Arts Class	111
One Teach, One Observe	112
Making Co-Teaching Work	112
Multitiered Systems of Support	114
References	119

7 Social and Emotional Learning — 121

Basics of Social-Emotional Learning	121
Adverse Childhood Experiences and Trauma	122
Social-Emotional Learning	124
Considerations for Supporting Students' Social and Emotional Learning	127
Trauma-Informed Social-Emotional-Learning Practices	127
Assessing the Situation	128
Safe Spaces	129
Mindfulness	129
Advisory Programs	131
Building Resilience	132
Resilience	132
Suggested Readings	135
References	135

8 Culturally Sustaining Pedagogy and Supporting Multilingual Learners — 137

Context for Culturally Sustaining Pedagogy	137

Defining Culturally Relevant, Responsive, and Sustaining Pedagogy	138
Culturally Responsive Teaching	140
Competency 1: Reflect on One's Cultural Lens	141
Competency 2: Recognize and Redress Bias in the System	141
Competency 3: Draw on Students' Culture to Shape Curriculum and Instruction	141
Competency 4: Bring Real-World Issues into the Classroom	142
Competency 5: Model High Expectations for All Students	142
Competency 6: Promote Respect for Student Differences	142
Competency 7: Collaborate with Families and the Local Community	142
Competency 8: Communicate in Linguistically and Culturally Responsive Ways	142
Across the Subject Areas	143
Social Studies	143
English Language Arts	144
Science	144
Mathematics	145
Standards in Practice	145
Social Studies	146
English Language Arts	147
Science	149
Mathematics	150
Connections in Other Subjects	152
Literature and Culturally Responsive Teaching	153
Individuals with Disabilities	153
Mental Health and Body Image	154
Social Injustice	154
Refugees	154
Japanese Internment Camps	154
LGBTQIA+	155
Strategies for Supporting English Learners	155
Encourage Authentic Talk	158
Develop Strong Language	159
Use Strong Discussion Prompts	159
Links to Standards, Other Resources, and Reading Recommendations	161
References	162
9 Middle School Curriculum and Pedagogy	**165**
Middle Grades Curriculum	165
Yearly Planning and Unit Planning	167
Lesson Planning	173
Three Stages of Backward Design	174
Learning Outcomes and Objectives	175
Instructional Objectives	175
Types of Objectives	176
Tips for Writing Objectives	176

	Instructional Models and Strategies	180
	Direct Instruction	180
	Indirect Instruction	181
	Experiential Learning	182
	Specific Instructional Strategies	182
	Discourse Practices	184
	Bloom's Taxonomy	184
	Webb's Depth of Knowledge	185
	Questioning Strategies	186
	Suggested Readings and Resources	191
	References	191
10	Differentiating Instruction for All Learners	193
	Basics of Differentiation	193
	What Differentiation Is . . . and Isn't	195
	Students: The Who of Differentiation	196
	Readiness	196
	Student Interest	197
	Learning Profile	198
	The What and the How of Differentiation	199
	Content	199
	Process	199
	Product	199
	Strategies for Differentiation	200
	Flexible Grouping	202
	Center or Station Teaching	202
	Learning Contracts, Choice Boards, and Menus	203
	Compacting	206
	Tiered Assignments	207
	Varied Questions	209
	Role-Audience-Format-Topic Assignments	209
	Literature Circles	210
	Journaling	212
	Conclusion	214
	Suggested Readings	215
	AMLE Reading Resources	215
	References	215
11	Assessment	217
	Connecting Assessment and Instruction	217
	The Era of Assessment and Accountability	217
	Varied and Ongoing Assessments	218
	Diagnostic or Preassessment	219
	Formative Assessment	219
	Summative Assessment	222
	Rubrics and Grades	224
	Grades	225

	Standards-Based Grading	226
	Rubrics	227
	Designing and Implementing Effective Rubrics	228
	Suggested Readings	230
	References	231
12	Literacy across the Disciplines	233
	Reading Comprehension	233
	Models of Reading	234
	The Simple View of Reading	234
	Scarborough's Reading Rope	235
	The Active View of Reading	236
	The Four-Part Processing Model	236
	Ehri's Phases of Word Reading	237
	Structured Literacy	238
	Writing Rope	238
	How the Models Work Together	239
	Strategy Instruction	240
	Reading Connections	240
	Literacy within the Disciplines	241
	What Is Disciplinary Literacy?	241
	Why Is Disciplinary Literacy Important?	242
	Speaking, Listening, and Language Connections	245
	Literacy in Multiple Languages	245
	Promoting Comprehension through Read-Alouds, Shared Readings, Close Reading, and Think-Alouds	246
	Read-Alouds	246
	Shared Reading	246
	Close Reading	247
	Think-Alouds	247
	Evidence-Based Practices	248
	Prompting Connections to Prior Knowledge	248
	Drawing Attention to Meaning	249
	Prompting for Effortful Thinking	251
	Using Examples and Nonexamples	252
	Questioning during Instruction and Strategies That Prompt Thinking	254
	Reading Strategies That Incorporate Questioning	261
	Vocabulary Development across the Curriculum	262
	Explicit Vocabulary Instruction	264
	Vocabulary Instruction in Action	265
	Use of Graphic Organizers	267
	Making and Taking Notes across the Curriculum	271
	Final Thoughts	273
	References	275

13	Classroom Dynamics:	279
	Strategies for Effective Discipline and Classroom Management	279
	Classroom Management Basics	279
	Culturally Responsive Discipline Practices	280
	Equity	282
	Systems	283
	Data	283
	Outcomes	283
	Practices	283
	Positive Behavioral Interventions and Supports Incentives	285
	Restorative-Discipline Practices	285
	Creating Classroom Communities: Relationships, Rules, and Routines	288
	Relationships	288
	Rules about Rules	290
	Routines and Procedures	291
	Silent Signal	294
	Teacher Presence and Persona	295
	Verbal Communication	297
	Physical Space	298
	Consistency	299
	Communicating with Families	300
	Climate of Safety	300
	Addressing Big Behaviors	300
	Practical Applications	301
	Scenario 1	303
	The Situation	303
	What Happened	303
	Reflection	304
	Scenario 2	304
	The Context	305
	What Happened	305
	Reflection	306
	Scenario 3	307
	Context	307
	What Happened	307
	Reflection	307
	School Codes of Conduct	308
	General Discipline Philosophy	308
	Resources and Recommended Readings	318
	Websites	318
	References	318
14	Philosophy and History of Middle Level Schools	321
	A Brief History	321
	Growth and Rationale of the Middle School	322
	Alexander's The Emergent Middle School (1968)	322

xiv CONTENTS

Carnegie Corporation's Turning Points: Preparing American Youth
for the 21st Century (1989) ... 324
The Contemporary Middle School ... 330
  Accomplishments and Developments Attributed to the Middle
  School Movement ... 330
  Working within Constraints ... 332
    School Lacks Interdisciplinary Teams or Does Not Use
    Interdisciplinary/Integrative Teaching ... 332
    School Lacks an Advisory Program ... 333
    School Lacks an Exploratory Program ... 333
    School Schedule Is Not Flexible ... 333
References ... 335

15 Middle School Organization and Structure ... 337
  Structures of Time ... 337
    Examples of School Schedules ... 340
  Structures of Place and Practice ... 342
    Grouping Students for Instruction ... 342
    Regrouping for Instruction ... 343
      Looping ... 343
    Interdisciplinary Teaming ... 344
      Inclusion and Co-Teaching ... 344
      Multitiered Systems of Supports and Positive Behavioral
      Interventions and Supports ... 345
  Structures of Curriculum and Programming ... 346
    Advisory Programs ... 346
    Exploratory and Enrichment Programs ... 348
    School and Community Partnerships in Support of Learning ... 349
  Structures of Health and Safety ... 349
    Comprehensive School Health Plan ... 350
    Restorative Discipline ... 351
    Mental-Health and Wellness Programs ... 351
    School Safety and Crisis Planning ... 352
  References ... 354

Glossary ... 357

Index ... 377

Online Resources

Visit https://textbooks.rowman.com/middle-school-today

Instructor Resources: Ancillary materials for the book include a series of PowerPoint presentations, each aligned with a specific chapter. These presentations are designed to enhance the learning experience by integrating key activities from the book, such as the "Pause and Reflect" prompts, which encourage students to think critically about the content, and the "Practice It" opportunities, which offer hands-on exercises to reinforce learning. Additionally, each presentation highlights key vocabulary terms, ensuring that students grasp essential concepts.

Student Resources: Electronic flashcards are available open-access to help students master key vocabulary in the text.

Acknowledgments

We are grateful to many people who have supported and guided us on this journey. First, we would like to thank our spouses and families for their endless support throughout this process from conception to fruition. Second, to Dr. Bruce Henderson and Dr. Tammy Barron, we express our gratitude for your lending, as contributing authors, your expertise in your specific areas of psychology and special education. Because of your contributions we feel confident that we are sharing best practices in these areas of expertise. We are also immensely thankful to our contributing teachers and students. To our teachers, thank you for sharing your resources, your ideas, and your stories with us. To our student contributors, we thank you for being open and honest with us as we asked you about your personal journeys through adolescence. Finally, to Heidi Buchanan and Dr. Dave Strahan, thank you for your reading of and feedback about our work.

CHAPTER 1

Introduction to Middle Level Teaching and a Theory of Learning

SETTING THE FOUNDATION FOR MIDDLE LEVEL EDUCATION

So, you want to teach. Welcome. We are so glad you are here.

And you want to teach **middle school**? Hooray! This amazing group of quirky, brilliant, funny, sometimes smelly, often emotionally charged human beings is simply at the best age to teach.

How do we know? Our team has worked with adolescent learners between eight and thirty years, and we are simply convinced they are the most fun.

But let's be honest for a moment. How many of us, when we say we want to teach—and middle school at that—are then bombarded with a litany of commentaries about how brave or crazy (or even more crass terms) we are to want to work with early adolescents? Let's start with a reflection exercise.

Grab a sheet of paper. On the left-hand side, write down all negative statements someone has said to you about becoming a teacher. Then put a star by the ones specific to teaching middle school. On the right-hand side, write down the positive statements you've been told about becoming a teacher. Star the ones specific to teaching middle school. Now compare the two lists—what do you notice? With any luck, some of you have long lists on the right-hand side with many stars filled with encouragement to join this noble profession. If we were betting, though, we would expect that your left-hand list is much longer and filled with stars about how hard, horrible, terrifying, underpaid, undervalued, etc. teaching middle school may be.

But you've arrived here to this book, which means you have at least a bourgeoning belief in the marvelousness of **adolescents**. We hope that, by the time you have finished reading this text, you feel you have a solid foundation in teaching adolescents well. We will do this by exploring the characteristics of adolescents and their identity development as well as by providing a myriad of teaching strategies for you, as a practicing teacher, to use every day to support diverse populations of adolescents in their academic and social-emotional learning pathways.

CHAPTER 1

Attributes of an Effective Middle School

Before we get started, we need to set some important context for the uniqueness of the middle school setting and acknowledge that working with adolescents doesn't occur only within a grade-six to grade-eight middle school setting. Some teachers may end up (or are currently) teaching in intermediate schools that specialize in some combination of fourth, fifth, and sixth grades. Or some of you may land in high schools that have big differences in size, structure, and organization but are still serving an adolescent population. To frame our work, it is important to know that we advocate for the *middle school concept*, which is built on the foundations of the **Association for Middle Level Education (AMLE)**, an organization driven by the goal of supporting educators in nurturing adolescents to their full potential. To do so, AMLE advocates for education that is responsive, challenging, empowering, equitable, and engaging, as defined in Figure 1.1.

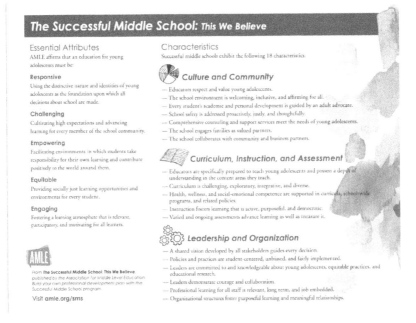

Figure 1.1 Characteristics of Successful Middle Schools as Defined by AMLE. Reprinted with Permission AMLE (2021)

The word *responsive*, or the phrase ***developmentally responsive***, will be used consistently throughout this text. As this term may seem ambiguous, let's operationally define it based on the longstanding literature base of middle level education. First used by Lipsitz (1984) in the publication *Successful Schools for Young Adolescents*, developmentally responsive schools were to carry out these things:

1) reduce the size of the focus groups;

2) personalize the quality of adult-student relationships;

3) give ample room for peer groups to flourish;

4) acknowledge diverse areas of competence;

5) involve students in participatory activities;

6) emphasize self-exploration and physical activity; and

7) encompass all these in a clearly defined, structured environment.

(Lipsitz, 1984, p. 199)

Ellerbrock (2016) explains the difficulties in defining *developmentally responsive*, as the term is broad and inclusive and was often misinterpreted as the middle school movement gained momentum. At its core, *developmental responsiveness* is applied to all decisions (policy, school organization, curriculum, instruction, and assessment) based on how they support the developmental characteristics of young adolescents.

Challenging curriculum does not mean curriculum that is difficult or more abstract. This attribute instead pertains to ensuring that all students have access and opportunity to learning outcomes and that teachers have high expectations of *all* students. **Empowerment** speaks to the role of adolescents in their own education. We think about building students' capacity for voice, choice, and responsibility in their education pathway. **Equitable** refers in this context to how schools and teachers ensure that *all* students have opportunities to reach their potential through socially just and inclusive environments. This includes how teachers differentiate learning for all students. All humans, especially adolescents, learn better when they are **engaged**. Motivation is a critical element of keeping students engaged as active learners in middle school and ensuring that their natural curiosities are sparked and that they have opportunities to explore.

AMLE also articulates eighteen characteristics of successful middle schools, clustered into three categories: Curriculum Instruction and Assessment; Leadership and Organization; and Culture and Community. We will reference these attributes and the sixteen characteristics throughout the text to make connections between theory and practical applications. These characteristics reinforce our ideas about adolescent development and instructional practices that will help teachers teach adolescents well. For an alignment of these attributes to the content in this book, see the chart in Figure 1.2.

A Theory of Learning

As we explore the fundamentals of teaching middle school, it is important to have a theory of learning that specifically relates to adolescents' unique development. Here we rely on expertise from cognitive psychology to help us situate adolescent learners within the frame of what we know about adolescent development. Educators often say that all learners learn in different ways, and this is somewhat misleading. The fundamental learning process is the same across learners of all ages. Simply, learning occurs when a student pays attention to new material and then connects that new material to what the student already has in memory.

CHAPTER 1

	Chapters	1. Adolescent Development	2. The Physical Self	3. The Academic Self	4. The Social Self	5. Creating Inclusive Environments	6. Social Emotional Learning	7. Culturally Sustaining Pedagogy	8. Middle School Curriculum	9. Middle School Pedagogy	10. Differentiating Instruction	11. Assessment in Middle School	12. Literacy Across the Disciplines	13. Classroom Dynamics	14. Philosophy & History of Middle Level Schools	15. Middle School Organization & Structure
Characteristics of Successful Middle Schools	***Curriculum, Instruction, and Assessment***															
	Value Young Adolescents	+	+	+	+	+	+		+	+	+	+	+	+	+	+
	Active Learning	+	+	+	+				+	+	+	+				+
	Challenging Curriculum	+	+	+				+	+	+	+	+	+	+	+	+
	Multiple Learning Approaches	+	+	+	+	+		+	+	+	+	+	+		+	+
	Varied Assessments	+		+		+			+	+	+	+				+
	Leadership and Organization															
	Shared Vision	+	+	+	+	+	+	+	+	+	+	+	+		+	+	+
	Committed Leaders														+	+	+
	Courageous and Collaborative Leaders														+	+	+
	Professional Development	+				+									+	+	+
	Organizational Structures	+	+	+	+	+	+	+	+						+		+
	Culture and Community															
	School Environment	+	+	+	+	+	+		+	+	+	+	+	+	+	+
	Adult Advocate	+	+	+	+		+								+		+
	Guidance Services	+		+	+		+								+		+
	Health and Wellness	+	+	+	+	+	+	+							+		
	Family Involvement					+		+							+		
	Community and Business					+		+									

Figure 1.2 Alignment of AMLE Characteristics with Book Chapters. Created by authors

Figure 1.3 Model of the Mind. Deans for Impact (2023). Science of Learning: Teacher Action Overview - Prompting for Effortful Thinking. Retrieved from: https://www.deansforimpact.org/files/assets/lbsdanchorcharteft.pdf Willingham, D. T. (2021). Why don't students like school?: A cognitive scientist answers questions about how the mind works and what it means for the classroom. John Wiley & Sons.

What does differ from learner to learner is what each attends and make connections to in addition to; in addition, learners' existing memories differ. We will briefly describe the attention, connection, and storage steps involved in learning and then discuss their implications, considering a recent review of the learning process (Dehaene, 2021). The basic parameters of the learning process have been known for a long time, and many detailed treatments are readily available for teachers (Bransford et al., 2005; Willingham, 2021). Figure 1.3 highlights the key components of attention and memory that are working parts of learners making connections and serves as our model of the mind (Deans for Impact, 2023; Willingham, 2021).

Attention is the indispensable first step. What is not attended to is not learned. There are two forms of attention. **Orienting attention** is an automatic response to novelty, uncertainty, incongruity, or surprise in the environment. Starting in infancy, we pay attention to things that are new and different. Attending to what is new is important to survival not only because new things might be dangerous but also because they often contain useful information. Clever teachers have always taken advantage of this feature of learners by keeping the physical and intellectual features of their classrooms and teaching full of variety and challenge.

The second form of attention is **selective attention**. Learners can choose goal-directed aspects of the environment. While orienting attention does not change with age (what is novel, unpredictable, or surprising does), selective attention becomes increasingly under the learner's control. Learners get better at searching systematically, attending to the more informative aspects of their environments, avoiding distractions, and getting faster and more exhaustive in their searches. By adolescence, most learners have become skilled at focusing their attention. However, none of us is immune to the distractions of a novel, changing environment. Take for example the power the Internet has on our attentional resources.

We make connections with **working memory**. Whatever is attended to enters consciousness or working memory, however fleetingly. In many ways, working memory is the main arena of learning. This is where learners either make connections between the new and old or do not; if they do not, the new material is not retained. There are many different strategies for processing information in working memory. They include using imagery (particularly powerful with younger learners), categorizing or classifying (using already available knowledge to sort new information), associating (making sensory or conceptual links between new and old information), or, most generally, elaborative rehearsal. Repetition or rehearsal (often called maintenance rehearsal) is not usually a good learning strategy (though see the section on procedural knowledge, below). Elaborative rehearsal is repetition with multiple connections of many different sensory and conceptual types, leading to understanding new material in the flexible ways it can be used across time and contexts. When we use elaborative forms of rehearsal, when we engage in strategic remembering, we are engaging in "deep processing" or "**deep learning**." When new information has been understood through many forms of meaningful elaboration, it is difficult to forget. When information is not understood, it is almost impossible to remember, no matter how often it is repeated. Effective teachers are those who have found many ways to get their students to understand and use new information.

An important feature of working memory is that it has a limited capacity. For over one hundred fifty years, psychologists have known that we can hold only five to nine units of information in consciousness at any one time. That span is even smaller in younger learners, and recent research suggests that it may be closer to three to five units for most kinds of information, even in adults. Short-term memory can be extended by **chunking** smaller units into larger units or by externalizing storage (e.g., writing things down, using graphics, etc.). However, the best way to overcome the limits of working memory is to store information in some form of longer-term memory as quickly as possible.

To retain what we learn, we use types of **long-term memory** storage. So, not everything we pay attention to is retained. It is when we engage working memory and, most of all, when we make meaning and understand that we store information in memory, that we learn. At least four forms of memory can be distinguished. However, as we examine each of these, it is important to note that, in most learning, these different forms of memory work together.

Semantic memory is propositional knowledge. Much of what is learned in school is stored in semantic memory. Semantic memory holds our propositional knowledge, facts, concepts, and strategies. It is our dictionary, our encyclopedia, our life instruction manuals. It is semantic memory that is central to math class, English class, social science and history classes, science class, and so much more. Storing semantic memories requires making strategic effort in working memory. Here is where deep processing leads to retention. The more connections and elaborations, the better.

Procedural memory involves skills. Whereas semantic memory is about what we know, procedural memory is about how to do things. It informs motor skills, which are needed for actions ranging from taking steps to hitting a ball, to playing a musical instrument. Procedural knowledge is involved in music class, physical-education class, woodworking, and many other domains requiring physical skills. Whereas repetition per se is not helpful in making semantic memories, practice, especially when it involves focused attention and feedback, is important in forming procedural memories.

Episodic memory involves experience. Some of what we experience has a strong sensory quality. We see, hear, smell, or taste it in our memories (for human beings, smells can be particularly sharp in memory). We remember particular events, often vividly. The knowledge of what a birthday is, for example, is in your semantic memory. The experience of your twenty-first birthday is in episodic memory. Particularly vivid episodic memories are called "flashbulb" memories. Episodic memories just happen; they are not the result of strategic practice. However, episodic memories may enhance the formation of semantic memories. That is one reason that hands-on experiences often lead to better learning.

Autobiographical memory refers to memories that are particularly tied to personal life experiences and identities. They are memories of events, like general episodic memories, but they are events we have experienced. An extreme version of autobiographical memory occurs in rare individuals who remember everything that has happened to them, by date and day of the week (these individuals do not have especially accurate semantic memories—for complete recall, the events must have happened to them).

Metacognition refers to a special type of semantic memory concerning what the mind knows about itself. This "cognition about cognition" or "metacognition" includes our knowledge of how to use strategies effectively, our awareness of whether we know something or not (metamemory or the feeling of knowing), and what we know about circumstances that enhance our memories.

Pause and Reflect: Think about your educational experiences. Can you make any connections between these concepts and specific instances in your own learning experiences in school?

Implications for Education

In the conclusion of his recent book *How We Learn: Why Brains Learn Better than any Machine . . . For Now*, Stanislas Dehaene provides thirteen "take-home messages to optimize children's potential," based on the principles of learning outlined above. Not all Dehaene's messages apply to the early adolescent, but most of them do. Here we share each of those messages, clustered by some commonalities, along with examples from our current classrooms, highlighting that these messages are not found just in isolation but also in everyday practice.

> ***Do not underestimate children.*** Dehaene focuses on the sometimes-unexpected cognitive capabilities of infants and young children. But this message applies to adolescents. Adolescents have often been seen as deficient in their thinking abilities: incapable of abstract thinking; too egocentric to think reasonably. Obviously, early adolescents do not know everything. Yet they are fully able, when motivated and supported to do so, to think clearly and logically.
>
> ***Rescind the idea that all children are different.*** Yes, students have different interests and different amounts and types of previously known information. Yet the learning process, as outlined above, is the same across learners. The key to teaching that leads to learning is engaging attention and working memory. All students should be challenged to broaden their interests and go beyond their current ways of thinking.
>
> ***Keep children active, curious, engaged, and autonomous.*** This message goes with the one about attention. Passivity is the enemy of learning. Some educators and psychologists think curiosity declines with age. Curiosity does not decline in environments where it is encouraged. Fear, coercion, and extrinsic rewards are not good motivators in school. Curiosity is.
>
> ***Pay attention to attention.*** The lesson for educators here is simple. Information that is not attended to is not learned. Teachers need to enlist novelty, incongruity, complexity, and surprise to elicit curiosity. They need to use appropriate degrees of intellectual challenge as a classroom norm.
>
> ***Help students deepen their thinking.*** Dehaene emphasizes what we know about the effectiveness of deep processing, the engagement of multiple meaningful connections in working memory. The notion here is that it is important to challenge students with novel, complex ideas. The challenge for teachers of adolescents is that, as the student's knowledge and thinking deepens, it is increasingly difficult for the teacher to keep up. The availability of extra-classroom resources and independent study is becoming increasingly important.

Connections in Practice: In Holly's Math 1 class, when we are exploring quadratic functions through the exploration of visual patterns, students are finding multiple ways to represent the patterns with expressions and graphs. Students began to express a natural curiosity and to wonder what would happen to the graphs as we changed parts of the expression. After asking them to think about some hypotheses, we made some adjustments to one expression and analyzed how the graph changed. They then started making predictions—some that worked, others that did not—and, through exploring their own wonderings, they were able to come to some important mathematical generalizations that frankly were not even part of the lesson aims for that day. As students began to ask more in-depth questions, we encouraged them to spend some more time investigating and deepening their thinking by writing in their weekly journal for that week.

> *Take advantage of the brains' sensitive periods.* Dehaene sees early childhood as a particular period of openness to learning, especially learning of second languages. We think all developmental periods are sensitive. Many of Dehaene's other messages reflect this fact.
>
> *Enrich the environment.* It is striking how barren the typical middle school or high school classroom is (college classrooms are often worse). Laboratories are an exception. Even more important than the physical environment is an intellectual environment rich in novel and complex ideas and opportunities to discuss and debate. Not all schools have the resources of a large city or a national park. But all schools have untapped resources in their environment. A teacher who gets students excited by having them read about what is under a rock ought to take them outside to turn over a rock.
>
> *Make every school day enjoyable.* In the right environments, early adolescents are natural learners. We are not talking about cheap thrills. Learners need novelty, but the best form of novelty is intellectual challenge. Like all of us, early adolescents want to be competent. When we successfully deal with a challenge, we are happy.

Connections in Practice: In Amanda Clapp's science class, students begin every day with a riddle that connects to the world. This is not only a great classroom warm-up to help provide routine and structure as a classroom management strategy. It also invokes curiosity, conversation, and critical-thinking skills, and the students enjoy the often-comical challenges. When Clapp's class does citizen science, the students are motivated by something bigger than themselves; they are sharing their observations with adult researchers from all over the world. Even though our campus is not set up to be child-friendly, we can still take part in projects that record changes in the world around us. Some projects that Clapp has joined with her students are phenology studies through the USA national phenology network (USAnpn org). The students pick a tree, or a tree per student, and record data weekly about how it changes. The kids pay attention to leaves and flowers, recording growth and falling on the website. The site generates beautiful graphs that reflect leafing out and flowering across North America, so the kids can see their part affecting the national data set. They got a grant for a few bird feeders and joined Cornell Lab of Ornithology's Feederwatch project. They record the birds at our feeders in the winter, and they share swag and updates. Both these projects are virtually free and require minimal outdoor space. Getting excited about the world around us leads to more civic action.

Encourage efforts. We live in a bottom-line world. School should be a special haven where the learning process should be at least as important as outcomes. What Dweck calls an incremental or growth mindset is important for students and teachers to hold. Errors should be seen as informative feedback, not as indicators of failure that discourage effort.

Accept and correct mistakes. Dehaene argues that errors should not be punished but should be corrected quickly. Feedback is essential for early adolescents but does not need to be quick in all instances. Adolescents need time to think about their errors and self-correct. They must also learn to tolerate ambiguity, a ubiquitous feature of all adult learning environments. Some delay of feedback can help learners find their own solutions.

Connections in Practice: Productive struggle means students are being challenged and working to meet their goals. In writing, students are often frustrated about how to get started, how to transition between topics, and how to provide enough information. We put scaffolds in place to support students in these areas, as needed, but create natural pauses for teachers to give encouraging feedback. For example, to write their own myth, students used a graphic organizer with boxes to add their characters, the lesson the myth would teach, and the setting. We immediately praised students for naming and writing the morals of their myth but the key to this praise was that it was concrete and specific. Before editing students' work, we praised them for their ideas and allowed them to write without structure. Then we taught a specific skill and started to make changes.

Set clear learning objectives. Dehaene is not calling for a narrow technology of measurable behavioral goals. He is arguing that students should know what is expected of them. This is important for adolescents because it fits with their growing metacognitive knowledge about how to learn and their goal-directed motivation.

Practice regularly. This message applies more to procedural knowledge than to semantic knowledge. Repetition enhances skills more than it does conceptual learning. The latter may occur in one or a few repetitions when it involves meaningful learning and understanding, most clearly in the classic "aha!" learning situations. It is difficult to forget what you truly understand (and impossible to remember what you do not understand). With frequent focused practice with feedback, skills also can be learned to a degree that they are difficult to forget (although one of us recently discovered that you can, indeed, forget the fine points of riding a bike).

Connections in Practice: These messages are simple but vital in practice. Learning in school shouldn't be a mystery to students. In our school, we ensure that teachers have a mechanism for students to know what is expected of them and what they should be learning. This happens in several ways, such as using "I can" statements, agendas being displayed, teachers introducing learning targets at the beginning of each lesson, or even having students keep track of their progress on standards with self-reflection structures. Students need opportunities to apply skills through practice. Keep in mind that doesn't necessarily mean loads of homework or worksheets.

> ***Let students sleep.*** Dehaene is more convinced than we are that research shows that sleep consolidates typical learning. However, the research showing that a lack of sleep affects attention is quite convincing. Most adolescents do not get enough sleep, and many believe it does not matter. They are wrong.

Connections in Practice: While teachers genuinely have little control over this message, as sleep happens more in the home than at school, it is crucial to be aware that sleep quality and quantity do affect how students function during their school day. For one, we must recognize that sleep-deprived adolescents will not be bringing their *A* game, so to speak, when it comes to participating, thinking, and making connections in a lesson. Second, while it sometimes feels offensive when a student falls asleep in class, it will happen from time to time, and it is essential to recognize that the student may not be getting enough sleep and, for whatever reason, there are times that it may be in the best interest of the child to allow him or her a nap during class. This does not mean, however, that students aren't held accountable for missed instruction, and teachers will need to follow up with students and support them later. It also is not necessarily an affront to our teaching and may simply reflect a basic need that requires attention.

The message that cuts across these thirteen messages is that the typical mismatch between adolescent students and their classrooms can be reduced if they are seen as active, curious, meaning makers who thrive in novel, challenging, supportive environments. Throughout this text we consistently encourage using an asset-based lens to learn about and understand adolescents. We hope that you will begin to build your own examples of connections in practice of these ideas as you begin working more in classroom settings.

How to Use This Book

This text has been designed to serve as a comprehensive foundation of middle level teaching for both teacher candidates and novice practicing teachers. The first large section of the book focuses on getting to know the ins and outs of adolescents and thinking about their physical, cognitive, and social identities. To be an effective teacher, we believe it is important to know our students well. These chapters help readers understand the students in their classrooms and address the uniqueness of those students as learners and as humans. Bolded terms are defined in the glossary.

Chapters are organized with the following elements:

- Learning outcomes
- Introduction of case students and/or teachers
- Chapter-specific content

- Pause-and-reflect discussion questions: framed to be used either individually or as discussion questions in class

- Plan it/practice it: A structure to apply newly covered content to a real-world example

- Applications and resources: examples, where applicable, are provided from classrooms to help students understand how to apply the principles of the content; students will then be able to start saving resources to build a toolkit for their later classroom use

- Suggested readings: supplemental readings that support the content in each chapter

This book is written with specific intentions for readers who are teacher educators, readers who are teacher candidates, and readers who are practicing teachers.

TEACHER EDUCATORS

It is our aim that this book provide a comprehensive lens into teaching middle school. Some chapters can be used alone, but other chapters are often referenced as background or applications of content. This book could be framed to use in a foundation's methods course, but we hope that it also can be used across a program. The beginning chapters (2–5) will help build an understanding of adolescents. The next section (chapters 6–8) is designed to build a context of middle school practices and policies, one that reflects what is present in middle schools today. The third section (chapters 9–13) is more application based and will provide more ideas for how to give students opportunities to plan and practice **instructional strategies**. Finally, the last section (chapters 14–15) is meant to build context for the middle school setting's uniqueness by digging into the history and philosophy of middle grade education and the organizational structures of middle schools. These chapters are at the end of the book so that teacher candidates can use all they have learned throughout the book to think more deeply about how the middle school concept applies to them. That said, these chapters are written in a way that their content could be used at the beginning of a course if the course is more oriented toward history and foundational principles. Ancillary materials are available to support the implementation of this text.

TEACHER CANDIDATES

This book is written to support teacher candidates by taking such readers on a progressive journey to build their understanding of adolescents and to provide them with a toolkit of applicable teaching strategies. The first section (chapters 2–5) will give an understanding of adolescents and how they are unique. This section is important in the journey toward becoming a middle grades teacher, as the most effective instructional strategies will not work for teachers without an understanding of adolescent development. The second section (chapters 6–8) will introduce a lot of terminology, policy, and current trends in middle school practices, and we have built in opportunities to plan and practice tasks related to these concepts. The third section (chapters 9–13) focuses more on the day-to-day teaching practices of effective middle school teachers. Here we explore many strategies and tools to use in daily teaching practice and address components of classroom management. The concluding section (chapters 14–15) gives readers an opportunity to think about the unique history and philosophy of middle school and to think through the organizational structures we use to fully implement the middle school concept.

PRACTICING TEACHERS

Practicing teachers can use the beginning section of this book (chapters 2–5) if they lack any background knowledge about adolescents or weren't prepared in a traditional teacher preparation program. The second section of the book (chapters 6–8) will provide a solid overview of current policy and practices, including many of the acronyms we so lovingly use in education. The third section of the book (chapters 9–13), on curriculum and instruction, may be the most useful for finding examples of and application opportunities for instructional strategies. For practicing teachers who are already in a traditional middle school, the concluding section (chapters 14–15) gives context and strategies for best practice in middle school—even for those who are not in a setting that fully implements the middle school model.

Meet the Authors

Picture 1.1 Holly Henderson Pinter. Photo, Nick Breedlove

Holly Henderson Pinter, PhD, is an associate professor of middle grades education at Western Carolina University. Dr. Pinter completed a PhD in 2013 at the University of Virginia. Her teaching and research center on implementing standards-based mathematical teaching practices, preservice teacher education policy and practice, and developmentally responsive middle level teaching. In addition to serving as the middle grades program coordinator and assistant director of the School of Teaching and Learning, Holly teaches methods and pedagogy courses in the middle grades department as well as serves as the Math 1 teacher and instructional liaison at the university's laboratory school, The Catamount School.

MIDDLE LEVEL TEACHING AND A THEORY OF LEARNING

Picture 1.2 Kim K. Winter. Photo, Western Carolina University

Kim K. Winter, PhD, is Dean of the College of Education and Allied Professions and Chancellor's Designee/Superintendent for the UNC-System lab school, The Catamount School, of Western Carolina University. She has served in other roles, including associate dean, associate chair, and middle level program director. Dr. Winter has taught a variety of university courses: middle level curriculum, instruction, and assessment; language arts and literacy methods; young-adolescent development; English learner methods; and young-adult literature. She has taught language arts and writing to both elementary and middle school students in Texas and Indiana. Her recent research projects include digital video analysis of and reflection on teaching among preservice teachers; alignment of state and national English standards; the study of deficit thinking among teacher candidates; performance-based assessment in teacher education; and the induction and retention of teachers.

Picture 1.3 Kayleigh Kassel. Photo, Megan Kassel

Kayleigh Kassel, MAEd, serves as the English Language Arts Teacher Leader at The Catamount School, a lab school, in Western North Carolina. In addition to teaching sixth, seventh, and eighth grades, she is an adjunct instructor for the College of Education at Western Carolina University. Mrs. Kassel has earned both a bachelor's degree and a master's degree from Western Carolina University in middle grades education with a concentration in literacy. Her research focus is on studying trauma-informed practices and the impact of adverse childhood experiences on students' needs and success.

Contributing Authors

Picture 1.4 Bruce Henderson. Photo, Judy Henderson

Bruce Henderson, PhD, received a bachelor of arts degree and a master's degree in psychology at Bucknell University. After working with young children for several years, he completed a PhD in child psychology at the Institute of Child Development at the University of Minnesota. In 1978, he accepted a job as an assistant professor of psychology at Western Carolina University. For forty-two years, he taught courses in child psychology and other areas and conducted research on a variety of topics, especially the development of curiosity and the development of memory. Over the years, he worked with many early-childhood organizations, the public schools, and the North Carolina Center for the Advancement of Teaching. He also worked on several national projects on teaching with the American Psychology Association. On the side, he took an interest in higher-education policy issues concerning the special status of comprehensive universities like Western Carolina University, publishing articles in many higher-education journals and a book, *Teaching at the People's University*, an introduction to such universities for new faculty. In December 2023, Routledge published his review of research on residential care: *Challenging the Conventional Wisdom about Residential Care for Children and Youth: A Good Place to Grow*.

Picture 1.5 Tammy Barron. Photo, CJ Barron (Dogstar Digital, LLC)

Tammy L Barron, PhD, is a professor at Western Carolina University and the special-education administrator of the laboratory school run by Western Carolina University. She has co-taught in various settings in preschool, elementary, secondary, and higher education in general and special education. Her research interests relate to policies and organizational behaviors that support practices that foster inclusion for students with disabilities. Dr. Barron has collaborated with school professionals to implement co-teaching and build collaboration in their schools. She strives to improve outcomes for students through increasing understanding and advocating for the needs of children, families, support staff, teachers, and administrators through research and practice.

Meet the Teachers

Many of the teachers included in this text are faculty at The Catamount School. Others are teachers from various places who volunteered their insight and expertise to contribute to the text. These are their real names as we wanted to celebrate and credit their work in the field. We are grateful for all that they do and all that they have to share with us.

Picture 1.6 Amanda Clapp. Kenan Fellows Program photo by Amneris Solano

Amanda Clapp, MAEd, is a twenty-year veteran science teacher. She has taught middle school and high school science as well as college science as an adjunct professor of middle school science methods. Ms. Clapp is a master teacher who has won multiple teaching awards and grants, including the Burroughs Wellcome Fund Career Award in STEM Teaching. She is a National Board–certified teacher and has two master's degrees in education in addition to two bachelor's degrees. Her expertise is in concepts related to project-based learning and STEM.

Picture 1.7 Meghan Rector. Photo, Holly Pinter

Meghan Rector, MEd, is the mathematics teacher for Western Carolina University's lab middle school, The Catamount School. Mrs. Rector completed a master of education program at Vanderbilt University, where she studied learning and design theories and the impact of their cohesion within traditional and nontraditional learning settings. She is an adjunct professor for Western Carolina's education department, where she has taught elementary math methods and middle school teacher preparation courses. Her teaching and research center around growing mathematical knowledge in preservice math teachers, the impact and implementation of culturally responsive math practices in the classroom, and the exploration of the impact of journaling on students' motivation, and identity with mathematics.

Picture 1.8 Morgan Nichols. Photo, Morgan Nichols

Morgan Nichols has been teaching for seven years. After receiving her bachelor's degree at Western Carolina University, she started her career teaching at a private school in Costa Rica. In her two years working in Costa Rica, she taught fourth grade and middle and high school social studies. More recently, she has worked in a middle school setting as an affective-needs special-education teacher. Affective-needs teachers work with students diagnosed with a significant emotional disability. Ms. Nichols now works as a career and academic counselor at the same middle school in Southwest Colorado.

Picture 1.9 Amy Wilt. Photo, Amy Wilt

Amy Wilt is a beginning science teacher in the triangle area of North Carolina. Mrs. Wilt graduated with honors from Western Carolina University where she received awards from the middle grades program as an outstanding teacher. She has presented at multiple state and national conferences. As a novice teacher, Amy exhibits strengths in project-based learning, resilience strategies, and restorative discipline practices.

Picture 1.10 Salem Parris. Photo, Western Carolina University

Salem Parris is an early-career middle grades social-studies teacher. She has a bachelor's degree in middle grades and has taught seventh- and eighth-grade science and social studies at a traditional middle school in western North Carolina. Ms. Parris was recognized early in her career by receiving the Beginning Teacher of the Year award for her school district.

Meet the Students

The students in this book are primarily students from The Catamount School. All students contributed their stories to our book with permission from their parents, and all assented to being included. The names provided are pseudonyms to protect their identities. Pictures included in this text do not necessarily represent student case studies.

Picture 1.11   Students Working. Photo, Western Carolina University

Gigi is a high-achieving seventh-grade student. She shows a strong work ethic and contributes to her classes by engaging in all activities and discussions. Gigi has shown a growth mindset, particularly in her academics, and strives for success. She takes part in electives and clubs that demand athleticism and teamwork. In both core classes and nonacademic classes, she is a leader and ensures that other students with similar and differing abilities are included.

Khalil is a young scholar. Due to a rich sense of culture within his family, Khalil's personal expectations about academics make grades a top priority. Khalil has a diverse set of skills, and he excels in both academics and extracurriculars like intramurals. Even as a seventh-grade student, he obtained the role of student-body president. Despite his success, Khalil consistently seeks positive affirmation from teachers to feel that he is showing mastery in all areas of his studies. He is diligent and driven to succeed and can be hard on himself if he isn't at the top of the class in all ways.

Claire is an eighth grader who excels in school and extracurricular activities. She is quick-witted and compassionate. In eighth grade, she took and excelled in Math 1 to earn credit for high school. Claire is intuitive and shows her friends and others vast amounts of empathy. Claire has a calm demeanor but is strong-willed in setting boundaries for herself to ensure that she achieves her goals. She has a supportive, albeit strict, home environment with deeply rooted cultural values from her Polish heritage. With her family background, Claire is well traveled and is fluent in her home language (Polish) as well as in English, which she has grown up with.

Dion is a charismatic eighth grader with enough personality to fill a room. He has a core group of close friends but also can sit with any group of humans to strike up a conversation. He is very socially driven, and social standing is important to him, as is being well liked by his teachers.

Brooklyn is an outspoken but big-hearted eighth grader who has faced significant trauma within her short life. Brooklyn began her year living with her birth mother. As the year progressed, this setting became an unstable environment for Brooklyn and her siblings. She was then moved to a foster-care placement, which has provided much more stability for her despite the lack of permanence. Brooklyn has a therapist with whom she meets regularly, and she uses the school counselor as needed. Her trauma affects her school behaviors academically, socially, and emotionally. She can discuss the growth she has made in school, with her peers, in coping in healthier ways, and in meeting the challenges and handling the setbacks she faces daily.

Larry is a sixth grader who is passionate about Dungeons and Dragons, reading, and creating games. He has found himself struggling with some peers as he and his classmates shifted from elementary to middle school but has learned to adapt and find his select niche of friends. Larry is an only child and lives with his family. In his home, he is surrounded by a multitude of farm animals that he loves and helps tend to!

Picture 1.12 Pep rally. Photo, Western Carolina University

Aaron is an expressive eighth grader with impressive artistic skills. Aaron demonstrates a wide range of emotions throughout their typical day. They are a nonbinary student who has sought out a community that is supportive of their individuality. Like many middle school students on the pathway to self-discovery, Aaron seeks attention from students and teachers alike as they search for a sense of belonging. Aaron's academic journey has been somewhat stagnant, and Aaron has not had much growth in core classes. For the majority of the year, they exhibited task-avoidant behaviors and was often distracted by their artwork or peers. One of the solutions to success for Aaron, that they also requested, was sitting close to the front of the room or alone as well as the use of earbuds with music to help them focus.

Liza is a quiet, thoughtful, and intelligent eighth grader who has an incredible support system at home. In addition, she has a strong core group of friends at school. Liza also takes on leadership roles in school, serving as her eighth-grade class's representative in the student-government association. She struggles with anxiety and obsessive-compulsive personality disorder (OCPD). Liza has a therapist with whom she meets regularly, and she sees the school counselor as needed. She has said that her mental-health needs impact her success at school, although she feels supported by the adults and friends she has found while at school. Despite her OCPD, she is a student who consistently keeps good grades and is generally successful.

Cade is a lively seventh grader who has massive energy whose emotive nature occasionally results in a whirlwind of emotional expression. Cade told us that, at the beginning of the school year, starting in a new school, he was consistently distracted, did not have strong peer relationships, was rude to teachers, and struggled with his grades. He would rush through his day, not consistently able to keep up with his belongings, sometimes having a negative interaction with a peer or two, and then also spouting out some mathematical brilliance along the way. After the first quarter, the teachers realized Cade would need more support related to his executive function and self-regulation skills.

Olivia is another energetic eighth grader who has consistently been a high performer in school. Olivia has an active social life and is incredibly involved in activities in and outside of school, including theater and the student-government association. Olivia developed a toolkit of strategies to help balance her busy life and uses strategies encouraged by teachers to help stay organized and on top of things. Her strategies include using a weekly organizer to track assignments and due dates.

Krystal is a rising eighth grader from an urban school in the region. She is Jamaican American and describes herself as a self-taught musician. She plays the piano, double bass, and the viola and is part of the school orchestra.

References

Bishop, P. A., & Harrison, L. M. (2021). *The successful middle school: This we believe, 5th edition*. Author.

Bransford, J., Derry, S., Berliner, D., Hammerness, K., & Beckett, K. L. (2005). Theories of learning and their roles in teaching. In L. Darling-Hammond & J. Bransford (Eds), *Preparing teachers for a changing world: What teachers should learn and be able to do*. Jossey-Bass, 40, 87.

Deans for Impact. (2023). Science of learning: Teacher action overview—prompting for effortful thinking. Retrieved from: https://www.deansforimpact.org/files/assets/lbsdanchorcharteft.pdf

Dehaene, S. (2021). *How we learn: Why brains learn better than any machine . . . for now.* Penguin.

Ellerbrock, C. R. (2016). Developmental responsiveness. In S. B. Mertens, M. M. Caskey, & N. Flowers (Eds.), *The encyclopedia of middle grades education* (2nd ed.). Information Age Publishing.

Lipsitz, J. (1984) *Successful schools for young adolescents.* Transaction Books.

Willingham, D. T. (2021). *Why don't students like school?: A cognitive scientist answers questions about how the mind works and what it means for the classroom.* John Wiley & Sons.

CHAPTER 2

Introduction to Early Adolescent Development

Learning Outcomes:

1. Identify and analyze key developmental issues in early adolescence.
2. Describe adolescents' abilities as abstract thinkers.
3. Explain how adolescents are active explorers.
4. Identify ways that adolescents make connections with parents and peers.
5. Describe factors that contribute to an environment in which adolescents thrive.

Developmental Issues in Early Adolescence

If you want to work effectively with middle schoolers, it helps to know how they think and why they behave the way they do. In the fifty years that **developmentalists** have taken adolescence seriously, many theories have been debated, empirically supported, or refuted in the textbooks of the field. Articles in scholarly journals in developmental psychology are full of data and theories describing stages of development, egocentrism, moral development, identity, and emotion inhibition, to name a few. Instead of getting into the details of these arguments, we will view adolescent development from a higher altitude. We will begin by addressing a set of issues that puts early adolescent development into a conceptual context. Then, we will present four themes that we are confident capture the essence of early adolescent development in terms consistent with recent developmental research but also are helpful to classroom teachers and others who work with middle schoolers. We will conclude the chapter by describing what we consider to be generalizations that characterize early adolescents while considering both the gaps in our knowledge and the reality of individual differences.

PROMISE, NOT PROBLEMS

One of the critical shifts of emphasis in research on early adolescence has been from a focus on adolescents' problems and deficits to a new appreciation for what adolescents can do (Qu, 2023). The Positive Youth Development orientation (Lerner et al., 2005) sees early adolescents as being "at promise" rather than "at risk"; Lerner and his colleagues' attention is on what adolescents are doing or are capable of doing rather than on their deficits or weaknesses. The themes we offer in this chapter are couched in this more positive tone and align with the instructional strategies we discuss throughout the text, emphasizing the utilization of **asset-based language**.

THE CONCEPT OF DEVELOPMENT

It is tempting to think about development as growth, maturation, or change. But none of those descriptors captures how development occurs (Harris, 1957). For example, a fertilized egg does not just get larger. Immediately following conception, changes in complexity begin to occur. Cells differentiate into different body parts and organs, all with distinct functions. Psychological development is also a matter of changes in complexity. Adolescents do not just know more than children, although they do; they think in different ways. Adolescents do not just have more relationships; their relationships with peers and adults are organized into more complex networks than are those of children. As we describe early adolescent development, we will return frequently to this notion of increases in complexity.

Early adolescence refers to the age range of ten to fourteen years. In this phase, as we will explore in this chapter and the next three, significant changes are characterized physically, cognitively, and socially. This is the phase of life in which humans transition from being childlike creatures into being more adultlike, with physically growing bodies and more complex thoughts. Below, we explore more distinctive factors that characterize early adolescence, and we particularly examine the connection between these factors and adolescents in school.

INDIVIDUAL DIFFERENCES

One generalization about early adolescence that is unlikely to be contradicted is that every individual adolescent is different in multiple ways. There are **individual differences** at all ages, but, when a younger child grows up in the evolutionarily expected "normal" environment, the breadth of differences is somewhat constrained. Starting with early adolescence, every statement about development must be qualified by reference to individual differences. There are no universal age ranges for developmental features. This is obvious regarding physical development (identifying an "average height" for sixth graders is meaningless) but applies to psychological development too. We will dig deeper into generalized aspects of physical, social, and cognitive **domains of development** in later chapters, but for the purpose of laying a foundation of understanding of adolescent development, note that each of the themes below, by their nature, contains an implicit expectation of differences.

CULTURAL DIFFERENCES

Like generalizations across individuals, generalizations about early adolescence get increasingly difficult to make across cultural or economic groups. The life experience of early adolescents who expect to go to college is likely to differ from that of those who expect to work in fields or mines. Much of the research on adolescents has been conducted within a narrow group that includes little cultural variety. Although that is changing, we will return in the chapter conclusion to the importance of environment-adolescent fit. It simply is dangerous to forget how environments influence early adolescents and the **cultural differences** that exist.

DOMAINS OF DEVELOPMENT

Developmental research and theory have historically been domain specific. The focus has been on cognitive development, social-personality development, or communication development. The themes in this chapter reflect that early adolescents do not develop in independent domains. For teachers, a cross-domain approach is more consistent with the fact that they are dealing with whole students. In fact, one of the problems with the school curricula is that some implicitly assume that students are cognitively, socially, emotionally, and linguistically the same. You will see in later chapters how any reference to physical changes is inextricably linked to social-development references.

COHORT DIFFERENCES

Individuals grow up during particular historical periods. Individuals are sometimes influenced by what are called "secular effects." The most well-known "secular effects" are the purported changes in age of first menstruation and eventual adult height, which have been linked to improved nutrition or other historical changes. There may be **cohort differences** (or effects) created by changes in media environments or the introduction of high-stakes testing. It is difficult but important to systematically study cohort effects (e.g., Twenge et al., 2017). Cohort differences are often based on speculation. But it surely would be a mistake to assume that they do not influence development at all.

PHYSICAL-PSYCHOLOGICAL CONNECTIONS

Perhaps because the physical changes that occur during early adolescence are so dramatic, there has been a tendency to attribute developmental changes in psychological domains directly to changes in the brain and body. Important changes, including the development of the brain parts that control impulse and emotional responses and sexual maturation (see Chapter 3 for more), occur during early adolescence. Those physical changes are important in themselves and often have important psychological influences. Presumably (unless we move to the realm of science fiction), all psychological experiences have a basis in the brain and body. Yet we do not want to suggest that early adolescent behavior and experience must be reduced to physical, anatomical language. At this point in our understanding, any single psychological phenomenon can be linked to multiple physical (or neuronal or hormonal) events, and multiple physical events can be linked to the same psychological phenomenon (Bessanta & Watts, 2012). Moreover, physical events occur in environments. It is likely to be many decades from now, if ever, when we can say that Cheryl bullied Jo because neurons in a particular part of her brain interacted with certain hormones over time (De Vos, 2016). For the purposes of this chapter on early adolescent development, we will take the tack that it is more useful to talk about planning for and inhibiting behaviors rather than about the maturation of particular brain structures.

It is clear from what we have outlined so far that the development of adolescents is multifaceted and includes physical, cognitive, social, emotional, and cultural attributes. No pathway in adolescent development is perfectly predictable; nor is it linear. This chapter will outline several themes that help educators create classroom environments to support each student on his or her developmental journey all the while knowing that your classroom of twenty-five students will have students who are at various points in their pathway.

Developmental Themes in Early Adolescence

Each major developmental period ("period" is better than "stage" here because developmental change is more gradual than the term "stage" implies) is characterized by themes, much like Erikson (1968) argued. Infancy reflects themes of attachment, exploration, and basic communication. The preschool years reflect **curiosity** about the environment, rapid learning, and socialization, especially by parents. Childhood is about the beginning of formal schooling, learning to read fluently, internalization of basic norms, and the start of friendships. We will use four similar themes that we see as characteristics of **early adolescence** and that provide the developmental bridge into later adolescence and adulthood.

As we explore these themes, we will use the cases of Khalil and Liza. Khalil is a young scholar. Due to a rich sense of culture within his family, Khalil's personal expectations about academics make grades a top priority for him. Khalil has a diverse set of skills, and he excels in both academics and extracurriculars like intramurals. Even as a seventh-grade student, he obtained the role of student-body president. Despite his success, Khalil consistently seeks positive affirmation from teachers to feel that he is demonstrating mastery in all areas of his studies. He is diligent and driven to succeed and can be hard on himself if he is not at the top of the class in all ways.

Liza is a quiet, thoughtful, and intelligent eighth grader who has a dedicated support system at home. In addition, she has a solid core group of friends at school. Liza also takes on leadership roles in school; for example, she is the eighth-grade class representative on the student-government association. She struggles with anxiety and obsessive-compulsive personality disorder (OCPD). Liza has a therapist with whom she meets regularly, and she sees the school counselor as needed. She has stated that her mental-health needs impact her success at school, although she feels supported by the adults and friends she has found while at school. Despite her OCPD, she is a student who consistently maintains good grades and is generally successful.

THEME 1: THINKING ABOUT POSSIBILITIES

Much of the early interest in early adolescent thinking can be traced to the work of Inhelder and Piaget (1958). They saw the change from childhood thinking to adolescent thinking as a qualitative change from the concrete thinking of childhood to a form of abstract thinking they called "formal operations." The change was characterized as going from being able to think only about single, isolated propositions about the real world to being able to coordinate multiple propositions at one time and even being able to think logically about the impossible, abstracted from real constraints, and being able to think about thinking.

Early Piagetian theorizing suggested that this change from concrete to abstract or formal operational thinking occurred abruptly and was applied by the thinker across domains, from math, to science, to moral issues. By the 1970s, even Piagetians began to consider the transition to more complex forms of thinking to be both more gradual and applicable to different domains in different ways. However, one important aspect of Piagetian theory has been retained and is still used to describe the development of formal operational thinking in early adolescents: the increasing ability to and the increasing predisposition to think about possibilities, not just concrete instances.

Possibility Generating

The ability to think about thinking, to think in terms of multiple possibilities and even impossibilities, is based on several fundamental changes in the early adolescent's abilities. Included are increases in the speed of mental processing, in processing efficiency, and, importantly, in the ability to resist interfering ideas and distractions. Early adolescents also grow in their abilities to plan ahead and regulate emotions. Although the research and theorizing in this area are highly complex, together these changes are seen as constituting what has been called "**executive functioning**" (e.g., Tervo-Clemmens et al., 2023).

An often-underappreciated factor in changes in adolescent thinking is the growth of adolescents' knowledge bases, changes in what is stored in their long-term memories (Ackerman, 2023). Long-term memory consists of different forms of memory, including procedural memory (the processes and skills of doing things, including physical and cognitive actions), declarative memory (the information we have about the world—the main concern of schools), and autobiographical memory (our memories of what happened to us personally). Enhanced processing speed, processing efficiency, and distraction avoidance improve working memory's ability to connect new information to existing declarative memory and encode it into a more sophisticated knowledge base.

Two of the best predictors of whether something new will be learned are what learners already know about the topic and how interested they are in the topic (Jansen et al., 2016). (Yet neither prior knowledge nor interest is typically assessed in school.) Often the knowledge bases early adolescents build have nothing to do with academic priorities. They may become experts on graphic novels, popular (or even unpopular) music, professional sports, or woodworking. Regardless of the content area, the ability to encode new information in memory can be facilitated by effective instruction and exposure, formally by teachers, coaches, or mentors, or informally by peers or media. Age-related improvements in executive functioning make it easier to make connections in working memory, but the richer the knowledge base, the easier it is to find more connections (Crone, 2017). The more you know, the more you are likely to come to know. The already knowledge rich get richer.

Deductive or Scientific Reasoning

Even preschool-aged children demonstrate some skills related to hypothesis testing and interpreting the results of the experiments they plan. But as late as the sixth grade, many students have difficulty in producing multiple hypotheses (Piekny & Maehler, 2013). The increases during early adolescence in the ability to generate possibilities leads to improvements in this ability in later adolescence and adulthood. However, even older adolescents and adults have difficulty in evaluating logical reasoning when their own backgrounds and beliefs (i.e., biases) are at issue. One's knowledge base is intricately involved in any reasoning.

As in many aspects of early adolescent thinking, there are enormous individual differences in scientific reasoning, dependent on processing speed, processing efficiency, knowledge base, and other abilities, especially reading comprehension skills and specific past educational experiences. For example, elementary-school students who have been engaged in inquiry learning tend to be better at scientific reasoning when they reach adolescence. In early adolescents, developing executive functioning and an increasing ability to deploy and execute cognitive resources and to resist distractions (including the aforementioned biases) result in improved and more effective scientific reasoning (Kuhn, 2009).

Decision-Making

Research on adolescent decision-making has focused on risk-taking. However, what more centrally reflects early adolescents' decision-making is their increasing ability to generate possibilities (Ciranka & van der Bos, 2021). As with scientific reasoning, the early adolescent's increasingly rich knowledge bases allow more complex mental representations that take into consideration social norms, culture, and scientific, technical, and statistical knowledge when making decisions. What appears to be "risky" may simply be what is possible without appropriate constraints. Regardless, early-adolescent decision-making reflects the generative quality of their thinking.

Theory of Mind

Theory of mind is a theoretical position that refers to the ability to understand that others have minds and to make inferences about what is going on in those minds. Developmental research on theory-of-mind abilities has concentrated on developments during infancy and early childhood. It has become clear, however, that theory-of-mind abilities continue to develop during adolescence and adulthood (Weimer et al., 2021). Mutually supportive executive and regulation skills help early adolescents to assess other minds. Refinements are especially apparent in social sensitivity skills. These changes influence how adolescents think about themselves and others. Like the other developments described in this theme, theory of mind is about possibilities.

Summary: Possibilities and the Building of Knowledge Bases

What early adolescents know determines not only what they think about but also what they are likely to learn in the future. Acquiring new knowledge involves the active engagement of working memory as new knowledge is connected to old knowledge. The early adolescent actively links, elaborates, imagines, and makes meaning with the rich possibilities offered in the environment. This process is increasingly under the control of the developing adolescent with a supportive environment. The degree to which this process takes place, and the direction in which it goes, depends on the individual's **motivation**.

To think about these components, let's look at Liza, who in an interview was reflective about her growth and change, particularly her academic growth and change, from sixth grade to the end of eighth grade. Liza spoke to us about working through the uncomfortable. Specifically, she shared with us how she has learned at our school to work on, work through, and complete high-quality projects with peers. Liza has noticed that in several of her classes in middle school she has been required to do large-scale, long-term projects. She reflected on how that experience has differed in the past few years from her earlier childhood experiences with projects. She remembers experiences from elementary school where she shared: "Back then it was rare that we got projects and we would get really excited but none of us know how to do a proper project . . . we never had them and I remember my first project on marine life and I was like, oh I have some research but I don't know how to use it . . . I've never done this before." She then reflected on a clear memory of another project she was assigned and remembered a project about a lighthouse that had to have a light that turned on: "The project is a big deal and there's a due date but you have two weeks to do it and everyone is panicking and we have the material but we didn't know how to build the structure and my mom was freaking out and we're trying to build it with clay and like it was bad it was not quality work." Now, three years later, she feels differently about her ability to tackle projects. She discussed with us her enjoyment of doing a school-wide PBL (problem-based learning) project where she was able to choose what she investigated but was given a clear structure and expectations of what needed to be completed. She expressed how difficult it is for her to talk in front of large groups of people but said that her work on this project helped her overcome that anxiety. She said the use of these projects is beneficial "because in real life you will have to present a lot, especially in college." For her project, she chose to investigate safety for people who are in the LGBTQIA+ community, which was of personal relevance to her as an individual. When we asked her about her personal connection to that particular project, she shared that she had people in her life that, while supportive, were uneducated about the topic, and she said, "I wanted to educate people, and just put it in simple terms so that parents and kids can understand what it means to be a part of the community, and [teach] terms that we should use and terms we shouldn't use just so people know."

Pause and Reflect: With this vignette, brainstorm evidence of the above elements (possibility generating, deductive/scientific reasoning, decision-making, and theory of mind) in Liza's school experience.

THEME 2: EARLY ADOLESCENTS ARE ACTIVE EXPLORERS

Our second theme is that early adolescents are active explorers—explorers of their environments and of themselves. Active exploration is not peculiar to adolescents; infants and children also explore. What is different in early adolescence is that the exploration goes deeper. No longer content with exploring novel surface features, early adolescents use their ability to generate possibilities, their increasingly complex physical and intellectual environments, and their expanding social worlds to elaborate and deepen their exploration.

Curiosity: Exploring the Physical and Intellectual Environment

The general curiosity and exploratory behavior exhibited during early and middle childhood are responses to environmental novelty. By early adolescence, much of the easily available novelty in the environment has been explored. Indeed, some research suggests a decline in general curiosity and exploration from the preschool years into adolescence. However, that decline may be at least partially illusory. Early adolescents can find the novel in the familiar (Litman, 2019). Interestingly, students who are in classrooms for the academically gifted do not show a decline in curiosity, and, in some studies, show increases (Gottfried & Gottfried, 2009). This lack of decline is tied more closely to the enriched environments of those classrooms than to psychometric intelligence (Henderson et al., 1982). Teachers and parents can provide environments specifically designed to offer novel ideas and experiences. Another important feature of early adolescent exploration is that it is more differentiated. Instead of being curious about anything and everything, early adolescents begin to specialize in areas of interest.

Focused Exploration: Interests

Psychologists who study interests often distinguish between situational and individual interests (Renninger & Hidi, 2019). Situational interests reflect curiosity triggered by environmental novelty. Individual interests, in contrast, emerge over time, sometimes because of repeated experiences of situational interests. But there is also evidence that individual personal interests appear early in development, well before adolescence, and that those interests remain relatively stable over time. For example, there is evidence that, early on, some children prefer interacting with objects whereas others prefer interacting with people (Su et al., 2009).

The most thoroughly studied view of individual differences in interests is **Holland's themes** (realistic, investigative, artistic, social, entrepreneurial, conventional). Supporters of this approach treat these themes as personality traits (Low et al., 2005). They influence the choices individuals make in their educational and occupational environments. There are overall increases with age in artistic, social, and entrepreneurial interests, possibly because of the availability of more educational support for specialization in those categories of interest. The one age period in which there is less stability in Holland themes is between eleven and fourteen years of age. It is not clear what factors are involved in the instability, but changes in schooling are likely involved. Wise teachers and parents use both situational and individual interests to motivate students and use developing individual interests to bridge what students are interested in to what they are not. For example, a teacher may teach fractions and percentages by using a student's interest in sports.

Exploring the Self: Identity Statuses

In addition to exploring environments and knowledge bases, early adolescents are actively exploring themselves, who they are in terms of values, occupational ambitions, and other aspects of self, and they explore their competencies (Ferrer-Wieder & Kroger, 2020). Based on Erikson's theoretical work and Marcia's elaborations on personality development, the concept of identity statuses dominated thinking about **identity development** for decades (Côté, 2009).

Marcia's identity theory includes four **identity statuses**: identity diffusion, foreclosure, moratorium, and identity achievement. The following briefly operationalizes each status:

- Diffusion: Those in identity diffusion do not have an identity and are likely to be quite confused about who they are.

- Foreclosure: This status presents more as a pseudo-identity, most likely adopted from a parent. Individuals in foreclosure are not actively exploring or questioning options and will not do so until some event, usually a crisis (e.g., a change in family structure or occupation) occurs.

- Moratorium: The moratorium status has some similarities to identity diffusion except that the adolescent's explorations are not conducted aimlessly or with great anxiety (i.e., they reflect the stereotypical actions of the average teen in "identity crisis"). The goal of identity development is the status of identity achievement.

- Achievement: In identity achievement, the individual has a sense of self-confidence, a commitment to important values, and at least some direction toward occupational goals.

To solidify this, let's look at a traditional developmental pattern through Marcia's identity statuses during adolescence: diffusion or foreclosure, moratorium, and, ultimately, achievement, with the healthiest sequence being moratorium to achievement. Recent research indicates that only a minority of college seniors have attained identity achievement, and a plurality of adults remain in foreclosure. Recent thinking about identity statuses reflects a return to Erikson's simpler two-step developmental version of the journey from identity confusion (some form of diffusion or moratorium) to identity resolution (identity achievement or foreclosure).

Although Marcia's four-status version retains some intuitive appeal for those who work with adolescents, for our purposes, two things remain important: 1) early adolescents are actively exploring their identities and exploration continues through adolescence and into adulthood; and 2) supportive environments, especially supportive families and schools, make identity resolution more likely to be achieved. There is considerable evidence that interaction with authoritative adults—those who are characterized by warmth, moderate means of discipline, high communication, and high expectations—increases the likelihood of an adolescent achieving identity resolution, whereas interaction with adults who are authoritarian or permissive does not. We will discuss much more about the identity development of adolescents in Chapter 5.

Exploring the Self: Self-Assessments

Early adolescents explore self-roles and make judgments about themselves. One of the more sophisticated perspectives on **self-assessments** is **Harter's (2012) multifaceted view of self-competencies**. In Harter's scheme, adolescents evaluate themselves in seven domains: academics, physical appearance, behavioral conduct, relationships with close friends, romantic appeal, job performance, and athletics. They also make assessments of their global self-worth. Friendship and romantic appeal are differentiations from a general social domain in childhood, and job issues appear first in adolescence. The prevalence of each domain in the early adolescent's assessment depends on how much the adolescent values the domain. For example, low assessments of athletic competence do not matter much if the individual is not interested in athletics. Perhaps not surprisingly, for early adolescents, the best predictor of assessments of global self-worth is how the individual assesses his or her physical appearance. This is true across age, sex, and level of academic competence. Even high self-assessments in academics or athletics do not cancel out the impact of low perceptions of physical appearance.

Despite stereotypes, assessments of self-worth do not uniformly decrease with age or entry into new schools. How supportive the home and school environments are matters. **Authoritative-democratic parenting** and high-quality teaching are both associated with more positive self-assessments. When there are age declines in self-assessments, they are more likely to occur with females and minority-group members.

Let's lean into Khalil's journey and share more about his background, interests, and what he has to say about them. We asked Khalil a myriad of questions about his middle school experiences, and he was able to articulate quite a bit about who he is as a middle schooler and to express confidence in his own skin while simultaneously expressing some doubt. We asked him where he felt he thrived in school—this could be academics or certain activities or parts of the day. Khalil was quick to reply that his best subject was math and instantly added that it was not English language arts. He expressed that, in English language arts, he finds himself always second guessing and does not feel confident in his answers. The reason math is his favorite relates to a memory of a babysitter who helped him work through his early lack of confidence in the subject. Khalil said, "When I was younger, right? I had this babysitter. I always sucked at math, but she always taught me math and since then I have always been good at it. Like if it is a [mental math] problem? It just comes to me." He then shared that he feels strong with problem-solving. We then asked Khalil to share some of the other activities he enjoys outside of school, and he quickly rattled off a list of hobbies, including fishing, basketball, football, and talking to friends on the phone. When asked about challenges he has faced, he just could not produce any, and, when we asked him to describe some projects or activities he has enjoyed in school, he could not narrow it down to one. He reflected on a project he worked on two years ago and excitedly told me the details of the human body (particularly the circulatory system). By the end of our conversation, we felt like we had successfully participated in a science lesson—and that was a project he had not touched in two years. When asked what was most important in his life, Khalil thought for just a moment before saying friends and family. When we asked him why, he said, "They just like support me. Everywhere."

Pause and Reflect: So now let's think—where do you think Khalil is on his identity journey, based on Marcia's identity statuses? What evidence from his story helps you decide? When you think about curiosity, interest, and self-assessment, how would you describe Khalil? Do you think his story is a typical middle school story? Why or not?

THEME 3: EARLY ADOLESCENTS MAKE CONNECTIONS

It will surprise no one that early adolescents are social beings. Most everything they do occurs in social contexts. Blakemore (2012) goes as far as to say that adolescents have "social brains." However, it may come as a surprise that the overall strength of the impact of peers on adolescent behavior is less and the relative impact of adults is greater than is often believed (Gilletta et al., 2021). But both are important (Oberle, 2023).

Parents

Although teachers, coaches, and mentors have an increasing role, parents remain the most influential adults in the lives of most early adolescents. Because the effects of other adults on development largely mimic parental influences, we will focus on key issues reflecting the research and theory on parenting.

The parallels between the developing autonomy of the two-year-old and that of the early adolescent are striking (Damon, 1983). At both ages, the need for the individual to become increasingly independent conflicts with parental expectations for control. While the degree of conflict at each age has sometimes been exaggerated, the developmental function of the conflict provides perspective. Social-personality development is about a balance between socialization and individuation. Socialization is the process by which the representatives of society, especially parents, help the toddler or the early adolescent learn how to fit in with the culture. Individuation is the process of developing an independent personality. Traditional psychological theories (especially those in the Freudian family) have seen socialization and individuation as inevitably clashing: too much socialization hinders individuation. More modern theories, including attachment theory, posit that appropriate socialization *facilitates* individuation. Here are some of the characteristics of connectedness to parents (and other adults) that do so (see Baumrind, 2013; Steinberg, 2014):

1. The style of parenting that optimally balances socialization and individuation during early adolescence is what has been variously called (originally by Baumrind) authoritative, democratic, or reciprocal. It is the style that is optimal at every age. Its features parental warmth and support, high communication, firm but negotiable control, and high expectations (for academics and conduct). This contrasts with authoritarian-autocratic parenting, which is high in control and low in warmth and communication, and with permissive parenting, which is low in control and expectations. As the child develops into an adolescent, an authoritative parent changes his or her level of control and expectations appropriately.

2. Those early adolescents who experience authoritative parenting have an important advantage. They are the individuals who are most likely to have internalized rules provided by parents and thus to have enhanced self-regulation skills. They develop communication and emotion modulation skills that allow them to deal successfully with challenges.

3. Early adolescents who have authoritative parents are those who are most likely to reach identity resolution, particularly in the form of identity achievement.

4. Authoritative parenting provides the early adolescent with a buffer to family disruptions, such as divorce. Divorce itself, not just the conflicts that precede the divorce, has been shown to negatively affect the adolescent's well-being, whether because of financial problems, dislocation, or declines in the quality of parenting practices.

5. Parent influences tend to be domain specific (Smetana, 2011). Early adolescents see parents as experts in some areas (e.g., health, academics) but not in other areas (e.g., dating and music preferences). Authoritative parents know this and are flexible enough to act on this knowledge.

Peer Influences

The research literature on peer influences is enormous. We provide here some generalizations from that literature that we think middle level teachers may find useful for interpreting what goes on in their classrooms. We will dig into peer dynamics in later chapters.

1. Although their impact may have been overstated (Giletta et al., 2021), peers do matter during early adolescence. Their influence, however, tends to be greatest on matters of immediate, and perhaps fleeting, importance. Peers are more influential in what an early adolescence is likely to wear or listen to than on an individual's job or college choice.

2. Early-adolescent peer relationships are unstable. They depend a great deal on propinquity (closeness in space), although technology is redefining propinquity. Friends are likely to be in the early adolescent's school or neighborhood. Mobility makes early-adolescent peer relationships fragile (Small & Adler, 2019).

3. Contrary to conventional wisdom, many of the influences of peers are positive (Laursen & Veenstra, 2023). The quality of adolescent friendships has been tied to psychological, and even physical, health (Ehrhardt & Schacter, 2024). Early adolescents learn social skills, including communication skills, negotiation skills, and social conventions from peers. They learn to take the perspective of others. Even conformity, often seen as a negative consequence of peer influence, facilitates compatibility and cohesion skills and the learning of conflict-resolution skills. Knowing when to conform and not to conform is a skill that is crucial to a balance between socialization and individuation.

4. When peers do have negative influences, such as on antisocial conduct, they tend to be specific to the peers they spend the most time with. A peer's negative influence is more likely to affect friends in the neighborhood rather than those who are just classmates and have less exposure to that peer. In extreme cases, the only way for parents to change peer-influenced bad behavior is to move (Steinberg, 1996). Because propinquity is so important to peer relations, it must be considered.

5. Early adolescents do not need a lot of friends. Popularity is not a guarantor of positive social development or adjustment. They do need one or two close friends (Rubin et al., 2015). During early adolescence, intimacy and self-disclosure are important and can be found with a small set of friends (Barzeva et al., 2022).

Let's revisit Khalil and think about what he shared about his friendships. Khalil was quick to name his two besties from his class. He explained that he had met James in fifth grade as they were at the same school together, but that he met Gigi (who you will meet in another chapter) as a sixth grader at our school. Khalil described the comfort of knowing James already as he transitioned to our school but was also quick to say that he just instantly had a strong bond with Gigi. We pressed Khalil a bit more to talk about what helped in forming that bond. His answer was simple—sports and math. This trio (whose friendship we can attest to witnessing) are glued together throughout the day. They often work on projects together when they are given a choice of who to work with. All three students had early aspirations in sixth grade to make it into Math 1 as eighth graders (which, by the way, they all have), and this shared goal kept them motivated into working on problem-solving together to prove they had what it takes to their teachers. When not working on academics, the three are found on the court or on the field playing whatever sport is available. We asked Khalil how his friendships have changed throughout middle school, and his response was short: "I've made some new friends; I've lost a few friends." This response was not given with any emotion attached, just a simple shoulder shrug and a seeming awareness that this was something natural to occur during this time.

Pause and Reflect: Take a moment to think back to the connections you built as an adolescent. Think specifically about the connections (or lack thereof) made at home with your family unit. How did your family impact your decisions, beliefs, and choices? Now think back to your friendships across sixth, seventh, and eighth grades: Where were there ebbs and flows in those relationships? What decisions, attitudes, and beliefs were impacted by your peers? Now, as an adult, can you identify where the positive peer and family influences (versus the negative influences) were? How have those things influenced you now as an adult?

THEME 4: THRIVING DEPENDS ON ADOLESCENT-ENVIRONMENT FIT

It is a truism that the development of children and youth is enhanced in environments that stimulate and support them. What shifts with age is where those environments are and what is in them. In early development, home is special. During adolescence, the most important environments are in school and community. We will focus here on schools. The degree to which the school environment fits the early adolescent is closely related to our other themes. Early adolescents thrive in environments that

1. ***are populated by adults who are sensitive to their needs*** (but not necessarily of their wants). Attachment provides a good model (Posada & Waters, 2018). The early adolescent sends off signals, and adults provide responses that are supportive of those needs. Young children send relatively simple signals. They cry or approach when they are hungry or fearful, and they get fed, held, or protected. During adolescence, the signals may be much harder to read and require much more complex responses from adults. The range of differences in signals, needs, and responses in a single classroom can be daunting. Teachers are not parents, but they are more successful to the degree that they act like authoritative parents, with high expectations and effective communication. Teachers who see their job as getting their students ready for college or the work world by toughening them up or leaving them to their own devices may forget they are dealing with individuals with diverse needs. Coaches who see their players as cogs in a system will miss important signals.

2. ***provide physical and intellectual resources capable of stimulating a wide range of interests.*** We know that curiosity and creativity occur in environments where there is novelty and variety. Yet many classrooms are characterized by sameness and scarceness. Middle school classrooms that ignore the wide range of possible tracks their students are on will discourage exploration and the growth of interests. A middle school classroom that encourages exploration is likely to look more like a workshop, a library, a laboratory, or a political convention than a typical classroom. In an environment designed to encourage exploration, teachers will not be the only adults in the classroom. Mentors, models, and experts from the community will represent a wide range of vocational and avocational possibilities.

3. ***are diverse.*** Homogeneous environments are the enemy of exploration and possibilities. That is as true of social environments as it is of physical environments. In safe school environments, guided by authoritative teachers, early adolescents can explore cultural, ethnic, class, and racial differences. There are also advantages to classrooms that are not age-graded as American schools usually are. Being able to learn with and teach peers at various developmental levels enriches social learning.

4. ***challenge the early adolescent's current way of thinking.*** Too many classrooms (all the way through college) are devoid of intellectual challenge. What is needed is not over-the-head difficulty but challenge at an optimal level, a level that is not too easy and not arbitrarily difficult. Long ago, Lev Vygotsky (1978) coined the term "zone of proximal development." Vygotsky thought that advances in cognitive development occurred when a learner encountered tasks that the learner could not do alone but could accomplish with the assistance of a teacher, mentor, or knowledgeable peer. Without the challenge of difficult tasks, real learning does not occur. Of course, because early adolescents are so social, what Vygotsky describes is often a preferred way of learning for them. The challenge for the teacher is to find each student's zone of proximal development and match it with appropriate help. That is more likely in an environment that is diverse.

Let's revisit Liza and dig more deeply into the school experiences that she shared with us. Kayleigh (one of the authors and Liza's English language arts teacher) completed Liza's interview, and Holly noticed a few crucial nuggets in Liza's experience as an outside listener. Liza has obsessive-compulsive personality disorder and what many might describe as crippling anxiety. First, Liza sat and talked with Kayleigh for an hour, openly sharing her firsthand experiences of both her struggles and her achievements. This alone shows the impact of having adult advocates to create a supportive and successful environment. Liza is a product of a post-pandemic class; she spent her sixth-grade year at home and did not return to an in-school setting until seventh grade. For her, the remote learning was a blessing in disguise as she had started to battle a ferocious anxiety about school shootings. She said it was often hard for her to leave her home and, when she did, she mostly did so in tears. Teachers at our school were very aware of and in tune with Liza's needs. She said she felt safe in our school, knowing that Counselor Kathy was always nearby to take Liza on a calming walk when, say, in the middle of class she would have the paralyzing and distracting thought of "You know what could happen right now? A school shooting." Teachers also built a relationship with and a routine for Liza so that she could process her feelings in a healthy manner before starting her day and thus stay engaged in her academics. And was she engaged! She talked openly about multiple projects, from a project on the revolution to her PBL project on LGBTQIA+ communities, projects that captivated her. When she talked about her electives, Liza's passion was palpable. Liza and Kayleigh had several minutes in their interview where they gushed over their love of books and the fact that she could be in a book club that allowed her to get lost in literature twice a week with her trusted teacher and peers from all three grade levels. Liza laughed and expressed how much fun her creative-writing elective was and how jealous some of her friends at other schools had been when she told them what activities she got to choose throughout the year.

Pause and Reflect: Look at what Liza has shared about her highs, her lows, and her learning environment. What do you notice about the environment of Liza's school? Make some evaluations based on the characteristics explored in this section. Think about your own experiences in middle school (or those you have observed if you do not remember)?

Conclusion

It was once common to describe adolescent development in terms of deficits (such as thinking that adolescents do not have abstract reasoning, the ability to take the perspective of another, or the ability to regulate emotions). While there is a grain of truth in each of those descriptions, we have chosen to focus on four themes that accentuate early adolescents' promise. However, early adolescents do have a deficit of experience and knowledge. There are many things they have not experienced and many things they do not know. They share that relative state of ignorance with most of us adults in many domains. Adolescents experience diverse cultures in important ways. But, across cultures, when early adolescents explore the possibilities in rich physical, intellectual, and social environments with the support of teachers and mentors, they overcome their deficit of experience.

One of us had a college roommate who grew up in the near suburbs of Washington, DC. When asked how often his school experience had availed him of the rich array of museums, galleries, libraries, and zoos (all available at no cost), the roommate said, "Never." How sad. But you do not need to live in our nation's capital to find rich sources to enhance exploration and the generation of possibilities. They are everywhere.

Pause and Reflect: The next three chapters, titled the Physical Self, the Academic Self, and the Social Self, will explore these ideas in more detail with applications for you in your work with middle school students. For now, reflect on the asset-based language of this chapter, and think about your position as a middle level educator. How does thinking about adolescents with the mindset of possibilities (rather than deficits) confirm and/or challenge your previous conceptions of adolescents? In what ways do these themes help your mindset as a future educator?

To summarize, let us revisit our learning outcomes:

1. **Identify and analyze key developmental issues in early adolescence.** Early adolescence (from ten to fourteen years of age) is a phase marked by intricate changes in social, cognitive, and physical aspects. This period is characterized by increasing complexity as adolescents begin to think in more intricate ways. We recognize the importance of recognizing cultural differences, the interconnectedness of developmental domains, and the potential influence of cohort effects on adolescent development. This pathway is not linear for adolescents, but teachers can support students along this pathway by using an assets-based lens, appreciating their capabilities and strengths, and fostering a positive outlook on adolescent development.

2. **Describe adolescents' abilities as abstract thinkers.** Researchers have shifted their understanding of early adolescence from the early notions of a sudden transition to abstract thinking toward an understanding that this transition is more of a gradual development in thinking abilities. We see early adolescents displaying an enhanced capacity to think about multiple constructs and abstract concepts with improved processing speed, improved processing efficiency, and improved executive functioning. Their personal interests and experiences play a pivotal role in their ability to generate hypotheses, engage in scientific reasoning, make decisions, and refine their theory of mind.

3. **Explain how adolescents are active explorers.** Early adolescents are active explorers of their environment, allowing them to deepen their curiosity and leveraging their ability to generate possibilities. While general curiosity may decline during early adolescence, early adolescents thrive at finding novelty in the familiar, especially when exposed to an enriched learning environment. Adolescents work toward focused exploration of their individual interests as teachers cultivate those interests, linking what may initially seem less interesting to something more engaging. Additionally, adolescents begin exploring their self-identities, and supportive environments play a crucial role in fostering positive self-perceptions.

4. **Identify ways that adolescents make connections with parents and peers.** Adolescents are inherently social beings, and peers and adults both play vital roles in development. Peers have some influence, especially in matters of immediate importance, but authoritative parenting remains an influential factor in early adolescents' lives, particularly in supporting self-regulation, identity development, and resilience. Peer relationships are often location dependent and have positive contributions to adolescents' development by fostering social skills, communication skills, conflict resolution ability, and so on. Popularity is not essential for adolescents, but having one or two close friends with shared interests (like Khalil's friendship trio) can be meaningful during this time of development.

5. **Describe factors that contribute to an environment in which adolescents fit and thrive.** Early adolescents thrive in environments that are sensitive to their needs, with adults as support. Their environments should offer physical and intellectual resources that stimulate exploration and varied interests. Diversity in social

and physical environments is imperative to foster exploration and understanding of cultural, ethnic, and developmental differences. Environments should provide challenges to students at an optimal level within students' zone of proximal development.

References

Ackerman, P. L. (2023). Intelligence: Moving beyond the lowest common denominator. *American Psychologist, 78*, 283–97. doi.org/10.1037/amp0001057.

Barzeva, S. A., Richards, J. S., Veenstra, R., Meeus, W. H. J., & Oldehinkel, A. J. (2022). Quality over quantity: A transactional model of social withdrawal and friendship development in late adolescence. *Social Development, 31*, 126–46. doi:0.1111/sode.12530.

Baumrind, D. (2013). Authoritative parenting revisited: History and current status. In R. E. Larzelere, A. S. Morris, & A. W. Harrist (Eds.), *Authoritative parenting: Synthesizing nurturance and discipline for optimal child development* (pp. 11–34). American Psychological Association. doi:10.1037/13948-002.

Bessanta, J., & Watts, R. (2012). The mismeasurement of youth: Why adolescent brain science is bad science. *Contemporary Social Science, 7*, 181–96. doi:10.1080/21582041.2012.691541.

Blakemore S. J. (2012). Development of the social brain in adolescence. *Journal of Royal Society of Medicine, 105*, 111–16. doi:10.1258/jrsm.2011.110221.

Ciranka, S., & van den Bos, W. (2021). Adolescent risk-taking in the context of exploration and social influence. *Developmental Review, 61*, 100979. doi:10.1016/j.dr.2021.100979.

Côté, J. E. (2009). Identity formation and self-development in adolescence. In R. M. Lerner & L. Steinberg (Eds.), *Handbook of adolescent psychology: Vol. 1, Individual bases of adolescent development* (pp. 266–304). John Wiley & Sons. doi:10.1002/9780470479193.adlpsy001010.

Crone, E. A. (2017). *The adolescent brain: Changes in learning, decision-making and social relations*. Routledge.

Damon, W. (1983). *Social and personality development: Infancy through adolescence*. W. W. Norton.

De Vos, J. (2016). *The metamorphoses of the brain: Neurologisation and its discontents*. Palgrave Macmillan. doi:10.1057/978-1-137-50557-6.

Ehrhardt, A. D., & Schacter, H. L. (2024). Connecting adolescent friendships to physical health outcomes: A narrative review. *Social Development, 33*, e12726. doi:10.1111/sode.12726.

Erikson, E. H. (1968). *Identity, youth, and crisis*. W. W. Norton.

Ferrer-Wieder, L., & Kroger, J. (2020). *Identity in adolescence: The balance between self and other*. Routledge.

Giletta, M., Choukas-Bradley, S., Maes, M., Linthicum, K. P., Card, N. A., & Prinstein, M. J. (2021). A meta-analysis of longitudinal peer influence effects in childhood and adolescence. *Psychological Bulletin, 147*, 719–47. doi:10.1037/bul0000329.

Gottfried, A. E., & Gottfried, A. W. (2009). Development of gifted motivation: Longitudinal research and applications. In L. Shavinina (Ed.), *International handbook on giftedness* (pp. 617–31). Springer Netherlands. doi:10.1007/978-1-4020-6162-2_30.

Harris, D. (Ed.). (1957). *The concept of development*. University of Minnesota Press.

Harter, S. (2012). *The construction of the self: Developmental and sociocultural foundations* (2nd ed.). The Guilford Press.

Henderson, B. B., Gold, S. R., & McCord, M. T. (1982). Daydreaming and curiosity in gifted and average children and adolescents. *Developmental Psychology, 18,* 576–82. doi:10.1037/0012-1649.18.4.576.

Inhelder, B., & Piaget, J. (1958). The growth of logical thinking: From childhood to adolescence. (A. Parsons & S. Milgram, Trans.). Basic Books. doi:10.1037/10034-000.

Jansen, M., Lüdtke, O., & Schroeders, U. (2016). Evidence for a positive relation between interest and achievement: Examining between-person and within-person variation in five domains. *Contemporary Educational Psychology, 46,* 116–27. doi:10.1016/j.cedpsych.2016.05.004.

Kuhn, D. (2009). Adolescent thinking. In R. M. Lerner & L. Steinberg (Eds.), *Handbook of adolescent psychology: Vol. 1, Individual bases of adolescent development* (pp. 152–86). John Wiley & Sons. doi:10.1002/9780470479193.adlpsy001007.

Larson, R. W., Wilson, S., & Rickman, A. (2009). Globalization, societal change, and adolescence across the world. In R. M. Lerner & L. Steinberg (Eds.), *Handbook of adolescent psychology: Vol. 2, Contextual influences on adolescent development* (pp. 590–622). John Wiley & Sons, Inc. https://doi.org/10.1002/9780470479193.adlpsy002018.

Laursen, B., & Veenstra, R. (2023). In defense of peer influence: The unheralded benefits of conformity. *Child Development Perspectives, 17,* 74–80. doi:10.1111/cdep.12477.

Lerner, R. M., Lerner, J. V., & Benson, J. B. (2011). Positive youth development: Research and applications for promoting thriving in adolescence. *Advances in Child Development and Behavior, 41,* 1–17. doi:10.1016/b978-0-12-386492-5.00001-4.

Litman, J. (2019). Curiosity: Nature, dimensionality, and determinants. In K. A. Renninger & S. Hidi (Eds.), *The Cambridge handbook of motivation and learning* (pp. 418–42). Cambridge University Press. doi:10.1017/9781316823279.

Low, K. S., Yoon, M., Roberts, B. W., & Rounds, J. (2005). The stability of vocational interests from early adolescence to middle adulthood: A quantitative review of longitudinal studies. *Psychological Bulletin, 131,* 713–37. doi:10.1037/0033-2909.131.5.713.

Oberle, E., Ji, X. R., Alkawaja, M., Molyneux, T. M., Kerai, S., Thomson, K. C., Guhn, M., Schonert-Reichl, K. A., & Gadermann, A. M. (2024). Connections matter: Adolescent social connectedness profiles and mental well-being over time. *Journal of Adolescence, 96,* 31–48. doi:10.1002/jad.12250.

Piekny, J., & Maehler, C. (2013). Scientific reasoning in early and middle childhood: The development of domain-general evidence evaluation, experimentation, and hypothesis generation skills. *British Journal of Developmental Psychology, 31,* 153–79. doi:10.1111/j.2044-835X.2012.02082.x.

Posada, G. E., & Waters, H. S. (2018). The mother-child attachment partnership in early childhood: Secure base behavioral and representational processes: I. Introduction: The co-construction of mother–child attachment relationships in early childhood. *Monographs of the Society for Research in Child Development, 83*(4), 7–21. doi:10.1111/mono.12388.

Qu, Y. (2023). Stereotypes of adolescence: Cultural differences, consequences, and intervention. *Child Development Perspectives, 17,* 136–41. doi:10.1111/cdep.12489.

Renninger, K. A., & Hidi, S. (2019). Interest development and motivation. In K. A. Renninger & S. Hidi (Eds.), *The Cambridge handbook of motivation and learning* (pp. 265–90). Cambridge University Press. doi:10.1017/9781316823279.013.

Rubin, K. H., Bukowski, W. M., & Parker, J. G. (2006). Peer Interactions, Relationships, and Groups. In N. Eisenberg, W. Damon, & R. M. Lerner (Eds.), *Handbook of child psychology: Social, emotional, and personality development* (pp. 571–645). John Wiley & Sons, Inc.

Small, M. L., & Adler, L. (2019). The role of space in the formation of social ties. *Annual Review of Sociology, 45,* 111–32. doi: 10.1146/annurev-soc-073018-022707

Smetana, J. G. (2011). *Adolescents, families, and social development— How teens construct their worlds*. Wiley Blackwell.

Steinberg, L. D. (1996). *Beyond the classroom: Why school reform has failed and what parents need to do*. Simon & Schuster.

Su, R., Rounds, J., & Armstrong, P. I. (2009). Men and things, women and people: A meta-analysis of sex differences in interests. *Psychological Bulletin, 135*, 859–84. https://doi.org/10.1037/a0017364

Tervo-Clemmens, B., Calabro, F. J., Parr, A. C., Fedor, J., Foran, W., & Luna, B. (2023). A canonical trajectory of executive function maturation from adolescence to adulthood. *Nature Communications, 14*, 6922. doi:10.1038/s41467-023-42540-8

Twenge, J. M., Carter, N. T., & Campbell, W. K. (2016). Age, time period, and birth cohort differences in self-esteem: Reexamining a cohort-sequential longitudinal study. *Journal of Personality and Social Psychology, 112*, No. 5, e9 – e17. doi:10.1037/psAge, Time Period, and Birth Cohort Differences in Self-Esteem:

Weimer, A. A., Warnell, K. R., Ettekal, I., Cartwright, K. B., Guajardo, N. R., & Liew, J. (2021). Correlates and antecedents of theory of mind development during middle childhood and adolescence: An integrated model. *Developmental Review, 59*, 100945. doi:10.1016/j.dr.2020.100945

Vygotsky, L. S. (1978). *Mind in society: The development of higher psychological processes*. Harvard University Press.

CHAPTER 3

The Physical Self

Learning Outcomes:

1. Describe the typical elements of puberty and the physical development of adolescents.
2. Describe ways to support adolescents' physical needs within the classroom setting.
3. Understand the various environmental factors that impact adolescents' physical well-being.

Defining Adolescence

Adolescence is a remarkable period between childhood and adulthood. This time encompasses a myriad of significant physical, psychological, and social changes. Within this phase not only the body but also the mind is changing rapidly. Adolescents begin to develop a social identity (even if it changes multiple times as they grow older). Independence becomes an emphasis in all contexts, and yet often adolescents simultaneously hold on to the routine and structure and adult influences in their life. Adolescence is characterized by a variety of new emotions, the exploration of personal values, and the defining of a moral compass to guide one's life within one's societal context. This chapter will focus primarily on physical development and practical implications for educators. We will also explore some notions of how physical development interrelates with social and cognitive development; we will delve more into those aspects in Chapter 4 and Chapter 5.

Meet Dion: Dion is a charismatic eighth grader with enough personality to fill a room. He has a core group of close friends but also can sit with any group and strike up a conversation. He has had typical experience in terms of physical development, having had several growth spurts and weight fluctuations as his body has matured over the last three years. In this chapter, he shares anecdotes to capture some of the on- and off-campus behaviors of himself and his peers.

Physical Development

As adults, it is essential to take a moment and reflect on our journey through **puberty**—the phase of life that carried a whirlwind of awkwardness and change. Remember those days when our bodies underwent remarkable transformations, leaving us feeling a little out of place in our own skin? We may be flooded with memories of the awkward in-between, also known as puberty. We remember feeling weirdly short or tall, compared with our peers; the appearance of acne on our previously smooth skin; strange sounds coming from our vocal cords as our voices dropped; or running to the bathroom when something felt weird, just to find out that our first period had arrived. Puberty introduced us to a world where our once-familiar bodies had a mind of their own. As we navigate through the complexities of adulthood, it is worth pausing to appreciate the journey we undertook, embracing the metamorphosis that shaped us into who we are today. Apart from the first two years of life, adolescence is the time of most rapid and significant physical changes. Thinking back to this time is also helpful to the middle school educator as the rapid changes in adolescent students impacts daily instructional practices and educator responses to students' behaviors.

Puberty is the stage in which adolescents reach sexual maturity. For female adolescents, this is indicated by the start of breast development, pubic hair growth, and menstrual cycles, typically occurring from ten to fourteen years of age. For male adolescents, puberty starts with maturation of the penis and testicles but is also highlighted by growing pubic hair and having voice changes, usually between the ages of twelve and sixteen. During this time, most adolescents will experience growth spurts which can make body movements clumsy and even painful (i.e., growing pains) (Wiles et al., 2006). We also know that all the changes of puberty can have an impact on the stress level of **transgender and nongender-conforming youth** (Bishop & Harrison, 2021). Table 3.1 gives generalized descriptions of the physical changes for each gender assigned at birth.

Table 3.1 Physical Changes during Puberty

Male	*Female*
-Enlargement of scrotum and testes	-Development of breast buds areola and nipple development
-Enlargement of penis	
-Hair growth in the pubic region	-Hair growth in the pubic region
-Limbs (hands, feet, legs, arms) develop ahead of the rest of the body	-Increase in hair growth other places including legs and armpits
	-Body changes shape: hips widen, more fat develops in buttocks and thighs
-Increase in hair growth other places including face, legs, and armpits	-Limbs (hands, feet, legs, arms) develop ahead of the rest of the body
-Voice changes and may "crack"	
-Will begin to have erections	-As hormones increase there may be oily skin and more sweating often acne occurs
-Begin to develop semen (often will be released during a nocturnal emission)	
	-Menstruation begins

Source: Stanford, https://www.stanfordchildrens.org/en/topic/default?id=puberty-adolescent-female-90-P01635, retrieved September 5, 2023

We might wonder why it is important to think about the potentially uncomfortable nature of the changes listed in Table 3.1. Think for a moment about the sheer amount of change happening physically to adolescents, not even considering the cognitive and social-emotional changes happening simultaneously. Taking a close look at this physical progression gives educators perspective about all the things that may be on an adolescent's mind—experiences that may feel more important to that adolescent than annotating a short story. Below, Holly shares a brief reflection on her puberty experience:

> If you had asked me a week ago to reflect on my adolescence, I would have said . . . I had a great middle school experience (which is predominantly true), but as I sat down to write this vignette, I started digging a little deeper into my memory and finding that puberty kind of sucked. And if I think about it now as an adult, I see where some of my adult behaviors and feelings, particularly about body image, have come from . . . so let's get into those repressed memories shall we?
>
> I was one of the unlucky ones who got to be one of the first to grow tall, towering over my peers, especially the boys in my class, and one of the first to get her period at the beginning of fifth grade. I was lucky, however, that this happened to me in the safety of my own home on a weekend morning when I could simply cry out for my mom (who I felt like I had never needed more). It did not matter that my mom had prepped me, and we had talked about it and read all the books . . . it is really disconcerting to go to the restroom and see a puddle of blood in your underwear. And just think—I WAS prepared by my mom. How many of my peers did not have that luxury of supportive and proactive family support? My best friend had been much unluckier in this endeavor—she got hers in 4th grade while wearing white shorts and in the middle of the school day. I won friend points that day for sacrificing my long sleeve shirt for her to tie around her waist as we walked to the office to call her mom. At least we had each other to talk to about the weird changes in our bodies, but there is just no getting around it being downright uncomfortable. And then oddly it became something we were proud of: oh well I have had mine for two years already, you are just getting yours now? As if period cramps and stuffing pieces of cotton into your body each month was an experience to be relished.
>
> Several of my close friends began to deal with horrible acne problems and many of my peers started getting braces and suddenly they no longer smiled fully as they were filled with embarrassment over their "metal mouths." And because tweens are just cruel sometimes, they were teased incessantly about them. I continued to tower over my male peers, an entire foot over my "boyfriend" at the time. Close dancing in the middle school cafeteria with his head pressed against my non-existent breasts had to have been [an] entertaining (or embarrassing?) sight for the chaperones. Because my sexual maturity had not caught up though, I was blissfully unaware that this might be inappropriate at the age of 12. I was captain of the cheerleading squad, but my hips and thighs had developed far beyond my peers so none of the school uniforms fit me. My mom had to sew an extra panel into the skirt just so I could get it to button. The hourglass shape I saw on the cover of

every magazine was a far reach for my purely rectangular body. I went on my first diet at the age of 12, constantly chasing a certain size or number on the scale. I had a sweatshirt perpetually tied around my waist to hide my belly and hips from even myself.

What did this mean for my interactions in school? I was a well-adjusted kid, but I definitely had an unhealthy obsession with my looks and a hatred of my body that would follow me into adulthood. I would get up at 5 AM each morning to painstakingly curl my hair (which I believed to be my best physical attribute), and I just felt extra aware of the space I took up in the world all the time . . . thinking as I sat down at my desk that my thighs spread too wide and would think of how to position myself in my chair for this to be less true. I was most certainly distracted and while I was a strong student, there is no doubt in my mind that I was not as present with my academic learning as I could have been.

Whether it is height, weight, skin, voice, level of athleticism (or lack thereof), teeth, glasses, breath, body odor, etc., there is some part of the pubertal process that is impacting how students function in school, and it is our job as their teachers to give them empathy and grace as they navigate that awkward in-between. Several teaching guides have suggested simple things like putting a mirror in the classroom to help lessen the constant requests to use the restroom. One of us has an entire section of her classroom devoted to boosting self-confidence with an array of lotion, floss, gum, hair ties, spray deodorant, etc. that students can use at their leisure to help them look and feel their best during the school day. While we may not be able to fully mitigate the obsession with appearance, we can easily give them an outlet to address this without leaving the classroom. It will be small things you cultivate in the culture of your classroom to best support students through these significant changes.

Pause and Reflect: Think back to your own journey through puberty—what aspects felt the worst? The most empowering? The most embarrassing? How did those changes affect your interaction with your world—think about your peer interactions as well as your interactions with adults.

Additional Factors: Nutrition, Metabolism, and Lifestyle
Our society has evolved in terms of how humans spend their time. The national **Youth Risk Behavior Survey (YRBS)** data over recent decades shows interesting trends related to physical activity and sedentary lifestyle behaviors. For example, there has been minimal change in the past fifteen or so years in the percentage of adolescents who were physically active for a total of at least sixty minutes per day on five or more days per week, hovering between 49 percent in 2011, down to 46 percent in 2017. Meanwhile, in the late 1990s, around 42 percent of adolescents reported watching more than three hours of television per day but in 2017 that statistic has dropped drastically to a mere 20 percent. Twenty percent in 1999 and 40 percent in 2017 spent more than three hours per day using computers or playing video games. Then add more recent statistics. According to the Kaiser Family Foundation, kids between the ages of eight and eighteen spend an average of 7.5 hours in front of a screen for *entertainment* each

THE PHYSICAL SELF   45

day. This number does not even consider the number of hours that students spend in front of screens at school or elsewhere each day on schoolwork and homework.

Then consider the nutritional needs and habits of adolescents as well as obesity trends in adolescents over the past fifty years. According to the National Health and Nutrition Examination Survey, obesity among adolescents is continually on the rise. For students aged twelve to nineteen, the percentage of adolescents who are obese has increased from 4.6 percent during the 1970s to 19.7 percent in 2020. The rate of increase has slowed in the past ten years but is still increasing. This gradual increase can be seen in Figure 3.1.

There is much comment about the "raging" hormones of adolescents and their related moody nature. Research indicates that this perception is exaggerated. Hormone levels are fluctuating as the body is developing. Sex hormones (testosterone and estradiol) as well as dehydroepiandrosterone (DHEA), and growth hormone are all changing rapidly during puberty (Peper & Dahl, 2013). Early studies made weak links between hormones and irritability and aggression, but these statistics only represent a small percentage of variance in terms of the effect of adolescence being the contributing factor. That said, there is evidence that the change in hormones as body mass increases may contribute to poor self-perception and, potentially, the development of eating disorders.

Sleep is another lifestyle factor impacting adolescents in the classroom. We know that, while we do not fully understand the relationship between puberty and circadian rhythms, there is evidence that sleep rhythms change during adolescence. Beyond biological factors, studies suggest correlations between the use of electronic media and later bedtimes; more use results in less sleep. There are two main arguments here. One is that the adolescents would choose to stay up late anyway—even if they did not use electronic media—and may use their devices only until they feel sleepy. There is also the argument that the lighted screens of devices make them unable to fall asleep. According to Willingham (2018), "the impact of typical levels of inadequate sleep on

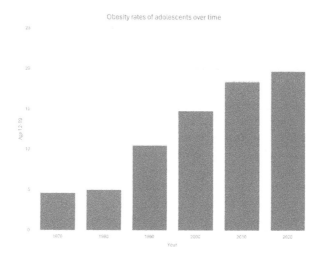

Figure 3.1 *Obesity rates of adolescents over time.* Created by authors

student learning is quite real, but it is not devastating. All the same, its impact lasts for years, and there is every reason to think that it is cumulative" (p. 38).

Knowing what we know about adolescents and their need to burn energy and move their bodies, it is important that we model healthy eating and movement for our students. We also need to be cognizant of ways to integrate students' learning about their bodies and their needs as well as implementing activities throughout the day that allow students to move beyond just a physical-education class. For starters, science teachers can capitalize on opportunities in their curriculum to teach about how students' bodies grow and develop and help students understand how to harness their own control about their healthy habits. Teachers can do some health challenges that focus on healthy habits—maybe a homeroom competition on who can spend the least amount of time on screens for a week, or who can do a total number of minutes of physical activity one week, or who can meet a healthy hydration challenge, which might include partnering with a community partner who could provide reusable water bottles to all students.

A program that encourages fitness and healthy lifestyles will go a long way in establishing foundational habits that will follow these students into adulthood. There is a tricky balance to be met here. We know that there are factors impacting obesity rates across racial and ethnic groups as well as barriers of poverty, food insecurity, and lack of access to food and health care that must be considered as well. **Body image** is of great concern during adolescence. Recent statistics highlight that 49 percent of boys and 57 percent of girls from eight to twelve years of age feel self-conscious about their bodies, and those numbers are even higher for those between thirteen and seventeen years of age, with 69 percent of boys and 73 percent of girls reporting self-consciousness as a concern (Natterson & Bennett, 2023). We have seen a big shift in social media toward the idea of **body positivity**. This movement, primarily driven by social media, encourages us to love our body, no matter the size and shape. This can be worrisome as, frankly, sometimes we do not love our body, and that is okay. A newer, potentially healthier view is that of **body neutrality**, which advocates for eliminating any perception of physical appearance being related to our self-worth. Whatever health program is implemented, it is important that the focus truly be on *health*, not appearance or external factors that adolescents already struggle with. The concept of body neutrality may help adolescents feel okay in their own skin, regardless of appearance, and truly focus attention on healthy habits that will decrease the chances of health risks along their path to adulthood. Almost thirty million people (about the population of Texas) in the United States have an eating disorder and approximately 95 percent of them are adolescents. Additionally, in alignment with *The Successful Middle School* (2021), **health and wellness programs** must be comprehensive, with sex education, including inclusive approaches supporting LGBTQIA+ students (Brinegar & Caskey, 2022). This is particularly important regarding body image, as the LGBTQIA+ population is two to four times more likely than their heterosexual peers to engage in weight-control behaviors (Natterson & Bennett, 2023). In addition to having a health program, schools also need to provide high-quality social-media literacy education to help adolescents navigate the potential manipulations utilized in social media, which influence feelings about lots of things, including body image.

Pause and Reflect: Think back to your own habits as an adolescent and compare them to your adult habits. Where did you learn your habits? Do you feel that your adolescent experience helped you build healthy habits to decrease health risk factors or not? If they did not, what do you think could have been implemented in your school programs to help you build a better foundation? How do you plan to model healthy behaviors for your future students?

The Adolescent Brain

Brain research is complex and multifaceted, and there is much we still do not know about the adolescent brain. Steinberg (2007) pointed to the fact that we have gotten it wrong—for well over a century; researchers have tried to explain adolescence (risk-taking during adolescence in particular) from a biological perspective, hoping to explain things we have not understood about this incredibly transformative period of life. While Steinberg asserts that we have far from a complete picture, we do have some potential directions of progress in this arena. Specifically, research conducted in recent decades has provided much more detail about the things we do know. We have all heard remarks about adolescents and young adults along the lines of "Well, their frontal cortex clearly isn't fully developed." This is often said in jest as a judgment of someone's lack of impulse control or poor decision-making. We do know that the **frontal cortex** (responsible for executive function and problem-solving), the **cerebellum** (responsible for coordination and movement), and the **amygdala** (responsible for emotion) are all undergoing massive change and development throughout the years of adolescence and young adulthood (Bahr 2017). We also know that these developmental pathways vary by individual and by gender. For female adolescents, the frontal cortex is typically fully developed two years prior to that of male adolescents (NPR, 2011). With a larger **corpus callosum**, adolescent girls may have more ability to easily switch between tasks and may have more abilities in language processing; in addition, their amygdalas may develop about eighteen months sooner than those of boys (Jensen, 2015). Adolescence is also when the corpus callosum and **myelination** processes occur, processes that are imperative to cognitive function.

For teachers, understanding the development of the brain is important as the frontal cortex, cerebellum, amygdala, corpus callosum, and myelination all impact students' motor, emotional, and cognitive functions. Will there be a quiz at the end of the chapter, asking you to define each of these and to explain their role in the brain? Absolutely not. The understanding is more conceptually based. For example, thinking about the frontal cortex's role in executive functioning highlights the need for teachers to plan activities to help enhance self-regulation and coordination. Knowing that the amygdala involves emotional processing underscores how important the classroom environment is and that students will need to learn emotion-regulation strategies. If we know that the corpus callosum has a role in integrating information, it helps us know that collaborative learning and multisensory methods should be used. And knowing that myelination impacts processing efficiency and processing speed helps us understand the importance of repetition and differentiated instruction. If we understand how the brain works during adolescence, we can utilize that knowledge to become better teachers for our students.

Brain research is everchanging, and it would be easy to quickly get into highly technical terms and curiosities (even more so than we already have). Steinberg (2007) cautions against premature generalization and oversimplification of brain research as "direct hormone–behavior linkages proved more difficult and less fertile than many scientists had hoped" (p. 81) and notes that the element of the environment is an important variable in the hormone–behavior manifestation. It is important for you as future educators to keep a pulse on the current research in terms of how it *potentially* impacts and alters teaching practices relevant to the adolescent brain. As we mentioned in Chapter 2, it is all too easy to fall into a reductionist trap when analyzing the complexities of the brain. One refreshing aspect of the last decade of research regarding the adolescent brain is the shift toward more asset-based thinking about adolescents. Take for example this quote from Galván (2021):

> Whereas early brain studies fueled the notion that the adolescent brain promoted problematic behavior, the contemporary perception is one of respect, awe, and appreciation for the opportunities, innovations, and adaptability that characterize adolescent brain. Both the scientific and nonscientific communities have been plagued by predictable cliché about rebellious attitudes, invincibility, and poor decision-making. But the tide is turning. (p.843)

See? Adolescents are not so bad after all.

Connecting Physical Self to Social Self

We have already explored some of the basic components of puberty and reflected on our own experiences during puberty. Some of these things are simply universal, and all humans will experience them. Some of the more social aspects of puberty, though, may be manifesting differently in contemporary generations than in earlier generations. Here we will argue that supporting adolescents through puberty may also be an evolving experience, one based on the generation we will begin teaching, which is now generation alpha. Generation alpha is the group of humans born between from 2010 through 2024. These students are already making their way through the school system, and their life point of view will influence how we teach and how we best support those students. As we explore the next section regarding **risky behaviors**, keep in mind this evolution of generational differences.

RISKY BEHAVIORS

Before digging into risky behaviors, let's set clear expectations of the word *risk*. What connotation does the word *risk* bring to mind? For many, the idea of risk brings up negative thoughts or feelings. Risk is associated with getting in trouble or getting hurt. Yet there are positive connotations of risk as well: taking a risk on trying something new and outside our comfort zone, taking a risk in trying a new food. These types of risks often have minimal or no negative consequences and potentially help encourage us to grow and adapt. So, as we explore "risky behaviors" of adolescents, keep in mind that there are an equal number of positive risk-taking opportunities that can help humans grow and flourish. Research supports the idea that risk-taking is heightened during adolescence and, while many studies have tried to explain why, most fall short of this. Steinberg (2007) argues that there is little that we can do to alter the biologically driven reward sensitivity that contributes to adolescent risk-taking. He suggests that altering environments may be easier. Focusing on explicit teaching of self-regulation skills may help too, although there is little research to show that doing so will be effective. Research does indicate that heightened engagement in risky behavior specifically contributes to several health risks that we will explore below (Boyer, 2006; Powers et al., 2022; Steinberg, 2007).

As defined by the **Center for Disease Control and Prevention (CDC)**, behaviors that are related to health risks include behaviors that contribute to unintentional injury or violence; tobacco, alcohol, and other drug use; sexual behaviors that contribute to unintended pregnancy and sexually transmitted illness or human immunodeficiency virus infection; unhealthy dietary behaviors; and physical inactivity (Underwood, 2020; Powers et al., 2022; and the CDC website). Patterns of data in each of these areas have changed over the past four decades or so, and we give updates on these trends below.

Suicide

Suicide among adolescents is an increasing concern in recent decades. The suicide rates for youth and young adults (ages 20–24) have increased 52.2 percent since 2000–2021 to become the second-leading cause of death for this age group. Youth and young adult suicides account for 15 percent of all suicides (CDC, 2023).

Keeping a pulse on students daily can be helpful in gauging students' mental health and their potential risk for dying by suicide. Encouraging students to share their feelings openly can be helpful. It is important for you, as a mandatory reporter, to disclose to students that, if they confide in a teacher something that must be reported, the teacher is obligated to do so. While we want our students to feel comfortable sharing information with us, we also need to ensure they do not feel betrayed if we do indeed have to report something. Also, know the limits of what you can do as a teacher. Bring in counselors, administrators, and outside community partners to help in supporting students if they are navigating a challenging time.

There are several critical components of preventative and proactive responses when a teacher feels a student might be exhibiting suicidal ideations. From a preventative standpoint, it is imperative to build a warm classroom environment with trust, where students feel safe, respected, and loved. Good middle schools integrate mental-health awareness into the curriculum, often in **advisory programs** or other social-emotional learning lessons.

Signs of suicidal ideation can be overtly obvious or, often, much more subtle. Often students will exhibit behavioral changes, such as withdrawing from friends, exhibiting moodiness, having an increased incidence of absences, or even giving away their personal possessions. We may notice students talking or writing more about death in various ways. They may also begin neglecting their hygiene or show changes in eating or sleeping habits.

If we see these kinds of changes in our students, it is crucial to act. If we have done our jobs well and have built strong relationships with students, we should be able to talk openly with students about our concerns. It is important to do so without judgment or being dismissive. Ask open-ended questions to help students express their thoughts and feelings. If you feel the student is in immediate danger, ensure that the student is not left alone. Then it is time to get professional help from appropriate resources, like a school counselor or a psychologist, and to work with parents and caregivers. Also, make sure the school has publicly posted resources for students, like the suicide and crisis lifeline (988 in the United States), which students can call or text. Schools often utilize reporting systems, like *Say Something*, whereby peers can anonymously report concerns about fellow classmates.

Pause and Reflect: Finding the right words in delicate situations can be difficult. Take a moment to script and, if possible, role-play a conversation with a student you feel may be exhibiting suicidal ideation. Practice your body language, tone, and questions. If you're working with a peer, give feedback to each other on these components.

Anxiety and Depression

Since the turn of the twenty-first century, there has been increased discussion of mental-health needs and pertinent issues related to mental health for both children and adults. In 2002, about 32 percent of adolescents met the requirements for an **anxiety disorder** of some kind, just in the United States. These disorders manifest differently during adolescence and typically include separation anxiety or some sort of specific or social phobia. Symptoms of anxiety disorders include stomachaches or headaches, which may not be easily recognized as symptoms of anxiety, and more cognitive symptoms, which may be reflected as defiant behavior rather than as worrying; worrying as a symptom of anxiety appears more in adults. We have also seen an increase in the incidence of depressive episodes in adolescents in recent decades. This is concerning on many levels; depression can lead to suicidal tendencies and physical disorders, such as diabetes (National Academies of Science, 2019).

Signs of anxiety include loss of interest in activities, changes in weight or appetite, changes in sleep, and exhibition of low energy. Students may also share that they have feelings of worthlessness, have trouble concentrating, or have thoughts of death or suicide. When we have students showing symptoms of anxiety, just as in our response to students showing suicidal ideation, we need to focus on establishing a comforting and trusting environment, talking to the students, recruiting help from school counselors, and working with parents to support students as they navigate their mental health. Figure 3.2 highlights several resources we can use when supporting students with anxiety or depression. Also, we recommend participating in mental-health first aid, as this gives teachers a strong toolkit for supporting students through a variety of issues.

THE PHYSICAL SELF 51

Mental Health America (MHA): Offers resources for understanding and supporting students with mental health issues.

National Alliance on Mental Illness (NAMI): Provides information on anxiety and depression, as well as resources for teachers.

Anxiety and Depression Association of America (ADAA): Offers resources for understanding anxiety and depression, including strategies for schools.

Centers for Disease Control and Prevention (CDC): Provides information on mental health in schools and strategies for supporting students.

American Psychological Association (APA): Offers resources for educators on supporting students with mental health issues.

School-Based Health Alliance: Provides resources and tools for integrating mental health services into schools.

Figure 3.2 *Resources for mental health.* Created by authors

Sex

We have discussed already how important a comprehensive sex-education program is for adolescents to be armed with the facts they need for healthy sexual behavior. We have seen some positive trends in terms of sex education and sex risk factors over recent decades. For starters, the teen birth rate has steadily declined. In fact, from 2007 to 2021, teenage birth rates (among those fifteen to seventeen years of age) declined 9 percent. On a broader scale, from 1990 to 2017, there has been a 73.6 percent decrease in teen pregnancy. Sexually active teenagers have shown more inclination to use of contraception, but there are also fewer teenagers reporting engaging in sex at all. The CDC data from the YRBS survey also indicate that teenagers reporting having had sex has fallen 17 percent since 2010. Some might argue that the COVID-19 pandemic may have contributed to recent declines, but there are long-range trends showing that adolescents in Generation Z and Generation Alpha are less likely to engage in sexual activity. Natterson and Bennett (2023) point out that there are some potential limitations to this data as well as that surveys often don't specify the degree or definition of sexual activity; therefore, it is tricky to interpret whether adolescents answer the way researchers anticipate. In contrast, when the CDC published a study in 2018, asking questions relating specifically to oral and anal sex, 30 percent of teenagers reported having engaged in oral sex and 11 percent reported having had anal sex. Our statistics, therefore, may not be as comprehensively representative as we assume. We must also acknowledge pornography as a factor in adolescents' sexual exploration. According to Natterson and Bennett (2023), the average age of first viewing of porn is twelve years of age for boys (and slightly later for girls). They report that sometimes the viewing is accidental but that it is often spurred by curiosity or used as an aid to masturbation. One potentially concerning statistic is that over half of the teenagers who have viewed porn report that the content often includes violent or aggressive behavior.

Another gap in research, as identified by Natterson and Bennett (2023), is lack of information about hookup culture. They identify how tricky it is for researchers to capture these elusive data due to just how hard it is to even define what hooking up means. Some people interpret hooking up as having sex while others infer it to mean everything but sex. There is also less linearity in hookup culture, where sex may happen before the dating or commitment part, which feels very different from conventional dating, going steady, which was the sex pathway of past generations. While a separate construct (addressed in a later chapter), another layer to hookup culture is **sexual fluidity**, where "sexual orientation is not fixed but changes depending on attraction and circumstance" (Natterson & Bennett, 2023, p. 217).

While we hope that students are having thorough conversations with parents at home, we must work to ensure that students have access to support and information to help them make informed decisions about their sexual identity. Work with health teachers to ensure that sex education is integrated into the curriculum to arm students with the information they need to make the best choices for themselves. As it stands in the United States, sex education is mandated in twenty-eight states and Washington, DC, and, when it is provided, there is variance in what content is required and emphasized. Table 3.2 highlights the requirements across the United States. Some states have specific constraints; for example, some states' mandated HIV education requires teaching that, among other behaviors, "homosexual activity" is considered to be "responsible for contact with the AIDS virus." Some states also prohibit teachers from responding to students' spontaneous questions in ways that conflict with the law's requirements. Iowa law prohibits teaching about sexually transmitted infections, gender identity, and sexual orientation before seventh grade. Florida law mandates teaching that a person's sex is binary and unchangeable and prohibits teaching about sexual orientation before ninth grade. It is important to do our best to provide information for our students while working within each state's legal constraints.

Tobacco and Drugs

Statistics from the CDC (2022) indicate that about 4.5 percent of middle school students report the use of tobacco products; 3.3 percent of middle school students report the use of e-cigarettes. Most statistics available refer to "all teenagers," so keep in mind that the following statistics include high school students. In terms of drugs,

Table 3.2 Requirements for Sex and HIV Education

When provided, sex education or HIV must:	Number of States
Be medically accurate	18
Be age appropriate	26 + DC
Be culturally appropriate and unbiased	10
When provided, sex education must include:	
Contraception	21 + DC
Abstinence	39 + DC (29 stress this, 10 cover it)
Importance of sex only within marriage	19
Sex education to include life skills on sexual consent, relationships, and prevention of violence	
Healthy relationships	31 + DC
Sexual decision-making and self-discipline	27 + DC
Refusal skills and personal boundaries	24 + DC
Consent	10 + DC
Dating and sexual violence prevention	38 + DC

Source: https://www.guttmacher.org/state-policy/explore/sex-and-hiv-education

the CDC reported in 2022 that over 30 percent of seniors reported having used marijuana, that 15 percent of high school students reported having used illicit or injection drugs (including cocaine, heroin, ecstasy, etc.), and that 14 percent of students reported having misused prescription opioids. At our school we have seen an increase in the use of vapes, more so than in the use of cigarettes or other drugs, and consistently enforcing consequences for this behavior is challenging due to how well students can hide them. Monitoring hallways, buses, and restrooms is important, as is having clear policies about vaping and consequences for policy violations. A comprehensive health program that explicitly teaches the facts and dangers of these drugs is a crucial part of helping our adolescents navigate and make healthy choices. Utilize the school nurse and local health departments to provide education to students about the associated risks of these substances. Having access to resources that support students who have engaged in risky behaviors is another important part of this system. Figure 3.3 shows several useful resources related to tobacco use for teachers.

We spoke with Dion to share his general perceptions of risky behaviors in school. While he feels that he does not dabble in anything particularly risky, he did share his experiences with his peers over his middle school years. Here are some of his thoughts:

> Nothing risky for me. But friends, I would say. Maybe sexual acts on the bus. Being on phones in class. Like sexting in class or at the dinner table, which my brother does. Smoking. Smoking in church and school. Being a rebel. Like just being a rebel in general, not following directions.

We asked how his peers seemed to get away with these behaviors without being caught. His response was that students hide things like vapes on their bodies consistently (maybe even in their shoes) and then escape to the bathroom to use them.

Figure 3.3 *Resources related to tobacco and vaping.* Created by authors

In class or on the bus they dabble by touching their thighs or using a blanket to hide what might be going on underneath the blanket.

According to Dion, social media is the root of much of the drama in school. He said,

> That is where all the trouble is like that. That's why fights start. It's like fights on reality TV because of social media. [For example, maybe you] find out your boyfriend or girlfriend is cheating on you or social media; it [is used for] everything. Like it's crazy. It's crazy off the streets. Social media is how people know almost everything. They will send screenshots of people saying, like someone saying, what they did in the bathroom with their boyfriend or girlfriend or whatever. That's how fights also start. It could be your text. You're texting someone, [then] they say something, screenshot it, send it to someone else. Like a text chain. It just keeps going. That's wrong. That is how everyone at school finds out about it.

Dion continued to explain how trust is destroyed among friend group members and that, when information they did not intend to give someone lands in that person's hands, things get blown out of proportion. So, according to Dion, risky behavior is indeed happening, and social media is fueling the fire. Now, is this representative of the general population? Not necessarily. Risky behaviors do exist in middle school, but many extreme behaviors are more the exception than the rule.

Pause and Reflect: Look back to the statistics about risky behaviors above, then also take a close look at what Dion shared with us (keeping in mind his perspective is one singular adolescent's point of view), and begin to think. What kinds of behaviors do you expect to see in middle schools? How well equipped do you feel in handling those behaviors? Name what resources you will need to help you in addressing health risk factors.

Interdependence: Physical, Social, and Cognitive Attributes of Adolescents

In surrounding chapters, we delve into global aspects of adolescent development, the development of academic identity, the development of social identity, and the physical experience of adolescence. We know that all these factors are related, so let's look at the big picture, cutting across these ideas to think about a snapshot of our "typical" students during the middle school years. These descriptions are generalizations, as we know that development is not a predictably linear process for adolescents and that some will develop in each area at different rates due to individual differences. That said, it is often helpful to think about trends we typically see at a certain age, as it impacts how each individual functions in a school setting. We will describe a generalized portrait and offer real-life insight into current middle school students, remembering from Chapter 2 that there will be marked individual differences.

The typical middle school student is beginning to think abstractly. This student's previously straightforward view of the world is evolving into a more intricate landscape of thoughts and ideas. Middle school students are becoming more concerned with social and political issues and enjoy exploring these more complex subjects and engaging in discussion as they navigate their opinions. **Peer relationships** are particularly important for middle school students, and a feeling of acceptance by peers is crucial to their mood and well-being. A typical middle school student maintains a close group of friends but is also grappling with curiosity about different social circles. Typically, middle school students are starting to want some independence from parents and begin to test boundaries there. Meanwhile, this student is going through massive physical changes, including growth spurts and changes to his or her physical attributes.

To summarize, let us revisit our learning outcomes:

1. **Describe typical elements of puberty and physical development of adolescents.** Puberty is a time of significant physical changes in adolescents, with sexual maturation of male adolescents (growth in the scrotum and the penis and growth of pubic hairs) and female adolescents (breast development, changes in body shape, and onset of menstruation). These changes have a potential impact on adolescents' self-esteem and how they interact with their environments.

2. **Describe ways to support adolescents' physical needs within the classroom setting.** Incorporating opportunities for movement into the curriculum can help students manage their energy. Teachers can do simple things like having mirrors in the classroom for students to be able to see themselves throughout the day. Schools need to have solid health programs to support students as they navigate the creation of healthy habits to support their physical and mental changes.

3. **Understand the various environmental factors that impact adolescents' physical well-being.** Environmental factors, such as screen time, sedentary lifestyles, and nutrition, play a critical role in adolescents' physical well-being. Emphasizing healthy choices, getting sufficient sleep, and managing stress are helpful for students to fight health risk factors. Ensuring that teachers model healthy behaviors, integrating health education into the curriculum, and promoting body-neutrality approaches in school will help students increase their physical well-being while avoiding negative undercurrents of appearance-related pressures.

Suggested Readings

Brinegar, K., & Caskey, M. M. (2022). *Developmental characteristics of young adolescents: Research summary.* Association for Middle Level Education.

Natterson, C., & Bennett, V. K. (2023). *This is so awkward: Modern puberty explained.* Rodale Books.

References

Brinegar, K., & Caskey, M. (2022). *Developmental characteristics of young adolescents: Research summary.* Association for Middle Level Education.

Farberman, R., & Bright, W. (2022). State of obesity 2022: Better policies for a healthier America. https://www.tfah.org/report-details/state-of-obesity-2022/.

Center for Disease Control and Prevention. (2023). Disparities in suicide. https://www.cdc.gov/suicide/facts/disparities-in-suicide.html.

Center for Disease Control and Prevention: National Center for Health Statistics. (2010). Obesity and overweight. http://www.cdc.gov/nchs/fastats/overwt.htm.

Centers for Disease Control and Prevention. (2022). Tobacco product use among middle and high school students—United States, 2022. *Morbidity and Mortality Weekly Report, 71*(45), 1429–35. https://doi.org/10.15585/mmwr.mm7145a1.

Center for Disease Control and Prevention. (2017). Trends in the prevalence of physical activity and sedentary behaviors national YRBS: 1991–2017. www.cdc.gov/yrbss.

Galván, A. (2021). Adolescent brain development and contextual influences: A decade in review. *Journal of Research on Adolescence, 31*(4), 843–69. https://doi.org/10.1111/jora.12687.

Hamilton, B., Martin, J. A., & Osterman, M. J. K. (2023). Vital statistics rapid release report no. 28 n June 2023 births: Provisional statistics for 2022. https://www.cdc.gov/nchs/products/index.htm.

Jensen, F. E., with Nutt, A. E. (2015). *The teenage brain: A neuroscientist's survival guide to raising adolescents and young adults.* HarperCollins Publishers.

Kaiser Family Foundation. https://www.kff.org/other/poll-finding/report-generation-m2-media-in-the-lives/.

National Academies of Sciences, Engineering, and Medicine. (2019). The promise of adolescence: Realizing opportunity for all youth. https://pubmed.ncbi.nlm.nih.gov/31449373/.

National Center for Health Statistics. National Health and Nutrition Examination Survey, 1999–2000 to 2017–2018. https://wwwn.cdc.gov/nchs/nhanes/Default.aspx.

Natterson, C., & Bennett, V. K. (2023). *This is so awkward: Modern puberty explained.* Rodale Books.

New, M. (2023). New CDC data show continued declines in teen sexual activity. https://www.nationalreview.com/corner/new-cdc-data-show-continued-declines-in-teen-sexual-activity/.

Peper, J. S., & Dahl, R. E. (2013). The teenage brain: Surging hormones—Brain-behavior interactions during puberty. *Current directions in psychological science, 22*(2), 134–39. https://doi.org/10.1177/0963721412473755.

VandenBos, G. R. (Ed.). (2007). *APA dictionary of psychology.* American Psychological Association.

CHAPTER 4

The Academic Self

Learning Outcomes:

1. Define and describe executive-function–related skills.

2. Define and describe self-regulation and self-directed learning and identify effective interventions for teaching those skills.

3. Describe strategies and interventions for supporting executive-function–related and self-regulation skills.

As students proceed through their educational journey, one of the complex learning experiences is learning how to "do" school. Beyond just learning core academic content, students are learning how to interact with their world—learning social norms; learning how to balance school requirements, such as homework, with other responsibilities; learning how to handle transitions; and learning to be prepared. These skills can be situated within a key set of cognitive abilities, including executive function, self-regulation, and motivation. In this chapter, we will explore the essential components of these skills by exploring foundational research and six lighting classroom strategies to help adolescents in each area. We will also utilize the cases of two students, Cade and Olivia, throughout the chapter to explore how teachers have supported them across the year. Let's meet the students:

Cade is a lively seventh grader with massive energy whose emotive nature occasionally results in a whirlwind of emotional expression. Cade admits that, at the beginning of the school year, starting in a new school, he was consistently distracted, did not have strong peer relationships, was rude to teachers, and struggled with his grades. He would rush through his day, was not able to consistently keep up with his belongings, would sometimes have a negative interaction with a peer or two, and then would spout out some mathematical brilliance along the way. After the first quarter, the teachers realized Cade needed more support related to his executive function and self-regulation skills.

Comparatively, Olivia is another energetic eighth grader who has consistently been a high performer in school. Olivia has an active social life and is incredibly involved in activities in and outside of school, including theater and the student-government association. Olivia has developed a toolkit of strategies to help balance her busy life and uses strategies encouraged by teachers to help stay organized. Her strategies include using a weekly organizer to track assignments and due dates.

Executive Function

Educational researchers and psychologists have long debated the definition of **executive function**, and more recent research utilizing technology to study the brain has only minorly helped hone the exact definition of executive function. Early work describes executive function as the process of meeting our goals—utilizing memory and attention to help us become adaptable and adjust to achieve (Eslinger, 1996). Several decades later, definitions of executive function utilize more specificity, including components such as attention and emotional regulation, initiation and inhibition, goal setting, planning and organization, flexibility, memory systems, and self-regulatory processes (Meltzer et al., 2018).

Executive-function–related skills are "higher-order cognitive processes essential for goal-oriented behavior and the self-regulation of attention, emotion, and behavior." (Carrera et al., 2019, p. 1). This includes cognitive processes like the ability to control responses to stimuli, working memory, and cognitive flexibility. While these skills begin developing from infancy, they gradually improve throughout childhood and adolescence. Research has shown that strong executive functioning for adolescents is highly dependent on those early experiences and that any sense of trauma or adversity in those early years impacts an adolescent's capacity for self-regulation (Carrera et al., 2019).

Executive functioning presents particular challenges for students with learning disabilities or ADHD or both (Denckla, 2018). Researchers highlight that students who transition from elementary to middle school with adequate academic skills may struggle due to the higher demand of executive-function skills in the middle school setting. For these students, what may be labeled by teachers as irresponsible, lazy, and unmotivated is realistically an immaturity of neurodevelopment. Developmental psychologists Moran and Gardner (2018) situate executive function as goal-directed behavior. They argue that executive function presents itself differently at various parts of life. Adolescents, for example, are most likely in the "apprentice" phase of executive function, meaning that the goals they are to achieve are likely set by parents and teachers rather than by themselves. These goals are situated within the student's social culture and are not introspective. Moran and Gardner use the analogy of *hill, skill,* and *will* describe executive function. *Hill* is the goal to be achieved, *skill* is related to the strategies and techniques to achieve the goal and *will* relates to the motivation and persistence toward achieving the goal. These parameters interact with each other but must work together to achieve the goal. For Cade, the hill is to be able to function better throughout his academic classes by not distracting peers, staying on task, and being kind and respectful to his teachers. The skill piece is built into the intervention (described later in this chapter) to support his changes in behavior, and Cade's will comes from the intrinsic and extrinsic motivation to achieve the goal. For extrinsic motivation, Cade's teachers use words of affirmation, encouragement, and rewards for his consistent improvement. Olivia's goal is to be an excellent student in all academic classes. She has developed and used additional teacher-created tools to stay organized; Olivia's executive functioning has developed to the point where she has sufficient intrinsic motivation and can achieve these goals without much external push from teachers.

When we think about the typical middle school classroom, it is important to consider how much executive functioning we expect from students. We require them to engage in long-term projects (sometimes even torturing them with collaborative group work), lengthy writing assignments, regular homework in multiple classes, and more. Often, middle school teachers assume that, because students have been in school for years and are maturing, they will automatically be able to manage all these activities. Teachers often focus on *what* students are learning and sometimes forget to focus on *how* they are learning—the strategies and techniques that students need to be academically successful need to be taught to and modeled for students. To access the science, mathematics, history, and language arts content through these varied learning opportunities, students will need help in learning to see the goal, in using skills to achieve the goal, and in finding the motivation and perseverance required to accomplish cognitively demanding tasks.

There are fundamental differences between the brains of adolescents and those of adults, particularly in the development of the frontal lobe, which is the part of the brain that helps humans control behavior. The frontal lobe is the largest part of the brain, and it experiences the most change during adolescence. Because the frontal lobe is not completely developed during the teenage years, the amygdala is utilized more for reasoning and problem-solving. This part of the brain is more responsible for emotional responses and reactions. The amygdala is not as sophisticated as the frontal lobe, which is responsible for abstract thoughts, impulse control, and moral judgments (Feinstein, 2014). Below we present potential examples of how being in this phase of frontal-lobe development may play out with adolescents.

Picture 4.1 Students collaborating. Photo, Western Carolina University

62   CHAPTER 4

Picture 4.2   Students getting feedback in ELA. Photo, Western Carolina University

EMOTIONAL OUTBURSTS

***Scenario 1*:** Sarah, a fourteen-year-old, is struggling with regulating her emotions. One day, her younger brother accidentally knocks over her favorite mug. In an instant, Sarah explodes in anger, yelling at him and throwing things around the room, unable to control her intense reaction to the minor incident.

Scenario 2: Alex, a twelve-year-old, is feeling overwhelmed by schoolwork and personal issues. During a math class, his frustration reaches a tipping point when he cannot solve a difficult problem. He slams his books on the desk, storms out of the classroom, and vents his anger by kicking a nearby locker, unable to manage his emotions appropriately.

SUSCEPTIBILITY TO PEER PRESSURE

Scenario 1: Jake, a fifteen-year-old, has always been conscious of fitting in with his friends. When his peer group starts experimenting with alcohol at parties, Jake feels pressured to join them, even though he knows it is against his better judgment and his parents' rules. He succumbs to peer pressure, disregarding the potential consequences and his own values.

Scenario 2: Emma, a thirteen-year-old, wants to be accepted by a popular group of girls at her new school. They convince her to shoplift a small item from a local store as a "test of loyalty." Despite feeling uneasy about it, Emma gives in to peer pressure, seeking their approval and failing to consider the legal and moral implications of her actions.

LACK OF EMPATHY

Scenario 1: Michael, a seventeen-year-old, witnesses a classmate, Amy, openly expressing her sadness after a difficult breakup. Instead of offering support or understanding, Michael mocks her and belittles her emotions in front of their peers. He fails to empathize with Amy's pain, focusing solely on gaining attention and reinforcing his own social standing.

Scenario 2: Lily, a sixteen-year-old, notices her best friend, Sarah, struggling with self-esteem issues and feeling left out at school. Instead of showing empathy and offering a listening ear, Lily dismisses Sarah's concerns, telling her to "just get over it" and not fully comprehending the emotional turmoil her friend is going through.

These are just a few plausible scenarios that exemplify the immaturity of the brain throughout adolescence.

Pause and Reflect: Look over the scenarios with a partner, and brainstorm plausible scenarios for each category (emotional outbursts, susceptibility to peer pressure, and lack of empathy). These can be from personal experience or made-up situations. Then brainstorm with your group about how you might address these scenarios as a teacher.

Holly's experiences with writing this chapter provide illustrations of executive function.

> For me, just beginning to draft this book was a daunting task. For weeks, months even, I would open the document, look at my book proposal, and

just stare at the blank screen. There is so much content to write about—which chapter do I start with? Some days I would start reading related articles and books that I knew I needed to dig into, but I did not have a structure or a process to get started. I would simply shut down and waste hours of available time—and I am an adult with three degrees in education and a fully developed frontal lobe. I need strategies to get myself started and to use my executive function toolkit. After reading a multitude of articles and books related to executive function, I realized I needed to organize the immense amount of information floating around in my head. So, I used a graphic organizer to get my initial ramblings on paper. I then created a structure of how to organize the resources I was using to support my ideas by listing the citation for each resource and my "notes and quotes" from each. I recognized that I needed to start with one chapter and not get overwhelmed by the need for 14 other chapters. Then I was finally able to put my fingers on the keyboard and start typing.

All learners, but particularly adolescents in middle school, need tangible strategies to tackle the tasks of "doing" school. These skills, of course, translate into skills that will make students turn into productive adults.

Pause and Reflect: To emphasize the importance of executive function in learning how to "do" school, reflect for a moment about yourself. Think back to a project, assignment, or task that you struggled to get started with or to complete. Perhaps you just looked at it and froze. Maybe the task felt so daunting that you instantly become overwhelmed and shut down. Does that experience make you lazy? Unmotivated? Or were you simply lacking a structure in your toolkit that would be helpful to complete the task? Try to think of examples of yourself as an adolescent versus as an adult. Brainstorm some ideas of what strategies you could have used in your toolkit for each instance.

Self-Regulation and Self-Directed Learning

Related to executive function, **self-regulation** is another set of complex mental processes that contribute to success in "doing" school. Cleary and Zimmerman (2004) describe self-regulation as involving a process for learners to utilize strategies or behaviors to achieve goals. Zimmerman first described self-regulated students as "metacognitively, motivationally, and behaviorally active participants in their own learning" (1986). Later, Zimmerman developed a cyclical model of self-regulation based on social cognitive research. In simpler terms, think of this cycle as "plan, practice, and evaluate." We know from research and anecdotal experience that mastering self-regulation can be challenging for adolescents. Zimmerman (1995) positions the thinking processes and challenges involved in learning self-regulation skills. Self-regulated learning includes deliberative and nondeliberative forms of cognitive engagement and highlights obstacles that hinder students' ability to self-regulate. Several examples of these hindrances include insufficient motivation, ineffective metacognitive self-monitoring, and inaccurate expectations and self-beliefs about learning. Self-regulation is complex, and there are many additional challenges to being successful in self-regulation. Because of this, we must be intentional in **modeling** and teaching strategies for students to build full capacity in these skills. Cleary and Zimmerman also discuss the disconnect between adolescents' development and their educational environments as students transition into middle school. While their brains are developing to a point where they desire more autonomy and choice, those are often restricted in the school environment, which will then impact students' motivation as well as their self-regulation skills.

Let's revisit Cade and think through how this cycle might work for his academic needs.

Plan it: Cade's teachers, Mrs. Rector and Ms. Clapp, meet with him to discuss his challenges and the need for improved self-regulation skills. They create a plan together to support Cade's executive function and help him develop better self-regulation strategies. The plan includes setting goals, creating a structured daily routine, and implementing strategies to improve focus and organization.

Practice it: Cade begins implementing the plan. Mrs. Rector and Ms. Clapp provide him with a checklist and a visual schedule to help him stay organized. They also introduce him to techniques, such as deep-breathing exercises and **mindfulness** activities, to help him manage his energy and focus better. Cade practices these strategies daily, both at school and at home.

Evaluate it: After a few weeks of practicing the strategies, Mrs. Rector and Ms. Clapp meet with Cade to evaluate his progress. They discuss his experiences, challenges, and successes. Cade acknowledges that he has been more aware of his distractions and has been making a conscious effort to stay focused. He shares that the visual schedule and checklist have helped him keep track of his belongings and assignments. Cade also mentions that he has noticed improvements in his relationships with peers and teachers, as he has been working on being more respectful and considerate.

Mrs. Rector and Ms. Clapp provide positive feedback, emphasizing Cade's growth and encouraging him to continue practicing self-regulation strategies. They adjust the plan based on his feedback, adding additional techniques like time-management strategies and self-reflection exercises. Over time, with consistent practice and evaluation, we see Cade's self-regulation skills improve. He becomes more organized, focused, and respectful in the classroom. Cade's grades also start to show improvement as he develops a more structured approach to his schoolwork. With ongoing support from his teachers and continued practice, Cade's self-regulation skills continue to strengthen, enabling him to navigate his academic and social responsibilities more effectively.

One example of how we have historically approached supporting self-regulation skills is the use of homework in schools. While past research has focused on the relationship between homework and achievement, little research has been done on how homework facilitates the development of self-regulation processes. Self-regulation of learning involves learners setting goals, selecting appropriate learning strategies, maintaining motivation, and monitoring and evaluating academic progress. Students who engage in self-regulatory processes while completing homework are more motivated and are higher achievers than those who do not use these processes. Ramdass and Zimmerman (2011) continue to explore how homework completion is associated with the development of various self-regulatory behaviors at elementary, middle school, high school, and college levels. They emphasize that, although homework has been criticized for not improving study skills, promoting self-discipline and responsibility, or enhancing students' academic achievement, it does provide opportunities for students to engage in a range of self-regulation processes, making it a classic form of practice in self-regulated learning. It is important to note that homework practices should be utilized with caution. The research regarding the effectiveness of homework on achievement is murky at best. In fact, as Cathy Vatterott (2018) reports, we can easily find outcomes both supporting and not supporting the value of doing homework, assuming we ignore the contradictory studies that also exist. We found that a certain amount of homework bears a positive relation to student achievement and that more homework is not better. For homework to be useful in building self-regulation skills, students must find the task to be valuable (and therefore be motivated to complete it), they must utilize their cognition (use effective strategies to complete the task), and then they must utilize metacognition to reflect (think about what they do and don't understand, based on this homework experience) (Cooper et al., 2006; Ramdass & Zimmerman, 2011). Good teachers are intentional about assigning homework that is related to a project where students have **voice and choice** and therefore are motivated and invested in the process. Good teachers may utilize concise review types of questions to hold students accountable but not to overwhelm them. A secondary consideration that could be the subject of a whole other book is to keep in mind that the intention of assigning homework is to give students feedback rather than to punitively grade them for compliance or for not yet understanding a topic. See the suggested readings at the end of this chapter to look more into this topic.

A closely related construct to self-regulation is **self-directed learning**. The concept of self-directed learning was developed by Malcom Knowles in the 1970s. While his investigations focused primarily on adult learners, his concepts are very easily applicable to middle school students. Self-directed learning is "a process in which individuals take the initiative, with or without the help of others, in diagnosing their learning needs, formulating learning goals, identifying human and material resources for learning, choosing and implementing appropriate learning strategies, and evaluating learning outcomes" (Knowles, 1975, p. 18). The distinction is that, in self-directed learning, the learner is the one choosing the task whereas, in self-regulated learning, activities and tasks are often chosen and guided by the teacher (Loyens et al., 2008). In a middle school classroom, self-directed learning will present itself as an independent project, a project-based learning activity, or other opportunities for students to have voice, choice, and control over how they approach a learning task.

Developing Academic Identity in the Classroom

Holly reflects on her early experiences teaching college.

> One of the first courses I taught when starting my assistant professor position at the university was a first-year seminar focused on education today.

The course was full of eighteen and nineteen-year-olds from various backgrounds, many first-generation college students. When they turned in their first big assignment, I realized I had made a world of assumptions about their ability to manage their time, organize their thoughts, and keep track of information. Despite a final deadline and a rubric provided for evaluation criteria, the products turned in were incredibly varied in structure, length, depth, etc. Even at the age of adulthood, many of my students were lacking in the underlying skills that would be imperative for their academic success in college. I realized that I would need to scaffold more opportunities in my class sessions to help students be more successful with final products. For example, the next semester I made sure to share a guiding document with clear tasks and deadlines with built in accountability for submitting pieces of the project before submitting the final project at the end of the semester. A few years later I went back to teaching middle school and I knew that if my college students struggled with these skills, my sixth, seventh, and eighth graders would also need structure and modeling of skills for things like keeping up with assignments, organizing notes and materials, how to study for assessments etc. So, I carefully modeled a consistent routine of how we would take notes. Students had tabs in their composition books with a section for building a glossary at the back. We practiced making headings and writing our "I can" statement each day with intentional use of examples and explanations. I thought I had everything covered. Then at the start of the second semester, I realized that while I had modeled and practiced the routine and had them set up for the first quarter, without continued reminders and practice, the skill had disappeared over the winter break. I discovered my error when I looked at students' notebooks and realized that instead of the clear labels I had encouraged, that there was simply a disorganized mess of random problems they had solved, followed by multiple blank pages and then more random problems with no headings and no context. I say this to emphasize that with all interactive modeling strategies that we share, it is important to remember that consistency and continual modeling are important for adolescents to truly utilize strategies toward academic success in the long term.

One potential starting point for teachers to measure the level of students' executive function and self-regulation is to utilize an assessment or a self-assessment in which students reflect on their own awareness of these skills. That said, there are several potential avenues for assessing these skills for students. A brief survey could easily be created, but there are already many existing resources. These types of activities and assessments can be a part of a larger school effort and accomplished during advisory with paired mini lessons on each concept. Programs such as REACH (Pekel, 2016) and Responsive Classroom for Middle School (Responsive Classroom, 2018) are two examples of programs with lessons and activities built in to support academic skills, including skills relating to executive function, self-regulation, and motivation. The structure of these advisory-like meetings typically includes students self-reflecting and assessing, brainstorming, and then engaging in a practical strategy for improvement.

Dawson and Guare (2018) list several other potential assessment measures, including a case history (usually an interview with teachers and parents), classroom observations, behavior checklists, and informal rating scales, as potential options for gauging initial skill levels prior to interventions being utilized. No matter which assessment tool is utilized, the generalized goals are to highlight specific strengths and weaknesses among executive-function–related skills; to identify previously utilized interventions and note whether they were effective; and to help tease apart the contexts in which problems are likely (or unlikely) to occur. This helps all the stakeholders be on the same page from the beginning and gives a solid starting point for designing an intervention. An example of this process is explored below when we revisit Cade and Olivia.

Attention can be given at a whole-group level by utilizing explicit instruction woven into core-content lessons. Meghan Hickey's (AMLE.org) music class, for example, had students self-assess using a modified tool (included in the suggested resources at the end of this chapter) from Dawson and Guare (2018) that targets areas of self-control, perseverance, and attention. Hickey then implemented interventions whereby students chose an area of growth either from the assessment results or based on their own interests. After implementing several mini lessons focused on topics such as organization, time management, and cognitive flexibility, Hickey had students reflect through journaling and the use of mantras. She would provide a journal prompt related to executive functioning for student response after each mini lesson. Examples of the prompts included, "Think about a moment in life that you really struggled with. Write about that moment. Would the mantra have helped you get through [that] challenging time?" or "Choose a song that relates to your mantra. Why did you choose this song?" In her reflection about this process, Hickey noted, as in my own previously mentioned experience, that students needed more support and reminders along the way to utilize those executive-functioning–related skills.

Interventions for Executive Functioning and Self-Regulation

So far, we have established ways to measure the existence of executive functioning and ways to incorporate executive-function–related skills within explicit whole-group instruction. We now shift our focus to targeted and individualized interventions. Dawson and Guare also emphasize two levels of intervention to help support students with weak executive-function–related skills—intervention may occur at the environment level or at the level of the individual. Changing multiple factors may have a positive impact on student success. It is a matter of changing the physical or social environment (think seating design and grouping structures) or altering the task for students (e.g., shortening tasks, giving choice, or providing a guiding structure). One powerful suggestion is to think about how we cue particular behaviors for students. For example, it may seem simple, but providing verbal reminders to the whole group, using proximity to and eye contact with students who may have underdeveloped executive-function–related skills can prompt students to actively think about what they need (e.g., to bring, to do, to write down). Also, do not underestimate the value of posted reminders.

This may be as simple as making sure there is a central place in the classroom for students to visualize the schedule or any needed reminders, such as reminders about getting permission forms signed or turning in homework.

Dawson and Guare (2018) outline several interventions to teach executive-function–related skills. The interventions they suggest are designed to address specific executive-function–related skills and can be adapted to suit different ages and skill levels. Below is a summary of these interventions:

1. **Self-monitoring:** Encourage students to keep track of their own behavior and progress by using a chart or a checklist. This intervention helps students develop self-awareness and self-regulation skills.

2. **Goal setting:** Help students set goals and create a plan of action to achieve them. This intervention improves planning and organization skills.

3. **Break down tasks:** Teach students to break down complex tasks into smaller, more manageable steps. This intervention enhances planning and problem-solving skills.

4. **Practice mindfulness:** Encourage students to practice mindfulness exercises, such as deep breathing or meditation, to help them focus and reduce stress. This intervention improves attention and self-regulation skills.

5. **Time management:** Teach students to use a planner or a schedule to manage their time effectively. This intervention helps improve planning and organization skills.

6. **Memory strategies:** Teach students memory strategies, such as visualization, association, or repetition, to help them remember valuable information. This intervention improves working memory and recall skills.

7. **Provide feedback:** Provide students with regular feedback on their progress and behavior. This intervention helps students develop self-awareness and self-regulation skills.

These interventions can be implemented in different settings, such as schools, homes, or clinics, and can be tailored to meet individual needs. By being taught executive-function–related skills, students can become more efficient and effective learners, which can lead to greater academic and personal success.

Holly has used several of these strategies in her middle school classroom over the last few years.

> One year I had a particularly excitable group of 6th graders who collectively struggled to get settled and back into an academic mindset when returning to the classroom after lunch. It was quickly apparent to me that my group needed a strategy to get settled and finish our class with strong focused effort. So, I started putting up a soundscape (from Calm or YouTube, or something I had recorded myself) to have some soothing music and a sense of an ocean, or a local waterfall in our region, or a rainstorm. Students then practiced entering the room after lunch quietly having a "mindful

minute" where they could put their head down, practice some breathing, or even draw in their notebooks. Students started to utilize the time in a meaningful way, some even utilizing some yoga stretches that I had taught them throughout the year. This use of mindfulness practices became a part of our culture, and the students would call me out if I skipped it. Another common strategy I utilized from this list is to break down tasks. My math classroom is structured to have a significant amount of exploration and collaboration time where students are investigating patterns to make mathematical generalizations. This often means being presented with a challenging task that may need to be chunked into smaller more manageable pieces for students to be able to feel successful.

Kayleigh also utilizes various strategies to promote self-monitoring, time management, memory retention, and effective feedback for students.

> To address behavior concerns, our team implemented a behavior chart utilized specifically for Nicole, a 7th-grade student who consistently arrives to class unprepared, dozes off during classes, and employs avoidance behaviors like frequent visits to the nurse's office. Nicole is encouraged to self-monitor by using a checklist that focuses on the identified concerns. By reviewing the percentage of checks earned in each class, Nicole can track her progress and earn a self-selected reward.
>
> To assist all students in managing their time and tasks, I use timers throughout the class. This allows the students to engage in discussions about how long they think is reasonable for different activities. The timers keep the class on track and serve as a model for effective time management.
>
> We often use memory strategies to enhance vocabulary retention. Students are encouraged to create mnemonic devices, such as associating a vocabulary word with its definition, synonyms, and symbolic representations. Additionally, the "3 S strategy" (subject, structure, and said) is a strategy I employ to aid in analyzing poems. Subject reminds students to extract the main idea and theme of the poem. Structure challenges students to think about the rhyme scheme, pacing, and the purpose of each stanza. Said is used to remind students to analyze the tone, word choice, and figurative language. To memorize prefixes, root words, and suffixes I use the alphabetical order of the initial letters in each component to help students recall and understand their meanings (p for prefix comes before r for root word which is then followed by s for suffix). I use this in additional examples including helping students associate vocabulary words with things they already know. For instance, the association of "fiction" with "fake" and "non-fiction" with "not fake" simplifies the comprehension of these terms.
>
> Feedback is provided to students in both formal and informal ways. Informal feedback is often given through small group discussions and parallel teaching during co-taught lessons. Whole-class reviews also offer opportunities for formal feedback. Writing conferences are conducted on a one-on-one or small group basis to address common issues that students may be facing in their writing. These varied feedback approaches ensure that

students receive guidance and support tailored to their individual needs, fostering their growth and development in the ELA classroom.

Pause and Reflect: Looking at the list of executive-function–related interventions and self-regulation strategies, can you think of yourself as an adolescent learner and think of any of these that were utilized by your teachers? Were there ones that you did not experience that may have been helpful to you? What characteristics of those interventions would have been particularly effective for you?

CADE AND OLIVIA'S INTERVENTIONS AND TOOLKITS

As we previously established, when Cade came to our school, he self-identified some struggles with peer relationships and behavior in class. After the first quarter, Cade's teachers knew they needed to do something concrete for Cade to find success in the classroom. They chose to implement a list for Cade to get checked off from each teacher throughout the day. Prior to making the checklist, Cade's core teachers met as a team and then again with Cade to discuss what *he needed* to have more support within class. This piece of the intervention is important, particularly at the middle school level, so that the student becomes a significant part of the discussion and builds a positive attitude. Cade having a voice and a sense of choice, rather than having something forced upon him, were key to his achieving success. After discussing his behavior needs with Cade, the teachers reached out to his family and asked his mom to come in for a meeting. Following the school's behavior plan system, teachers had all noted the same patterns of off-task, distracted, and disrespectful behavior that Cade had engaged in. While talking to his mom, teachers acknowledged that Cade's individual executive-function–related skills were low. Every time teachers gave him explicit instructions individually, he was much better at meeting expectations; however, he still failed to initiate these behaviors on his own. The goal was to explicitly identify a few actions that Cade most needed to improve and take ownership of throughout the school day. Figure 4.1 is a copy of the checklist Cade and his teachers created. Note that this is a widely flexible tool and should cater specifically to each individual child.

Cade expressed that, before he had the checklist, he had a lot of distractions, was rude to teachers, and had bad grades. He reflected that the checklist has helped him stay on task, start without adult prompting, and reduce peer interruption. Cade's relationship with his teachers improved as they noticed he was changing. Cade also indicated that the checklist has also taught him that following a structure helps him to "get somewhere" (i.e., achieve his life goals). His teachers have witnessed a vast improvement in Cade's behavior, self-awareness, and overall responses to adults and peers. He became responsible for bringing his checklist to document his behavior and keeping up with his progress in each class. The largest improvement teachers noticed was that Cade's self-awareness has increased dramatically. When his successes or concerns with the checklist were evaluated at the end of each period, he noticed the same successes or areas for improvement as his teachers did.

GOAL: SUCCESSFULLY COMPLETE 2 OF THE 3 BEHAVIORS DURING EACH CLASS PERIOD, WORKING TOWARD COMPLETING 3 OUT OF 3 SUCCESSFULLY
BEHAVIORS OF FOCUS: 1) STARTING TASKS ON OUR OWN 2) STAYING ON TASK
3) LESS INTERRUPTING OF MY PEERS
1/3 – EARNS 2 TICKETS   2/3 – EARNS 7 TICKETS   3/3 – EARNS 10 TICKETS

Monday	Starting a task without adult	Staying on Task	Less Peer Interruptions
ELA			
Math			
Science			
Social Studies			
Tuesday	Starting a task without adult	Staying on Task	Less Peer Interruptions
ELA			
Math			
Science			
Social Studies			
Wednesday	Starting a task without adult	Staying on Task	Less Peer Interruptions
ELA			
Math			
Science			
Social Studies			
Thursday	Starting a task without adult	Staying on Task	Less Peer Interruptions
ELA			
Math			
Science			
Social Studies			
Friday	Starting a task without adult	Staying on Task	Less Peer Interruptions
ELA			
Math			
Science			
Social Studies			

Figure 4.1 *Cade's Checklist.* **Created by authors**

The checklist has helped Cade set goals and has provided him with structure, which will be helpful as he plans to join the army in the future. Olivia's experience is less teacher-directed and more self-directed. Olivia shared with us that she begins her week each week by sitting down in homeroom to establish tasks for the week. The teachers have created a weekly to-do list in which all assignments that students will need to accomplish in every content area that week have been compiled. Within this to-do list, teachers also manage a document where students can find any assignments they have missed. Olivia takes her agenda book and goes through the to-do list, making note of when certain things need to be turned in for each teacher. She then thinks through what of this list she will need peer and teacher support for and works to accomplish those tasks during the study hall times provided throughout the week. At this point, she can figure out which tasks she can accomplish outside of school hours between her dance and theater classes. Olivia self-reports that she is strong with self-regulation but also really depends on the tools her teachers have provided to stay on top of things. Olivia shared that she is a bit nervous about transitioning to the early college (a high school experience where students simultaneously earn an associate's degree) next year as she knows the homework and expectations will be greater; the tools we have in place may not be there, and she will have to find new strategies to stay organized.

There will always be a diverse set of learners in every classroom, and it is important to build capacity for a variety of strategies for learners while also working to equip students to self-select strategies that are most effective for them. While Olivia needs less structure, we also see that she really appreciates tools when they are offered. Cade's success in seventh grade has been hugely impacted by the checklist intervention. It is just as important to remember that no tool is a one-size-fits-all; our job as middle level educators is to provide individualized attention to build a strong capacity for executive-function–related and self-regulation skills.

To summarize, let us revisit our chapter objectives:

1. **Define and describe executive-function–related skills.** Executive function is the process of meeting our goals utilizing memory and attention to help us become adaptable and adjust to achieve. More specifically, executive function includes attention and emotion regulation, initiation and inhibition, goal setting, planning and organization, flexibility, memory systems, and self-regulatory processes. Executive-function–related skills include cognitive processes like the ability to control responses to stimuli, working memory, and cognitive flexibility. These skills often need to be explicitly modeled and taught to students to set them up for success.

2. **Define and describe self-regulation and self-directed learning and identify effective interventions for teaching those skills.** Self-regulation involves a process for learners to use strategies or behaviors to achieve goals. A simple model for this is Zimmerman's "plan it, practice it, and evaluate it" cycle. Self-regulation of learning involves learners setting goals, selecting appropriate learning strategies, maintaining motivation, and monitoring and evaluating academic progress. Self-directed learning is when learners identify and monitor their progress on a self-selected task.

3. **Describe strategies and interventions for supporting executive-function–related and self-regulation skills.** Teachers are encouraged to utilize self-assessment with students to identify needs they have regarding executive-function–related skills. To access content through these varied learning opportunities, students will need help in learning to see the goal, in using skills to achieve the goal, and in finding the motivation and perseverance required to accomplish cognitively demanding tasks. Adolescent brains are not fully developed, and, therefore, students need support in building strategies such as mindfulness, self-monitoring, and memory strategies.

Suggested Readings and Resources

Dawson, P., & Guare, R. (2018). *Executive skills in children and adolescents: A practical guide to assessment and intervention* (3rd ed.). Guilford Press. https://www.amle.org/looking-at-executive-function/. https://www.amle.org/wp-content/uploads/2022/06/Appendix-A-Mantras_Updated.pdf.
Vatterott, C. (2018). *Rethinking homework: Best practices that support diverse needs*. Ascd.

References

Burriss, K. G., & Snead, D. (2017). Middle school students' perceptions regarding the motivation and effectiveness of homework. *School Community Journal, 27*(2), 193–210.

Carrera, P., Jiménez-Morago, J. M., Román, M., & León, E. (2019). Caregiver ratings of executive functions among foster children in middle childhood: Associations with early adversity and school adjustment. *Children and Youth Services Review, 106.* https://doi.org/10.1016/j.childyouth.2019.104495.

Cleary, T. J., & Zimmerman, B. J. (2004). Self-regulation empowerment program: A school-based program to enhance self-regulated and self-motivated cycles of student learning. *Psychology in the Schools, 41*(5), 537–50. https://doi.org/10.1002/pits.10177.

Cooper, H., Robinson, J. C., & Patall, E. A. (2006). Does homework improve academic achievement? A synthesis of research, 1987–2003. *Review of educational research, 76*(1), 1–62. https://doi.org/10.3102/00346543076001001.

Dawson, P., & Guare, R. (2018). *Executive skills in children and adolescents: A practical guide to assessment and intervention* (3rd ed.). Guilford Press.

Denckla, M. B. (2018). Executive function: Binding together the definitions of attention-deficit/hyperactivity disorder and learning disabilities. In L. Meltzer (Ed.), *Executive function in education: From theory to practice* (2nd ed., pp. 5–24). Guilford Publications.

Eslinger, P. J. (1996). Conceptualizing, describing, and measuring components of executive function: A summary. In G. R. Lyon & N. A. Krasnegor (Eds.), *Attention, memory, and executive function* (pp. 367–95). Paul H Brookes Publishing Co.

Feinstein, S. (Ed.). (2014). *From the brain to the classroom: The encyclopedia of learning: The encyclopedia of learning.* ABC-CLIO.

Hickey, M. (n.d.). Post-pandemic challenges: the use of mantras on executive functioning skills. https://www.amle.org/post-pandemic-challenges-the-use-of-mantras-on-executive-functioning-skills/.

Knowles, M. (1975). Self-directed learning: a guide for learners and teachers. Association Press.

Loyens, S. M. M., Magda, J., & Rikers, R. J. (2008). Self-directed learning in problem-based learning and its relationships with self-regulated learning. *Educational Psychology Review, 20*(4), 411–27. https://doi.org/10.1007/s10648-008-9082-7.

Meltzer, L., Pollica, L. S., & Barzillai, M. (2018). Executive function in the classroom. In L. Meltzer (Ed.), *Executive function in education: From theory to practice* (2nd ed., pp 165–93). Guilford Press.

Pekel, K. (2016). *The REACH strategies guidebook: approaches and activities to strengthen academic motivation.* Search Institute.

Ramdass, D., & Zimmerman, B. J. (2011). Developing self-regulation skills: The important role of homework. *Journal of advanced academics, 22*(2), 194–218.

University of Delaware Center for Research in Education & Social Policy. (2018). Responsive Classroom. (P18-003.5). University of Delaware.

Vatterott, C. (2018). *Rethinking homework: Best practices that support diverse needs.* Ascd.

Zimmerman, B. J., & Pons, M. M. (1986). Development of a structured interview for assessing student use of self-regulated learning strategies. *American educational research journal, 23*(4), 614–28. https://doi.org/10.2307/1163093.

Zimmerman, B. J. (1995). Self-regulation involves more than metacognition: A social cognitive perspective. *Educational psychologist, 30*(4), 217–21. https://doi.org/10.1207/s15326985ep30048.

CHAPTER 5

The Social Self
DEVELOPING IDENTITY

Learning Outcomes:

1. Recognize contemporary realities of social and emotional development of adolescents.

2. Understand and plan ways to support adolescents as they navigate identity development.

3. Address contemporary issues related to ethnic, cultural, and racial identity and gender and sexual identity in educational settings effectively.

Introduction to Social Identity

Beyond the angst of physical changes, amidst the learning curve of how to "do" school, there are incredible changes in the social and emotional development of adolescents. The physical and social-emotional realms intersect, and those intersections may be messy or awkward. Social and emotional development are deeply rooted in the physical and academic selves as discussed in previous chapters. As we saw in the general exploration of adolescence in Chapter 2, these three threads of development (physical, social, and emotional) are closely intertwined, and what is happening say, in physical development, may very well impact some aspects of social development, such as self-esteem and confidence, among other attributes. There are many misconceptions in society regarding these creatures we call adolescents. How many times was saying to someone, "I want to teach middle school" met with a response indicative of pity or disgust? Comments like "Oh wow, that is just such a hard age! All those raging hormones and the moodiness . . . ." In some ways, the societal perceptions of adolescence have a self-fulfilling prophecy and potential for causing negative impacts. Our students internalize those external perceptions while navigating self-exploration and working toward adulthood. To dig into these ideas, we will use case reflections from the author and middle schoolers Aaron, Larry, Liza, and Krystal throughout the chapter.

Aaron is an expressive eighth grader with impressive artistic skills. They are a **nonbinary** student who has worked through a significant amount of identity work during middle school. Aaron has had a wide range of academic experiences and cites their struggle with **ADHD** as a key factor in their struggles. Later in this chapter, we will share a bit about their **gender and sexuality identity** journey.

Larry is a sixth grader who is passionate about Dungeons and Dragons, reading, and creating games. He has found himself struggling in his relationships with some peers as he and his classmates shifted from elementary to middle school but has learned to adapt and has found his group of friends. Larry is an only child and lives with his family. In his home, he is surrounded by farm animals that he loves and helps tend to.

Liza, the eighth grader whom you met in Chapter 2, visits us in this chapter as a self-identified asexual member of the **LGBTQIA+** community. In this chapter, she will share with us some of her perceptions of the needs in education for informing students about ways to include and support LGBTQIA+ humans in our classroom communities.

Krystal is a rising eighth grader from an urban school in the region. She is Jamaican American and describes herself as a self-taught musician. She plays the piano, double bass, and the viola and is part of the school orchestra. In this chapter, she and her mom, Zoe, share some of their journeys in developing and supporting **cultural identity**.

Defining Identity

First, we need to define identity, which has been conceptualized in many ways. Erikson's early work was mentioned in Chapter 2. It situates identity development within the individual and within the community and the community's culture. Also in Chapter 2, we discussed several other theories of identity development, such as Marcia's theories. The common theme among them is the consideration of the individual, the community, and the significant amount of growth and change occurring during the adolescent years. Saltman (2005) describes identity as "an individual, internal endeavor for youth facilitated by well-meaning parents, teachers, and other adults" (p. 238). The important developing components of adolescence are based on the individual but are very much influenced by the social environment. This emphasizes our role as educators within this journey. This chapter will address peer dynamics and relationship building and offer middle grades educators a lens through which to envision inclusive and supportive environments. There are contemporary needs for supporting students in their ethnic or cultural identity and for supporting students experiencing shifts in their gender and sexual identities. As we explore these ideas, we'd like to encourage one important distinction: the differentiation of identity formation from identity construction. We will argue here that identity is constructed as a dynamic creation within a social context rather than a prescribed linear unfolding. It is a process of self-definition in response to the people around us. This emphasizes the importance of an educator's role in helping adolescents on their identity-development path.

There are many reasons for us, as middle level educators, to investigate the social-identity development of adolescents. One is that school is a primary place to find **social belonging**. Students spend a significant amount of their time in the school setting, and it is the one place where they can be guaranteed to develop and practice social skills. Teachers can help shape the context and can be especially influential when they work with colleagues to create supportive learning situations and respond to individuals.

Let's think for a moment about where our students go after they graduate and move on. Some of them will go to college, and some will go straight into the workforce. Many will have entered some form of the workforce while in high school with part-time jobs. These part-time jobs may have involved fast-food restaurant work, work in grocery-store check-out lines, or work stocking for various businesses. Later, such work may have provided students with a link to more career-oriented positions in corporations, engineering firms, academia, and the like. Regardless of which pathway these students choose, having good social skills is a necessary component in meeting the requirements of most positions. Even remote workers are likely still to be on a *team* in some capacity and will need to develop social and collaborative skills to help them function properly on those teams. In this and later chapters, we will explore some primary mechanisms to help build these skills in our middle school classrooms.

Factors Contributing to Social Identity

Middle school is the time when adolescents are beginning to attain more abstract thinking skills, and they begin applying those thinking skills to situate how they see themselves fitting into the world. They begin to develop their own moral compass and their own personal belief system, experimenting with different forms of self-expression, and trying on different styles and attitudes to see what fits. Their use of a particular style or attitude may be fleeting as they decide which aspects of self-expression are true to themselves. Their experiments may be of small, nuanced aspects of self-expression, like hairstyle or taste in music; however, their experiments, even those involving seemingly small things, may delve into significant explorations of sexuality, gender, culture, and race. Middle school years tend to be the beginning of this exploration phase (as previously noted, no identity pathway is consistent with a particular timeline). Research has shown that the final stages and much of the "work" of identity development happens in later adolescence and into young adulthood (Steinberg & Morris, 2001). There are many factors that contribute to how adolescents explore identity: peer and family relationships, cultural and ethnic considerations, and sexual- and gender-identity constructs. While this list is not exhaustive, these are key areas in which middle level teachers can provide support.

Pause and Reflect: If you are able, try to find a few photographs of yourself from sixth, seventh, and eighth grades. Look closely at the photographs—who is in them with you? Reflect on your relationships with the humans in the picture. Look closely at what you are wearing. How does this reflect your current style of dress now? Looking back, can you hypothesize anything about where you were in your own identity-development progression?

Identity and Peer Relationships

Peer relationships get a lot of attention when it comes to middle school, and often that attention is misguided. We know from our exploration in the physical self that adolescents are most certainly battling some physical or hormonal changes, and we know anecdotally that some students may exhibit moodiness that influences their interactions with the world. But we also know that this is not a one-size-fits-all model and that individual differences in peer relationships will certainly manifest differently for each adolescent. From Chapter 2, we know that adolescents make connections and that certainly includes connections with peers. Research provides some insight into the complex nature of peer relationships. For one, we know that social experiences within families impact social relationships with peers. Studies have shown that warm, caring, and supportive families have adolescents who are more socially competent and who have more friends (Lieberman et al., 1999). The nature of the family relationship may determine whether an adolescent is more influenced by family or by peers.

Peer interactions can be both positive and negative. Take a moment to think back to some of your closest relationships as an adolescent. If you are like Holly, you feel like some days were like a rollercoaster with close friendships while, in other periods, those friendships felt like the most grounding force in your life. Recent research on the stability of friendships for adolescents sheds some light on this rollercoaster experience. Peers have the potential to influence academic and social behaviors positively or to instigate problem behaviors (such as the health risk behaviors explained in Chapter 3). Adults often discuss the concept of "**peer pressure**" with a connotation that peers are actively coercive in their influence, but the research suggests that the "pressure" experienced by adolescents is more based on their desire to emulate the behaviors of someone they admire or respect than on pressure exerted by that person. (Susman et al., 1994; Steinberg & Morris, 2001). Adolescents will gravitate toward friends with similar attitudes and identities.

Adolescents who have developed new friendships and widened their friendship circle at school report greater satisfaction regarding friendships and stronger self-confidence in their social skills for making new friends. In fact, evidence shows that making new friendships *and* losing other friendships is potentially a positive experience for adolescents as they explore different avenues that better fit who they are in that moment (Ferguson et al., 2022). So, we may notice that Zuri is Sofia's best friend this week, but a few weeks down the line, when Sofia has made the volleyball team and is exploring a new part of her identity, it may be that Sofia's teammates on the volleyball team become her closer friends.

When we interviewed sixth grader Larry, much of what he shared with us pertained to friendships—the highs, the lows, and all the changes. Larry reflected on how helpful it was coming to our school with a few peers he had known for years, as it helped him feel more comfortable while settling into his unfamiliar environment.

THE SOCIAL SELF   79

Picture 5.1   8th graders in cafeteria. Photo, Holly Pinter

However, within a month or so of starting school he noticed that things were changing, and he was not sure how to feel about it. His old friends had also met new people, and suddenly they were choosing to hang out with others. Larry stated that it was hard at times to deal with the hurt feelings of his changing peer groups, noting slight changes like who sat with who at lunch. He also noticed that he had to learn throughout the year to handle some peers that were just simply on his nerves at times. Because his teachers had him working in small groups often, he said he had to learn how to deal with those peers he did not have a good relationship with and still try to be productive. When I asked him if there was anything from the year that he wished would have gone differently, his answer was about friends—just about friends. He felt that he did not necessarily handle the changes in his friend group well, and he lamented the loss of certain friendships but also seemed to be enjoying new friendships that had developed from his Dungeons and Dragons club. When Larry talked about being a seventh grader next year, he described wanting to learn how to be more productive in group projects—particularly our school-wide project-based learning endeavor.

Pause and Reflect: Look at the experience of Larry as a sixth grader. As a future educator how can you observe and notice the shifting dynamics of peer groups? How will you support your students through these challenging times and help heal hurt feelings while also helping someone like Larry develop new friendships?

Cultural, Ethnic, and Racial Identity

Related to the importance of family relationships in adolescents' social-identity development is the development of ethnic and cultural identity. Early work in the 1990s highlighted that having a strong **ethnic identity** is associated with having higher self-esteem among minority adolescents. While much of this early work focused on Black adolescents, more recent studies have studied Latino, indigenous, and Asian youth. Immigration, familial ethnic identity, and ethnicity experiences in school will vary widely. Several possibilities may emerge. Adolescents may reject their own culture while attempting to assimilate into the majority culture, or they may fully reject the majority culture, or they may reach some interim position, a "blend." Research conducted in the late 1990s indicates that this blend, or **biculturalism**, may provide a more positive psychological adjustment (Steinberg & Morris, 2001). More recently however, we have found that the focus on **assimilation** of cultures can be problematic and may contribute to some of the historical trends of **systemic racism** (Busey and Gainer, 2021). We must be mindful of supporting students in the development of their **racial identity**. Historically, discourse related to racial-identity development has been absent from middle level education, even from important documents like early versions of "This We Believe" (2010). Many of the middle level curricula and policy documents are heavily **Eurocentric** in nature. Researchers, however, have attended to the distinction of racial-identity development in recent decades. Ward (1990), for example, states that the "integration of the individual's personal identity with one's racial identity is a necessary and inevitable developmental task of growing up Black in white America" (p. 218).

These complex ideas have important implications for middle level educators, particularly with the implementation of curriculum materials. Brinegar and Caskey (2022) emphasize the importance of implementing social-emotional practices that are culturally responsive in nature, as practices that "center compliance and assimilation are harmful to the social-emotional development of young adolescents, particularly those with marginalized identities who are most harmed by such policies" (para 23). Educators still have a lot of work to do to learn about systemic racial issues that are pervasive in our practice and curriculum materials. Chamberlain underscores why this is so important in our practice:

> Nevertheless, from the beginning students learn whether their background is "good enough" and if their culture's contribution is not valued, they

connect this to their personal identities. In a period when young adolescent students are eager to explore, their opportunities to explore are limited. At a time when students are anxious to address social issues and be involved in community action, their ability to develop pride in their culture is thwarted by curricula designed to support the dominant culture. (2003, p. 48)

Studies in just the past decade indicate strong stigma when it comes to teacher interactions with minority students. Busey and Gainer (2021) describe studies within the last decade that indicate that white teachers have lower expectations of students of color when it comes to academics, including a misguided conception of students of color as being noncompliant. Historically, this has meant that students of color are not placed in academically gifted settings and are often pushed toward vocational tracks rather than college-preparation tracks. Well into the twenty-first century, it is imperative that middle level educators reflect on mainstream discourses related to race and culture and work toward building environments where *all* students feel they belong and have pathways to succeed.

Picture 5.2 Students collaborating. Photo, Western Carolina University

We talked with Krystal, and her mother, Zoe, about identity development from both a student and a parent perspective. As Krystal shared her stories about her identity development related to teachers, she focused mostly on how teachers could better support her academically, with little to no reference to her cultural background. She articulated ways that teachers could better support learning with tangible supports for students who don't instantly "get it" during the lesson. She continued to share stories of and some frustrations about not feeling academically supported in school at times and wishing teachers would work more to understand the individual differences of learners in the classroom. Listening to her daughter share these things, Zoe shared an emphasis on relationship building with teachers. She shared,

> At some point [teachers] have to start treating our young adults as humans, and they also have to humanize the experience of all of our students . . . everything my daughter tells me is secondhand information because it didn't happen to me. I'm having that experience for the very first time and it doesn't feel good, it doesn't feel good in my body sometimes. It's not even logical or practical some of the things that happen. One of the things that I think first, is that [teachers] have to start treating them like human beings. They have to stop telling and start showing. You have to show my child you care.

Zoe expressed concrete reasoning for why building these relationships is so important in school, "A lot of our students are going through a lot there was trauma there's generational trauma there's community trauma . . . how do we bridge that gap?" Zoe emphasized the potential overuse of things like in-school suspension and other inequitable discipline policies,

> Why would you bring someone to a place [like school] and then isolate them? What that is doing that is evoking the lowest emotion in the universe. Our students are already in fight or flight because in the neighborhood where we live we live in. Between the different housing communities there [may be] gunshots, there's a fire department, there's the hospital, there is the ambulance, and sometimes things are happening where they live it's outside their window. Then we expect a child to turn up, put on a book bag, and show up smiling? Why should a child need to exercise so much resilience when they are physiologically in fight or flight mode every single day just based on their ethnicity, based on their zip code, or based on their socioeconomic standard a way of living?

Zoe also articulated multiple instances over the course of Krystal's educational career where Krystal got in trouble simply by her proximity to situations, based on the community she lives in.

We continually recognize and encourage relationship building with our adolescent students as we widely recognize the power that has in the overall experience of our students. Hearing this perspective from a parent, recognizing the external factors that impact our students daily, is an important reminder to stay alert and aware of our students' experiences in and outside of the classroom, experiences that may impact their daily functioning in our classrooms. We also talked with Krystal about peer dynamics and thinking about her identity development from that perspective. She shared a bit about the ever-changing group dynamics of her friendships over the years, noting that she also has a core group of friends who are similar in race but, possibly, different in cultural backgrounds. She shared,

> I mean I hang around a lot of kids that my mom would classify as hood rats. I don't think they're hood rats; I think they just do what their dad or their mom does, and I guess that's what makes them the way they are. Obviously, as like a Black girl, I hang around with other Black girls and other Black boys. I would say I hang around with other people [too], but you know

that's kind of like the main groups, you know? It's not saying that we can't merge, it's just like it's always been like the main group, and my main group consists of people that live in, I guess, the hood. I guess that's OK, but I don't see them as that. I think that they're just the people that do whatever their parents do or family whoever they live with.

Zoe also called attention to cultural differences within the community sharing that she may parent differently because of her cultural background and that it is important for schools to recognize differences in expectations that parents may have for their children and recognize the challenges of working together to support all students amidst these differences from home to school.

MICROAGGRESSIONS

Related to cultural, ethnic, racial, gender, and sexual identities, it is important for teachers to be mindful of persistent and pervasive issues related to microaggressions in schools. Microaggressions are admittedly a contentious area of education, but we argue it is an important consideration for educators. Dr. Derald Wing Sue defines microaggressions: "Microaggressions are the everyday verbal, nonverbal, and environmental slights, snubs, or insults, whether intentional or unintentional, which communicate hostile, derogatory, or negative messages to target persons based solely upon their marginalized group membership" (Sue, 2010). These microaggressions can be targeted toward persons, based on their race, religion, gender (and gender expression), sexuality, or nationality. They may be exhibited by students (and therefore addressed by teachers), but they may also be exhibited by adults in schools, both in and outside of the classroom. Below is a list of just *some* of the microaggressions reported by students (list adapted from Portman et al., n.d.):

- Failing to pronounce names properly, even after being corrected
- Having low expectations for students of particular groups, such as students from particular neighborhoods
- Validating students of one gender, class, or race while seemingly ignoring other students
- Anticipating students' emotions based on students' gender, race, sexual orientation, or ethnicity
- Singling students out and/or outing students in class because of their backgrounds or potential disabilities
- Using heteronormative metaphors
- Assuming gender
- Assuming that all students have access to and are proficient in the use of technology related to school activities and academic work

Microaggressions are particularly problematic because we are often unaware that we are even doing them. Let's think about some of these situations that may seem subtle but have massive insinuation that could very easily have negative impacts on our students:

- Expressing confusion that a student of Asian descent is not a more self-regulated and high-achieving student
- Seeming surprised when a girl achieves a higher score on a math test than a boy because "boys are better at math" or when a boy prefers theater-arts club over intramurals
- Using a nickname for a student because the teacher "just can't seem to" pronounce his name correctly
- Assigning significant amounts of homework that need resources or technology and assuming that all students have access to those resources
- Assigning only books with a white protagonist
- Making generalized comments about cultures or backgrounds
- Making comments giving thanks to God publicly in class, knowing that many of our students do not practice Christian faith

Two things need to be at the forefront of our minds here—one is being mindful of the unintentional microaggressions that may pass our mouths from time to time. The key is to then acknowledge it, apologize for it if necessary, and then make intentions toward eradicating that from future practice. The second thing is to be mindful of students in our classrooms who may also be expressing microaggressions. Teaching our populations about microaggressions and holding all students and adults accountable will help build a much healthier classroom community and a sense of belonging for all.

Pause and Reflect: Based on your reading here, where have you witnessed microaggressions in your life? Can you be reflective about potential times in your life that you've unintentionally (or intentionally) expressed a microaggression? Brainstorm how you can work to battle this in your future teaching.

Sexual and Gender Identity

Early adolescents may start to explore their sexuality and romantic feelings toward others. In this section, we will make the distinction between **sexual orientation** and **gender identity**. The premise of gender identity is very personal in nature while sexual orientation is more interpersonal. We will give the gist of both concepts as they are pertinent to the populations we may teach. First, let's tackle sexual orientation and define the wide range of options along the way. The most current results from the CDC (Centers for Disease Control) youth risk behavior survey data (2021) indicate that approximately 75 percent of students identify as heterosexual. For some, this is a time of exploring sexual orientation and gender expression. The data identifies about 3 percent of students identifying as gay or lesbian; 12 percent, as bisexual; and 9 percent, as other or questioning. Table 5.1 defines each letter of the LGBTQIA+ acronym.

Currently the average age for gay youth to come out is fourteen (down from the mid-twenties for previous generations). There are many related social issues for lesbian, gay, bisexual, transgender, and queer (LGBTQIA+) students as they navigate this experience. LGBTQIA+ youth report disproportionate levels of bullying, negative peer associations, and truancy. Research conducted in the early 2000s found that LGBTQIA+ youth (particularly bisexual youth) have more negative psychological and educational outcomes, while other research suggests that many of those students report few to no

Table 5.1 Sexual Orientation Terms

L = Lesbian	A woman who is emotionally, romantically, or sexually attracted to another woman.
G = Gay	A person who is emotionally, romantically, or sexually attracted to members of the same gender.
B = Bisexual	A person who is emotionally, romantically, or sexually attracted to more than one sex, gender, or gender identity.
T = Transgender/Transsexual	Transgender is a term for people whose gender identity and/or gender expression is different from cultural expectations based on their sex assigned at birth. This is separate from any specific sexual orientation. Transsexual is a more historic term for folks who have changed or desire to change their bodies using medical interventions.
Q = Queer/Questioning	A term to express a wide spectrum of identities and orientations countering the mainstream.
I = Intersex	People who are born with differences in their sex traits and reproductive anatomy.
A = Asexual/Ally	Asexual refers to a complete or partial lack of sexual attraction or lack of interest in sexual activity with others. Ally is a term used to describe someone who is actively supportive of the LGBTQ+ community. This includes straight cisgendered allies as well as members of the LGBTQ+ community who are allies for other components (such as lesbians supporting transgender humans)
+ (P) = Pansexual	This is a term for someone who may feel emotional, romantic, or sexual attraction to people of any gender.

Source: Natterson & Bennett, 2023, p. 270

concerns about mental health and education. Just as all adolescents have a variety of individual differences, the LGBTQIA+ population does as well. Another study (McGuire et al., 2010) suggests that transgender youth have challenges in perceived feelings of safety due to the pervasive harassment they endure. Some research has tracked absences among LGBTQIA+ youth and, not surprisingly, there are more unexcused absences for these students (22 percent report skipping school), potentially due to their lack of a sense of belonging in their school environments. Robinson and Espelage (2011) report that these levels of truancy are more prevalent in middle school, which means middle level educators need to be on high alert for early intervention in supporting these students. The school's culture of acceptance and support must be modeled by adults, as 63 percent of LGBTQIA+ students report hearing homophobic remarks from school staff. All stakeholders must have critical conversations to create a sense of belonging for all students. While there have been great strides in the general acceptance of LGBTQIA+ youth in recent decades, there are still persistent stigmas and even troublesome political movements on the horizon. Just think, in the past twenty years the world has made a large shift in the perception of the LGBTQIA+ community. The Netherlands paved the way by legislating same-sex marriages in 2001, and now over thirty countries have followed suit. In the United States, most youth support same-sex marriages (National Academies of Sciences, Engineering, and Medicine, 2019).

We have seen an evolution in the discourse and vocabulary surrounding gender identity and sexual orientation. Many youths may begin to explore gender-nonconforming or nonbinary expressions of identity, and they are potentially using pronouns that are different from the ones associated with their sex assigned at birth. As we mentioned, sexual orientations have broadened to include pansexual, bisexual, queer, and others, and even relationship structures have broadened to include polyamorous, ethically nonmonogamous, and so on. In terms of gender identity, Table 5.2 highlights

Table 5.2 Gender Identity Terms

Nonbinary	People who do not identify with binary male or female options. Other terms that may be utilized to describe nonbinary include genderqueer, genderfluid, gender nonconforming, or gender diverse.
Cisgender	A person who identifies as the culturally defined norms of their gender assigned at birth.
Transgender	A person who identifies with a gender other than that they were assigned at birth.
Gender expansive	A person whose self-expression and behavior does not align with societal expectations of that gender.
Gender diverse	A broad term that includes all transgender, nonbinary, and gender expansive people.
Gender dysphoria	A clinical term describing the distress caused when gender identity and gender assigned at birth are out of sync. It is often used by psychologists as a diagnosis.

Source: Natterson & Bennett, 2023, pages 285–86

the definitions of terms utilized across the nonbinary gender spectrum. Information about these expressions and structures has become widely available through the Internet and social media, and our youth now have a vocabulary to utilize as they explore various expressions along their identity pathway. It is important that we teach them to be critical consumers of information they find to make sure they are using high-quality information to make choices. While some trends among adults may not feel like they pertain to adolescents, our students have wide exposure to such trends, and teachers should be aware of what students may talk about or begin to engage with.

Providing support for our students in this fluid expression can be difficult in the political climate of many of our schools. State legislation regarding curriculum materials and some bills, such as the "Don't Say Gay" bill in Florida and the Parents Bill of Rights (and similar bills in other states), are putting very specific constraints on schools, constraints that sometimes conflict with the advice provided in guiding documents in our field. For example, *The Successful Middle School: This We Believe* (2021) guides us to be more comprehensively inclusive and supportive of our students. These bills have potential to impact educators' ability to build trust and relationships with transgender students as they require school staff to report information about students' sexual orientation to parents even if students have not come out to their parents yet. Below are some resources for facilitating conversations with students and families to put the adolescent's well-being front and center. Our job is to ensure that *all* students feel welcome and supported in our classrooms. Even our adolescents recognize the importance of building capacity for respect and awareness in our classrooms. Liza shared her perceptions with us, and a snippet of her thoughts follow.

In our interview with Liza, she shared how important it has been for her to be exposed to conversations and literature that helped her understand herself more and to recognize that what she was feeling on her identity journey was totally okay. Liza identifies as an asexual female. She has had many healthy conversations with her parents about sex, and she feels adamant that it just doesn't fit for her. While her parents indicated that she may feel differently when she is older, Liza, at this point, simply says—nope, no thank you. And she feels that those explicit conversations with her parents have helped her navigate some aspects of her identity. She says that, without those conversations, she may have felt pressured toward acquiescence to what is deemed to be "normal." Liza described situations where she has known gay men to date women because they haven't felt that their environment has supported them in exploring what feels natural to them. Because of this Liza feels passionate about the need for education and exposure in school. Liza said, "School is supposed to prepare you for life . . . and [sexuality and gender] is included in life . . . it is a big part of people's lives is learning things about themselves and respecting other people, and learning about other people's lives and respecting that. I think that is appropriate. Even though a parent might be upset that their child knows these things . . . We don't want to know about the terrible things in history (like wars), but it is important to know that." What Liza recognizes is that our students need to have exposure to widely varying resources that allow them, in a safe space, to explore their own identities and that provide them with a vocabulary to begin to describe it. Such resources should also allow students to build compassion and understanding of others along the way.

88　CHAPTER 5

We had the opportunity to sit down and talk with Aaron about their journey in gender- and sexual-identity development. While Holly was not Aaron's teacher, she had a strong rapport with this student just from getting to know them throughout the year. Aaron often found solace in talking with the adults in the school and depended on those interactions to help support them through the day. Below are several snippets of Holly's interview with Aaron. We started the discussion by exploring gender identity and having Aaron reflect on when Aaron's shift began.

> I started feeling that I was not meant to be female when I was about eight or nine, because things just weren't really setting up for me. And I went through several "phases" before coming out as nonbinary. But first I believed that I was a trans male. I used, I think, three different names, which was, I hate this first one. I don't know why I picked it, but I chose Kyle. I went through Kyle, Thomas, and Levi. I enjoyed Levi for a little bit, but it still didn't feel right. And then, I believe, seventh grade, which was last year, I was feeling a gender fluid and a nonbinary.

I then asked Aaron to flesh out their decision process a bit more—it was clear that they were experimenting and trying things on to find the right fit, so I asked them what this process was like for them. Aaron replied,

> I did research because whenever I thought that was a trans male for example, I did [a] bunch of research on binders. I figured out safer ways to use binders and figured out that taping is very dangerous. It can harm you even more than binders. It basically just does not help, and I figured out that if you use two sports bras, or just like, actually the bra I'm using right now, it's basically like a binder. But it doesn't like, compress your chest, and you can still exercise in it.

We then shifted our conversation to explore sexual-identity development, asking Aaron to reflect on their decisions related to sexuality, while we simultaneously explored gender identity.

> I am bi curious, which means I do like men kind of, but I do like females more. Deciding my sexuality was extremely difficult for me from the age of ten to now. I went through several phases of sexuality. I went through straight because, yeah. And then I dated my first girlfriend. So, then I was like, okay, wait, am I lesbian or am I straight? I'm confused. So, then I was down that path of being a lesbian. And then I went down the path of being pan, because I was like screw it, "hearts not parts, right?" Then I went down the path of being bi which I'm still kind of in, back to lesbian and back to bi. It was just a journey.

So, even in the four years that Aaron has been exploring, there seems to still be a fluid nature as they continues to have new experiences and to explore different relationships, gender identities, and gender expressions. I asked Aaron to think about ways educators can better support LGBTQIA+ youth in schools. They expressed a few key things—primarily is to be respectful of pronouns. Aaron said it can be frustrating when they have told someone multiple times what pronouns they use and that person continues to use other pronouns. Or, even more so, it is frustrating when (particularly adults) use their "dead" (previous) name. They also shared with me the importance of protecting their privacy. Aaron shared that, in their previous school, a teacher outed them to their entire class as gay, which then led to bullying experiences that eventually pushed Aaron to leave the school in search of a safer environment.

Pause and Reflect: Looking through the details of Aaron's journey, what resonates with you? What questions do you have? If anything about this feels uncomfortable to you, brainstorm how you will reconcile your personal feelings and opinions by openly including Aaron in your community. How would you work to support Aaron in the classroom?

Supporting Identity Development in Our Classrooms

Considering the factors that contribute to identity development for adolescents, it is important that educators foster classroom environments that allow for a safe space for exploration and experimentation, provide explicit instruction on navigating challenging conversations, and give all students a sense of belonging in the classroom. Finnan and Kombe (2011) suggest that a positive sense of belonging is associated with a welcoming community for all students. They state that this fosters a community of acceptance of group members with differences in culture, economic status, or gender, which allows adolescents to build trusting relationships even when differing opinions are expressed. It is also important to just honor the journey of each individual student. This is the age where adolescents try different things on to see what fits—these things may be clothing style, certain friend circles, certain activities, or gender identity or gender expression. Try not to hold too tightly to any one aspect, and just support the students as their explorations ebb and flow, knowing that they will ultimately settle on what truly fits them best and that their journeys may come to fruition, far beyond their middle school years. Focus your feedback to students on providing them ways to research, resources to support them, and, simply, a safe space to just be.

Brinegar and Caskey (2022) make several key recommendations for supporting adolescents' identity development. They suggest three key opportunities, including "(a) formal and non-formal educational experiences, (b) organizational structures that promote affiliation among peers (e.g., affinity groups), and (c) experiences to explore an array of interests" (para 30, 2022). To accomplish this, various experiences must be structured within and outside of the school day for adolescents to explore identity. Within the school day, activities and experiences can be created within core-content classes but also within advisory and in-school clubs. Extracurricular clubs and activities, such as a straight-gay-alliance club or other student-led clubs that provide a safe space for exploration and conversation among peers, can also be utilized.

One example of implementation within core instruction is described by Martha Caldwell (2012) in her account of implementing in her classroom a unit of study related to race, class, and gender as an avenue for identity exploration. Caldwell describes the norms of the classroom, emphasizing ground rules for respect. She uses the term *cognitive dissonance* for students to process what may be an uncomfortable or awkward conversation, noting that discomfort is part of thinking about innovative ideas. The work in this project positions students to think about social justice and the idea of fairness, noting that, as adolescents are developing their own moral compass, young adolescents simply want the world to be a better place and are in a space to actively think about how they might contribute as global citizens. Caldwell states, "Successful global citizens must have a healthy appreciation for other cultures and understand that the dynamic potential of diversity lies in considering multiple perspectives and synthesizing collaborative solutions" (p. 13).

As a second example, let's look at a larger school structure to see how a school dictates the use of time, which can provide an opportunity to intentionally support identity development of our adolescents. Embedded in the mission and vision of our school is a focus on the whole child, the whole school, and the whole community. This model privileges the use of social-emotional support and student voice and choice as avenues for directing student programming. Integrated into the weekly schedule are several key components to supporting adolescent identity development. First, we offer two noncore-curriculum opportunities so that students may engage in something of interest to them; we offer electives that students choose from a list that rotates throughout the year. Second, we have clubs, which provide another student-selected and interest-based opportunity. Each club focuses on a topic, such as outdoor education, art, ukulele, chorus, theater arts, journalism, robotics, and intramurals to name a few. As student interests shift, the school works to offer electives and clubs related to those new interests.

Students also engage in an advisory program that is focused on developing social and emotional competencies. This is driven by our guidance counselor, another key link in the chain of identity support. Within the core curriculum, there is a school-wide focus on and investment in project-based learning, which relies heavily on critical thinking.

At times, our school has also had a straight-gay-alliance club that is sponsored by a teacher but functions as a student-driven after-school resource. We have found that, in certain years when we have had a larger population of students exploring sexual and gender identity, this group offered a safe space for those students to have constructive discussions about their feelings and sense of identity.

These examples barely skim the surface of what is possible. We encourage teachers to have explicit conversations at minimum at the team level, if not at the school level, to evaluate and brainstorm ideas about how to support student identity, recognizing that those needs may be different from year to year as each cohort of students may have differences from the cohort of the year before. Take, for example, the massive resurgence of Dungeons and Dragons (likely influenced by the show *Stranger Things*). While a Dungeons and Dragons club may not have thrived at our school ten years ago, it is certainly thriving now.

Resources for Supporting Identity Development

In this section, we will recommend some basics for supporting identity development within the school day. We include resources for exploring advisory programs, resources for supporting LGBTQIA+ populations, and positive development of cultural, ethnic, and racial identities. Please note that our recommendations of resources are truly the starting point and that more resources are being created and shared all the time. Stay diligent in the power of the internet and keep researching consistently to get the most up-to-date information.

ADVISORY PROGRAMS

There are many curricula for advisory programs that have an associated cost, but please note that paying for a curriculum isn't necessary to have a high-quality advisory program. In Chapter 7, you can find more about the core characteristics of a strong advisory program. Table 5.3 lists a few of the curriculum packages for middle school advisory programs. Each of these programs aims to build skills for cognitive and social development. Table 5.3 also lists several supplementary resources from AMLE for nonprescriptive perspectives.

SUPPORTING LGBTQIA+ STUDENTS

There are many advocacy groups and nonprofit resources available to support LGBTQIA+ youth. For example, one helpful resource for professional development—to help educators build inclusive and supportive classroom environments—is Welcoming Schools. Welcoming Schools is built from an antiracist perspective, with a focus on policy and practice. Their aim is to build school communities and support them in embracing family diversity, promoting LGBTQIA+ and gender inclusivity, preventing bias-based bullying, and providing specific support to transgender and nonbinary students. Table 5.4 has several recommended groups with descriptions of what they provide.

To provide a tangible example from one of these sources, Welcoming Schools, Figure 5.1 and Figure 5.2 provide a school checklist so that educators may see just how well schools measure up in terms of creating a gender-inclusive environment. This checklist encourages schools to think about the climate, policies and procedures, professional development, resources and materials, confidentiality, and school events. The last resource listed, from Gender Spectrum, is a detailed gender-identity–related support plan that could be immensely helpful in supporting students. This document emphasizes providing a lot of autonomy and voice for students to make sure teachers and administrators know how to best support them. It not only accounts for their preferred name and pronouns but also outlines who in their world knows what so that the unfortunate incident that Aaron experienced (of being outed to their class) does not occur. It also facilitates an important conversation about dead names. In many of the systems used in school for, say, testing purposes, using a student's chosen name is often not an option. However, there are places, such as in a learning management system like Canvas, where chosen names can be altered easily. Having a structure like that provided by the Gender Spectrum program pushes students and teachers to be very explicit about needs and preferences. There are many small but powerful adjustments to be made to make schools more inclusive for all, for example, using the Welcoming Schools checklist about the language used at school events. Rather than using language like "ladies and gentleman" or "mom and dad," educators should use more inclusive terms, such as "families" and "students." This is a small step that can make a significant impact on many students' feeling of belonging.

Table 5.3 Advisory Program Examples and Resources

Program/Resource	Website	Description
The Search Institute	https://searchinstitute.org/	This group focuses on developmental relationships between teachers and students. They use a framework, REACH, to implement strategies for students related to relationships, effort, aspirations, cognition, and heart. The materials include surveys to measure student perceptions and lessons to implement strategies.
Responsive Classroom	https://responsiveclassroom.org/	The Responsive Classroom approach is based on social and emotional learning with a student-centered vision for teaching and discipline. For middle school there is a specific advisory program to support implementation of those principles.
Second Step	https://www.secondstep.org/middle-school-curriculum	This is a comprehensive SEL (Social Emotional Learning) advisory curriculum for middle school focused on building life skills, relationship building, empathy, antibullying, mindset, and emotions.
AMLE	https://www.amle.org/video/daily-tiered-advisory-supports-students-no-matter-their-needs/	Video about Daily, Tiered Advisory Supports Students No Matter their Needs
AMLE	https://www.amle.org/why-advisory/	Article describing why middle level educators use advisory
AMLE	https://www.amle.org/play-move-calm-think-an-advisory-approach-with-student-choice-at-the-center/	Play, Move, Calm, Think: An Advisory Approach with Student Choice at the Center
AMLE	https://www.amle.org/an-advisory-program-for-the-whole-child-and-whole-school/	An Advisory Program for the Whole Child and Whole School
AMLE	https://www.amle.org/podcast/the-evolution-of-advisory/	A podcast describing the evolution of advisory

Table 5.4 LGBTQIA+ Organizations and Resources

Organization	Website	Description
Welcoming Schools	https://welcomingschools.org/	Support school communities to embrace family diversity, promote LGBTQIA+ and gender inclusivity, prevent bias-based bullying, and provide specific support to transgender and nonbinary students
US Department of Health and Human Services Center for Disease Control and Prevention	https://www.cdc.gov/healthyyouth/disparities/mai/pdf/LGBTQ_Inclusivity-508.pdf	A self-assessment tool to support schools and districts in addressing the needs of LGBTQIA+ students and in encouraging practices that are safe and inclusive for all youth
GLAAD	https://glaad.org/	GLAAD is a nonprofit organization whose aim is ensuring fair and inclusive representation for LGBTQIA+ acceptance
The Trevor Project	https://www.thetrevorproject.org/	The Trevor Project's specific aim is ending suicide among LGBTQ youth; it offers crisis support and advocacy, and its website includes a myriad of resources for LGBTQ youth
GLSEN	https://www.glsen.org/	GLSEN aims to support LGBTQ youth through a safe, supportive, and inclusive education; it provides many resources for educators and information about inclusive curriculum, policies, and educator development
Gender Spectrum		Gender support plan
AMLE	https://www.amle.org/co-constructing-inclusive-environments/	Article about what it truly means to build an inclusive environment
AMLE	https://www.amle.org/lgbtqia-what-do-the-letters-mean-and-how-do-i-support-my-students/	Article explaining the definition of LGBTQIA+ and how to support students in school
AMLE	https://www.amle.org/statement-in-support-of-learning-environments-that-meet-the-social-emotional-needs-of-our-lgbtq-students/	Position statement of AMLE for supporting LGBTQIA+ students

94 CHAPTER 5

Figure 5.1 *Welcoming schools checklist part 1*. Reprinted with permission from Human Rights Campaign Foundation (2023)

SUPPORTING CULTURAL-, ETHNIC-, AND RACIAL-IDENTITY DEVELOPMENT

There is no arguing that cultural and racial inequities are a large factor in our schools. Organizations and researchers continue to work diligently to better the situation but, in the meantime, challenges persist. Table 5.5 is again a brief list of resources that may be helpful in building capacity for addressing these challenges.

Practice It: Get in a group of three, and collectively dig into one of the resources listed in Table 5.1, Table 5.2, and Table 5.3, making sure that each of you is looking at a different one. Create a list of the strengths and weaknesses of this source. Then jigsaw, take your expert information, and meet up with others who explored a different resource. Share your findings with your new group.

School Events

- Is gender-inclusive language such as "families" and "students" used on all event communications in lieu of "Mom and Dad," "Ladies and Gentlemen" or "Girls and Boys"?
- Are event organizers educated about students' First Amendment right to attend events with a date of any gender or sexual orientation?
- Do staff and educators treat all families with respect and avoid stereotyping or judgment when communicating with two-mom and two-dad, single-parent, racially diverse and/or multi-linguistic families
- Does your school have at least one staff member who is ensuring that every student feels welcome at school events such as prom and homecoming?

LGBTQ+ Inclusive Material and Resources

- Is your school's sexual health curriculum inclusive of all sexual orientations and gender identities?
- Does your school's academic curriculum include a full spectrum of gender identity and sexual orientation perspectives, voices, histories and current events?
- Does your school's library include books and resources about people with a broad spectrum of gender identities and sexual orientations?
- Do educators and students create classroom and school displays that show a wide range of occupations and achievements for all genders and sexual orientations?
- Do educators use lesson plans and classroom examples designed to expand your students' understanding of gender and sexuality?
- Do educators create opportunities for your class to examine social media and books to increase their media literacy around LGBTQ+ topics?

Professional Development

- Does your school or school district provide ongoing professional development for educators that increase critical skills to address bias-based bullying behaviors regarding gender identity, gender expression and sexual orientation?
- Are educators and staff members specifically trained to prevent and respond to bullying incidents involving gender identity, gender expression, and sexual orientation?

Confidentiality

- Are educators and staff aware that under FERPA they must protect the confidentiality of students related to their gender identity and sexual orientation and show great caution not to share students' sexual orientation or gender identities without that student's permission, even to the student's family?
- Do school privacy policies explicitly assert the confidentiality of information pertaining to students' sexual orientations and gender identities?

WelcomingSchools.org | HRC.org   © 2021 Human Rights Campaign Foundation Welcoming School

Figure 5.2 *Welcoming schools checklist part* 2. Reprinted with permission from Human Rights Campaign Foundation (2023)

Conclusion

It is no wonder people that think of adolescence as stressful and challenging, given the complexities of psychological development. Figuring out who one is and who one wants to be is a daunting task, and educators can provide supportive environments to help students disentangle all the messy pieces in this process. From an academic standpoint, we must support them in learning how to navigate information, such as how to do research and how to filter high-quality information from misinformation. From a physical perspective, we must arm them with information about the changes in their bodies and help them feel normal when everything just feels different (and maybe have a stash of spray deodorant in the school office because there is no smell quite like seventh graders after physical-education class). Socially, we must work to build trusting

Table 5.5 Organizations and Resources for Cultural, Ethnic, and Racial Identity

Organization	Website	Description
Harvard: Adolescent ethnic-racial identity development lab (AERIDLAB)	https://umana-taylorlab.gse.harvard.edu/	AERIDLAB focuses on sociocultural ecological approaches to understanding ethnic-racial identity development in adolescence; its resources include a wide variety of "you may be wondering" pages to address challenging management issues in classrooms; it also provides scales related to racial identity, familial and cultural socialization, and discrimination-related coping strategies
The Equity Collaborative	https://theequitycollaborative.com/resources/supporting-positive-racial-identity-development/	Resources and coaching for educators, based on ideals of equity, including maintaining culturally responsive practices, analyzing implicit bias, and understanding systemic oppression
PBIS Apps	https://www.pbisapps.org/articles/microaggressions-whats-the-big-deal-and-what-do-i-do-about-them	Article with supporting video about microaggressions in classrooms and discussion of micro interventions
AMLE	https://www.amle.org/microaggressions-in-the-classroom/	Article by Rick Wormeli about microaggressions in schools

relationships with students so they can safely explore the nuances of identity without judgment. All of this is on top of our adhering to the standards and teaching the curriculum of core subjects. This work is so important to the larger picture. Cycling back to the common thread seen in many chapters of this text, we revisit this principle: basic needs must be met before students will learn. Creating an environment in which they may be themselves (whatever that may mean on that day) is a crucial step for students to be ready for academic rigor.

To summarize, let us revisit our learning outcomes:

1. **Recognize contemporary realities of social and emotional development of adolescents.** Middle school is the time when adolescents are beginning to have more abstract thinking skills, and they begin applying those thinking skills to situate how they see themselves fitting into the world. They begin to develop their own moral compass and their own personal belief system, and they often start experimenting with different forms of self-expression, trying on different styles and attitudes to see what fits. Sometimes this means that their adoption of a particular style or attitude is fleeting, as they decide which aspects of self-expression are true to themselves or not. Adolescents in the twenty-first century are surrounded by social media and peer influences and, as they are exposed to thoughts and opinions other than those of their families, they are adapting and developing their own more independent views and identities. Many students are grappling with their cultural and racial identities as well as with gender identity and expression.

2. **Understand and plan ways to support adolescents as they navigate identity development.** Teachers have a significant role in helping adolescents define their place in the world. As students begin to think more abstractly and to outwardly grapple with big ideas, teachers need to support them by teaching core content and social-emotional content that will help students navigate this journey. Teaching students how to research (including how to find high-quality sources and how to fact-check), providing students with resources (both human and informational) to address their inquiries, and providing a safe nonjudgmental space in which students may explore are key to supporting identity development. Students need formal and informal educational experiences as well as organizational structures that allow students to affiliate among like peers. They also need to have experiences in which they may explore a variety of interests.

3. **Address contemporary issues related to ethnic, cultural, racial, gender, and sexual identity in educational settings effectively.** Creating a safe space for adolescents includes respecting where they are in their identity journey. Many students will need to have norms established and would benefit from having opportunities for healthy discourse related to more sensitive aspects of identity development, including ethnic, cultural, and racial identity as well as gender and sexual identity. Be mindful of creating an environment that provides a sense of belonging for all students by evaluating your own biases and examining how to use language in the classroom to establish an inclusive space.

References

AMLE (2023). Amle.org

Brinegar, K., & Caskey, M. (2022). Developmental characteristics of young adolescents: Research summary. https://www.amle.org/developmental-characteristics-of-young-adolescents/.

Busey, C. L., & Gainer, J. (2021). Arrested development: How This We Believe utilizes colorblind narratives and racialization to socially construct early adolescent development. *The Urban Review*. https://doi.org/10.1007/s11256-021-00604-3.

Caldwell, M. (2012) Inquiry into identity: Teaching critical thinking through a study of race, class, and gender. *Middle School Journal*, *43*(4), 6–15. https://doi.org/10.1080/00940771.2012.11461815.

Chamberlain, K. (2003). Middle schools for a diverse society. Peter Lang Publishing.

Ferguson, S., Brass, N. R., Medina, M. A., & Ryan, A. M. (2022). The role of school friendship stability, instability, and network size in early adolescents' social adjustment. *Developmental Psychology*, *58*(5), 950–62. https://doi.org/10.1037/dev0001328.

Finnan, C., & Kombe, D. (2011) Accelerating struggling students' learning through identity redevelopment. *Middle School Journal*, *42*(4), 4–12, https://doi.org/10.1080/00940771.2011.11461769.

Lieberman, M., Doyle, A. B., & Markiewicz, D. (1999). Developmental patterns in security of attachment to mother and father in late childhood and early adolescence: Associations with peer relations. *Child Development*, *70*(1), 202–13. https://doi.org/10.1111/1467-8624.00015.

McGuire, J. K., Anderson, C. R., Toomey, R. B., & Russell, S. T. (2010). School climate for transgender youth: A mixed method investigation of student experiences and school responses. *Journal of Youth and Adolescence*, *39*, 1175–88. https://doi.org/10.1007/s10964-010-9540-7.

National Academies of Sciences, Engineering, and Medicine 2019. The promise of adolescence: Realizing opportunity for all youth. The National Academies Press. https://doi.org/10.17226/25388.

Natterson, C., & Bennett, V. K. (2023). *This is so awkward: Modern puberty explained*. Rodale Books.

Portman, J., Bui, T. T., Ogaz, J., and Trevino, J. (n.d). *Microaggressions in the classroom*. University of Denver. http://otl.du.edu/wp content/uploads/2013/03/MicroAggressionsInClassroom-DUCME.pdf.

Robinson, J. P., & Espelage, D.L., (2011). Inequities in educational and psychological outcomes between LGBTQ and straight students in middle and high school. *Educational Researcher*, *40*(7), 315–30. https://doi.org/10.3102/0013189x11422112.

Sue, D. W. (2010). Microaggressions: More than just race. *Psychology Today*, *17*.

Ward, J. V. (1990). Racial identity formation and transformation. In C. Gilligan, N. P. Lyons, & T. J. Hanmer (Eds.), *Making connections: The relational worlds of adolescent girls at Emma Willard School* (pp. 214–26). Harvard University Press.

CHAPTER 6

Creating Inclusive Environments
SUPPORTING DIVERSE POPULATIONS

Learning Outcomes:

1. Recognize the components of special-education principles in middle school, including universal design for learning, individualized education programs, and 504 plans.

2. Understand the models of co-teaching and how to implement them.

3. Distinguish between the different tiers of multitiered systems of support, and apply them to practical settings.

Setting the Stage for Inclusive Learning Environments

In the previous chapters, we did a deep dive into the intricacies of adolescent development and identity development. These chapters build the foundation of understanding the students who enter our classrooms daily. In these next few chapters, we will shift toward focusing on more specific aspects of the adolescent learner within the school setting. Here the focus will be more toward instructional practices and ideas that best support all learners. This topic is timely, given that, over the past thirty years, the number of students with disabilities who are primarily educated in general-education classrooms has steadily increased. For example, in 2000, 46.5 percent of students aged six through twenty-one served under the Individuals with Disabilities Education Act (IDEA) spent at least 80 percent of their school day in general-education settings. By the 2021–2022 school year, this percentage reached 66.7 percent (Office of Special Education Programs [OSEP], 2004, 2024). Here we explore the complicated network of support utilized to build inclusive environments that support students.

There is a multifaceted system that schools use to achieve the goal of designing inclusive classrooms that support all students. . In this chapter, we will explore **universal design for learning (UDL)**; policies and practices related to special-education services, including **individualized education plans (IEPs)** and **504 plans**; **co-teaching** models and applications of co-teaching models; and, finally, **multitiered systems of support (MTSS)**. While each is distinct, these systems work together to monitor and support the individualized needs of all learners.

Universal Design for Learning

UDL has simultaneously emerged, alongside differentiation plans and policies such as IEPs and 504s, as an instructional framework that aligns well in an inclusive classroom. UDL is based on a proactive design of instruction to ensure access for all learners. UDL aims to eliminate unnecessary barriers to learning as students access the curriculum. The premise depends on flexible learning environments that present material in a variety of ways, giving students options among which to choose what helps them the most.

UDL is a teaching approach that works to accommodate the needs and abilities of all learners and eliminates unnecessary hurdles in the learning process. This means developing a flexible learning environment in which information is presented in multiple ways, students engage in learning in a variety of ways, and students are provided

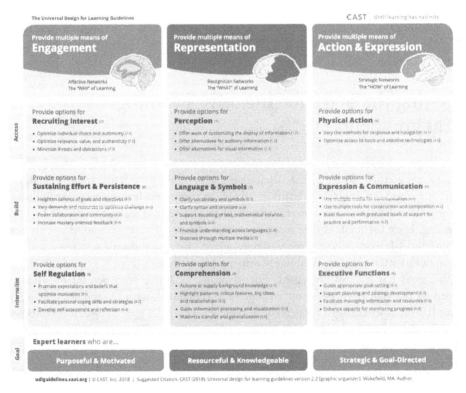

Figure 6.1 *Principles of UDL*. © 2018 CAST, Inc. Used with permission. All rights reserved. Reference: CAST (2018). Universal design for learning guidelines version 2.2 [graphic organizer]. Wakefield, MA: Author.

options when demonstrating their learning. Additionally, the use of UDL eradicates the need for special educators to constantly adapt and modify materials to fit the needs of individual learners because the materials were designed with all learners in mind. It is a *smarter not harder* approach: using one lesson that has been designed to be accessible to all learners means everyone wins.

There are three principles of UDL: engagement, representation, and action and expression. The graphic organizer in Figure 6.1 highlights how these factors build and interact as instructional activities are designed.

Special-Education and Related Services in Middle School

This section explores major principles of special-education services and policies in middle school. Specifically, we will discuss the trends of **inclusive practices** and **specially designed instruction (SDI)** and examine how teachers utilize **collaboration** to identify specific practices to support the needs of all students. We will review the historical background for special-education identification and policies as well as how these concepts align with UDL. We will examine differentiation and strategies for supporting other subgroups of students, including multilingual learners and those who are **gifted** or **twice exceptional**.

LAWS GOVERNING SPECIAL-EDUCATION SERVICES

Middle school students who are identified as having a disability receive special-education services in many ways. On the continuum of placement are restrictive environments and nonrestrictive environments as possible locations for receipt of special-education services. Students placed in restrictive environments may receive services at home or in separate classrooms. Students placed in less restrictive options may receive some or all of their special-education services in general-education classrooms. IDEA has been the primary law governing special education for nearly fifty years. Since its inception in 1975 as the Education of All Handicapped Children Act (EAHCA), it has mandated that school personnel— including administrators, **special-education teachers**, **general-education teachers**, school psychologists, and related-service providers—collaborate with parents in developing and implementing special-education programs. Although IDEA does not explicitly use the term "collaboration," it requires that school personnel and parents work together to address each student's individualized needs. This collaboration is essential for fulfilling IDEA's mandate to provide a **free appropriate public education (FAPE)** for all eligible students with disabilities in the **least restrictive environment (LRE)**. In the early years of inclusive education, soon after the law was enacted, the goal of placing children in the LRE often resulted in what was referred to as *mainstreaming* students and sometimes resulted in students being included in the general-education setting during noninstructional portions of the school day. Although the term *mainstreaming* is used in a few places still today, it has been replaced by the term *inclusive education* to emphasize the full membership to the learning community that is necessary to help students reach their full potential. Without SDI, students have limited access to the curriculum, as King-Sears et al. (2021) found in a study illustrating that, often, accommodations and modifications are confused with specially designed instruction in the classroom. We know that students today should be delivered appropriate instruction if SDI is implemented well. Many teachers strive to serve a diverse group of students with a wide range of abilities through SDI.

This aligns with the policies and procedures defined in the law. Under EAHCA, Congress established the right for every eligible student with a disability to receive a FAPE and has been the driving force for increased access to the general curriculum for all students in the public school system. In the same way, Congress aimed to ensure that students with disabilities received individualized education through the development of IEPs. The law mandated that, for each student with a disability, a team of school personnel and the student's parents collaborate to create an IEP. Collaboration is broadly defined as the act of individuals or groups working together to achieve a common goal or purpose. This is a critical component of supporting all students in our classrooms. At the root of collaboration is recognition that two minds are better than one and that the ultimate product created by two teachers will be stronger than a product created in isolation. This builds on the middle school concept, which is highly collaborative by design. Strong collaboration is based on mutual goals, parity, voluntariness, shared responsibility for decisions, shared accountability for outcomes, and shared resources (Friend, 2023).

> The term 'special education' means access to instruction [emphasis added], at no cost to parents, to meet the unique needs of a child with a disability, including (A) instruction conducted in the classroom, in the home, in hospitals and institutions, and in other settings; and (B) instruction in physical education. (IDEA, 20 U.S.C. 1400 et seq., 34 C.F.R. pt. 339).

First, SDI is based on students' present level of academic and functional performance (often referred to as PLAFP, PLOP, or a similar acronym) and should be related to an IEP goal or learner characteristic (e.g., receptive language disorder). Second, it generally involves changes in content (i.e., not modifying a standard but changing the learning activities that are used to reach the standard), changes in methodology (i.e., using a research-based model of instruction or a specific technique or strategy that addresses the learner's needs), or a change in delivery (e.g., in the setting or the group size) (IDEA, 20 U.S.C. 1400 et seq., 34 C.F.R. pt. 339). In addition, it is deliberate; SDI in co-taught classes is planned and mapped onto the general-curriculum lessons, data are collected, and adjustments are made as needed. For interventions to and extensions of lessons to be coined *SDI* these supports must be planned by the exceptional children's teacher. However, in a co-taught classroom, both teachers are involved in SDI delivery by teaching the lesson together, but this is the dimension of instruction on which special educators take the lead

PRACTICES SUPPORTING EFFECTIVE SPECIALLY DESIGNED INSTRUCTION IN MIDDLE SCHOOL

The premise of inclusion is a philosophy and educational approach that views all students, regardless of ability or background (including students with disabilities, multilingual learners, culturally diverse students, and students with typical development), as an integral part of the school community. Schools that use inclusive practices ensure that all students can participate in the general-education classroom and out-of-class activities (Vanderbilt, 2023). As mentioned earlier in the chapter, UDL tools are necessary accommodations and may enhance the core instruction from a UDL perspective, but they could be provided by the general-education teacher even if the special educator were not present. SDI goes a bit deeper to ensure that special-education services are delivered and often includes co-teaching. Questions co-teachers should ask themselves are these: "How have we changed our teaching in order to facilitate the learning of students with disabilities?"; and "How is our co-taught lesson instructionally more intensive than the same lesson taught by one teacher?"

CO-TEACHING

The co-teaching model, which began appearing in professional literature in the late 1980s and early 1990s (Friend et al., 1993; Klingner & Vaughn, 1999), has expanded with evolving expectations set by IDEA reauthorizations, in 1997; the Individual with Disabilities Education Improvement Act (IDEIA), in 2004; the Elementary and Secondary Education Act (No Child Left Behind Act [NCLB]), in 2001; and the Every Student Succeeds Act (ESSA), in 2015. Today, co-teaching is encouraged in most states, though it is not universally required (Office of Special Education Programs, 2024). Since the mid-1980s, educators have collaborated to include students with disabilities in general-education settings through co-teaching. For much of that time, emphasis was placed on developing strong teacher partnerships and effectively grouping learners on the premise that, if the teachers worked together and delivered instruction in small, flexible groups, students with disabilities would thrive (e.g., Bauwens et al., 1989).

Most professionals are familiar with the key concepts of co-teaching. It is a collaborative service-delivery model in which two professionals jointly deliver, in a shared classroom space, general instruction for all learners and SDI for students with disabilities (and sometimes for other struggling learners) (Friend, 2021). They also share accountability for learner outcomes. Co-teaching may occur for the entirety of a subject (e.g., English/language arts, algebra), a class period or half of a block-scheduled class, and usually (but not necessarily) every time that instruction occurs. Co-teachers operate from the principle of role reciprocity, meaning general educators lead in the development of the general-curriculum instruction, but special educators participate in its delivery. Similarly, special educators lead in the development of the specially designed instruction, but general educators participate in its delivery. Partners hold themselves mutually accountable for academic and other outcomes for all students.

Co-teaching has evolved over the past four decades. It is now conceptualized as a service-delivery option designed to accomplish three goals: 1) access to the general curriculum, 2) education in the LRE, and 3) improved student outcomes (Friend & Barron, 2014; Poon et al., 2013; Scruggs & Mastropieri, 1996). Not surprisingly, attention has gradually shifted to the quality of the instruction students with disabilities receive in co-taught classes. Contemporary expectations are that co-teachers provide the research-based specialized instruction to which students are entitled because doing so enables them to reach state academic standards and to prepare for adult life. Specifically, teachers should not focus on trying to have the same role but rather have parity and implement a true blending of expertise (Beninghof, 2016).

Co-teaching is an important and crucial inclusion practice in middle grades instruction. Co-teaching is primarily utilized in English language arts and math classrooms, as those content areas tend to be aligned to most IEP goals, but some schools

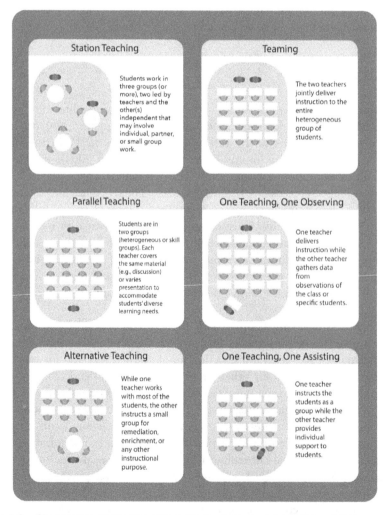

Figure 6.2 *Six Models of Co-Teaching.* Note: Adapted from Friend & Barron, 2020

creatively design co-teaching schedules to also support science and social-studies classes. Co-teaching also exists in other partnerships beyond general education and special education. Other common teaching partnerships you might experience in your classroom include general education paired with English language support, speech-language, literacy or math coaches, or even gifted educators.

The various models of co-teaching can be used within each teaching partnership. It is important to note that co-teaching is a dynamic practice that may look different daily, as it should be responsive to students' needs within a unit of instruction. There are six models of co-teaching: **team teaching**, **parallel teaching**, **station teaching**, **alternative teaching**, **one teach one assist**, and **one teach one observe**. Figure 6.2 gives a visual representation of each model. Table 6.1 highlights the key components of each model along with some challenges and benefits of each.

Although six co-teaching approaches are widely accepted, three are considered high-yield and should be used most frequently, while the other three are limited-yield. The three high-yield approaches are parallel teaching, station teaching, and alternative teaching (Friend & Barron, 2014). In all three approaches, teachers are co-instructing and can provide students with multiple access points to the content. Using the high-yield approaches is essential and can be effective in increasing engagement and making use of UDL strategies and embedding SDI to be feasible in each unit of study. This should not result in students with IEPs frequently being isolated; teachers must remember that not every student needs every intervention, and some students without IEPs can benefit by participating in some interventions.

When they are modeling, general-education teachers usually carefully explain the steps in the process being demonstrated, discuss their rationale, relate the current learning to past or personal experiences, and apply it to students' lives. After some practice, most learners understand the modeled process and can apply it in their independent work, but some students focus on extraneous details instead of the essential steps explained and can become confused.

In an example of using the parallel approach, the teachers would determine which students need to be taught in specific ways. The general-education teacher would take half of the class and, to prepare students for writing a paragraph about reproduction in turtles, would model how to comprehend information by reading a passage about how turtles reproduce in the ocean. The general-education teacher would relate the passage to her personal experience of going to the aquarium and then would encourage students to describe their own life connections to sea turtles. A teacher would then pose questions testing students' comprehension of the text. Students answering such comprehension questions, such as questions about the process of sea-turtle reproduction, as shared in the text, would understand the details of the passage without confusing it with the additional connections made and would differentiate which details were found in the passage and which were examples shared by the teacher and their classmates to help them remember.

A special-education teacher would take a slightly different approach to modeling, knowing that some students with disabilities may be unable to pick out and remember key concepts if the teacher elaborates too much or he or the students make several connections to their own lives. The special-education teacher first would model without

Table 6.1 Benefits and Frequencies of Each Model

Model	Description	Benefits	Challenges	Frequency
Parallel teaching	This model utilizes the same instruction but by dividing the group into two small groups. Each teacher independently teaches the same lesson to half of the class.	Its primary benefit is a smaller setting, which allows teachers to keep closer tabs on student understanding and results in more individualized attention for each student. This maximizes opportunities for student engagement and allows minimization of behavior challenges due to the smaller number of students.	Both teachers must be able to deliver the same instruction, which puts pressure on the content knowledge of the special-education teacher and the ability of general educators to address the needs of students receiving special education. Teachers must pace their instruction similarly. Maintaining reasonable noise levels and creating an adequate physical setup in the classroom can be challenging.	Frequent
Team teaching	Both teachers are simultaneously working with the large group, sharing responsibility for delivering instruction. In this model, both teachers are fully engaged and equally responsible for components of instructional delivery.	Strong engagement of the classroom as the dynamic of the team teachers keeps students' attention. This model also allows for two voices delivering the same content and building on each other's ideas, which may support the multiple ways students understand the content.	Ensuring equitable responsibility takes significant communication and planning. As both teachers are working with the large group, there may be fewer opportunities to notice the subtle needs of individual students.	Occasional
Station teaching	Typically, teachers divide the content for the day and divide the large group into three small groups (based on a particular academic need, randomly, or purposefully to support social dynamics). Students rotate through each teacher's station as well as an independent station.	This model allows teachers time and space to keep a closer eye on student understanding as they work with smaller groups at a time. Organizing groups to address a specific academic skill allows teachers to focus more deeply on that specific need for students. This also fosters a highly interactive environment.	Activities within each station must function independently of one another. If students start at the independent station, it is imperative that they may not have needed station one or two first. Timing and coordination can be challenging, and station teaching requires careful planning. Noise in the classroom is an additional challenge.	Frequent

Alternative teaching	One teacher manages the large group while the other teacher works with an intentional small group for a specific purpose.	This model allows teachers to provide enrichment, remediation, or assessment to small groups of students with specific needs.	This model can cause the stigma of a "pullout" setting. To be effective, this model cannot only utilize the same small group of students every time.	Occasional
One teach, one assist	One teacher does the large-group instruction while the other teacher is available to assist individual students as needed.	A teacher is always available for students. The assisting teacher may also recognize when students need help while the leading teacher is otherwise occupied.	This model can cause an imbalanced power dynamic, especially if the same teacher is leading instruction all the time and is seen as the "real" teacher while the other is seen as the "assistant" teacher.	Seldom
One teach, one observe	In this model, one teacher focuses on delivery of instruction while the other observes, typically focusing on collecting data related to academic, behavior, or social skills.	This model allows for data collection that teachers normally would not have time to accomplish.		Frequent use for brief periods of time

Source: Adapted from M. Friend and T. _._ Barron, "Co-teaching: Inclusion and Increased Student Achievement," *Proven Programs in Education: Classroom Management & Assessment* (Corwin, 2014).

interruption and then would perhaps model several times with students participating while incorporating explanations and scaffolds as needed. The special-education teacher would determine when gradual release of supports and scaffolds is appropriate. Using the same example, the special-education teacher would perhaps use the mnemonic device *WINDOW* to helps students comprehend a text and write a paragraph with details about sea-turtle reproduction. In the special-education teacher's group, the teacher would perhaps say something like this:

> I need to be sure my summary of the article on how sea turtles reproduce is accurate. WINDOW will help me do that. I wrote WINDOW on the side of the page which will help me remember all the steps. First—W—I must write a topic sentence. That is easy, I think about the prompt and write a sentence about that . . . I did it. Now, what is I next? I know—I—is for information; I list what is important . . . Sea turtles are endangered, there are seven types of sea turtles, sea turtles lay eggs in sand on the beach . . . After an adult female sea turtle nests, she returns to the sea, leaving her nest and the amount of time the egg takes to hatch varies among the distinct species and is influenced by environmental conditions such as the temperature of the sand . . . only one in one thousand hatchlings survives to adulthood. What do I do next? —N—is for number the pieces of information. That is easy! Next, I do—D—which is develop sentences. That is harder but I do it . . . Wow, now I have many sentences about sea turtles! Now I do—O—which means I organize sentences with transition words and then—W—write an ending sentence.

In addition, as the students work independently, the special-education teacher would provide immediate scaffolds and feedback and close the instruction with a summary of the strategy, asking students how they could further use it. Students may be provided with a video of the special-education teacher modeling to refer to while working independently.

Planning for Specially Designed Instruction Implementation

Co-teachers must plan to implement the three high-yield approaches explained in the example above. How much time they need is driven by several factors, including their prior experience together or with other partners and the options available for electronic, asynchronous planning. The planning process includes the general-education teacher sharing the goals of the upcoming units of study as well as any areas of difficulty that students have had in the past. The co-teachers review what they know about students' skills thus far through formative or summative assessment, and the special-education teacher shares information related to specific students with disabilities that determines the SDI needed for the upcoming instruction. Co-teachers make grouping and instructional decisions based on data and share this information with students and parents or caregivers. Many students are motivated when they keep track of their academic growth, and parents are appreciative of your efforts to carefully analyze. Also keep administrators in the loop.

Pause and Reflect: Think back to your middle school experiences or other classroom experiences you can identify. Can you remember having classes with a co-teaching model? If so, think through how those experiences did or did not support you as a learner. If they were not helpful, think with your teacher brain about adjustments that could have made this more beneficial for you. If you did experience positive co-taught settings, see if you can remember specific instances that supported you. Share these memories and compare these memories with those of your peers.

Let's explore some examples of each of these structures within real-world classroom examples. Here Holly and Kayleigh share examples from our math and language-arts classrooms of how we have utilized each model.

PARALLEL TEACHING IN KAYLEIGH'S ELA CLASS

Parallel teaching in our English language-arts classroom allows students to get the same instruction but in smaller groups. We use parallel teaching to teach minilessons and to read short stories regularly. It allows us to go at the pace of our small groups while providing all students with the same content. In parallel teaching, all the work occurs upfront. To plan this, we sit down with the text we plan to analyze and annotate it for the specific focus of that lesson. For example, when reading "Tell-Tale Heart" by Edgar Allen Poe, we focus on plot development. Before working with students, we color-code and dictate each portion of the text we want to point out, any questions we should ask, and stopping points. We use the same graphic organizers and structures. The benefit of this is that we can group kids according to their pace, their reading ability, their behavior, and in a myriad of other ways. Parallel teaching in this way allows more students to engage in the lesson and permits teachers to work closely with them. A worry that I had and have when working with new co-teachers or student teachers is that one of us would finish the lesson more quickly than the other would finish. Unfortunately, this does happen occasionally, but as time goes on it gets better. To prepare for this scenario, we also have prepared consistent practices and extension activities, and we have prepared and practiced ways to reinforce reading strategies. An example would be going back in the text and looking for other literary elements that were not the focus. Parallel teaching allows for students to have more opportunities to read aloud, to be formatively observed, and to get the extra help they need.

TEAM TEACHING IN HOLLY'S MATH CLASS

In our school we have two tracks for eighth-grade math. Many of our students take traditional eighth-grade math, and a subset of eighth graders, those who meet specific criteria, take the Math 1 course, which gives these students potential to earn high-school math credit. Much of the curriculum of the two tracks overlaps, and, so, I, Dr.

Pinter, teach Math 1, and the eighth-grade math teacher, Mrs. Rector, typically use the first month or so of school to team teach. We sit down together and plan a unit of instruction for all students, regardless of which course they are enrolled in. In this model, we plan the unit and teach it together. While we do not necessarily script who is responsible for each piece of a lesson (if you are new co-teachers, doing so may be helpful), we do just tend to piggyback off each other throughout the lesson. Much of our communication is happening on the spot as Mrs. Rector may launch the lesson with a warmup but then say, "Dr. Pinter, do you want to get them started on ___?" Then, maybe after I have led the students through our next task, I say, "Mrs. Rector, do you have anything to add?" We found that we utilize this more formal language more as we first get started but, ultimately, because we have sat down and thought through the entire plan so thoroughly, we very much find a groove of just building on each other and naturally and seamlessly threading things together. A very tangible example is that, in our unit of linear functions, I may be asking probing questions, such as "What do you notice?"; "What do you wonder?"; and "How do you know?" And, while I am using the task on the interactive whiteboard, in the background, Mrs. Rector is making a summary table of what students share. This allows me to be very present in the task at hand, working to plan my next questions, while we are solidifying and generalizing student thinking with Mrs. Rector's notes on the board.

STATION TEACHING IN HOLLY'S MATH CLASS

Station teaching is a powerful model that is primarily frontloaded in terms of the time and effort to make an efficient and effective lesson. When seventh graders were working on a unit of integer operations, I noticed that some of my students were mastering the content quite quickly, while some of my students displayed some targeted needs, particularly with subtracting integers. I realized this in doing a mid-unit assessment where I found patterns in misconceptions among a small group of students in their subtraction tasks. Meanwhile, I realized that a different set of my students was struggling only when given a set of mixed problems (addition, subtraction, multiplication, and division). So, I planned two different targeted minilessons, using some models (tape diagrams and colored counters) to address each of these needs. I grouped students accordingly and planned three stations—one where I could deliver the targeted minilesson based on specific needs, a second where my inclusion co-teacher could work on some application word problems with each group, and then a third station where students had differentiated assignments on *Formative*, an online learning platform, "formative," in which they were practicing and building on skills from a previous unit. To make this successful, I had to ensure that I had looked at data; grouped students accordingly; created two minilessons to address students' needs; and checked that each student had been assigned the appropriate differentiated independent-station assignment. In addition, I needed to ensure that my co-teacher had also planned appropriate tasks for her station. Then we had to make some decisions, including whether it would be easier for the teachers or the students to move stations. In this case, since I was working with manipulatives (such as colored counters), we decided students would move and teachers would stay put. On other occasions, especially with groups of students who struggled to transition, we would find it easier for the teacher to be the one moving from group to group. This model has been highly successful for us to differentiate for students but does require teachers to be 100 percent prepared.

ALTERNATIVE TEACHING IN KAYLEIGH'S ENGLISH LANGUAGE ARTS CLASS

Alternative teaching is used in English language arts when students read on different grade levels, when students have been substantially absent, or when a small group of students struggles with the same skill. It is imperative to ensure that alternative teaching is not always used for students who have disabilities alone, separating them from their peers, but, rather, is used as a strategic tool to help students who are struggling to grasp a specific concept. When writing, we have used alternative groups to work with students who we realized had difficulties in recognizing and capitalizing proper nouns. When the core of our class moved on to another grammatical element, my co-teacher spent another couple of days reteaching and reviewing proper nouns with this small group of students. This exemplifies using the alternative teaching method to simultaneously instruct students with differentiated materials. The other use of alternative teaching is to modify instruction. When students were writing theme essays, the core expectation of our lesson was for students to compare the development of theme throughout two of the three texts we read. However, to modify the lesson for our students who are striving writers and readers, we altered the task for them and they were instructed to draft an essay about the development of theme in a singular text. This modified assignment required alternative teaching because the structure of the essay, the graphic organizers to be used to prepare the essay, and the overall format of the essay were different from those for the original assignment. The format of alternative teaching also allows for students to succeed in some areas and get specific, targeted teaching and reteaching in areas of concern for their individual needs.

ONE TEACH, ONE ASSIST IN KAYLEIGH'S ENGLISH LANGUAGE ARTS CLASS

When used properly one teach, one assist is an effective teaching practice. The one-teach,-one-assist strategy ensures that both teachers are fully engaged in working with students, but their roles look different. One common misconception is that the core teacher always leads the main instruction, and the support or exceptional children's teacher always assists. That can lead to students viewing the teachers as a "real teacher" and "a helper," which is what we usually see happen. In best practice, the leading teacher changes. Even when teachers are newly working together and learning how to collaborate well, this is a quick strategy to begin. During warm-ups and any routine activities, this can be easily implemented. For example, we watch CNN10 daily with students, and they write paragraphs, analyze vocabulary, and practice using text features. My co-teacher and I take turns leading this activity, while the other assists students that day. Students see that both teachers are capable of the same practices, are there to help all students, and maintain the same expectations.

ONE TEACH, ONE OBSERVE

As mentioned in the table, this model can be used frequently but for brief periods of time. It is seldom used for an entire class period of instruction; its incidence of use depends on the data to be gathered. I remember a student in my last block of the day who had been doing well in all his other classes but, when he came to math class, he struggled to make it through the class period without being removed from the room for being disruptive. His behavior was impeding his own learning and that of others. So, we had my co-teacher do a **functional behavior assessment (FBA)**, and she spent the entire day following this student around and taking significant notes about how he behaved throughout the day in all our classrooms so that we could then analyze the data to find patterns of his most and least successful moments throughout the day. We found that his struggle with my class was primarily that it was after physical-education class, and he was simply wound up. So, we implemented a system whereby my co-teacher would intercept him on the way back from physical-education class and take him for a very short walk to get water, and then we would give him a fidget toy to utilize at the start of class. We also relocated him to one of the café tables in the room so that he could choose to stand if he wanted. He was also assigned to that table alone so that he could begin class without extra distractions. Then, when we started more collaborative work, he would move to a table with his peers. This gave him just a few minutes at the beginning of each class to decompress and settle back into the learning environment. But those minute details of how he was functioning in the classroom were fundamental to our finding a solution. Therefore, it was worth the time and effort for my co-teacher to conduct the FBA.

Making Co-Teaching Work

There are a few imperative aspects of implementing co-teaching well. The relationship between a general educator and his or her co-teaching partner functions much like a dating or marriage relationship. Parity is a vital component of these relationships—you are equals in your classroom, and functioning any other way is setting yourself up for failure or at least a lot of frustration. Why is this difficult? Well, for starters, there is often the feeling of, "but I am the content expert, and it is *my* classroom." And yes, while your training developed your pedagogical skills and content knowledge in your area of academic concentration, your co-teacher has an incredible skill set as well as particular knowledge in the areas of differentiation, modifications, and individualization of instruction. As with many healthy marriages, it is this balance of different skills that builds a complete and happy home, and trust in and communication with your co-teaching partner is key. Small shifts may be necessary in the way you communicate—instead of "my kids" and "your kids," it must become "our kids" and "our plans," for example. To give some long-term context, Holly reflects on her varied experiences and growth as a co-teacher.

> I was fresh out of [earning] my college degree and teaching seventh-grade math. I was assigned an inclusion teacher who was to spend every day with me during my inclusion block at the start of each day. Dating myself a little here, co-teaching was not something I was trained for in college as it was not a widely used practice in middle school settings. I was a brand-new teacher, and I had no clue how to utilize this extra human in my room. I fumbled my way along with giving her a task to do each day—she facilitated the warmup each day and then spent the rest of class assisting students one-on-one as I delivered instruction to the whole group. I had a superficial relationship with her at best and while she was lovely to work alongside, I can now say we did not utilize our skill sets to best serve those students. It was very much "my students" and "her students." We even split the grading up rather than by assignment by hers versus mine. The second year I had a second co-teacher who brought her IEP paperwork to my classroom and sat in the corner daily, only intervening when I had a particularly bad moment with a behavior management issue. This was by far my most unhealthy co-teaching relationship and those students were barely served with the co-teaching model . . . let's be real there was zero co-teaching happening. My third year I turned a corner, and it was primarily because of my third co-teacher, I fondly call her Mama Mackey as she shepherded me into a much healthier co-teaching environment. Mrs. Mackey was a seasoned special education teacher who knew her math content and that she had the skills to support content instruction and the differentiated needs of our students. The first lesson I learned in making this relationship work is to find time to co-plan. I cannot emphasize enough how important this practice is. Luckily for us, our administration had ensured that we had a common planning time. And while I was one of four teachers, she co-taught with; Mrs. Mackey guaranteed that we would have one day each week that we would sit down to plan together. While I usually said what I had planned based on our district pacing guide, I was pleasantly surprised in the amount of voice Mrs. Mackey brought to the table in terms of ideas and strategies to use with our students. Instead of being on my own with instructional design, I suddenly had this collaborative voice to bounce ideas with and to design instruction that was going to meet the needs of our students. We were careful to decide who oversaw what parts of each lesson and we worked hard to implement solid team teaching.
>
> Over a decade later I can reflect on this time with Mama Mackey and be incredibly grateful for the shift she made in my instructional practice as a co-teacher. But look carefully at how I described what we did . . . we team taught. And while we were able to make that work well, now that I know more about co-teaching, I realize that we still had a lot of room to grow. Over a decade later when I came back to the classroom full-time, I worked with several other co-teachers. This time I approached things differently . . . instruction started to look different daily depending on the needs of my

students. Where I would have thought that station teaching was only for elementary classrooms, I began to realize this was a way to target specific skills or tasks to smaller groups. This was helpful at times when I was teaching eighth-grade math and Math 1 simultaneously as I needed to differentiate and do enrichment with my Math 1 students but also provided targeted interventions to my grade-eight students. And even in this time I had varied experiences . . . I worked with one teacher who really struggled with the middle school mathematics content, and while I wanted to use parallel teaching regularly, this meant that she and I had to set extra time within the week where I could work with her on the content of the lesson, so she felt comfortable implementing it with half of the class. And because of my unpleasant experience during my second year, I had written off the positive purposes of a one teach one observe model and had to be reminded by my co-teacher that those occasional observations gave us tangible data to use to better support students. To be a good co-teacher you must be flexible, communicative, and caring with your co-teaching partner and remember that each of you will bring your own personality and skill set to the classroom and work together to maximize that experience.

MULTITIERED SYSTEMS OF SUPPORT

MTSS is a concept that blends elements of academic/instructional and behavioral support for students. In many ways, it is the contemporary blending of special-education supports with general education to provide, when needed, targeted interventions for *all* students. The structure focuses on instructional practices from a prevention and intervention perspective, using data to inform instruction and identify needed supports for students. Typically, MTSS is structured into three tiers: core, supplemental, and intensive. At the bottom of the pyramid is the core, tier 1, serving the needs of most students; these are instructional activities, done at the classroom level. Here, teachers focus on gathering data based on interest and abilities and using that data to drive instructional decisions. Here, we will see many of the differentiated instruction strategies that we explore in Chapter 10. Key components of this tier are progress monitoring and data collection; a debriefing with the instructional team follows so that team members' understanding of such data informs the next instructional decisions and so that they recognize which students need attention at the second tier. The second tier, consisting of targeted group interventions, is aimed at providing additional support to small groups whose members may not yet need individualized interventions. Such *supplemental* interventions typically serve about 15 percent of students. At this level, teachers recognize themes in academic, behavioral, or social-emotional needs for which a portion of the student population needs scaffolds. Teachers spend time explicitly teaching skills to and reinforcing expectations for students, helping them build capacity for consistency. Tier 3, consisting of *intensive* interventions, serves approximately 5 percent of the population and is focused on targeted individual interventions. Once again, MTSS is a complex network of supports for behavior, academics, and social-emotional needs, and the interventions could address any or all of those three areas. This is where we start to see overlap with and connections to the

PBIS (the Positive Behavior and Intervention System), which may be used to supporting behavior (see Chapter 13), academics, self-regulation (see Chapter 4), differentiation (see Chapter 10), and social-emotional needs (see Chapter 7). MTSS structures vary widely by school and district but have the same basic tiers: core, supplemental, and intensive. To provide an example, we share a brief outline of the three-tiered model at our school:

Tier 1: Class-Wide Core Instructional Activities

- Assist teachers in gathering individual student data on interests and concerns to assist with core instruction development
- Assist teachers in developing and implementing core instruction with differentiation as needed
- Assist teachers in monthly progress-monitoring data collection related to class-wide student academic and social/emotional progress
- Review and analyze progress-monitoring data to identify a need for changes in core instruction and/or need for additional student support; the focus will be on the performance level and the progress rate

Tier 2: Small-Group Supplemental Intervention Activities

- Use classroom progress-monitoring data and other data available to identify students who meet specific academic and/or behavioral-emotional criteria, indicating a need for small-group interventions to address these needs
- Assist teachers in identifying additional data needed to understand the needs of students identified as needing additional small-group interventions, including student feedback on their needs
- Assist teachers in identifying goals for level of performance or rate of progress and developing and implementing small-group interventions to address the needs identified
- Assist teachers in measuring fidelity of intervention implementation
- Assist teachers in weekly progress-monitoring data collection related to small-group intervention implementation
- Review and analyze progress-monitoring data to identify a need for change to small-group interventions and/or need additional student support

Tier 3: Individual Intensive Intervention Activities

- Use small-group progress-monitoring data and other data available to identify students who have received academic and/or behavioral-emotional small-group interventions but have not met the goals set for the level of performance or rate of progress, indicating need for individual student interventions to address these needs

- Assist teachers in identifying additional data needed to understand the needs of the individual child identified as needing an individual intervention, including student feedback on their needs

- Assist teachers in identifying goals for level of performance or rate of progress for individual students and develop and implement individual interventions to address the need identified

- Assist teachers in measuring fidelity of intervention implementation

- Assist teachers in weekly progress-monitoring data collection related to individual intervention implementation

- Review and analyze progress-monitoring data to identify a need for change to individual interventions and/or need for additional student supports

MTSS takes a village to implement well, and data collection must be organized in such a way that the data are meaningful when analyzed in MTSS team meetings but also not overwhelming for teachers to collect.

Here is a more tangible example from our school about the structure and implementation of MTSS protocols.

Every single student in the school is part of tier 1, the core, and receives high-quality and standards-based instruction within all academic blocks. Tier-1 instruction is data based, and teachers use data to determine student success and to plan next steps in instruction. Any student who is not progressing at an acceptable rate to meet or exceed growth targets for the year will receive a tier-2 intervention. All tier-2 interventions are delivered with research-based strategies addressing the skills most needed in a small group. All tier-2 interventions are teacher led, and progress is assessed every ten days. Once progress is seen, students may move back into tier 1 or continue to receive tier-2 instructions. If progress is not sufficient, the student will have layered support added and will receive an individual or smaller-group intervention. If progress is still insufficient, the team may determine that the frequency or the duration (or both) of interventions needs to be changed. Increasing in frequency or duration of tier-2 interventions would make them tier-3 interventions.

To address students' behavior, all students receive instruction in PBIS and participate in a ticket system. Any unsuccessful student, as determined by data collected from minor discipline forms, will receive layered tier-2 support to address specific behaviors. Some examples include individual incentive plans, target-behavior-tracking tools, and family–school team meetings. For behavior, tier 3 usually layers on more frequent and intense versions of the same interventions but can include a functional behavior assessment and/or a behavior intervention plan.

Behavior, tier 2/3: incentive plan, behavior tracking system

Social-emotional learning, tier 2/3: individual and group counseling

English language arts, tier 2/3: repeated reading, small group in context vocabulary with Frayer model

Math, tier 2/3: scaffolded math in small group, addressing skills that were biggest deficit

Below are both examples of tier-3 interventions. These students received this instruction to address serious behavior and academic needs that were associated with a lack of progress in core-content learning. Per the layered approach of the MTSS framework, these students also received tier-2 interventions during a dedicated time for those to be provided schoolwide.

Donovan is a seventh-grade student with an IEP. He is eligible under the category of autism. He receives special-education services in math, reading, written expression, and social-emotional needs. To serve him academically, Donovan is in a co-taught class for English language arts and math, with a core and a special-education teacher. To meet his social-emotional needs, he is in an advisory program, he can meet with a counselor when he or an adult decides he needs to do so, and he practices strategies individually or guided by an adult, as needed. For example, he commonly uses the "take-five" strategy in the cooldown space. Sometimes this is a self-requested strategy, and other times it is prompted by his teachers. He uses a weighted blanket, sets a five-minute timer, processes his behaviors with an adult when the interval is complete, and is generally able to calmly return to class.

To accommodate students' social-emotional needs, each tier looks different. Students receiving tier-1 services would be taught how to use "calm down" spaces, fidgets, and in-classroom tools. This could be a teacher- and counselor-led practice done during homeroom or advisory periods. A student receiving tier-1 services would be able to acknowledge his or her feelings and self-regulate without an adult. A student receiving tier-2 services may need additional one-on-one instruction on self-regulation strategies that he or she may practice with the exceptional children's teacher or the guidance counselor. Students receiving tier-3 services, such as Donovan, may need to receive prompting from an adult to acknowledge their behaviors and elevation of their stress before they reach an outburst and may consistently display outbursts. Such students usually need adult assistance to help them reset and return to class.

Drake is a seventh-grade student who has an IEP and who is eligible for services under the emotional disability category. He has behavior goals and requires special-education services to support reaching these goals. To support and monitor progress toward these goals, he uses an incentive plan. He carries around a behavior checklist that he presents to each of his teachers. The sheet has three to four goals that reflect the areas of behavioral concern; these goals are set by both Drake and the special-education team. At the end of each period, teachers give Drake a full point, half a point, or zero points, depending on how his behavior has reached the expectations set in his plan. If he receives two of three points, he is deemed to meet a goal.. During the first semester, Drake had three goals to work on; progress toward these goals would reflect growth in those areas. At his most recent IEP meeting, his incentive plan was modified to reflect his most recent behavior needs and to provide an incentive he was willing to work toward.

Regarding behavioral systems, a student receiving tier-1 services easily adheres to school-wide behavioral systems and can follow a PBIS system. For example, such a student may earn points or tickets for positive behavior, accumulation of which will result in an award like outside time or a treat. Students receiving tier-2 services may receive assistance with meeting school-wide expectations, such as being prepared for class, which would allow them to receive their ticket or point. A support for such students would be to provide them with an individual, tangible note that lists the specific supplies they need for the day. A tier-3 intervention like Drake's is one that acknowledges that the student's behavior requires more support. Such students have specific goals they need to focus on. It is best to select no more than three or four goals to focus on for a set period. Such students still receive incentives and awards. However, such students also receive guidance from an adult and are provided with periods during which they may reflect on their behavior as well as individual time to learn replacement behaviors or ways to cope by working with an adult.

This chapter explores some broad concepts of learning, the unique populations we serve, and the structures we use to best serve those students. Much of the content here will feel much more real once you are actually working in the classroom, but our aim here is to give exposure to some of the current best practices and the language that's associated with those practices to give you a bit of a head start on some big ideas. Let's revisit this chapter's learning outcomes.

1. **Recognize the components of special-education principles in middle school, including UDL, IEPs, and 504 plans.** Middle school special-education principles encompass SDI, which is mandated by federal law, focusing on individualized instruction to meet the unique needs of students with disabilities, as outlined in their IEPs. Collaboration between general- and special-education teachers is essential for effective SDI delivery, while practices such as UDL ensure inclusive environments by proactively designing instruction to accommodate diverse learners through flexible learning options aligned with engagement, representation, and action and expression principles.

2. **Understand the models of co-teaching and how to implement them.** Co-teaching is a collaborative model whereby two educators jointly deliver instruction, including SDI for students with disabilities, in a shared classroom space with shared accountability for learner outcomes. There are six models of co-teaching, with three considered to be high-yield approaches: parallel teaching, station teaching, and alternative teaching. The high-yield approaches should be utilized most frequently to increase engagement in and access to the curriculum while embedding SDI effectively within each unit of study. Doing so requires co-teachers to coordinate and make careful plans that are based on students' needs and assessment data.

3. **Distinguish between the different tiers of MTSS and apply them to practical settings.** MTSS encompasses three tiers, with tier 1 focusing on class-wide core instructional activities, tier 2 providing small-group supplemental interventions, and tier 3 offering individual intensive interventions and addressing academic,

behavioral, and social-emotional needs. Through a structured approach involving data-driven decision-making and layered interventions, MTSS aims to ensure that all students receive appropriate support to succeed academically and behaviorally.

References

Bauwens, J., Hourcade, J. J., & Friend, M. (1989). Cooperative teaching: A model for general and special education integration. *Remedial and Special Education, 10*(2), 17–22. https://doi.org/10.1177/074193258901000205.

Beninghof, A. M. (2016). To clone or not to clone? *Educational Leadership, 73*(4), 10–15.

CAST. (2018). Universal design for learning guidelines version 2.2. Retrieved from http://udlguidelines.cast.org.

Covey, S. M. R., & Merrill, R. R. (2006). *The speed of trust: the one thing that changes everything.* Free Press.

Diaz-Rico, L. (2019). *A course for teaching English learners*, 3rd Edition. Pearson.

Friend, M., Reising, M., & Cook, L. (1993). Co-teaching: An overview of the past, a glimpse at the present, and considerations for the future. *Preventing School Failure, 37*(4), 6–10.

Friend, M. (2021). *Interactions: Collaboration skills for school professionals* (9th edition). Pearson.

Friend, M., & Barron, T. L. (2014). Co-teaching: Inclusion and increased student achievement. In Robert E. Slavin, Ed., *Proven programs in education: Classroom management & assessment.* Corwin.

IDEA, 20 U.S.C. 1400 et seq., 34 C.F.R. pt. 339.

King-Sears, M. E., Stefanidis, A., Berkeley, S., & Strogilos, V. (2021). Does co-teaching improve academic achievement for students with disabilities? A meta-analysis. *Educational Research Review, 34*, 100405.

Klingner, J. K., & Vaughn, S. (1999). Students' perceptions of instruction in inclusion classrooms: Implications for students with learning disabilities. *Exceptional Children, 66*(1), 23–37.

Office of Special Education Programs. (2014). *32nd annual report to Congress on the implementation of the Individuals with Disabilities Education Act, 2010.* U.S. Department of Education, Office of Special Education and Rehabilitative Services.

Office of Special Education Programs. (2024). *45th annual report to Congress on the implementation of the Individuals with Disabilities Education Act, 2023.* U.S. Department of Education, Office of Special Education and Rehabilitative Services.

Poon-McBrayer, K. F., & Wong, P. M. (2013). Inclusive education services for children and youth with disabilities: Values, roles and challenges of school leaders. *Children and Youth Services Review, 35*(9), 1520–25.doi.org/10.1016/j.childyouth.2013.06.009.

Scruggs, T. E., & Mastropieri, M. A. (1996). Teacher perceptions of mainstreaming/inclusion, 1958–1995: A research synthesis. *Exceptional Children, 63*(1), 59–74. https://doi.org/10.1177/001440299606300106.

U.S. Department of Education. (n.d.). History: Twenty-five years of progress in educating children with disabilities through IDEA. Retrieved October 2011, from http://www2.ed.gov/policy/speced/leg/idea/history.html.

Vanderbilt University. (2023). *Creating an Inclusive School Environment: A Model for School Leaders.* https://iris.peabody.vanderbilt.edu/module/incl/.

CHAPTER 7

Social and Emotional Learning

Learning Outcomes:

1. Understand the social and emotional skills needed to support adolescents.

2. Identify trauma and barriers that young adolescents experience and their impact on adolescents' ability to learn.

3. Explore trauma-informed practices and their application in creating a safe and inclusive learning environment for students who have experienced trauma.

4. Recognize the diverse models of and approaches to implementing advisory programs, recognizing the importance of addressing social and emotional needs and tailoring lessons to issues relevant to the student population.

5. Understand resilience as a neurobiological response to stress, recognize its impact on adolescents' emotional well-being and learning, and learn strategies for helping students stay within their resilience zone.

Basics of Social-Emotional Learning

Adolescence is a time when important social and emotional changes are occurring. In earlier chapters we saw how adolescents make connections to peers and adults, exploring their self-perceptions and identities and responding to environments that challenge them. Cognitive developments, like increases in abstract thinking, improvements in decision-making, and a greater ability to understand what is going on in others' minds, all support these social and emotional developments. Traditionally, we have seen the business of schools as being academic achievement. Over the past thirty years, teachers, psychologists, and other professionals have explicitly recognized the need to focus on the social and emotional aspects of development, not only because they are important in themselves but also because they are intimately connected to academic achievement. About half of the states in the United States have implemented required competencies or standards related to social and emotional skills. Positive Youth Development (Shek et al., 2019) and Social Emotional Learning (Durlak et al., 2015) are two frameworks that provide programmatic school interventions to support adolescent social and emotional development in concrete ways.

In this chapter, we will use the Social Emotional Learning framework to explore the fundamental components of social and emotional well-being, with a focus on teachable emotional and social skills. We will look at the trauma experienced by many students, **trauma-informed practices** for reaching those students, and how effective interventions can lead to resilient students. Along the way, we will analyze the similarities and differences between two students, Brooklyn and Liza, whose backgrounds and experiences are quite different. We will then evaluate the impact of students' needs on their academic success and resiliency. Finally, we will review strategies that help students cope within their learning environments.

Adverse Childhood Experiences and Trauma

Trauma affects much of the population in some capacity although this impact may be different for each person. Young adolescents are developing their attention span, resiliency, and relationships, all traits affecting their success in school. The Substance Abuse and Mental Health Services Administration (SAMHSA) defines trauma as "an event, series of events, or set of circumstances that is experienced by an individual as physically or emotionally harmful or life threatening and that has lasting adverse effects on the individual's functioning and mental, physical, social, emotional, or spiritual well-being"(U.S. Department of Health and Human Services, Substance Abuse and Mental Health Services Administration, 2014, p. 7). In all schools, educators encounter students who have previously experienced or are currently experiencing traumatic events or **Adverse Childhood Experiences (ACEs)**. ACEs that lead to childhood trauma include physical and emotional abuse and neglect and parental violence, depression, substance abuse, and incarceration. Those childhood experiences have been shown to be highly related to a wide range of physical and mental-health problems in adolescence and adulthood, problems such as obesity, disease, ADHD, and both internalizing and externalizing behavior problems. The implications of trauma may be seen immediately or may persist into adulthood and can become obstacles to learning, peer and teacher relationships, and mental health. Some trauma is direct and explicit, including physical, sexual, and emotional abuse, but, other times, trauma is more implicit and is hidden to the outside world. Regardless of the source of trauma, teachers must use **trauma-informed practices**, which are specific practices that have been developed and implemented and that show responsiveness to individuals' trauma and stress factors.

Students who have experienced trauma may display various behaviors in the classroom. Students may be distrustful of peers and adults, or they appear to be withdrawn and unable to appropriately respond to social cues. These students often harbor a lot of guilt and shame, leading to negative self-perceptions. These students may struggle to regulate their emotions and behaviors. Jennings (2019) lists several trauma responses that we see in middle school—**hyperarousal**, **hypervigilance**, and **dissociation** are among those most common. Hyperarousal may be displayed as irritability, aggression, risky behavior, or difficulty in concentrating. Hypervigilance often appears as a constant tenseness or always feeling "on guard" or at high alert. Dissociation presents itself as separation from one's thoughts, emotions, bodily sensations, or overall sense of self.

These represent two extreme ends of the spectrum of behaviors we might see—on the end of hyperarousal/hypervigilance, we see agitation and potential overreaction while dissociation will look quieter and more withdrawn. Then there are the myriad other behaviors that are not related to trauma but are often noted. Jennings discusses four common behaviors:

- Attention lapses: students may have trouble maintaining attention as their brains are filtering through what information is relevant and what information is irrelevant and any unexpected information may cause students to become agitated or embarrassed or frozen like a "deer in headlights."

- Deficits in expressive language: When students are anxious, they may not be able to articulate their feelings into words. And when students feel that they are not heard or understood they may also become irritable or completely shut down.

- Difficulty taking another perspective: Students may struggle with textual inferences, thinking about how others completed/solved problems, and participating in classroom discourse. This leads to students seeming socially lost and unable to connect well with peers (which may lead them to either become victims or perpetrators of bullying).

- Difficulty with **sequential memory**: when students are exposed to trauma their memories are categorized as an episode of random events rather than a sequentially organized line of events. Students normally develop sequential memory with predictable environments and routines which may be lacking for students in chaotic unstable home environments. Sequential memory is important for reading, writing, and oral communication. (Jennings, 2019, p. 34–35).

When working with students who have been exposed to trauma, it is also important to be mindful of triggers that might cause students to be retraumatized. Sometimes these triggers are subtle and other times more overtly notable. Students may also respond differently, depending on the source of their original trauma. For some, loud noises or chaotic environments may be triggering, while, for others, being alone and quiet might be the trigger. In the school context, there are several common triggers for students experiencing trauma. For example, punishment can be triggering for many students, especially if they have experienced physical or verbal abuse. While a teacher may raise his voice purposefully to redirect a student, that tone may trigger a student to feel fearful and become either agitated or dissociated.

Pause and Reflect: While you may or may not have experienced trauma in your life, most of us can identify things that may trigger certain responses or reactions. Take a moment to reflect on at least one instance where something triggered you in some way.

Think about how your response/reaction manifested. Thinking now as an adult, can you identify the root cause of the trigger? How will these kinds of experiences impact your interactions with students in your classroom?

Brooklyn is a rising ninth grader. At the start of Brooklyn's eighth-grade year, she was living with her birth mother and her many siblings and stepfather in a chaotic and unstable environment. Sometimes, Brooklyn would be dressed in sweats, with her hoodie pulled up, and would be withdrawn from peers; on such days, she often would be sleeping through classes. On other days, she would have on full makeup and would exhibit much more aggressive behavior toward peers and teachers. She would react quickly and loudly to small redirections from teachers and would shout a litany of curses toward whoever rubbed her the wrong way at any moment. When she chose to engage in her academic classes, teachers noted immense capacity for problem-solving and making inferences and strong writing skills. However, it was rare that Brooklyn made it through a full day without some sort of behavior that impeded not only her own success but also the success of others.

Pause and Reflect: Take a moment to think about the brief description of Brooklyn and the behaviors that she exhibited in school. Then look back to the previous section, and see if you can identify the types of behaviors Brooklyn displayed. Brainstorm how you might want to address these behaviors. Keep the list handy; we will revisit this case later in the chapter.

At some point in the year, Brooklyn was moved to a foster-care placement. While, initially, her behaviors became even more exacerbated, after some time in the structured and stable environment, we noticed fewer days with "big" behaviors. Brooklyn currently has a therapist she meets with regularly, and she utilizes the school counselor as needed. At this point as a rising ninth grader, she can articulate how she has grown in school, how she has developed relationships with her peers, and how she is coping in healthier ways. She can think reflectively about the challenges and setbacks she faces daily.

Social-Emotional Learning

The effects of trauma, while detrimental, can be minimized by implementing trauma-informed instructional practices within schools. Over the past thirty years, many interventions have been designed to address the skills, attitudes, and behaviors that are needed for those who have experienced trauma to reach their academic potential. **Social-emotional learning** is defined, as is the process of acquiring and applying knowledge, skills, and attitudes to develop emotional intelligence, manage emotions, and achieve personal and collective goals, fostering empathy and enabling students to maintain healthy relationships and make responsible decisions in education and life. To explore the fundamentals of SEL we will rely heavily on the framework created by the **Collaborative for Academic, Social, and Emotional Learning (CASEL)**, which is widely used in education by researchers and practitioners. Durlak et al. (2015)

showed that the early use of school-wide SEL interventions—with all students in the school, not just those who had demonstrably shown the effects of trauma—improved students' social and emotional skills (e.g., empathy, decision-making, conflict resolution), attitudes about themselves (e.g., **self-efficacy** and self-management), relationships with their teachers and peers, and relations with their communities. Their academic achievement also improved. A similar, more recent analysis of second-generation SEL interventions (Cipriano et al., 2023) showed similar positive results and broadened the positive outcomes to include perceptions of school climate and safety and general school functioning.

In the SEL framework, there are five "clusters" of competencies related to SEL skills: **self-awareness, self-management, social awareness, relationship skills, and responsible decision-making.** To demonstrate competence in *self-awareness*, students must understand their emotions and personal values and how those interact across contexts. To do this, students must be able to self-assess strengths and weaknesses, acknowledge biases, and use a **growth mindset** to work toward personal goals. To show elevated levels of self-awareness, students must be able to reconcile how thoughts, feelings, values, and actions are intertwined with one another and their social identity. To demonstrate competence in *self-management*, students need to effectively handle their emotions to achieve their goals. Examples of this would include the ability to delay gratification, to manage stress, to control impulses, and to persevere in the face of challenges. Proficiency in *social awareness* includes the ability to grasp viewpoints of individuals, to demonstrate empathy and compassion for others, and to comprehend the historical and social standards of conduct in various situations. Students should be able to identify resources and support systems within their family, their school, and the community. *Relationship skills* relate to the capacity to create and sustain positive nurturing connections and adeptly maneuver through new environments. Highlights of relationship skills include the abilities of effective communication, active listening, cooperative teamwork, collaborative problem-solving, constructive conflict resolution, and adaptability within various social and cultural dynamics. *Responsible decision-making* entails the ability to make considerate decisions concerning one's own conduct in various circumstances. This would include students' ability to weigh ethical principles and safety considerations and assess benefits and repercussions of actions.

Pause and Reflect: Look at the five clusters of social and emotional learning skills. Where do you recognize strengths in yourself? Where do you see areas of need among the skills? Reflect on your home and schooling experience—where did you gain most of the SEL competencies?

While many would argue that SEL skills should be taught at home, which is a valid premise, there is an authentic space in schools in which to build these competencies as well. In fact, many of them seamlessly intertwine with what we teach. In math classes, we expect students to work in small cooperative groups with other students, which helps build relationship skills. In social studies classes, we explore multiple points of view of historical events, so such classes are a natural place to build social-awareness skills. Development of responsible decision-making and self-management is sprinkled throughout the school day as students learn to regulate their emotions and make decisions that help them meet their goals. Educators have a massive influence on building these skills every day by using best teaching practices. We also know that all the best curriculum and instruction in the world will not positively impact students if their basic needs are not met. For young adolescents, having shelter, food, and an environment in which they feel safe is outside of their control. Free and reduced lunch programs at school are important but do not reduce a student's stress about availability of food in the evening, on weekends, or during breaks from school. Nor do such programs ensure that, if the students qualify, their parents will complete the paperwork required to utilize this service. If these basic needs are not met, students often will exhibit behaviors that impede their academic success. Sometimes the easiest fix for a student's poor attitude is a snack.

Pause and Reflect: What needs of yours were and were not met consistently during your childhood? How did having those needs met impact your daily life at school each day and throughout your school year?

To better illustrate this complex system, we will utilize Dr. Dan Siegel's hand model of the brain (see Figure 7.1). First, we need to understand several components of the structure of our brains, using one of our hands as a model. Our wrist represents the spinal cord where our brain sits. The palm represents the inner brainstem (responsible for basic bodily functions like breathing and heart function). In this model, the thumb represents the amygdala (responsible for emotions) and, when the thumb rests on the palm, we form the limbic system, which also includes the brain's hippocampus (responsible for memory). These parts essentially make up our downstairs brain. Meanwhile, our fingers are the cerebral cortex (responsible for sensory responses and directing motor activity) and the prefrontal cortex (responsible for regulating thoughts and emotions), which make up the upstairs brain. When our fingers cover our thumb, we have our full brain model, with our upstairs brain and downstairs brain connected, enabling the sending of all the messages that are necessary to stay in a regulated state. This is when our brain is a thinking brain. When a stressor is introduced, however, the brain may become dysregulated. In the hand model, this is viewed as "flipping our lid" as the cerebral cortex and prefrontal cortex are no longer connected to the downstairs brain, and the brain enters an offline status. Our amygdala is sensing danger, but our prefrontal cortex cannot communicate to the body whether the stressor is indeed a danger to us. Realistically, any stressor, not only instances of real danger, can cause this, and the fact that the prefrontal cortex is not fully developed until adulthood means that adolescents sometimes struggle to regulate this brain interaction and to remain in the resilient zone. To get our dysregulated brain back to being in a regulated, thinking status, we must employ coping strategies. We will explore some of these strategies in a later section.

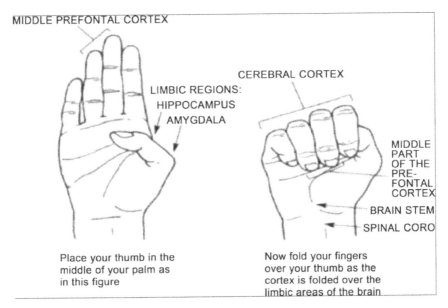

Figure 7.1 Siegel's Hand Model of the Brain. Available via license: Creative Commons Attribution 4.0 International

Considerations for Supporting Students' Social and Emotional Learning

The research on SEL (Durlak et al., 2011; Cipriano et al., 2023) indicates that the most effective interventions use instruction that is sequenced step by step, involves active forms of learning, provides sufficient time, and has explicit learning goals. Skills are explicitly taught, modelled, applied, practiced, and integrated with all instruction. In the next section, we address several components of how to support students' social and emotional learning within the school context using trauma-informed SEL practices. We explore how to set up safe spaces for students to utilize when they are no longer functioning in their resilience zone, then we share some mindfulness practices, which students may use to regulate their emotions as well as some reset activities for students who have "flipped their lid." We end with a focus on advisory periods as a practical context for embedding SEL skills into the school day.

TRAUMA-INFORMED SOCIAL-EMOTIONAL-LEARNING PRACTICES

Trauma is defined as the result of one or more events that leads to an emotional response such as stress, discomfort, frustration, fear, vulnerability, lack of control, and so on. Students in our classrooms arrive with diverse types of traumas, some of which are disclosed and some of which are unknown. Students' trauma and other social and emotional needs impact their academic performance and ability to collaborate throughout the school day. All students need to feel safe at school; this feeling is the foundation for motivation to learn. When we do not feel safe, it is challenging to focus on learning. Our students need to have trust in us as leaders to ensure they have a safe and supportive learning environment. From a macro level, much of this is addressed in a high-quality **MTSS** implementation (see Chapter 6 for more details on MTSS). Trauma-informed practices include an extensive list of good teaching practices explored in other chapters. Some of those include building relationships, using an assets-based approach to teaching, using **restorative practices**, and collaborating with families. According to SAMHSA (2014), there are six key principles of building trauma-informed practices in schools:

1. Safety: Prioritize creation of an environment that is physically and emotionally trustworthy to students.

2. Trustworthiness and Transparency: Provide open communication with students making decisions transparent with the goal of building trust through clear and honest information.

3. Peer Support: Recognize the value of individuals with lived experiences in supporting and empathizing with others who have faced trauma.

4. Collaboration and Mutuality: Build relationships that emphasize collaboration and shared decision making.

5. Empowerment, Voice, and Choice: Build capacity for students to feel empowered to advocate for themselves and as much as possible minimize power differentials.

6. Cultural, Historical, and Gender issues: Actively defy cultural biases and stereotypes and utilize culturally responsive practices.

Next, we will zoom in on a few specific practices that help educators and others working with students who have trauma to help them adapt to everyday situations in the classroom and situations that push them outside of their resiliency zone.

ASSESSING THE SITUATION

We know from our exploration of puberty in Chapter 3 that adolescents have immaturely developed frontal lobes and, therefore, sometimes make choices that are unrealistic and have emotions that are exaggerated. Their perception of a problem may be distorted. When encountering a problem, the role of an educator or a counselor is to help the student identify the problem, describe a specific word for the emotion the student is feeling, and prompt the student to brainstorm his or her own positive coping strategies. Assessing the situation is a great starting point in mediating a child's needs.

Questions to ask yourself:

1. What is the magnitude of the problem?
2. What steps can we take to solve this problem?
3. What barriers of anxiety, fear, or frustration will be removed to address this concern?

(Ginsburg & Jablow, 2015)

SAFE SPACES

A **safe space** for students is inclusive and allows them to utilize the strategies they have learned. In our classrooms, this feeling of a safe space can be created by having a corner or secluded location in the classroom for students. At our school, we have two designated cooldown spaces. One is located within our counselor's area. The other is in a small area between two classrooms within the office of one of our administrators. Not only is the space itself important but the resources it offers are also vital. When students take a break on their own, they may sit with their tough feelings in a way that escalates their concerns. They may replay the thoughts in their heads, relive the situation that is their stressor, express a physical outburst, or internalize their emotions and shut down.

Resources for students should be ones that help students regulate their emotions. There should be assorted options for students to choose from. However, they should be taught how to effectively use the space and items. For example, a timer should be provided for students to monitor their own time spent there. This provides students with responsibility if they have taken the initiative to request a break. Additional options for the space can be drawing or coloring pages, often with affirmations or calming words; reflection sheets; or fidgets. For students who need additional comfort, we provide weighted blankets as well. This helps some of our students with autism and special sensory needs and some of our students with anxiety. Engaging in these options engages students' bodies with movement and redirects their thoughts to a positive perspective.

MINDFULNESS

Mindfulness can be characterized in many ways. Practicing mindfulness often involves taking a pause in one's life; it serves as a moment to breathe and reflect. In the classroom, this practice is paired with a growth mindset, the belief that growth or development is possible and accessible to everyone. When one searches the Internet, one finds a myriad of free and paid resources to support teachers as they implement mindful moments. These moments are purposeful breaks to allow students to start, reset, or end their days. Because of the effects of trauma on mental health, these moments are imperative for some students.

Imagine that it is 1:45 p.m. and that eighth graders have participated in their exploratory programs, physical education, and lunch. These parts of the school day are essential elements in students' well-rounded education. But these sometimes-less-structured times of the day also tend to get students riled and excited. The abrupt transition back to a language arts class in which they begin class with reading may require them to take a moment to pause and reflect, to calm their bodies, and to focus.

Practice It: Read the following script with a peer or your class. Reflect on how your body felt prior to and following the reading. What could you add or adapt to fit the environment you are in?

Welcome to class. Let's take some time to reset today. To find a moment in our day that we can allow ourselves to rest and find a few minutes of peace in all the commotion and emotion you have experienced today. Find a comfortable seat or position that will allow you to relax your body. If you feel comfortable, close your eyes. Begin to focus on your breathing. Notice how your chest rises and falls. Breathe in. Hold for 5, 4, 3, 2, 1 and slowly release your breath for 5, 4, 3, 2, 1. Again, breathe in deeply. Hold for 5, 4, 3, 2, 1 and slowly release your breath for 5, 4, 3, 2, 1. While you continue to breathe, think of the events that took place in your life. What can you let go of as we sit here? What can you remind yourself of that is not yours to carry? As we breathe in together one last time, allow yourself to find the calmness you are feeling, hold on to it, and let it carry you throughout the rest of class. Let us take one final deep breath, hold for 5, 4, 3, 2, 1 and slowly release your breath for 5, 4, 3, 2, 1. Be reminded that in this room you are safe, cared for.

Some of the benefits of mindfulness are relieving stress, anxiety, pain, and depression and improving attention and sleep (Mayo Clinic, 2022). Teachers can adapt the focus and message of each mindfulness moment by including quotes that reflect what students are doing or need to hear, prompting students to imagine a place in which they feel safe or happy throughout the breathing process. Alternatively, teachers may allow students to move around the room or go outside for a new setting.

Using mindfulness strategies does not need to take a significant amount of time. Sometimes just having students acknowledge and sense their surroundings helps students reset. Perhaps we ask students to notice what is grounding them to the earth—notice the sensations of what is supporting them (their feet, their legs, etc.). Or we ask students to orient themselves in their environment by just looking around and noticing anything that catches their eyes (focus on having them move their entire head and neck as they do this to get the physical movement). Perhaps we just encourage our students to take a sip of water. Another strategy is having students practice bilateral coordination that crosses their midline. This improves coordination and fine motor skills. It is a therapeutic tool that leads to **emotional regulation**. It forces the left and right sides of the brain to work together. Here are a few simple time-efficient strategies that we utilize in our school to reset our minds and bodies:

- Snap and Wink: Individuals snap with their right hand and blink their left eye. Then they switch back and forth.

- Gotcha: Individuals form a circle, each person's right hand should be held up flat, like a plate, and, using their left hand, individuals should place their index finger in the palm of their neighbor's right hand. On the count of three, the players use their right hand to try to clasp their neighbor's index finger while trying to keep the other neighbor from capturing their own index finger.

- Rock, Paper, Scissors: In this version of the game, students pair off and then compete. The loser of the pair becomes his partner's "cheerleader" and cheers the partner on as the partner competes with the winner of another pair. After each game, the losing partner joins the cheering team of the player who continues to win, and play continues until there is a single winner.

- Push against a wall: This simple grounding exercise helps students calm their nervous system. To do this exercise students stand with their feet about hip distance apart a short distance away from the wall. They then press their palms into the wall moving energy from the head down to the lower body. This allows students to feel grounded and guide their minds away from anxious thoughts.

ADVISORY PROGRAMS

Advisory programs are a foundational part of the middle school concept. While advisory programs are not explicitly aimed toward enhancing social and emotional learning or implementing trauma-informed practices, when done well, such programs can address many of the things we have described throughout this chapter. In an advisory program, students can be supported and can build relationships with adults in the school setting. Advisory programs can and often do look different in various schools, and here we recognize several models that are utilized. One option is for all the students to be divided into small groups, with each group being assigned to school staff members, such as core teachers, noncore teachers, counselors, and other school support staff. The premise is to build a small group so that each child has a trusted adult in whom he or she can confide when necessary. Another common structure is for teachers to lead advisory lessons during an extended homeroom time. This model is ideal in many ways as it builds a strong and consistent community. Many schools choose to utilize a purchased program (such as Second Step or Responsive Classroom), or schools may have teachers design advisory lessons on their own. The topics within a unit in an advisory program vary according to grade-level concerns and development. Topics may include having a growth mindset, building positive peer relationships, making mistakes, communicating individual needs, dating, and other topics that are relevant to students' life experiences. Another, less common, model is for the school counselor(s) to run an advisory program. In larger schools, this may be a challenge but would consist of the counselors teaching a whole class of students. In these experiences, counselors may follow a program or lead lessons from resources they have curated.

At our school, our counselor chose to administer a school-wide survey to students to see what topics our population wanted to explore. This gave students more buy-in to the advisory class and provided clear guidance to our counselor on how to frame her lessons. Our counselor also utilized data from her check-in meetings with students to note what topics were most pertinent to our group. For example, this year, most meetings she had with students related to conflict with peers or with family. Therefore, she then designed lessons on how to handle conflict with others. Other common topics included stress management, issues related to anxiety and depression, as well as LGBTQIA+ issues and body-image issues. There are, of course, pros and cons to each advisory model. Having a purchased program is helpful as the lesson plans are already fleshed out with resources, and teachers implement the lessons. But there is also a lack of flexibility in this model. Using a model of creating lessons results in a more individualized approach to meeting specific needs of the population, but creating things from scratch is also very time-consuming and can be overwhelming on top of an already full plate of responsibilities.

You first met Liza in Chapter 2. In this chapter, we will focus on Liza's support network. Remember that Liza is a quiet, thoughtful, and intelligent eighth grader who has an incredible support system at home, has a strong group of friends, participates in leadership roles with student government, and struggles with anxiety and OCPD; these struggles impact her social and emotional needs at home and at school. Liza has a therapist she meets with regularly, and she sees the school counselor as needed. We remember that her mental-health needs impact her success at school, although she feels supported by the adults and friends she has found while at school. Despite her OCPD, she is a student who consistently maintains good grades and is successful.

Despite the support Liza has at school and at home, her OCPD impacts her comfort at school. As a result, she still missed a few days of school due to her mental health. She said that she occasionally feels uncomfortable in the lunchroom because she notices others eating food with textures or smells that impact her OCPD. Likewise, a disagreement with a peer can cause her to feel dysregulated. Her brain goes into overdrive in these situations, causing her to lose focus in class and to need time to reset.

Pause and Reflect: If Liza were in your homeroom and you were responsible for designing your advisory lessons, what topics do you feel would be helpful for Liza? While Liza is more open to receiving counseling and participating in advisory, Brooklyn is resistant to participating in advisory. She does not want to be vulnerable among her peers. In what ways could her advisory leader hook her? Additionally, based on the earlier description of Brooklyn's situation, what other trauma-informed practices do you think might be most useful to support her?

BUILDING RESILIENCE

Students typically develop protective adaptive skills from good parenting (in the family setting), social networks, and friendships; they thus become resilient. Students who have experienced trauma in their family and neighborhood environments can begin to develop **resilience** when they have safe and supportive schools (Racine et al., 2022; Souers & Hall, 2016). SEL, when it is integrated into instruction for all students, has been shown to make schools feel safe and supportive. The mindsets encouraged by SEL promote resilience because students begin to understand that these practices influence their environments to develop positive growth mindsets (Bronfenbrenner, 2004; Yeager & Dweck, 2012).

Resilience

There is a common misconception about what it means to be resilient. Likely this is because, according to the common definition, resilience is likened to toughness—the

SOCIAL AND EMOTIONAL LEARNING   133

ability to overcome some sort of adversity or to be flexible (will bend but not break). And, while at its core there is some truth to that, being resilient is more related to the body's **nervous system** response to stress, trauma, or triggers. A developmental view of resilience is that it is successful adaptation to adversity as the product of systems working together to result in successful adaptations to adversity. The interaction of attachment, mastery motivation and self-efficacy, and self-management systems results in what Masten (2014) calls the "ordinary magic" of resilience.

In this section, we explore what it means to be in the **resilience zone** and the implications of resilience for the adolescents in our classrooms. Figure 7.2 (adapted from the Community Resiliency Model developed by the Trauma Resource Institute) illustrates the resilience zone as well as what happens when we are no longer in that zone.

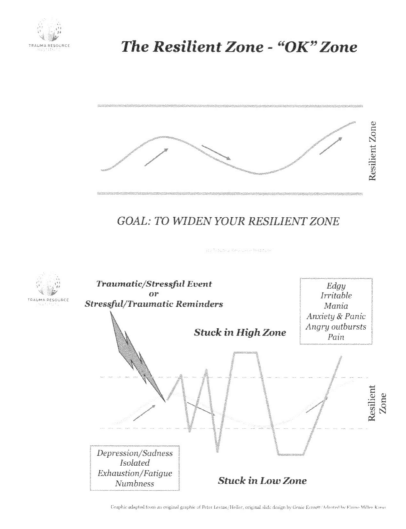

Figure 7.2 The Resilence Zone. "The Community Resiliency Model (CRM)® developed by the Trauma Resource Institute"

The resilience zone is a state of well-being we aim to be in most of the time. In this zone we can handle the stressors of life. There is potential to be a little muffled or angry, or a little sad. But, in this state of being, anger is not amping us up significantly and sadness is not causing us to spiral into a depressed state. In the resilience zone we can easily calm ourselves and continue moving through the day despite the ebbs and flows of these feelings. Sometimes, though, events or triggers cause us to leave our resilience zone and either become amped up or shut down. What is at play here is a complex interplay of components of the nervous system. Our nervous system is comprised of the brain, the spinal cord, and a network of nerves. The system's purpose is to send and receive messages between the brain and the body. Our brain controls all the body's functions and, therefore, when our brain experiences stress, there are often physical manifestations of that stress. Think of the common phrase "fight, flight, or freeze," and we recognize the physical reactions to stress.

To summarize, let's revisit our learning outcomes:

1. **Understand the social and emotional skills adolescents need.** According to CASEL, there are five clusters of SEL competencies: self-awareness, self-management, social awareness, relationship skills, and responsible decision-making. These skills cover a myriad of aspects, like emotional understanding, impulse control, empathy, and ethical decision-making. SEL should be integrated throughout the school experience.

2. **Identify trauma and barriers that young adolescents experience and their impact on adolescents' ability to learn.** Trauma, whether direct or implicit, including adverse childhood experiences, can have immediate and long-lasting effects on students. It may impact academic achievement, peer and teacher relationships, and mental health, making it essential for educators to implement trauma-informed practices to mitigate these challenges.

3. **Explore trauma-informed practices and their application in creating a safe and inclusive learning environment for students who have experienced trauma.** Many strategies can be utilized to support all students but especially those who have experienced trauma. Use of mindfulness practices, emphasis on safe spaces, use of resilience tools, and implementation of advisory programs are all practical strategies for supporting students' well-being.

4. **Recognize the diverse models of and approaches to implementing advisory programs, recognizing the importance of addressing social and emotional needs and tailoring lessons to issues relevant to the student population.** Advisory programs have various structures and models, but all advisory programs should emphasize students having a trusted adult in the building. Advisory programs can effectively address social, emotional, and developmental concerns of middle school students.

5. **Understand resilience as a neurobiological response to stress, recognize its impact on adolescents' emotional well-being and learning, and learn strategies for helping students stay within their resilience zone.** Remaining in the

resilience zone allows students to manage stress effectively. A complex interplay of components within the nervous system allows students either to remain regulated (in a regulated state) or to become amped up or shut down (in a dysregulated state). Using mindfulness strategies, such as taking a walk, orienting, and grounding, among others, may help students remain within the resilience mode and cope with stress.

Suggested Readings

Jennings, P. A. (2019). *The trauma-sensitive classroom: Building resilience with compassionate teaching*. WW Norton & Company.

Green, A. L., Ferrante, S., Boaz, T. L., Kutash, K., & Wheeldon-Reece, B. (2021). Social and emotional learning during early adolescence: Effectiveness of a classroom based SEL program for middle school students. *Psychology in the Schools*, *58*(6), 1056–69.

AMLE Resources and Readings

Bowerman, M. Navigating the gray: Trauma in the middle grades. https://www.amle.org/navigating-the-gray-trauma-in-the-middle-grades/

Fagel, P. How to build a resilient school community. https://www.amle.org/how-to-build-a-resilient-school-community/

Finch, P. A. Cultivating a culture of belonging in our school. https://www.amle.org/cultivating-a-culture-of-belonging-in-our-school/

References

Bronfenbrenner, U. (Ed.). (2004). *Making human beings human: Bioecological perspectives on human development*. SAGE Publications, Inc.

Cipriano, C., Strambler, M. J., Naples, L. H., Ha, C., Kirk, M., Wood, M., Sehgal, K., Zieher, A. K., Eveleigh, A., McCarthy, M., Funaro, M., Ponnock, A., Chow, J. C., & Durlak, J. (2023). The state of evidence for social and emotional learning: A contemporary meta-analysis of universal school-based SEL interventions. *Child Development*, *94*(5), 1181–1204. https://doi.org/10.1111/cdev.13968

Durlak, J. A., Domitrovich, C. E., Weissberg, R. P., & Gullotta, T. P. (Eds.) (2015). *Handbook of social and emotional learning: Research and practice*. Guilford Press.

Durlak, J. A., Weissberg, R. P., Dymnicki, A. B., Taylor, R. D., & Schellinger, K. B. (2011). The impact of enhancing students' social and emotional learning: A meta-analysis of school-based universal interventions. *Child Development*, *82*(1), 405–32. https://doi.org/10.1111/j.1467-8624.2010.01564

Ginsburg, K. R., & Jablow, M. M. (2015). *Building resilience in children and teens: Giving kids roots and wings*. American Academy of Pediatrics.

Jennings, P. A. (2019). *The trauma-sensitive classroom: Building resilience with compassionate teaching*. W. W. Norton & Company.

Masten, A. S. (2014). *Ordinary magic: Resilience in development*. The Guilford Press.

The Mayo Clinic. (2022). *Can mindfulness exercises help me?* Mayo Clinic. https://www.mayoclinic.org/healthy-lifestyle/consumer-health/in-depth/mindfulness-exercises/art

-20046356#:~:text=Mindfulness%20is%20a%20type%20of,mind%20and%20help%20reduce%20stress

Racine, N., Eirich, R., & Madigan, S. (2022). Fostering resilience in children who have been maltreated: A review and call for translational research. *Canadian Psychology/Psychologie Canadienne, 63*, 203–13. https://doi.org/10.1037/cap0000312

Shek, D. T. L, Dou, D., Zhu, X., & Chai, W. (2019). Positive youth development: Current perspectives. *Adolescent Health, Medicine and Therapeutics, 10*, 131–41. https://doi.org/10.1111/j.1750-8606.2011.00219.x

Souers, K., & Hall, P. (2016). *Fostering resilient learners: Strategies for creating a trauma-sensitive classroom.* Hawker Brownlow Education.

U.S. Department of Health and Human Services, Substance Abuse and Mental Health Services Administration. (2014). SAMHSA's concept of trauma and guidance for trauma-informed approach. https://store.samhsa.gov/system/files/sma14-4884.pdf

CHAPTER 8

Culturally Sustaining Pedagogy and Supporting Multilingual Learners

Learning Outcomes:

1. Articulate the concept of culturally relevant, responsive, and sustaining pedagogy.

2. Analyze culturally responsive teaching strategies and examples that can be integrated into subject areas.

3. Describe the benefits of culturally responsive teaching that impact both academics and well-being.

4. Identify strategies for supporting multilingual learners.

Context for Culturally Sustaining Pedagogy

Equality, equity, and **diversity** are common contemporary topics when discussing education. Unfortunately, the narrative surrounding these subjects can be controversial. Analyzing each of these concepts first requires clear operational definitions, identification of their role in the classroom, and investigation of the ways in which our students are impacted by these concepts in schools, as well as within their families, homes, and communities. Equality is ensuring individuals and groups are given the same resources or have the exact same opportunities. Equity recognizes that everyone has different circumstances, and being equitable means allocating the resources and opportunities as needed to ensure better outcomes for all individuals. Equity requires us to analyze and assess situations in order to make accommodations necessary to meet the needs of all—helping students receive what they need to achieve their academic and social potential. To explore and examine equity in education, we will analyze ways teachers can be culturally responsive across core and noncore subjects.

Differences among individuals and groups include those in race, ethnicity, culture, language, gender, religion, sexual orientation, socioeconomic status, family lifestyle and dynamics, and more. Although not limited to only these attributes, diverse aspects of students and their lives are imperative to discuss when teachers create equitable curriculum and education. This chapter will examine the impact of family dynamics, cultures, and communities on our students and their education. We will reflect upon inequities in our education system and will consider our roles and responsibilities as educators in providing safe, equitable, and inclusive classrooms. Russell has argued that, "through critical analysis of how we define, redefine, and refine the notion of family, we gain new vantage points on the complexities and possibilities of contemporary families, especially those that are marginal and marginalized" (2019, p. 358). This author also writes that our personal perspectives on healthy families are rooted in the context of our individual experiences. If we combine what we know from our experiences as educators with literature on contemporary families, we might be able to rethink the meaning of family in a way that contributes to the understanding and potential of not only marginal families but of all families. Advocacy work and the actions of educators and families related to schools, policies, and communities may shape the family's health.

Pause and Reflect: Consider your definitions of equality and equity before reading this introduction. What resonates with you now, reading this as a future teacher?

If you are able, find a peer to discuss these questions with. If you are alone, jot down notes about your responses to these questions to guide your thinking about this chapter's content.

- What are some examples of cultural or other types of diversity in your classroom or classrooms you have observed? Why are they relevant to your teaching?

- Why might bringing your students' languages into the classroom, and allowing them to use their home language at times, be beneficial to your students?

- What kinds of supports would help your students and their communities feel welcome at your school and in your classroom?

- How might you bring additional outside perspectives into your classroom or connect them to your content area?

- How might a survey or questionnaire help you establish a rapport with students and/or build strong relationships with their families?

- If you encourage students to talk in pairs or small groups before sharing their own experiences with the whole class, would more students participate or share and why?

- We know that teachers can boost lesson content by drawing connections with real-world issues, asking students to use opinions and existing knowledge to address them. Can you think of an example?

Defining Culturally Relevant, Responsive, and Sustaining Pedagogy

In the early 1990s, Gloria Ladson-Billings forged a pathway of research that reframed how we discuss issues related to historically marginalized students. When she found terms such as *disadvantaged, at-risk,* or *underachieving,* or any other set of deficit-based labels, she began to push back and charge us to think about what *can* these students do. What *success* can we find to highlight? She then started investigating classrooms where she saw teachers having success with students and shortly after came the premise of **culturally relevant pedagogy**. Ladson Billings original definition of culturally relevant pedagogy is a "theoretical model that not only addresses student achievement but also helps students to accept and affirm their cultural identity while developing critical perspectives that challenge inequities that schools (and other institutions) perpetuate" (1995, p. 469). It is important to situate this work within the context of teaching adolescents, as there has been some critique in recent decades about how middle level education has largely ignored the specific needs of students with diverse backgrounds, privileging whiteness within many of the theories and practices implemented in schools (Hurd et al., 2018).

Ladson-Billings's initial work on culturally relevant pedagogy has evolved with the work of other researchers to encompass elements of culture. Geneva Gay continued this work and used the term *culturally responsive* to encourage the field toward a shift in pedagogical practice to better serve students who are not white and not middle class (2018). Gay's work emphasizes meeting the needs of all students, which we know is good teaching; however, we also need to be intentional about embracing multiculturalism in our classrooms. In her words, she says doing so is both routine and radical.

> Routine because it does for Native American, Latino, Asian American, African American, and low-income students what traditional instructional ideologies and actions do for middle-class European Americans. That is, it filters curriculum content and teaching strategies through their cultural frames of reference to make the content more personally meaningful and easier to master. . . . radical because it makes explicit the previously implicit role of culture in teaching and learning, and it insists that educational institutions accept the legitimacy and viability of ethnic-group cultures in improving learning outcomes. (2018, p. 32)

Joining the culturally relevant/responsive framework, Django Paris coined the term **culturally sustaining pedagogy**, which he first defined in 2012, stating,

> Culturally sustaining pedagogy seeks to perpetuate and foster—to sustain—linguistic, literate, and cultural pluralism as part of the democratic project of schooling. In the face of current policies and practices that have the explicit goal of creating a monocultural and monolingual society, research and practice need equally explicit resistances that embrace cultural pluralism and cultural equality. (Paris, 2012, p. 93)

Paris goes on to explain that our teaching methods must extend beyond merely acknowledging or being relevant to the cultural experiences of students. Teachers need to actively support students' buffer in preserving the cultural and linguistic aspects of their communities while providing access to the dominant cultural norms.

CULTURALLY RESPONSIVE TEACHING

Culturally responsive teaching is the pedagogy in which equity, inclusion, and diversity are taught. As teachers, to support students we develop skills and strategies that are related to cultural factors that also play a role in facilitating learning. Culturally responsive teaching involves connecting academics to students' daily lives, cultural backgrounds, and concerns in ways that support engagement, achievement, and empowerment. It is the implementation of using our students' cultures, customs, and belief systems to allow students to feel recognized and presented in our classrooms. Being culturally responsive means embracing the identities of our students. And, if we are truly responding to the developmental needs of our students, particularly those of our marginalized students, then we must be culturally responsive as well (Brinegar, Harrison, & Hurd, 2019). Research shows that culturally responsive teaching

- focuses on student-centered classrooms;
- allows the needs of students to be better met;
- builds empathy and confidence of students;
- promotes global awareness; and
- teaches students about advocacy for both their selves and others.

According to Geneva Gay, teaching that is "culturally responsive" requires educators to move from thinking only about teaching content to also thinking about teaching *students*. Culturally responsive teaching involves ways of educating students that are based on principles of **social justice**. A key purpose of culturally responsive teaching is to provide all students, regardless of their gender, race, ethnicity, or first language, with learning opportunities (Ladson-Billings, 1995). Others have characterized this trait as teaching *with* social justice (Moje, 2007). An equally important purpose is the idea of teaching *for* social justice. Teaching with social justice refers to teaching in socially just ways and focuses on the process of teaching that includes providing access to learning opportunities. Teaching for social justice leads to more socially just outcomes and is intended to address and correct unjustified power differences in society.

The benefits of culturally responsive teaching impact both academics and well-being. Academic benefits include improved student attendance, overall student grades, and performance on assessments; higher graduation rates; greater interest in school; and even increased motivation to learn. Benefits related to overall well-being include having the opportunity to learn about the cultural backgrounds, history, and traditions that are associated with positive racial and ethnic identities. This can impact students' self-esteem and ability to overcome discrimination. Learning about racism and other social issues in school has the potential to shield students of color from some of the negative academic and mental outcomes of discrimination. Finally, students who learn to value diversity in school are more likely to have positive attitudes toward people of different backgrounds. In September 2020, New America published *Culturally Responsive Teaching: A Reflective Guide* to help fa-

cilitate self-appraisal, goal setting, and critical conversations across the core **culturally responsive teaching competencies**. While educators cannot single-handedly make schools less segregated and more equitable, they can ensure that students feel valued and affirmed in schools, by the curriculum, and in their interactions with peers. They can promote engagement and achievement by connecting curriculum to students' daily lives, cultural backgrounds, and concerns. They can deploy rigorous activities that help students make sense of the world around them and become agents for positive change. They can call attention to educational injustice and work to bolster opportunities for all learners. Culturally responsive teachers do these things and more.

Competency 1: Reflect on One's Cultural Lens

Culturally responsive teachers consider their own life experiences and identity groups (such as race, ethnicity, socioeconomic status, sexual orientation, and gender) and how they influence their beliefs and actions. We all possess internalized biases that shape our instruction and interactions with students, families, and colleagues. Culturally responsive teachers reflect on how they think and act and know that they may unintentionally use stereotypes (i.e., overgeneralized beliefs about certain groups) and commit microaggressions (e.g., subtle comments or unintentionally discriminatory actions).

Competency 2: Recognize and Redress Bias in the System

Culturally responsive teachers understand the difference between personal and systemic bias. These teachers work to understand better how identity markers, such as those assigned by race, ethnicity, ability, socioeconomic status, and gender, influence the opportunities that students receive. Taking advantage of the wide variety of resources and learning opportunities is the best way for teachers to become culturally responsive.

Competency 3: Draw on Students' Culture to Shape Curriculum and Instruction

Culturally responsive teachers believe that their students' cultural backgrounds and knowledge can help build and connect new learning—creating a kind of cultural scaffolding by providing links between concepts and students' cultural knowledge and lived experiences. Student input is important to these teachers as they build assignments, activities, and assessments. These teachers can analyze resources (i.e., curriculum, textbooks, and other sources of information) to ensure they do not perpetuate stereotypes or lack representation. Additional resources, such as newspapers, articles, songs, comics, games (and more), may complement the curriculum to reflect characters, themes, and experiences that are relatable to students. These resources might be called "mirrors" or "windows" into history, and using them in teaching shows students that their and their identity groups' experiences and traditions are as important as those of culturally dominant groups.

Competency 4: Bring Real-World Issues into the Classroom

Addressing the "so what?" factor of instruction by helping students see how the knowledge and skills they learn in school are valuable to their lives, families, and their communities is vital for culturally responsive teachers. These teachers are thinking about what content and concepts have to do with their students' lives, how their teaching connects to issues that students are passionate about, how information can be used to take action, and so on. They present relevant and complex problems rigorously to students and ask them to find solutions that incorporate consideration of bias and discrimination. Families, community members, and students are part of the planning process.

Competency 5: Model High Expectations for All Students

Culturally responsive teachers believe all students can learn and become highly successful. Such educators understand that students from marginalized groups are vulnerable to negative stereotypes about their intelligence, academic ability, and behavior and that these stereotypes can influence educators' instructional choices and expectations about students although educators may not be conscious of this influence. Our expectations and choices impact students' perceptions about their abilities.

Competency 6: Promote Respect for Student Differences

Culturally responsive teachers cultivate learning environments that are respectful, inclusive, and affirming. They promote such environments by modeling how to engage across differences and with respect for all forms of diversity. These teachers consider how learners from different backgrounds might experience the environment, encourage students to reflect on their own experience with bias, and help students value their own and others' cultures and develop a sense of responsibility for addressing prejudice and mistreatment when they encounter it. Compassionate classroom and school communities can improve students' academic performance and sense of belonging in school.

Competency 7: Collaborate with Families and the Local Community

Culturally responsive teachers believe parents want to be involved and remove barriers to family engagement. They understand that past trauma that families might have experienced in interfacing with schools can influence their involvement. These teachers search for ways to learn more about their students' families, including the families' cultures, values, and expectations for their child's education, and see themselves as part of the community.

Competency 8: Communicate in Linguistically and Culturally Responsive Ways

Students and families feel welcome and are more inclined to participate in school when teachers are culturally and linguistically sensitive. Culturally responsive teachers want to understand how culture influences communication, in both verbal and nonverbal ways. They respect and accommodate multilingual students and families and advocate for translation services and language resources.

Pause and Reflect: Think about your future educator role, specifically about promoting social justice within the classroom (and beyond). What are your ideas for actively addressing unjust power differences and promoting positive change? What ideas do you have to ensure all your students feel valued, affirmed, and empowered in your classroom?

ACROSS THE SUBJECT AREAS

Culturally responsive teaching should happen within and across the subject areas. Although legislation to staunch inclusive and equitable practice has become more prevalent, the need for culturally responsive teaching continues to exist. These practices impact the classroom environment and dynamics and the relationships among peers and between students and teachers.

Social Studies

The National Council for the Social Studies (NCSS) presents ten themes that relate directly to culturally responsive teaching:

1. Culture
2. Time, continuity, and change
3. People, places, and environments
4. Individual development and identity
5. Individuals, groups, and institutions
6. Power, authority, and governance
7. Production, distribution, and consumption
8. Science, technology, and society
9. Global connections
10. Civic ideals and practices

The scope of these concepts is infinite as history continues to build daily and the themes themselves set expectations for students to learn about their own as well as other people's cultures, belief systems, and local communities. Students explore worldwide views of family dynamics, governments (democratic and nondemocratic), civic responsibilities, economics, geography, and the history of continents. According to NCSS's introduction of the standards (p. 1), the "themes represent strands that should thread through a social studies program, from grades pre–K through 12, as appropriate at each level. While at some grades and for some courses, specific themes will be more dominant than others, all the themes are highly interrelated."

English Language Arts

When teaching English language arts, culturally responsive teaching is implemented into a myriad of standards. The overall goal of English language arts is developing one's ability to use a wide repertoire of tools for communicating one's own ideas, experiences, and perspectives and for receiving, interpreting, analyzing, and evaluating the communication of others. Students learn communication skills through wide reading of literature and practice writing in various modes and for varied audiences and purposes. Learners can practice social skills and communication techniques through debate, literature circles (also referred to as book groups), and varied classroom discussion techniques, such as Socratic seminars. The National Council for Teaching English (NCTE) standards cover research, calling for students to gather, analyze, and synthesize information from both past and present societies and cultures. Students must assess primary and secondary sources, read passages and books, and evaluate various digital resources that reflect culturally relevant teaching.

Science

The National Science Teachers Association (NSTA) standards cover life science, earth and space science, and physical science. NSTA strongly advocates for culturally relevant practice in science classrooms. It is not just name dropping the work of Black, indigenous, and other people of color (BIPOC) scientists and is more about integrating opportunities for students to connect with culture within exploration of science standards. Here is an abbreviated list of suggestions of strategies to bolster the cultural relevance of science lessons:

- Promote equity and mutual respect among students.

- Assist students in becoming socially and politically conscious (i.e., identify and extinguish myths about other cultures).

- Show interest in and encourage use of students' native language through using vocabulary to better communicate with them.

- Make sure the school environment contains evidence of contributions or work from individuals with diverse backgrounds regularly rather than just during a special week or month.

- Use classroom materials that include stories and perspectives from diverse cultures as well as materials provided in native languages represented in the classroom.

- Increase the number of learning activities that are relevant to the real world during science lessons.

- Acknowledge students' differences as well as their commonalities.

- Have genuine respect for students' abilities and talents and the cultural gifts they bring to science classes.
- Send messages of high expectations and rid ourselves of the deficiency model where we see ourselves as "white saviors" to rescue BIPOC students. (MacKenzie et al., 2021)

Mathematics

The National Council of Teachers of Mathematics (NCTM) standards include standards for teaching number and operations, algebra, geometry, data analysis and probability, and measurement. A growing body of research supports the use of culturally relevant mathematics teaching (CRMT) as a vital component to equitable teaching practice in the mathematics classroom. This body of research specifies four foundational components of CRMT: knowledge, communication, relationships/trust, and constant reflection and revision (Bonner, 2021). Knowledge is defined not just as content and pedagogical knowledge but also as the knowledge of students and community members. Findings encourage educators to use community assets to provide enriching experience for adolescents. Communication is about how we utilize our knowledge of our students and community to ensure that we interact with students appropriately, ensuring we instill a belief that all students can do mathematics and build on the funds of knowledge that students bring to the classroom. Relationships and trust are built in and outside of the classroom, with teachers immersing themselves in the community to build relationship with parents and empowering those parents through open lines of communication to work together to support their children's needs. Good teachers are reflective practitioners and use the practice of reflection to revise and enrich their teaching practices. In CRMT, teachers think deeply about their own backgrounds and experiences with race and culture and reflect on how these factors impact their interactions with the world. Culturally responsive teachers actively reflect on their interactions with students and parents and revise their behavior as needed to be more responsive to students. At its core, culturally sustaining mathematics instruction attends to three primary goals: to advance young adolescent learners' mathematical thinking; to promote equity in young adolescent learners' mathematical classroom learning experiences; and to attend to young adolescents' characteristics, needs, and interests (Ellerbrock & Vomvoridi-Ivanovic, 2019).

Pause and Reflect: What aspects of your educational experiences that you recall made you feel connected to your own community and communities throughout the world? Think about projects and activities that portrayed aspects of culture and community, such as faith, government, and traditions.

Standards in Practice

In this next section, we provide brief but tangible examples of activities we can utilize in middle school classrooms to embrace culturally relevant practice. These, of course, are only the beginning; good teachers think creatively about small and big ways to create learning environments that embrace equity and inclusiveness of our diverse populations.

SOCIAL STUDIES

The NCSS declares that "The aim of social studies is the promotion of civic competence—the knowledge, intellectual processes, and democratic dispositions required of students to be active and engaged participants in public life" (2010). This means students need to move beyond rote memorization of dates and names of people throughout history and be active and engaged learners. To demonstrate this practice, some social-studies educators introduce the concept of democracy and engagement by creating classroom contracts. In addition to being a behavior-management system, classroom contracts allow students to create a space in which they feel valued and for which they feel responsible. Social-studies teachers can take this a step further by creating smaller learning expectations with students before they do various tasks. For example, prior to doing group projects, students can design procedures alongside their teacher for what good group work looks, feels, and sounds like. This protocol can be used over and over, giving students consistency and ownership.

Engaging students in a "country project" is one way to embody the qualities discussed above in instruction. While this project can be conducted differently, here is one way to do it: After studying the governments, laws, policies, economies, cultures, and institutions of countries around the world, students design their own country. Students analyze primary and secondary texts, watch documentaries, and gather resources through their own research.

Expectations:

1. Name: What is the country called?

2. Flag with a seal or symbol: What does the flag represent about the country?

3. Origin: When was the country established? What (i.e., war with another country, etc.) caused the development of the country?

4. Government: What is the type of government and why was this type selected?

5. Laws: What are the major laws (like the bill of rights) of the society?

6. Past events: What do the country's citizens do as a community? How do their activities impact relationships?

7. Holidays: Which days are celebrated throughout the entire nation? What do the holidays represent? How are they celebrated?

8. Demographics: What is the population of and what are the groups within the country?

9. Environment: Draw or otherwise create a map of the country. What are the topographical features?

10. Communication and language: What are the main languages? What is respect? How does body language impact communication?
11. Family culture: What are the family norms? Do multiple generations live within a household?
12. Food: What are popular foods? How (using utensils, their hands, etc.) do people eat? How is food viewed? Are specific foods designated for occasions like birthdays or religious holidays?
13. Religion: What are the various religious belief systems (polytheism, monotheism, etc.)?

ENGLISH LANGUAGE ARTS

Kayleigh shares here how she integrates learning about global issues and current events with practicing basic writing skills. These examples illustrate how interdisciplinary connections can easily be made, especially with social studies and science.

> I begin each class by watching CNN10, a free ten-minute news show. Below are the daily instructions I use with class as well as a few differentiated graphic organizers for students. In addition to this resource there are rubrics based on standards-based grading practices which allow students to see the expectations set for them and provide a space for teachers to add feedback. Immediate or timely feedback is imperative to supporting students' growth.

The graphic organizers in Table 8.1 and Table 8.2 serve the same purpose of assessing students' writing and connecting them to global citizenship skills, but they are also in formats that allow students to have a resource that best meets their individual needs. The first graphic organizer focuses on student analysis of main ideas and key details of the digital media. The second graphic organizer focuses on student analysis of the main idea and key details of the digital media and anticipates a deeper investigation of the show's context. The portion of the assessment that challenges students to research and reflect requires that students select a national or global event covered in the show they want to learn and research more about. Students must reflect on the importance of the event to the world and make connections to their life, texts we read, and other events they have learned about. They also must share their own point of view and propose questions about the topic.

The first example illustrates the lack of wheelchair access in Paris, where the 2024 Olympics were held. Partially due to the age of the city transportation systems, many temporary vacation rentals are not easily accessible for those who utilize wheelchairs in their daily lives. Students found that they could make empathetic connections to the situation and became curious about potential solution pathways, such as the technology or development required to make the city more accessible. They brainstormed ideas to adapt places locally and globally to make the world more physically accessible. This basic task serves as an example of creating culturally responsive classrooms that empower students to think and explore independently and could even be extended through other nonfiction texts and research.

Table 8.1 Graphic Organizer 1: CNN 10 Paragraph of the Day

Sentence Starters • The main idea of CNN 10 is . . . • Today's show focused on portraying . . . • The topic of CNN today was . . . • The episode centered around . . .	**Main Idea**
Sentence Starters • Reporters said . . . • It was surprising that . . . • I wonder if . . . • I realized that . . . • I was confused by . . . • The interviews conducted throughout the show conveyed . . .	**Supporting Details**
Notes while viewing:	
CNN 10 Paragraph of the Day Rubric **Levels & Expectations of Performance**	
1	Identify the main idea of the news broadcast.
2	Identify the main idea and multiple supporting details. The paragraph may have multiple grammatical errors.
3	Identify the main idea and multiple accurate and relevant supporting details within a paragraph format. The paragraph should contain few to no grammatical errors (fewer than five). A vocabulary word that is essential to the text is provided and described.
4	Identify the main idea and multiple accurate and relevant supporting details within a paragraph format including indenting. The paragraph should contain few to no grammatical errors (fewer than three). Research a topic related to the main idea portrayed. Provide, describe, and explain a vocabulary word that is essential to the text.
Comments & Grade	

Table 8.2 *Graphic Organizer 2:* CNN Infographic Newspaper

Title: CNN 10 Explorer	
Imagery Caption:	**Key Vocabulary** **Word:** **Definition:** **Connection to text/story:**
Story Headline **Main Idea:** **Two or More Key Details:**	**Trivia Question**
Extension: Research or Impact	
CNN 10 Infographic—News Paper—Rubric **Levels & Expectations of Performance**	
1	Identify the main idea of the news broadcast.
2	Identify the main idea and multiple supporting details. The paragraph may have multiple grammatical errors.
3	Identify the main idea and multiple accurate and relevant supporting details within a paragraph format. The paragraph should contain few to no grammatical errors (fewer than five). Provide and describe a vocabulary word that is essential to the text.
4	Identify the main idea and multiple accurate and relevant supporting details within a paragraph format including indenting. The paragraph should contain few to no grammatical errors (fewer than three). Research a topic related to the main idea portrayed. Provide, describe, and explain a vocabulary word that is essential to the text.
Comments & Grade	

SCIENCE

Following are examples of systemic social inequalities that can be explored in science classes using culturally relevant pedagogy.

Students learn that less than 3 percent of water on the Earth is drinkable. Effective teachers use this fact to build exploration activities to help students understand concepts like disparities in access to water. Further exploration may include investigations of the economy, government, geographic location, living conditions, and climate. In science, these concepts can be researched and taught in a way that empowers students to learn more about their environments and those around the world. In rural areas, for example, many families use a well as their water source. "In North Carolina, water insecurity may be caused by a lack of household connections, water distribution infrastructure, unprotected water resources that threaten water quality, unaffordable water, or a combination of these factors" (Sohns, 2023). Well water can cause problems for families who struggle financially and cannot afford the proper resources to maintain their well and ensure the quality of the water. In urban areas, safe access to drinking water can be an equity issue, especially for marginalized and minority communities (Sohns, 2023). Water issues impact people on local, national, and global levels.

Another systemic social inequality faced by some of our students is poor living conditions or inadequate maintenance of government-controlled utilities. A well-known example is the water crisis in Flint, Michigan. The crisis was declared a state of emergency in 2016 but continues to impact the residences of Flint today. In an area inhabited by people of color, with significant rates of poverty, Flint residents faced these disparities without significant help from local government even though the crisis has resulted in considerable physical, social, and emotional health concerns. After legal experts and other groups across the nation became aware of the issue, outrage and subsequent advocacy led to some improvements. The Flint water crisis is one of many examples in which people of color and those in poverty suffered injustice. In science, students can study water quality while researching and learning about the injustices individuals face across the nation and the world, make connections to their own communities, and learn about advocacy and cultural awareness.

MATHEMATICS

Students must have opportunities to engage in cognitively demanding tasks that allow them to develop depth in their conceptual learning, and they need structures and routines that allow them to engage through active participation and discourse. Good teachers promote equity through promoting shared authority among the learners (and teacher) and value all student contributions, supporting English-language learners and using culture- or community-based funds of knowledge by engaging in topics that are relevant to them. To implement culturally sustaining practices, teachers need to make personal connections with students and empower them as active participants in the learning process.

Holly shares here a couple of examples of how she uses culturally relevant practices in her mathematics classroom. Note that these just scratch the surface but can provide an initial step.

> There are both large and small adjustments we can make in the mathematics classroom to embrace and support the diverse cultures represented in our students. First, I want to emphasize the subtle things like immersing students in problems. Many, if not most math teachers are using some sort of curriculum resources that outline problems using a myriad of names. Good curriculum resources already ensure that there is diversity in the names of

the "characters" in our problems. For example, we use a lot of Diego, Jada, Priya, and Lin, who are common characters in the curriculum resource I use. And I use those names often, but I also make sure to change the names to the students in front of me. I also try not to be random. If the problem is related to playing sports or riding a bike for example, I ensure that I use Adam as he is an outdoor sports enthusiast. Or when I have problems related to siblings, I make sure I use the names of the twins in my class as it makes the context more relatable to the small community of learners in my room. Another great strategy is having the students contribute to making tasks adjustments. We can easily present a task to our students and have them re-design the task to be something more meaningful and relevant to them. This in and of itself meets the three goals outline[d] by Ellerbrock and Vomvoridi-Ivanovic (2019) by advancing thinking through cognitive demand as they have to make the mathematical connections to build a context that makes sense, it gives them voice and choice which is helpful in addressing individual needs of adolescents and gives access to all learners through an open ended task.

Being aware of the content we use in our problem contexts is important. For example, in one curriculum resource there is an investigation about the subway system and how people are charged per ride but also must pay a small fee for the card they load their rides onto. We happen to live in a very rural place where many of our students have not had the opportunity to ride on a subway. So, we may choose to alter the context to something more meaningful to that group of learners, or we may also take the opportunity to investigate and discuss the differences between our rural experiences and others' urban experiences. This helps students make connections to things outside of their own experience and culture.

Another one of the easiest ways to make connections is to utilize existing datasets from around the world. One rich resource that can be explored is a Swedish-based website, gapminder.com, which houses a plethora of data sets on topics like life expectancy by country, world population, and income. One particularly interesting project providing topics for exploration is called *Dollar Street*. This project collected data from over 250 families in fifty countries. The researchers visited homes and collected thirty thousand photos, sorting the homes by income. Students might explore commonalities (e.g., thinking about where we sleep, eat, go to the bathroom, etc.). They might also explore how solutions around basic needs may look different around the world and in various contexts. More than one hundred topics are included in the *Dollar Street* database, enabling students to explore cultures and find similarities and differences in everyday life around the world. Other investigations into topics that address social injustice and inequity include activities such as the "parable of the polygons" (https://ncase.me/polygons/), which explores segregation through mathematical models to investigate bias.

Pause and Reflect: Look at your content standards for one grade level. By yourself or with a peer, brainstorm how you can expand upon your standards and implement culturally specific topics into your activities.

CONNECTIONS IN OTHER SUBJECTS

Building culturally responsive classrooms in noncore classrooms may not always be easy but could offer numerous ways to connect to the world. The arts provide a rich avenue for exploring connections. World-wide, individuals from diverse backgrounds and cultures enjoy the same artistic styles, music, language studies, cooking, agricultural studies, physical education and activities, psychological studies, technology, and many other passions. These aspects of life connect us to individuals who may live a life entirely different from our own yet who share some of the same likes and passions. Our governments, languages, religious beliefs and traditions, ethnicities, and race may differ, or these elements may connect us as well.

Students should have opportunities to explore these concepts outside of math, science, language-arts, and social-studies classes. Allowing students to self-select electives and clubs is one key step to building culturally responsive schools. Students find their passions, build self-confidence, develop independence, and are encouraged to learn new things in these classes. Societies use song and dance to represent their cultures. Geography and time periods are two elements that influence these practices. In music and dance classes, students may learn about native dances, playing African drums, such as the dejembe, or studying songs, like national anthems. In language courses, students analyze their own languages, which may give students an opportunity to feel included if they have the option to use a language that is their home or first language.

Kayleigh shares an experience from early in her teaching career:

> In my early years of teaching, I had an eighth-grade student move from Mexico to my rural community with her family. She knew very few words in English. In a school that was predominantly white, she voiced feeling uncomfortable in class and not being able to understand what she was learning. During electives, she took Spanish, her home language. Observing her entire demeanor shift in that environment signified the importance of inclusion and the value of culturally responsive teaching, in which students can see themselves in what they learn. I had the privilege of observing her connect to students who spoke English as their home language and were learning Spanish. It created mutual understanding of struggling and learning something new and allowed these students to empathize with one another.

Additional areas in which students can investigate and connect with other societies may include food, physical activities, and technology. These are aspects of everyday life for everyone. In home economics (often referred to as family and consumer sciences) and foods classes, students may connect with others by sharing recipes from their own cultures and discussing family traditions. These classes present students with the opportunity to explore what other communities eat and even how they eat. For example, some cultures eat with their hands, and others use utensils; some pray before they eat; and some eat raw foods and insects, which are delicacies for them and may be unusual for others. Even flavors and spices are connected to specific communities. Traditions, cultures, communities, and customs vary, but we can all use the things that represent us to bind us together with others.

Literature and Culturally Responsive Teaching

Using diverse literature allows teachers to implement many facets of the eight culturally sustaining teaching competencies into their classrooms. Classrooms and school libraries should reflect students in the school but should also introduce them to cultures unlike their own. Libraries should obtain high-interest texts that expose students to various religious and ethnic groups and to social issues, such as poverty, racism, climate concerns, and other controversial topics in the nation. Young adult literature is often reflected through the lenses of young adults, showing students age-appropriate examples of concerns. Seeing themselves reflected in the texts they read also empowers students to follow their aspirations and meet their goals. Even for striving readers, there are graphic novels with grade-level and culturally appropriate content to present students with the opportunity to learn about themselves and others. The discussions around literature are tense as book-banning laws restrict the texts schools can possess. It is possible to incorporate diverse texts into classrooms. Below are popular young adult books, paired with the communities they represent.

Individuals with Disabilities

- *Counting by 7s* by Holly Goldberg Sloan
- *Fish in a Tree* by Lynda Mullaly Hunt
- *Out of My Mind* by Sharon M. Draper
- *The War That Saved My Life* by Kimberly Brubaker Bradley
- *Wonder* by R. J. Palacio
- *The Extraordinary Life of Sam Hell* by Robert Dugoni
- *You're Welcome, Universe* by Whitney Gardner
- *What about Will* by Ellen Hopkins
- *The Magical Imperfect* by Chris Baron
- *Good Enough* by Jean Petro-Roy
- *The Real Boy* by Anne Ursu
- *The Silence between Us* by Alison Gervais
- *Unbroken: 13 Stories Starring Disabled Teens* edited by Marieke Nijkamp
- *Song for a Whale* by Lynne Kelly
- *Brave Enough* by Katy Gardner

Mental Health and Body Image

- *Trowbridge Road* by Marcella Pixley
- *The Science of Breakable Things* by Tae Keller
- *A Work in Progress* by Jarrett Lerner
- *Ab(solutely) Normal: Short Stories that Smash Mental Health Stereotypes* edited by Nora Shalaway Carpenter and Rocky Callen
- *Under Rose-Tainted Skies* by Louise Gornall
- *Finding Audrey* by Sophie Kinsella
- *The Seventh Most Important Thing* by Shelly Pearsall

Social Injustice

- *Ghost Boys* by Jewel Parker Rhodes
- *The Hate U Give* by Angie Thomas
- *All American Boys* by Jason Reynolds and Brendan Kiely
- *Long Way Down* by Jason Reynolds
- *Stamped: Racism, Antiracism, and You* by Jason Reynolds and Ibram X. Kendi
- *Monday's Not Coming* by Tiffany Jackson
- As always, Colorín Colorado has many resources. Here is one link with examples: https://www.colorincolorado.org/booklist/digging-deeper-books-about-social-issues-middle-grades

Refugees

- *Don't Ask Me Where I'm From* by Jennifer De Leon
- *Other Words from Home* by Jasmine Warga
- *Refugee* by Alan Gratz

Japanese Internment Camps

- *They Called Us Enemy* by George Takai (graphic novel)
- *The Journal of Ben Uchida* by Barry Denenberg
- *Farewell to Manzanar* by James D. Houston and Jeanne Wakatsuki Houston

LGBTQIA+

- *The Girl from the Sea* by Molly Knox Ostertag (graphic novel)
- *They Both Die at the End* by Adam Silvera
- *We Deserve Monuments* by Jas Hammonds
- *Melissa (previously published as George)* by Alex Gino
- https://www.amle.org/effective-instructional-practices-for-diverse-learners/)

Strategies for Supporting English Learners

> "Trust is the glue of life. It's the most essential ingredient in effective communication. It's the foundational principle that holds all relationships." (Covey & Merrell, 2006)

Although the teaching profession includes educators from many subgroups and cultures in the United States as well as from those in other countries, the core of the profession remains white, middle class, and, usually, monolingual. According to the US Department of Education, the percentage of public-school students in the United States who were **English learners (ELs)** increased overall between fall 2010 (9.2 percent, or 4.5 million students) and fall 2020 (10.3 percent, or 5 million students). Because teachers in the United States are increasingly expected to educate students whose native languages are not English and whose cultural backgrounds vary from that of the American mainstream culture, they can benefit from preparation that includes specialized methods and strategies for the effective education of culturally and linguistically diverse students. The linguistic and cultural variety of ELs suggests that more and more teachers serve as intercultural and interlinguistic educators—those who can reach out to learners from a variety of backgrounds and offer effective learning experiences (Diaz-Rico, 2019). It is important that we listen to our **deficit monitor**. As humans, we are potentially predisposed to biased, prejudiced, ignorant, misinformed, or deficit-based thinking about others. It is mostly subconscious, so we need a signal to bring it to our awareness.

With this awareness, we can make the choice to engage in thinking that is based on deficits or to engage in thinking that is responsive. Before developing cultural knowledge and awareness about others, we must first uncover and examine personal, social, and cultural identities. Culture is a shared system of meanings, beliefs, values, and behaviors through which we interpret our experiences. Culture is learned, collective, and changes over time. Culture is understood to be "what we know that everyone like us knows." It is organized within an identifiable community or group. This includes the ways that communities use language, interact with one another, take turns to talk, relate to time and space, and approach learning. Culture is "learned behavior," passed down through family, community, and **heritage**. Heritage comes in two parts: complexities and intangibles. Because of this, it is essential for us (as teachers) to think about and reflect on who our students are and what they bring to the classroom. Validation and affirmation of students' home (indigenous) culture and home language for the purpose of building and bridging the student to success in the culture of the student's school and the culture of mainstream society are crucial. Supports that are culturally and linguistically responsive help bring English learners to where they need to be academically. We are building—making the connections between the home culture and language and the school culture and language through instructional strategies and learning activities. And we are bridging—giving opportunities for situational appropriateness or utilizing appropriate cultural or linguistic behavior. Students who are most in need of **building** and **bridging** are often part of an underserved population, which includes any student who is not successful academically, socially, and/or behaviorally in school because the school as an institution is not being responsive to that student. It is important that teachers are not just responsive, but culturally responsive, which means the classroom and instruction is student-centered, communication is two-way, there is a lowered **affective filter**, and elements of culture and language are considered. *Affective filter* is the term Stephen Krashen has used to refer to the complex of negative emotional and motivational factors that may interfere with the reception and processing of **comprehensible input**. Such factors include anxiety, self-consciousness, boredom, annoyance, alienation, and so on. The affective filter is an invisible psychological filter that facilitates or hinders language production in a second language. When students' affective filter is high, it may inhibit students' success in acquiring a second language. On the other hand, a low affective filter facilitates risk-taking behavior in practicing and learning a second language.

Collaborative Summarizing helps students develop **oracy** and effectively make use of purposeful dialogue with a partner and a group to create a common product. The strategy includes five steps, which allow ELs to read, think, exchange information, and negotiate through dialogue. The teacher first selects a text that is appropriate for the students' independent reading level and determines the language demands. The purpose of reading the passage is to utilize the information to make meaning through oracy, language functions, and content or to acquire background knowledge. The six steps are as follows:

1. The teacher models how to identify the big ideas in the text (e.g., important people, things, or ideas, what is occurring, and details). Then, the students individually read the text and determine three to five big ideas. Students typically utilize a graphic organizer to record their information. Using those big ideas, students write a fifteen-word summary.

2. Students find a partner with whom to have a dialogue, and they, together, create a negotiated list that reflects agreement on three to six important ideas. They then collaboratively write a fifteen-word summary. Teachers can strategically pair up students, or students can choose. Students use **sentence frames** to support the function of negotiating and intentionally use academic language correctly. The purpose of students' negotiating with their partner is to identify who or what is most important in the passage and to identify what the subject is doing.

3. Each pair meets with another pair to read each other's summary, to write a common summary for the new group of four, and to add it to their graphic organizer.

4. Each group of four chooses another group of four to repeat the renegotiating process. The group will add their new summary to their graphic organizer.

5. Groups are asked to edit their summaries for meaning, language, and word choice. This could be an optional step because the focus of Collaborative Summarizing is utilizing purposeful dialogue to practice oracy.

6. One student from the group is chosen to present the summary to the class. ELs have varying comfort levels in reading in front of a class, so they should be given time to practice in their group first.

There are many categories of culturally and linguistically responsive teaching, a few of which include use of the following:

- attention signals, used strategically
- protocols for responding
- protocols for discussing
- movement activities
- extended collaboration activities
- tiering vocabulary words
- reinforcement activities
- culturally responsive supplemental text
- engaging read alouds
- effective literacy strategies across content areas
- opportunities for linguistic codeswitching (situational appropriateness)
- sentence lifting for situational appropriateness
- retellings for situational appropriateness
- role-playing for situational appropriateness
- teachable moments for situational appropriateness

When it comes to working with ELs, understanding **language structure** and use builds teachers' confidence and provides them with essential tools to help their students learn. Language is complex and arbitrary. The relationships between the sounds and the meanings of spoken languages and between gestures and meanings of sign languages are not caused by any natural reason. Language is open-ended, and all human languages have structure; they use a finite set of sounds or gestures that are combined to form meaningful elements or words, which themselves form an infinite set of sentences. Achieving proficiency in English is a multifaceted task. It is not only about learning to read and write but also about listening and speaking to gain information and demonstrate knowledge. Even more, the ability to think both critically and creatively is necessary.

The teacher's role is to integrate these separate, but interrelated, skills. This role also includes the ability to set up situations in which students feel a sense of purpose and can engage in real communication. Keep in mind that listening alone has varied purposes, including to repeat, to understand, or for communication. Being able to talk and express your thoughts clearly is vital in life. Yet too many students are graduating without sufficient experience with group discussions or with arguing their ideas effectively, and they are finding themselves unprepared for the communication demands of college and their careers. How can we prepare our students for these rigors? To lay a better foundation for this learning, we can do a few things: we can value oral language development, we can value communication of ideas over grammatical correctness, and we can value oral language as a powerful way to learn and remember content.

Pause and Reflect: How might students communicate without words in your classroom? How might you have students collaborate so that they can demonstrate comprehension via words as well as an alternative means of communication?

Some broad categories (think big-picture mindsets) that support oral language, might include what follows.

ENCOURAGE AUTHENTIC TALK

ELs may lack the confidence and/or ability to participate fully in class. Teachers need to set up environments that challenge students to use language. We must also remember that fluency is more important than accuracy. While older students can benefit from feedback on recurring errors, error correction is not necessary. Adapting current activities to include more authentic, original, and extended discussions gives students opportunities to contribute more than one sentence to a conversation. Sometimes, we miss the opportunity to encourage language development. For example, many teachers use some form of a jigsaw activity, in which students get into expert groups, read a text, and answer questions or fill in charts. They then go to mixed home groups to share their information. Yet, often what happens is this: students just read aloud what another student has copied from a resource—and opportunities for oral language development are lost. To improve this strategy, you can have the experts engage in a discussion of what to put, in their own words, onto paper. Then, they can rehearse what they will say—covering their papers to avoid reading aloud. Then, in home groups, you can have each person glance at his or her notes, cover them again, and share with the other group members, who listen and take notes. You can even ask students to try to speak in paragraphs, starting with a general claim or topic sentence and then supporting the claim or topic sentence with evidence sentences.

DEVELOP STRONG LANGUAGE

Use activities that allow students to develop a "stronger and clearer" answer as they talk to different partners successively in an activity. Instead of the all-too-common whole-class discussion, with the teacher asking questions and a few students answering, ask a question, and have students talk to three different partners. Or have students talk in separate groups. A few strategies are offered here as examples.

- 1-3-6 protocol: First, ask students to individually (1) tackle the challenge (any topic/subject). Second, form groups of three (3) in which students combine sets and agree on one list. Third, join two groups together to form groups of six (6), and instruct them to combine the two lists into a final list, prioritizing by teacher-determined parameters. An important aspect of this strategy is that students should not say the same thing each time; rather, they need to build on the language and ideas of previous partner(s) to improve, expand, clarify, and support their evolving answer each time they share it.
- Interview grid: Students talk with one different partner each time, making their answers stronger and clearer each time, taking minimal, if any, notes on the chart. Note that this activity can also work using inner-outer conversation circles or **debrief circles**.
- Debrief circles: This strategy is used to debrief a lesson or experience with students. Facilitate questions in a small group or a circle at the end of an event to encourage students to reflect on their experiences. Quotes can be used to stimulate discussion. This technique helps to deepen student engagement as it offers relevance, a sense of control, interaction, and dialogue.
- Opinion formation cards: Students receive a quotation from the text (before it is read) that includes evidence for one side or the other of an issue. Students share their quotations and their evolving opinions, with reasons and evidence for them.
- Opinion continuum: Students share where they fall on the continuum of a two-sided issue and why. They then engage in conversation with partners. At the end of the session, they share if they shifted at all along the continuum, based on their conversations with partners.

USE STRONG DISCUSSION PROMPTS

Try to use discussion prompts that foster evaluation in some way. Evaluation is usually needed for ranking, prioritizing, and choosing. For example, if a teacher asks for evidence of a theme or a claim, many students just find the first three remotely adequate pieces of evidence they can and stop there. But, if a teacher prompts students to rank the evidence from strongest to weakest, or to find the most influential cause of some war, the result is often deeper thinking and better conversation. An example of this might include the following prompt: how did the Civil War affect families in the

South? This prompt could be edited to encourage students to evaluate and discuss their opinions and to consider whether they are based on evidence. The resulting, edited prompt may be as follows: how did the Civil War most affect families in the South? When students evaluate various answers, their ideas often differ. If teachers allow time to argue and negotiate the ideas, lots of learning can happen.

The most-used evidence-based categories of strategies that support ELs include the following (many of which are recognizable as effective strategies for all populations):

- Connecting concepts to background knowledge
- Utilizing visuals
- Increasing student talking time
- Using multiple modalities
- Demonstrating use of **inductive reasoning** (making broad generalizations or drawing a principle from a body of observations)
- Using sentence frames
- Communicating with other professionals, including those who teach English as a second language or who teach English learners
- Providing comprehensible input (e.g., slowing down and enunciating clearly; avoiding figurative language and idioms; using gestures and total physical response
- Increasing interactions
- Setting routines
- Working together
- Summarizing collaboratively
- Explicitly teaching important or essential content vocabulary
- Teaching language skills across and throughout the curriculum

Many resources can be found online. One of the most well-known reputable sites is colorincolorado.org. This site includes everything from glossaries and general information on supports for English learners to strategies and resources for both schools and families. Others include esl-lounge.com, wordwall.net, edutopia.org, readwritethink.org, and amle.org.

Culturally responsive teaching is the pedagogy in which equity, inclusion, and diversity are taught. To support students, we, as teachers, develop skills and strategies that are related to cultural factors that also play a role in facilitating learning. Culturally responsive teaching involves connecting academics to students' daily lives, cultural backgrounds, and concerns in ways that support engagement, achievement, and empowerment. Good teachers use tools such as the eighth competencies for culturally responsive teaching to ensure that students feel valued and affirmed in schools, by the curriculum, and in their interactions with peers.

To summarize, let's revisit our learning outcomes:

1. **Articulate the concept of culturally relevant, responsive, and sustaining pedagogy.** Culturally relevant, responsive, and sustaining pedagogy affirms diverse cultural identities while also challenging systemic inequities in the education system. Good teachers integrate students' cultural backgrounds into classroom instruction to promote social justice and respect for diversity.

2. **Analyze culturally responsive teaching strategies and examples that can be integrated into subject areas.** Culturally responsive teaching should be integrated across subject areas. In social studies, this entails embracing ten themes outlined by the NCSS, fostering an understanding of culture, history, and societal dynamics. In English language arts, culturally responsive teaching encompasses promoting communication skills through reading diverse literature, using recommended writing practices, and critically analyzing global issues. Similarly, in science and mathematics, educators can incorporate culturally relevant examples, such as exploring disparities in access to resources or using diverse datasets, to empower students to connect learning to their own experiences and broader societal contexts.

3. **Describe the benefits of culturally responsive teaching that impact both academics and well-being.** Academic benefits include improved student attendance, overall student grades, and performance on assessments; higher graduation rates; greater interest in school; and even increased motivation to learn. Benefits related to students' overall well-being include students having the opportunity to learn about their cultural background and about history and traditions associated with positive racial and ethnic identities. This can impact students' self-esteem and ability to overcome discrimination. Students who learn to value diversity in school are more likely to have positive attitudes toward people of diverse backgrounds. Culturally responsive teachers deploy rigorous activities that help students make sense of the world around them and become agents for positive change. They call attention to educational injustice and work to bolster opportunities for all learners.

4. **Identify strategies for supporting ELs.** To effectively support ELs, teachers should prioritize using culturally and linguistically responsive teaching strategies, such as building trust, understanding students' cultural backgrounds, and valuing oral language development. Using strategies like collaborative summarizing, total physical response, and strong discussion prompts help foster language proficiency and engagement while honoring students' diverse linguistic and cultural backgrounds, promoting meaningful learning experiences for ELs.

Links to Standards, Other Resources, and Reading Recommendations

National Council for Social Studies Standards: https://www.socialstudies.org/standards/national-curriculum-standards-social-studies

National Council for Teachers of English Standards: https://cdn.ncte.org/nctefiles/resources/books/sample/standardsdoc.pdf.
https://ncte.org/resources/standards/ncte-ira-standards-for-the-english-language-arts/
National Science Teachers Association Standards:
https://my.nsta.org/ngss/AccessStandardsByTopic.
National Council of Teachers of Mathematics Standards:
https://www.nctm.org/Standards-and-Positions/Principles-and-Standards/.
CNN 10 episode referenced: https://www.cnn.com/2023/06/11/europe/paris-france-olympics-mood-cmd-intl/index.html.
Science connection:
https://www.who.int/news/item/18-06-2019-1-in-3-people-globally-do-not-have-access-to-safe-drinking-water-unicef-who.
Article about water quality: https://www.sciencedirect.com/science/article/abs/pii/S0301479723003882.
Flint Michigan water crisis: https://www.cdc.gov/nceh/casper/pdf-html/flint_water_crisis_pdf.html#:~:text=On%20April%2025%2C%202014%2C%20the,contaminants%20into%20municipal%20drinking%20water.
https://www.nrdc.org/stories/flint-water-crisis-everything-you-need-know#summary
https://www.amle.org/12-questions-to-ask-when-designing-culturally-and-historically-responsive-curriculum/.

References

Bonner, Emily P. (2021). "Practicing culturally responsive mathematics teaching." *Mathematics Teacher: Learning and Teaching PK–12, 114*(1), 6–15. https://doi.org/10.5951/mtlt.2020.0119.

Brinegar, K., Harrison, L., & Hurd, L. (Eds.) (2019). *Equity and cultural responsiveness in the middle grades.* Information Age Publishing.

Diaz-Rico, L. (2019). *A course for teaching English learners, 3rd Edition.* Pearson.

Gay, G. (2018). *Culturally responsive teaching: Theory, research, and practice.* Teachers College Press.

Ellerbrock, C., & Vomvoridi-Ivanovic, E. (2019). A framework for responsive middle level mathematics teaching. In K. Brinegar, L. Harrison, & E. Hurd, Eds., *Equity & Cultural Responsiveness in the Middle Grades* (pp. 45–68). Information Age Publishing.

Ladson-Billings, G. (1995). Toward a theory of culturally relevant pedagogy. *American Educational Research Journal, 32*(3), 465–91. https://doi.org/10.2307/1163320.

MacKenzie, A. H., Lindeman, P., Thomas, W., Lorrain, C., Parker, J., Shugart, E., & Sheldrake, J. (2021). Editor's corner: Why culturally relevant science teaching is vital in our classrooms. *The Science Teacher, 89*(2), 6–8. https://doi.org/10.1080/00368555.2021.12293644.

Moje, E. B. (2007). Developing socially just subject-matter instruction: A review of the literature on disciplinary literacy teaching. *Difference, Diversity, and Distinctiveness in Education, 31,* 1–44. https://doi.org/10.3102/0091732x07300046.

National Council for Social Studies. (2010). *National curriculum standards for social studies: Introduction.* https://www.socialstudies.org/standards/national-curriculum-standards-social-studies-introduction

Paris, D. (2012). Culturally sustaining pedagogy: A needed change in stance, terminology, and practice. *Educational Researcher, 41*(3), 93–97. doi:10.3102/0013189X12441244

Russell, S. T. (2019). Social justice and the future of healthy families: Sociocultural changes and challenges. *Family Relations: Interdisciplinary journal of Applied Family Science, 68*(3), 358–70. doi: 10.1111/fare.12358. PMID: 31736531; PMCID: PMC6857837. https://www.ncbi.nlm.nih.gov/pmc/articles/PMC6857837/.

Sohns, A. (2023). Differential exposure to drinking water contaminants in North Carolina: Evidence from structural topic modeling and water quality data. *Journal of Environmental Management, 336*(15), 117600. https://doi.org/10.1016/j.jenvman.2023.117600.

CHAPTER 9

Middle School Curriculum and Pedagogy

Learning Outcomes:

1. Deepen students' critical thinking, creativity, and decision-making skills through a middle grades curriculum that is challenging, exploratory, integrative, and diverse.

2. Develop the ability to collaboratively create a cohesive curriculum plan for the academic year, ensuring a logical progression of learning.

3. Explore the concept of designing lessons by starting with clear learning outcomes and working backward to create purposeful activities and assessments.

4. Identify appropriate instructional strategies to support student learning.

5. Develop skills for facilitating and engaging in productive whole-group discussions, fostering critical thinking and classroom discourse and questioning techniques.

In this chapter, we establish the key features of middle school curriculum, based on AMLE (Association for Middle Level Education) principles. We also explore the fundamental models and strategies for making that instruction come to life. Pedagogy is defined as the method and practice of teaching, especially as an academic subject. In this chapter, we will share the basics of instructional approaches, including how to create a **yearly plan**, a **unit plan**, and daily lesson plans. We will investigate different instructional strategies for the delivery and exploration of content. Also, we share high-leverage practices used across content areas to enact curriculum elements of relevance, challenge, integration, and exploration. Specifically, we will investigate practices related to discourse and the use of digital tools.

Middle Grades Curriculum

Above all else, the middle school curriculum should be challenging, exploratory, integrative, and diverse. The curriculum embraces every planned aspect of a school's educational program. An effective middle level curriculum is distinguished by including learning activities that appeal to young adolescents, by being exploratory and challenging, and by incorporating student-generated questions and concerns. According to AMLE, as educators, it is our responsibility to use knowledge of the distinct nature and identities of young adolescents when planning and implementing middle level curriculum and when selecting and using instructional strategies. We aim to help students make connections between subjects by using real-world applications, fostering critical thinking, encouraging creativity, and developing decision-making skills. Middle school curriculum also aims to support health and wellness, including social-emotional development of adolescents, which helps growth as a well-rounded individual. A middle grades curriculum provides a gateway for students to "learn about matters of personal, social, moral, and ethical significance" (Bishop & Harrison, p. 27). It addresses external expectations, such as state or local **standards**, and offers young adolescents opportunities to ask and investigate answers to questions. The curriculum also "introduces students to multiple, diverse perspectives and viewpoints" (p. 27).

A challenging curriculum is one that addresses substantive concepts and skills and is appropriately geared to each student's level of understanding and readiness (Bishop & Harrison, 2021). Developing curriculum to challenge each student requires significant planning, flexibility, and collaboration among educators, families, and the students themselves. Middle school teachers must be aware of the developmental and identity-related diversity of their learners and of their students' prior experiences, social and cultural backgrounds, and learning preferences. This knowledge specifically informs curriculum design (p. 28).

An *exploratory* curriculum directly reflects the curious, adventuresome nature of young adolescents. Exploration is not a classification of content; rather, it is an expansive attitude toward and an expansive approach to developing curriculum and instruction. Middle school is a time for students to explore and learn about themselves and the world around them. If youth pass through early adolescence without broad, exploratory experiences, their future lives may be needlessly restricted. They deserve chances to ascertain their special interests and aptitudes and to engage in activities that will broaden their views of the world and of themselves. This is particularly true for students who may not have access to such opportunities outside of school.

An *integrative* curriculum focuses on coherent ideas and concepts, irrespective of arbitrary subject boundaries, and enables students to see connections and real-world applications (AMLE, n.d.). When students examine problems and have identified and taken steps to solve them, students develop critical thinking, decision-making, creativity, and other deeper **learning outcomes**. "Educators support students' understanding of local, national, and global civic responsibilities and co-facilitate opportunities for them to demonstrate active citizenship through participation in endeavors that benefit their schools and broader communities" (Bishop & Harrison, 2021, p. 30).

Middle school curriculum integrates students' own backgrounds to help them see how they can use what they are learning right now while also focusing on what they will need in the future. Thoughtfully designed interdisciplinary experiences help students see the integrated nature of knowledge and the many connections that link various topics, concepts, and subjects.

Learning may be strengthened or augmented when curriculum is planned and implemented by an **interdisciplinary team** of teachers.

> In successful middle schools, students make decisions about curricular goals and content, and explore curriculum through a range of modes, including apprenticeships, independent study, small group work, and special interest experiences. Making curriculum integrative and relevant, however, does not mean limiting topics and material to students' pre-existing interests. Successful middle schools also foster new interests and open doors to new knowledge and opportunities. Youth benefit from studying concepts and learning skills in areas that interest them and those determined by adults. As young adolescents develop greater independence, they help make curriculum relevant by personalizing and taking increasing ownership of their education. (Bishop & Harrison, 2021, p. 31)

A diverse and relevant curriculum enables students to "pursue answers to questions they have about themselves, content, and the world" (NMSA, 2010, p. 22). An increased awareness of diversity and stereotypes can be developed while also broadening young adolescents' ability to understand power and privilege, including how they may differ among various groups. Young adolescents "reflect on and question how their own cultural and social identity groups relate to and differ from other groups" (Bishop & Harrison, 2021, p. 31). Questioning and self-investigation are important. Providing opportunities for this to occur in school may prevent students from developing faulty or misinformed views of their own worth and the worth of others. Impactful middle school teachers recognize that these thoughts around exploration of identity evolve over time and support students in better understanding the world around them. A diverse curriculum requires educators to design learning that builds on and sustains students' cultural and linguistic backgrounds and experiences while adding new material. Of course, it is essential for middle school teachers to develop the ability to affirm and support students as they understand and acknowledge their own privileges, such as those associated with race, social class, and identity.

YEARLY PLANNING AND UNIT PLANNING

Planning is fundamental to a successful classroom. The national and state standards that guide our planning are wide-ranging, are often open-ended, and can be overwhelming. Standards tell us what students should know and be able to do within a content area across grade levels—the end goal of instruction. All states have mandated state standards (which may also include **national standards**). Some districts may also include scope and sequence frameworks, or even **pacing guides** (especially common for math). Mapping out a plan to thoroughly teach the complete set of standards is necessary to ensure achievable pacing and depth of learning.

Yearly planning is not a prescriptive process, and teachers need to figure out a system that works well for their thinking process. To help us with this, we have shared here a set of examples including teachers from each content area as they describe their personal approach to creating a yearly plan. Each teacher discusses the **scope** (what to teach, based on standards) and the **sequence** (the order of what is taught). Essentially think of this as the high-altitude view of the year.

There are several factors to consider when deciding how to structure a yearly plan. Deciding on a logical progression, say in math, is important if there are important prerequisite skills that need to build over the course of the year. But, in English language arts, for example, the **content standards** are very fluid and flexible and could be clustered, based on specific themes or particular book studies. The national social-studies standards are already organized into ten themes, and teachers must decide what resources to use to meet them. The science standards lend themselves to clustered themes as well, but the order in which they are taught is less important. Interdisciplinary teams also need to consider **cross-curricular opportunities** to build **interdisciplinary units** or project-based learning units.

In terms of designing units, again there is no one-size-fits-all method, and some teachers will find that their teams, schools, or districts may require the use of common materials and the pacing of those materials. For those who are working in environments with full autonomy over planning, there is a basic structure to help approach this process. First, think of a way to encapsulate the unit—this may be a theme, such as dystopian literature, space, ancient Egypt, or linear functions. Then comes the time to dig into the standards. This process is more streamlined in some subjects than in others, as there may be many standards that can fit in with dystopian literature. Once the standards are established, a great next step is designing the **assessment** for the unit. This helps ensure that all the learning activities throughout the unit are well aligned to both the standards and the assessment itself. Then, the last step is to identify and flesh out daily activities and explorations to help students understand the content.

Amanda Clapp teaches sixth-, seventh-, and eighth-grade science. Orchestrating yearly plans for each grade level is a massively complex task with lots of moving parts. We asked her to share her process for this, and she discussed the constraints and flexibility embedded within her content area. There are clusters of objectives that need to hang together within a unit, but the order of the units is less important. Some years, things like partnership activities with other schools and community partners are what dictates when she does a certain unit; sometimes collaborations with other teachers on the team to build interdisciplinary units dictate when she does a certain unit; and sometimes she just knows a group well and feels strongly that starting the year with a certain unit may be most effective. Her process is to start with a skeleton template like the one provided in Table 9.1. This simple structure aligns standards by week, provides a space to include activities, and has a column to list necessary vocabulary for that standard. She repeats this process for each quarter to flesh out a yearly plan. Table 9.1 shows her sketch for the third quarter of seventh grade. From here she fleshes out the units and creates a tracking document for students to self-assess their understanding along the way. Figure 9.1 is an example template for an eighth-grade geology unit.

Table 9.1 Third-Quarter Seventh-Grade Science Planning

	Standards	Activities	Vocabulary
20 Jan. 8	**Cells** I can explain how cells are the smallest building blocks of organisms; I can compare plant and animal cells **7.L.1.2**	**Microscope labs, history**	Prokaryote, eukaryote, nucleus, organelle, structure, function
21 Jan. 16	**Cells** I can identify major organelles **7.L.1.2**	**Cell analogy project**	Nucleus, membrane, cytoplasm, lysosome, ribosome, Golgi, endoplasmic reticulum, vacuole, cell wall, mitochondria
22 Jan. 22	**Cells** I can compare unicellular organisms based on their structures **7.L.1.1**	**Microscope labs**	Euglena, protist, ameba, pseudopod, flagellum, cilia, paramecium, volvox, algae, locomotion, feeding, eyespot, microscope parts
23 Jan. 29	**Human body** I can describe the hierarchical structure of living things; I can describe the structure and function of the digestive system **7.L.1.3**	**Digestive system analogy, distance, cracker lab**	Cell, tissue, organ, system, organism, specialized cell, neuron, blood cell, muscle cell, osteoblast, skin cell, hierarchy, mechanical versus chemical digestion, absorption, surface area
24 Feb. 5	**Human body** I can describe the structure and function of the respiratory system **7.L.1.4**	**Heart diagram, model lungs.**	Oxygen, carbon dioxide, surface area, lung, alveoli, oxygenated, diaphragm
25 Feb. 12	**Human body** I can describe the structure and function of the circulatory system **7L.1.4**	**Heart dissection**	Vein, artery, capillary, heart, atrium, ventricle, vena cava, pulmonary veins, hemoglobin, platelets, white blood cells
26 Feb 20	**Human body** I can describe the structure and function of the excretory system **7.L.1.4**	**Problem-based learning: improve a system of your choice**	Bones, muscle, skin, adaptation
27 Feb. 26	**Human body** I can explain how the systems work together to keep humans alive **7.L.1.4**		Structure, function

(Continued)

Table 9.1 (Continued)

	Standards	Activities	Vocabulary
28 March 4	**Human body** I can compare sexual and asexual reproduction **7.L.2.1**	**Flipbook and hands**	Asexual reproduction, sexual reproduction, mitosis, interphase, cell cycle, prophase, metaphase, anaphase, telophase, cytokinesis
29 March 11	**Human body** I can compare sexual and asexual reproduction **7.L.2.1**		Meiosis, sperm, egg, ovary, testis, fertilization, embryo, fetus, placenta

Unit Overview Sheet: Geology

Over three weeks, we will investigate the evidence of geologic time, including relative and absolute dating. We will do a variety of activities to understand the age of the Earth and plate tectonics.

Essential Questions

How old is Earth?	What is the evidence for Earth's age?	How has the lithosphere changed over time?

Learning Target 1
I can use relative and absolute dating to determine the age of Earth (8.E.2.1).
This means I can explain how to use superposition and radioactive dating to determine rock ages.

Rate your level of Understanding: 1 | 2 | 3 | 4
Dates:

Your Proof:

Learning Target 2
I can use clues to read stratigraphic sections of rock and use proxy data for the past conditions (8.E.2.2).
This means I can explain the use of fossils, ice cores, faults, and igneous rock formations as evidence of the history of Earth and its changing life forms.

Rate your level of Understanding: 1 | 2 | 3 | 4
Dates:

Your Proof:

Learning Target 3
I can explain evolution (8.L.4.1).
This means I can summarize the use of evidence drawn from geology, fossils, and comparative anatomy to form the basis for biological classification systems and the theory of evolution.

Rate your level of Understanding: 1 | 2 | 3 | 4
Dates:

Your Proof:

Vocabulary to Master
- Geologic time
- Relative Dating
- Absolute dating
- Radioactive Decay
- Fossilization
- Homology
- Analogy
- Ice core
- Stratigraphy
- Superposition
- Crosscutting
- Rock Cycle

Figure 9.1 8th grade Geology Unit Overview. Amanda Clapp

Kayleigh Kassel (one of the authors) teaches sixth-, seventh-, and eighth-grade English language arts. Her planning is dynamic and changes yearly, as she tailors much of her instructional planning to the individual learners in the classroom. In English language arts, sixth-grade students need to know what the concepts are and how to identify them. Seventh-grade students need to also create their own examples of each concept they studied. Eighth-grade students focus on authors' craft and word choice to examine why an author would develop the text using the selected structure. Each grade level shares similar standards about citing text evidence, analyzing word choice, noticing figurative language, identifying the main idea, interpreting the theme, and tracking plot development. Kayleigh has general themes and practices she follows when planning but adapts them when she is teaching some units, based on when students are learning content in other classes. Here we share her general structures for seventh-grade English language arts:

- **First quarter:** Students draft an essay that describes them and study figurative language, mood, and tone, beginning with poems and moving into short stories. Then students study character development, character types, point of view (perspective), and the impact of setting on texts throughout short stories.

- **Second quarter:** Students study nonfiction reading strategies, conduct research, and write argumentative essays.

- **Third quarter:** Students participate in literature circles on historical fiction (which correlates to their social-studies content during this time). They practice fiction-reading strategies and study character development and the development of theme over time. During this time, we also connect content to World War II and nonfiction primary and secondary sources.

- **Fourth quarter:** Students study mixed-genre units. Each week is centered around a single theme, and students read fiction, nonfiction, and poetry texts then focus on a single literary device.

Salem Parris is an eighth-grade social-studies teacher in a traditional middle school setting. Her district uses a regionally adopted curriculum guide that provides her with the resources she needs while still leaving room for some choice in what activities she uses. Salem said that, historically, units were often done chronologically but that these added resources she is using are built around themes. For example, there may be a unit on revolutions, and the students would investigate revolutions that occurred across time in various parts of the world. History can be overwhelming if teachers try to teach every event, every period, and every part of the world. This thematic approach allows exploration of a few key events surrounding an idea and helps students build a toolkit for how to think about the world. Salem also emphasizes her role as a reading teacher. Her students use primary and secondary sources to investigate historical concepts and explicit reading strategies, such as annotating passages to help her students understand those texts' content.

Meghan Rector also teaches sixth, seventh, and eighth grade, but her content area is math. Because she is a math teacher, much of her yearly planning is more restrictive than it would be if she taught in another content area. She reflects here on her yearly planning process from two different perspectives—one where she taught in a large district with common pacing guides and another where she has full autonomy to choose.

In the large district, the school level required content-area professional learning communities (PLCs), and, from each school, a representative served on the district-wide PLC. At this level, PLC members gathered input from teachers on curriculum choices, but mostly all teachers were expected to follow the district-required pacing guide and to use common assessments in their classrooms. They would then meet monthly with their school-level PLCs and with the district-wide PLCs to discuss student responses. Teachers would then use that data to group students for targeted interventions to help small groups to continue to make progress.

Her process is much different in her current setting where she has full autonomy over instructional and curriculum decisions. To begin, she gathers all the curriculum resources she has been exposed to over the years, including EngageNY, Connected Mathematics Project, and Open Up Resources/Illustrative Mathematics, and she selects the tasks from each resource that she prefers to address each content standard. From there she does a crosswalk process to decide which units to do and when to do them. One driving factor in making such decisions is timing the units to match up with the state-level check-in assessments that happen three times a year before end-of-grade testing ends. In her estimation, the sixth-grade curriculum is the most disconnected (meaning that it does not build in a natural progression), and therefore she has more choice in the order of the content. Seventh- and eighth-grade curricula have more of a linear progression of skills, and many of those standards need to be taught in a certain order. Other factors in her yearly planning are the co-planning with the inclusion teacher and any interns she is hosting and any collaborative project-based learning she is doing with her team. In Figure 9.2, we see an example of the spreadsheet Meghan utilizes to plan one quarter of instruction for one grade level.

What we see here are the perspectives of four quite different individuals who all have varied processes they use to create their yearly plan. These plans vary in the level of detail, structure, and organization. This should indicate that there is no prescriptive one-size-fits-all approach to yearly and unit planning. That said, yearly planning is a crucial and critical step that good teachers use to set themselves up for success.

Week of	Topic	Strand Covered (RP, NS, EE, G, SP)	Standards Covered
Aug 16th (3 days)	Beginning of School Expectataions/ Group & Partner Norms/ MTC Problems		
Aug 21st	MTC Problems/ Area (Off coordinate plan)/ Area Pre-test		
Aug 28th	Area (Decomposing Shapes) (figures in coordinate plane)	G	6.G.1, 6.G.3
Sept 5th (4 days)	Coordinate Plane (all Quadrants)	NS	6.NS.6, 6.NS.8, 6.G.3
Sept 11th (4 days)	Volume of Rect. Prisms (Done Whole #'s will now do fractional)	G	6.G.2
Sept 18th	SA of prisms and pyramids using nets	G	6.G.4
Sept 25th	Introduce Ratios	RP	6.RP.1
Oct 2nd (4 days)	Equivalent Ratios (# lines, tables, graphs)	RP	6.RP.2, 6.RP.3
Oct 9th	Finding Unit Ratios/Rates	RP	6.RP.2
Oct 17th (4 days) (Check In 1)	Ratio Word Problems/ Review	RP	6.RP.3, 6.NS.9
Oct 23rd	Long Division	NS	6.NS.2

Figure 9.2 Yearly planning for 6th grade mathematics. Created by authors

While this may feel overwhelming to a beginning teacher who is just learning content standards, this process becomes easier and more streamlined from year to year. It is important to reflect on and refine one's plan each year, though, to ensure best practices are used.

Pause and Reflect: Before we launch into the section on **lesson planning**, take a moment to jot down what your conception is of how to plan a lesson. What do you feel is necessary to have in each lesson? What things might vary from one lesson plan to another? We will revisit these first conceptions later in the chapter.

LESSON PLANNING

Teachers typically approach lesson design in a "forward design" manner, meaning they consider the learning activities (how to teach the content), develop assessments around their learning activities, then try to draw connections to the **learning goals** of the course. In contrast, the **backward design** approach has teachers consider the learning goals of the course first. These learning goals represent the knowledge and skills that instructors want their students to have learned when they leave the course. Once the learning goals have been established, the second stage involves consideration of assessment. The backward design framework implies that teachers should consider these overarching learning goals and how students will be assessed *prior* to consideration of how to teach the content. For this reason, backward design is considered a much more purposeful approach to lesson planning than traditional methods of design.

Backward design is focused primarily on student learning and understanding. When teachers are designing lessons, units, or courses, they often focus on the activities and instruction rather than on the outputs of the instruction. Therefore, it could be said that teachers often focus more on teaching than learning. This perspective can lead to the misconception that learning is the activity when, in fact, learning stems from a careful reflection on the meaning of the activity.

To reiterate an earlier point, backward design is beneficial to teachers because it innately encourages intentionality during the lesson design process. The teacher is continually encouraged to establish the purpose of doing something before implementing it into the curriculum. Therefore, backward design is an effective way of providing guidance for instruction and designing lessons, units, and courses. Once the learning goals, or desired results, have been identified, teachers will have an easier time developing assessments and instruction around grounded learning outcomes.

The incorporation of backward design also lends itself to transparent and explicit instruction. If the teacher has defined the course's learning goals, he has a better idea of what he wants the students to get out of learning activities. If learning goals have been meticulously defined, the possibility of doing certain activities and tasks for the sake of doing them is eliminated. Every task and piece of instruction has a purpose that fits with the lesson's overarching goals. Teaching is not just about engaging students in content but also about ensuring students have the resources necessary to understand. Student learning and understanding can be assessed more accurately through a backward design approach, since it leverages what students will need to know and understand during the design process to progress.

THREE STAGES OF BACKWARD DESIGN

Identify the desired results. Consider the learning goals of the lesson, unit, or course. Wiggins and McTighe provide a useful process for establishing curricular priorities. They suggest that teachers ask themselves the following three questions as they increasingly focus on the most valuable content. What should learners hear, read, view, explore, or otherwise encounter? This knowledge is considered knowledge worth being familiar with. Information that answers this question is the lowest-priority content information mentioned in the lesson, unit, or course. What knowledge and skills should learners master? What is important for learners to know and be able to do? Examples include facts, concepts, principles, processes, strategies, and methods students should know when they leave the course. What are big ideas and important understandings learners should retain? These are called enduring understandings because they represent ideas students need to remember after they have completed the lesson or class.

Determine what is acceptable evidence. Consider the assessments and performance tasks students will complete to show evidence of understanding and learning. In the earlier stage, the focus was on the learning goals so that there is a sharp vision of what evidence students can provide to show that they have achieved or have started to attain the goals of the course. At this stage, it is important to consider a wide range of assessment methods to ensure that students are being assessed on their achievement of the goals the teacher wants them to reach. Sometimes, the assessments do not match the learning goals, which can be a frustrating experience for both students and teachers. Assessment methods relating to the learning goals of the class may include papers, short-answer quizzes, free-response questions, practice assignments or problems, lab projects, group projects, etc. (more on this in Chapter 11, which focuses on assessment). Consider the following two questions at this stage:

- How will I know if students have achieved the desired results?
- What will I accept as evidence of student understanding and proficiency?

Plan learning experiences and instruction. In the final stage of backward design, teachers begin to consider how they will teach. This is when instructional strategies and learning activities should be created. With the learning goals and assessment methods established, the teacher will have a well-defined vision of which strategies would work best to provide students with the resources and information necessary to reach the goals of the course. Consider the questions below:

- What enabling knowledge (facts, concepts, principles) and skills (processes, procedures, strategies) will students need to perform effectively and achieve desired results?
- What activities will equip students with the needed knowledge and skills?
- What will need to be taught and coached, and how should it best be taught, given performance goals?
- What materials and resources are best suited to accomplish these goals?

Leverage the various instructional strategies, such as group discussion, interactive **direct instruction**, think-pair shares, flipped classroom, cooperative/team-based/project-based learning, guided note-taking, and guided inquiry for problem-solving.

Pause and Reflect: After reading this section on backwards design, how is this process similar to and different from your original conceptions of lesson planning? What are the connections you see between planning and the five essential attributes of middle level curriculum (responsive, challenging, empowering, equitable, and engaging)?

Now that we have a framework in mind for planning lessons, let's begin to think more specifically about what our plans address—**student learning outcomes** and objectives.

LEARNING OUTCOMES AND OBJECTIVES

When first planning for instruction, teachers often focus on the selection of content, teaching method, and instructional materials. These are all essential elements of instructional planning, but the entire process is more effective if attention is first directed toward learning outcomes and **instructional objectives**.

- What are the intended *learning outcomes* of the instruction?
- How can we *describe*, in performance terms, what students are like when they have learned what is expected of them?

Good curriculum matters for good **differentiation**. A big idea or principle of differentiated instruction is clarity of learning goals, which means saying what you want students to know, understand, and be able to do. Clarifying our intended learning outcomes provides a basis for instructional planning and sets the stage for both teaching and assessment. Differentiation does not suggest that a teacher can be all things to all individuals at all times. It does, however, mandate that a teacher create a reasonable range of approaches to learning much of the time, so that most students find the teaching provided to fit their learning needs much of the time. Differentiation is not a strategy or something you do sometimes. It is a way of thinking about teaching and learning (more on differentiation in Chapter 10). The essentials to planning a solid lesson include the following three steps:

1. State the general objective and define it in terms of student performance.
2. Provide a variety of learning experiences directed toward the general objective.
3. Assess student achievement using a variety of assessment methods.

Instructional Objectives

Instructional objectives are specific, measurable, short-term, observable student behaviors. An objective is a description of a performance you want learners to be able to exhibit before you consider them competent. It describes an intended result of instruction rather than the process of instruction itself. A learning objective should focus on student performance (e.g., knowledge/skill acquisition or reinforcement). What is it that your students should be able to do at the end of the class session and course that they could not do before? It is important to make clear the intended learning outcome rather than what form the instruction will take.

Action verbs that are specific, such as *list, describe, report, compare, demonstrate, and analyze*, should state the behaviors students will be expected to perform. Well-written learning objectives can give students precise statements of what is expected of them and provide guidelines for assessing student progress. Our goal for students is learning, and, if students do not know what they should be able to do at the end of class, then it will be difficult for them to reach that goal. Clearly defined objectives form the foundation for selecting appropriate content, learning activities, and assessment measures. If objectives of the course are not clearly understood by both the instructor and the students, if learning activities do not relate to the objectives and the content that the instructor thinks are important, then the instructor's methods of assessment, which are supposed to indicate to both the learners and the instructor how effective the learning and teaching process have been, will be, at best, misleading and, at worst, irrelevant or unfair. Think about the lesson you will be teaching. What would you like each student to know and to be able to do when he or she has completed the lesson? Here we provide the types of objectives along with some helpful tips for writing effective objectives.

Types of Objectives

- **Cognitive**: understandings, awarenesses, insights (e.g., "List and explain . . ."). This includes information recall, conceptual understanding, and problem-solving.

- **Psychomotor**: specific integrational skills (e.g., "Dissect a frog so that the following organs are clearly displayed . . ."; "Take a replicable blood-pressure reading by appropriately using a sphygmomanometer").

- **Affective**: attitudes, appreciations, relationships.

TIPS FOR WRITING OBJECTIVES

- How specific and detailed objectives should be depends on what they are intended to be used for. Objectives for sequencing a unit plan will be more general than those for specifying a lesson plan.

- Do not make writing objectives tedious, trivial, time-consuming, or mechanical. Keep them simple, unambiguous, and clearly focused as a guide to learning.

- Express them in terms of student performance, behavior, and achievement, not in terms of what the teacher will be doing.

- Identify the type of activity in which competence is required (e.g., "Dissect . . .").

- Specify the criteria or standards by which competence in the activity will be assessed (e.g., "Dissect a frog so that the following organs are clearly displayed . . .").

Table 9.2 Chunking a Standard

The students will be able to	tell and record time on a digital clock and analog clock to the hour and half hour	by writing the times correctly in a story.
Audience: standard introduction for an objective	Behavior/action: described in a verb and is measurable and can be assessed; what is the learner to do?	Condition to be met by the students to demonstrate that the objective has been achieved
Hint: focus on what the students, not the teacher, must do	Content: description of the subject matter to be learned Hint: must specify observable and measurable behaviors	Hint: describes the curriculum circumstances, situation, or setting

- Use specific words or phrases, such as know, think, appreciate, learn, comprehend, remember, perceive, understand, be aware of, be familiar with, have knowledge of, grasp the significance, are not measurable, and should be avoided.

Let's break this down to tangible attributes. Table 9.2 chunks the objective into thinking through the audience, the action, and the condition to be met. Use this idea to evaluate this sample objective:

The students will be able to tell and record time on a digital clock and on an analog clock to the hour and the half hour by writing the times in a story.

Many teachers struggle when starting to write effective objectives. Often, the issues are that objectives are not observable or measurable or are too general or vague. Here is a list of some examples that DO NOT adequately specify the audience, the behavior or verb, or the condition:

- Students will appreciate the beauty of a circuit.
- Students will really understand relativity theory.
- Students will be familiar with the law.
- Students will understand the process of osmosis.
- Students will enjoy speaking French.
- Students will change the spark plugs on an engine.
- Students will learn about erosion.
- Students will learn the life stages of a frog.
- Students will explain the results of World War I and World War II.
- Students will review patterns.
- Students will increase their reading ability.
- Students will gain knowledge of basic principles.
- Students will learn symbols on a weather map.

One effective strategy for writing objectives is to clearly indicate the instructional outcomes and use the concept of what "students will be able to . . ." (SWBAT) do at the end of instruction. The following list highlights examples that ARE observable or measurable objectives (but is certainly not exhaustive):

- Students will label the four life stages of a frog.
- Students will compare the results of World War I and World War II, using a Venn Diagram.
- Students will order color blocks into a pattern.
- Students will recall the four major food groups without error.
- From a "story problem" description, students will convert the story to a mathematical manipulation needed to solve the problem.
- Students will multiply fractions in class with 90 percent accuracy.
- Students will read a presidential debate and point out the passages that attack a political opponent personally rather than the opponent's political programs.
- Students will point out the positive and negative points presented in an argument for the abolition of guns.
- Students will write a different but plausible ending to a short story.
- After studying the current economic policies of the United States, student groups will design their own goals for fiscal and monetary policies.
- Students will design a series of chemical operations to separate quantitatively the elements in a solution.
- Students will use the principles of society to evaluate the US economic system.
- Given any research study, students will evaluate the appropriateness of the conclusions reached, based on the data presented.
- SWBAT predicts weather from a weather map (using the symbols).
- SWBAT conducts simple probability experiments by determining the number of outcomes and make simple predictions.
- SWBAT makes decisions about how to approach problems.
- SWBAT analyzes problems by identifying relationships, distinguishing relevant from irrelevant information, sequencing and prioritizing information, and observing patterns.
- SWBAT knows plants and animals have structures that serve different functions in growth, survival, and reproduction.

Table 9.3 Words for Each Level of Bloom's Taxonomy

Lower-Level Cognitive Outcomes

Knowledge	Recalling
Comprehension	Translating
Application	Interpreting
	Estimating
	Comparing
	Classifying
	Applying

Higher-Level Thinking Skills

Analysis	Identifying
Synthesis	Analyzing
Evaluation	Inferring
	Relating
	Formulating
	Generating
	Judging

Affective Outcomes

Attitudes	Listening
Interests	Responding
Appreciations	Participating
Adjustments	Seeking
	Demonstrating
	Relating
	Valuing

Performance Outcomes

Procedure	Speaking
Product	Drawing
Procedure and product	Computing
Problem solving	Writing
	Constructing
	Demonstrating
	Operating
	Performing
	Originating

As we design our objectives, we may categorize our outcomes based on lower-cognitive-level outcomes, higher-level thinking skills, affective outcomes, or performance outcomes. Table 9.3 provides some associated words with each of the categories of **Bloom's Taxonomy**, which we explore more in depth later.

We notice that our design of our objectives is inextricably linked to other parts of lesson planning. Here are some questions to consider as we make our plans.

- How will I provide a review of items previously mastered so the students will retain them?

- How will I promote future generalizations when a simple acquisition has been reached?
- How will I accommodate the students' cultural, social, and linguistic backgrounds?
- How will I break the skill or concept into at least three to five teachable parts?
- How will I vary my instructional approach or techniques to accommodate different students?
- How will I assess student learning throughout the lesson and at the end?

INSTRUCTIONAL MODELS AND STRATEGIES

As we are designing lesson plans, we must think with intention about the instructional models and strategies we want to use to achieve learning outcomes. So, what do we mean by instructional model or strategy? Instructional models and strategies are the methods used to reach our learning outcomes. The list of instructional models and strategies is long and there simply is not room to include them all. There are multiple frameworks that are common to categorize and explore **instructional strategies**, and here we pull from commonly utilized frameworks to help begin building a toolkit of methods to use in the classroom.

Several considerations for choosing the appropriate instructional strategy for a given lesson follow: How does the strategy support student learning of this specific learning outcome? What kind of feedback from and assessment of student learning can be provided by this instructional model or strategy? Will this instructional model or strategy be challenging, relevant, and accessible to all students? There are also factors to consider, such as teacher personality, class personality (also known as classroom-management considerations), and content considerations. For example, one of the authors is a mathematics educator, and, every time she reads something about direct instruction, or *I do, we do, you do*, she feels like she may die a little inside. But, for teaching reading strategy explicitly, that method is considered to be effective in the field of English language arts. **Experiential learning**, for example, may be more easily integrated into science and social-studies classes with experiments and field trips. As we explore each model, think about how it could be used in each content area or at a certain point within a unit of instruction. All these models have merit and purpose, if they are chosen with intention, and, frankly, instruction should be varied, incorporating different models.

Direct Instruction

Direct instruction is defined by the National Direct Instruction Institute as "a model for teaching that emphasizes well-developed and carefully planned lessons designed around small learning increments and clearly defined and prescribed teaching tasks. It is based on the theory that clear instruction eliminating misinterpretations can improve and accelerate learning." The premise is to use explicit teaching and modeling and, then, **guided practice** and some independent practice and assessment. It is often referred to as a gradual-release model. Direct instruction is most effective for teaching basic academic skills. Teachers who utilize direct instruction effectively know that, even within this simple structure, variation is key. Here are some ideas of how to support students with the direct instruction model.

Introduction/review: An introductory activity is usually used to activate prior learning or do a quick preassessment. This could be reviewing the previous day's exit ticket, having students begin a Know, Want to Know, Learn (KWL) chart, front-loading information using graphic organizers, note-taking, and so on.

Demonstration/modeling (I do): In this part of a direct-instruction lesson, teachers use modeling, questioning, and cuing to scaffold student learning. The types of strategies used in this section include notetaking (like Cornell notes), graphic organizers, think-pair-shares, think alouds, and anticipation guides.

Guided practice (we do): This section of the lesson is where we start to see the gradual release of students to work more collaboratively and/or independently. Teachers are monitoring and providing feedback. Here, activities might include students finding some sort of similarities and differences (more on this later) or discovering patterns and making connections. Here, cooperative learning groups may play a key role, and students may explore various representations of knowledge.

Independent practice (you do): In this final phase of a direct-instruction lesson, we expect students to show proficiency in the learning objective. Students should be able to generalize and use problem-solving skills. This may be quick and formative—using exit tickets or whole-group summary information, adding the "L" to the KWL chart, or completing some sort of application task.

Indirect Instruction

Indirect instruction is a more student-centered approach that centralizes on active engagement and discovery. These strategies are inquiry based and include problem-based learning and project-based learning. While problem-based learning and project-based learning share many similarities, each has a few distinctive qualities that we will describe below.

Problem-based learning is centered on a specific problem or scenario (usually with relevant real-world connections) that requires investigation and exploration. These tasks are often open-ended, and students may use doing research and asking questions to approach the problem. The teacher's role tends to be more as a facilitator as the learning is student driven and constructed. These tasks are often smaller and more efficiently explored than are project-based learning experiences.

Project-based learning involves a more extended process beyond the singular situation of **problem-based learning**. There may be a larger product or a longer investigation time. Oftentimes these are interdisciplinary projects that integrate multiple content areas. This is an increasingly popular model and can be powerful in building student motivation and engagement. In our school, we utilize project-based learning at the classroom, team, and school level. Our science teacher consistently implements project-based learning that is specific to science instruction but then also has students

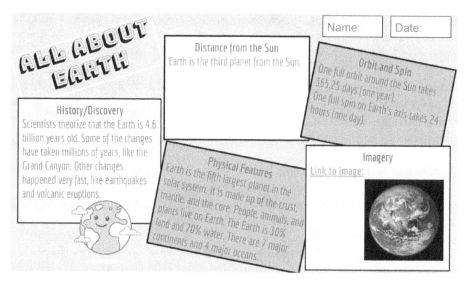

Figure 9.3 Assignment example connection with ELA and Science Earth PBL. Created by authors

collaborate with others. For example, the sixth graders do an interdisciplinary project about space. In English language arts, they explore nonfiction texts to build vocabulary, while, in science, they explore space through activities like planning, designing, and making a physical model of a moon base. In English language arts, they later write a narrative about living on their base for their planet, and they must include true facts about a planet in our solar system, using some of the research they collected in both English language arts and science. In science, they study infographics and, in English language arts, they create their own. In Figure 9.3, we share examples of student work used across both content areas.

Experiential Learning

Another innovative instructional-strategy category is experiential learning. In this realm, students learn through having hands-on learning experiences. In this model, students are engaged in investigating, experimenting, problem-solving, and building on natural curiosities. The teacher's role is to select the experience, pose problems, and then set boundaries and give resources to students. Once students are engaged in the experience, the teacher monitors to support students' ability to make connections and take part in reflective opportunities where they can synthesize their learning. In the middle school setting, experiential learning is typically tied to intentionally chosen field trips or service-learning opportunities.

Specific Instructional Strategies

Within each of these models of instruction, there are opportunities to use a plethora of specific instructional strategies for students to deepen their understanding of a concept. There are specific strategies and also some general strategies to use within each content area. While, as we mentioned previously, the list of these strategies is expansive and not limited to what we suggest here, sometimes it is helpful to have a simple starting point from which to grow. Here we suggest starting with a classic resource, Marzano et al.'s (2001) work, which outlines nine instructional strategies for learning. Here we share a brief description of each strategy and an example of each.

1. Identifying similarities and differences: With this instructional strategy students analyze and compare information on a particular topic or idea and then generalize demonstrating a deeper understanding.
2. Example: Students are asked to compare different species of plants, analyzing and identifying their structures and adaptation to environments.
3. Summarizing and note-taking: This instructional strategy requires students to organize or condense information to help comprehension and retention of information.
4. Example: During a unit about a specific historical period, students may explore key events that they then summarize, taking notes about the primary causes and effects of those events.
5. Reinforcing effort and providing recognition: Good teachers promote a growth mindset in students by acknowledging students' efforts, using specific feedback and praise to motivate students in their persistence toward learning.
6. Example: In a math class, a teacher gives specific praise to a student who persisted in problem-solving by saying something like, "I like that you used a table as a strategy to track your thinking here." This may then be followed up by a question or a statement to continue the student's thinking further.
7. Homework and practice: Use of homework and practice should emphasize intentional and purposeful homework that helps reinforce and/or extend learning in meaningful ways.
8. Example: In a math class, students have a once-per-week assignment that is based on reviewing previously learned units to keep their skills fresh.
9. Nonlinguistic representations: This strategy emphasizes the use of nonverbal tools, including the use of visuals and graphic organizers, to support understanding and memory.
10. Example: Students may create graphic organizers, using symbols and labels to illustrate the water cycle.
11. Cooperative learning: Collaboration is the cornerstone of cooperative learning. This strategy uses partner and group formations to foster shared responsibility for academic tasks as well as to build capacities in social skills.
12. Example: During a group project in science, students collaborate on the creation of a dynamic presentation about disease by divvying up research responsibilities and collectively contributing to the presentation.

13. Setting objectives and providing feedback: The focus of this strategy is transparency of learning goals for students and giving students explicit and constructive feedback to help them progress in their understanding of content.

14. Example: In an English-language-arts class, students may be asked to write personal writing goals for an essay, and the teacher then gives feedback about progress, highlighting strengths and areas of growth.

15. Generating and testing hypotheses: This strategy encourages students to formulate and test hypotheses as a method for developing critical-thinking skills.

16. Example: In a math class, students have found through guided discovery a working formula for finding the area of a parallelogram. They then test this hypothesis to see if the formula works for all parallelograms.

17. Cues, questions, and advance organizers: Teachers use cues and questions that emphasize key concepts, with an emphasis on prioritizing essential information and allowing ample wait time for students to process information.

18. Example: In a math class, the teacher uses an advance organizer to introduce a new concept, providing students with a framework for organizing their thoughts before using the framework on a set of problems.

Discourse Practices

Research about how we use discourse, or talk, in classrooms has evolved over recent decades. The shift of classrooms from teacher directed to student centered has demanded change in pedagogical practices to better foster student learning. Here we dig into several quintessential frameworks that underpin the contemporary structures we use to increase the cognitive demand and rigor of our instructional design as well as classroom conversations. We then explore strategies for practical application. To set context, we will explore Bloom's taxonomy (revised) and **Webb's Depth of Knowledge (DOK)** as frameworks for promoting rigorous discourse practices.

BLOOM'S TAXONOMY

Bloom's revised taxonomy provides an updated model of Benjamin Bloom's original framework describing a progression of cognitive processes. The updated version encompasses a more diverse set of these cognitive processes, with an emphasis on critical thinking, problem-solving, and creativity in learning. The Vanderbilt Teaching Center (2023) provides a helpful graphic, as seen in Figure 9.4, to show the progression in rigor from the bottom layer, "remember," to the upper tip of the pyramid, "create." This is a valuable tool for educators not only to structure assessments but also to implement curriculum. Meaningful discussions come from the promotion of higher-order thinking skills. As students progress through the taxonomy, they develop the ability to articulate ideas, analyze complex concepts, evaluate different perspectives, and construct and express their own knowledge, which then enhances comprehension and retention of content.

Bloom's Taxonomy

Create — Produce new or original work
Design, assemble, conjecture, develop, formulate, investigate

Evaluate — Justify a stand or decision
appraise, argue, defend, judge, select, support, value, critique

Analyze — Draw connections among ideas
differentiate, organize, compare, distinguish, experiment

Apply — Use information in new situations
solve, use, demonstrate, operate, sketch

Understand — Explain ideas or concepts
classify, explain, recognize, select

Remember — Recall facts and concepts
define, list, memorize, state

Figure 9.4 Revised Bloom's Taxonomy Inspired by the Vanderbilt University Center for Teaching.

WEBB'S DEPTH OF KNOWLEDGE

A related framework is Webb's Depth of Knowledge, which is a useful tool in designing cognitively demanding tasks. While this section is focused primarily on the discourse of the classroom, we think it is important to consider the framing of the activities used in classrooms in line with how discussion is then fostered. Figure 9.5 details the focus of the four Depth of Knowledge levels: recall/reproduce, skill/concept, strategic thinking, and extending thinking.

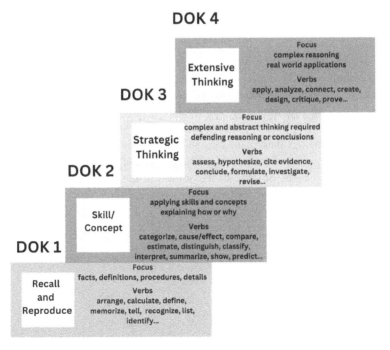

Figure 9.5 Webb's Depth of Knowledge Framework. Created by authors

Pause and Reflect: Look at both the revised Bloom's taxonomy and Webb's Depth of Knowledge frameworks closely, with special attention to the verbs used in each model. Where do you see alignment? Where do you see differences? How do you think these might help you in crafting questions to engage learners?

QUESTIONING STRATEGIES

Now that we have the basics of these two frameworks, let's think about how to use question stems to bolster the rigor of our lessons. In traditional direct instruction, much of the conversation in classrooms would be in what we refer to as an initiate, response, evaluate (IRE) structure. Take, for example, an interchange like this:

Mr. Rogers: "Tommy, what is one cause of the American civil war?"

Tommy: "Economic differences."

Mr. Rogers: "Good job."

This simple bidirectional conversation is between a teacher and one student rather than emphasizing more collective and collaborative discourse. Good teachers know how to use a variety of question structures in a myriad of ways to include more students in the conversation and at a deeper level. While there will certainly be a time and place in most lessons to include remember and recall types of questions, most of our questions should push students a bit more to engage in more meaningful thinking about content. Teachers categorize questions into low- and high-level questions. Low-level questions are usually from the remember and understand levels of Bloom's taxonomy; some are from the apply level. These questions might be aimed at establishing student comprehension, be used as a diagnostic tool to evaluate student strengths and weaknesses, or be used to review content. The high-level questions are more oriented toward the analyze, evaluate, and create levels. These questions are targeted to encourage more critical thinking and problem-solving, and they may spur more discussions.

To get an idea of what these questions may look like, see Table 9.4, which has examples of questions stemming at each level of Bloom's taxonomy.

As teachers develop lesson plans, especially in the beginning, scripting can be a useful (albeit sometimes painful to use) tool to ensure the implementation of good questioning to support student learning. Things for teachers to ask themselves include the following: What is the purpose of the questions? Can I phrase questions that trigger more than yes or no answers to extend the content focus of my question? One of us likes to script high-level questions out initially, then predict student responses, and then script additional questions that then scaffold the learning for students through reinforcement or probing questions.

Table 9.4 Question Stems for Bloom's Taxonomy

Bloom's Level	Possible Question Stems
Remember	Describe what happens when_____. How would you identify_____? How would you define_____? How would you recognize_____? List the _____ in order. What do you remember about_____? What/where/when/who/how is (are) _____? Which one_____? Why did _____?
Understand	Elaborate on_____. How can you describe_____? How would you compare/contrast_____? How would you differentiate between_____ and _____? How would you generalize_____? What can you infer from_____? What did you observe_____? What is the main idea of _____? What would happen if _____?
Apply	How would you develop_____? How would you modify_____? How would you demonstrate_____? How would you solve_____? What examples can you find that _____? What other way would you choose to ____? Why does _____ work?
Analyze	Discuss the pros and cons of _____. How is _____ connected to _____? How would you explain _____? What are the advantages and disadvantages of _____? What can you infer _____? What can you point out about _____? What evidence can you find that _____? What ideas support_____? What is your analysis of _____? Why do you think _____?
Evaluate	Create a ___ to explain_____. Devise a way to_____. How would you generate a plan to_____? How would you improve_____? What alternative would you suggest for____? What could you invent_____? What would happen if _____?
Create	Determine the value of _____. How could you verify_____? How would you determine which facts_____? How would you grade_____? Rank the importance of _____. Rate the _____. Explain your rating. What choice would you have made_____? Explain your reasoning. What criteria would you use to assess_____? What data were used to evaluate_____? What information would you use to prioritize_____? What is the most important_____? Tell me why. What is your favorite_____? Why? What would you suggest_____? What is your opinion of _____? Support your response.

Here Holly shares an example of one of her math lessons, one in which she asks scripted questions, using a scaffolded approach.

> In my math classroom I like for students to explore visual patterns that can build the foundation for understanding linear and quadratic functions. This task below is one of the first tasks I use in the linear function unit, and the instructional goal is very exploratory in nature—I want to understand how students see patterns and help them make connections between visual and algebraic representations of those patterns. Students are given this [See Figure 9.6].
>
> The task itself has several open-ended questions built in, but I need to think about how my students may respond and think through the kinds of reinforcement and probing they need to make the necessary connections. Here is what I do. I look at the first question in the task "Describe a pattern you see in the cube building," and I try to think through the different ways my students may visualize that task. Some may see the original cube from building one and then a "growing" arm of the same side in five directions, noting that the length of the arm is equal to the building number ($5n+1$). Other students may see five equal-size arms but then a need to take away the "overlap" on that center cube. Then, another pathway is that students may find a pattern and create the expression $4(n - 1) + n$ where $4(n - 1)$ represents the number of cubes in the four visible arms and n is the number of blocks in the center tower. So here I think about what I want to know from my students as they begin working, knowing that some of my students will be instantly ready to create these expressions while others may struggle to get started or to be able to think of ways to represent their thinking.
>
> So, I might ask a student struggling to get started, "What do you notice? How many cubes are in each of the buildings?" Then to keep them moving forward, I ask questions to advance their thinking, such as "Where do you 'see' the building growing? What is not changing from one building to the next? Is there a strategy you can use to track your thinking?"
>
> I hope they might use a table to track their thinking. If so, I may assess their understanding with questions like, "How did you find your table values? What patterns do you notice?" And then I try to push them further by validating them and advancing them: "You said it adds five each time . . . but what if you do not know the building number?"
>
> For students who quickly get to an expression, my questions need to vary to push them to make the mathematical connections. I assess what they know with questions like, "How did you get this expression? Explain what each term of your expression represents in the buildings." And then I might advance their thinking by asking, "How does the length of an arm relate to the building number? Can you simplify your expressions? Can you relate your simplified expression to the buildings?"
>
> Note that all these questions are for one lesson and one task. But also notice, who is doing the work? Who is doing the thinking? Students are. My job is to have them actively engaged so that they are the ones making the connections through the facilitation of my questioning. While it would be much easier for me to just tell them if they do not notice automatically, it is much more powerful for the connections to be made by students.

MIDDLE SCHOOL CURRICULUM AND PEDAGOGY 189

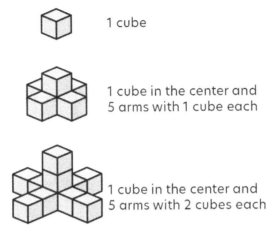

Study the sequence of cube building shown. What pattern do you notice?

Use the pattern to construct the next building in the sequence.

Think about your steps as you construct your building. The labels show one way you might think about the pattern.

a. Describe a pattern you see in the cube buildings.

b. Use your pattern to write an expression for the number of cubes in the nth building where n is an integer.

c. Use your expression to find the number of cubes in the 5th building.

e. Look for a different pattern in the buildings. Describe the pattern, and use it to write a different expression for the number of cubes in the nth building.

From *Connected Mathematics*® 4 (Phillips et al., 2025) Reprinted with permission.

Figure 9.6 Counting Cubes Task. From Connected Mathematics® 4 (Phillips et al., 2025). Reprinted with permission.

Practice It: Here is a set of tasks, one from each content area. You may use these or create your own. Choose the task for your content area, and design scripted questions you could use when implementing this lesson. If possible, try your questions out with a peer who can then give you feedback.

- **Math:** Create your own proportional relationship. Create a poster with a context, a table, a graph, and a word problem to show a real-world proportional relationship.

- **Science:** Introduce the concept of climate change, explaining the long-term shifts in temperature, precipitation patterns, and other aspects affected by human activity and natural processes. Lead a whole-group conversation, followed by small-group exploration and research.

- **Social studies:** Students explore the results of the 2016 presidential election and analyze the differences between the results of the popular vote and the results from the electoral college, using these resources. Explain to students how the electoral college works, and use resources such as the following: https://www.fec.gov/introduction-campaign-finance/election-results-and-voting-information/ and https://www.archives.gov/electoral-college. Then facilitate a debate among students about whether we should keep or change our electoral college structure.

English language arts: In a unit focused on author's craft, students read "Lamb to the Slaughter" by Roald Dahl. (It can be found here for free: https://theshortstory.co.uk/devsitegkl/wp-content/uploads/2015/06/Short-stories-Roald-Dhal-Lamb-to-the-Slaughter.pdf.) The focus is to first investigate what the author did to orchestrate how the reader experiences the story. Irony is used as the primary figurative language technique. Create a graphic organizer or activity to help students identify how irony is developed throughout the text.

To conclude this chapter, let's revisit our learning outcomes.

1. **Develop the ability to collaboratively create a cohesive curriculum plan for the academic year, ensuring a logical progression of learning.** Planning is a complex process of developing both long- and short-term goals. Teachers must first understand the standards and objectives across content areas. Then, they use logical progressions and sequencing to develop yearly plans. This process requires flexibility to tailor plans to individual learners while ensuring alignment with assessments and instructional goals.

2. **Explore the concept of designing lessons by starting with clear learning outcomes and working backward to create purposeful activities and assessments.** A learning objective should focus on student performance (e.g., knowledge/skill acquisition or reinforcement). What is it that your students should be able to do at the end of the class session and course that they could not do before? It is important to make clear the intended learning outcome rather than what form the instruction will take.

3. **Identify appropriate instructional strategies to support student learning.** There are many instructional strategies to use with students, and each has a time and a place to best support students. When teaching an explicit skill or strategy, direct instruction may be the best choice. At other times, we want students to explore and investigate, and more indirect methods, such as project-based learning or experiential learning, may be more appropriate.

4. **Develop skills for facilitating and engaging in productive whole-group discussions, fostering critical thinking, classroom discourse, and questioning techniques.** Good teachers know how to use a variety of question structures in a myriad of ways to include more students in the conversation and at a deeper level. While there will undoubtedly be a time and place in most lessons to include remember and recall questions, most of our questions should push students to engage in meaningful thinking about content.

Suggested Readings and Resources

https://education.illinoisstate.edu/downloads/casei/5-02-Revised%20Blooms.pdf
https://www.lessonplanningwithpurpose.com/.
Farber, K., & Bishop, P. (2018). Service learning in the middle grades: Learning by doing and caring. *RMLE Online*, *41*(2), 1–15. https://doi.org/10.1080/19404476.2017.1415600.

References

Anderson, L. W., & Krathwohl, D. R. (Eds.). (2001). *A taxonomy for learning, teaching and assessing: A revision of Bloom's taxonomy of educational outcomes: Complete edition*. Longman.

Armstrong, P. (2010). Bloom's taxonomy. Vanderbilt University Center for Teaching. Retrieved October 28, 2023, from https://cft.vanderbilt.edu/guides-sub-pages/blooms-taxonomy/.

Association for Middle Level Education. (n.d.). *Curriculum integration*. Retrieved July 12, 2024, from https://www.amle.org/curriculum integration/#:~:text=An%20integrative%20curriculum%20focuses%20on,rigorous%2C%20in%2Ddepth%20study.

Bishop, P. A., & Harrison, L. M. (2021). *The successful middle school: This we believe*. Association for Middle Level Education.

Bowen, R. S. (2017). Understanding by design. Vanderbilt University Center for Teaching. Retrieved November 21, 2023, from https://cft.vanderbilt.edu/understanding-by-design/.

Marzano, R. J., Pickering, D., & Pollock, J. E. (2001). *Classroom instruction that works: Research-based strategies for increasing student achievement*. Association for Supervision and Curriculum Development.

National Middle School Association & Believe, T. W. (2010). *Keys to educating young adolescents*. National Middle School Association.

CHAPTER 10

Differentiating Instruction for All Learners

Learning Outcomes:

1. Understand the concept of differentiated instruction, and recognize different ways to differentiate instruction, based on product, process, content, or learning environment.

2. Identify strategies for differentiated instruction (tiered assignments, flexible grouping, etc.).

3. Apply differentiated instruction principles: practice lesson-plan design to incorporate strategies (lesson complexity, multiple-pathways-of-mastery demonstration, individual learning goals, etc.).

Basics of Differentiation

Differentiated instruction is based on the principle of **responsiveness**. Being responsive means that we are meeting our students where they are and utilizing practical strategies to move students forward in their understanding. To differentiate well, teachers must consider several factors beyond simply what they are teaching. They must also consider who they are teaching and how they can build a productive learning environment in which those students can thrive. In this chapter, we explore the basic principles of differentiation and tackle some misconceptions and myths along the way. We will then begin to explore adaptable differentiation strategies to utilize in the middle school setting across content areas. We will build a toolkit for you to take into your classroom and utilize in a variety of ways to best support your students.

Carol Ann Tomlinson has spent her career studying differentiated instruction (Tomlinson, 2003, 2014, 2017, 2023). Her research has identified several factors related to the implementation and effectiveness of differentiation. Teachers must consider the student: their **interests**, **learning needs**, and **readiness** for instruction. Students come to school with their own individual curiosities and passions and can discover new curiosities and passions. Connecting instruction to students' interests enhances students' intrinsic motivation and persistence and provides them with content to stimulate their natural curiosities. Learning needs reflect how students learn best and most efficiently. And readiness for instruction reflects what a student already knows and can do at that time. Tomlinson describes differentiation as a clockwork of cogs, emphasizing the interrelatedness of elements for effective differentiation. These cogs represent what the student seeks, how the teacher responds, and the use of curriculum and instruction as the vehicle for differentiating instruction. What students seek includes a sense of belonging (affirmation): feeling safe and accepted and knowing that their perspectives and interests are welcome in our classrooms. They want to feel that they are connected to others, that they have a place in the community (contribution), and that there is significance in those contributions (purpose). Students also want some sense of choice and dependable pathways to being successful (power). Then, students want to feel a sense of accomplishment from their success in doing the challenging work they do (challenge). Complementary to these elements is how teachers respond to students. This includes establishing a sense of respect for students, creating an atmosphere in which students know that this community is theirs and that they are valuable (invitation). There is a sense that the activities within the classroom are worthy and important and will also push students to grow (opportunity). Teachers work hard to support students and help them succeed (investment) and will encourage students to continually grow and adapt pathways, as needed (persistence). For teachers, there is emphasis on being a reflective practitioner and continuously evaluating how things are working and how it can be better (reflection). The last cog focuses on how curriculum and instruction are the vehicle. Here, we must recognize that what we study is foundational to becoming expert in a particular discipline (important), and we must make explicit to both the teacher and the student how what we study builds capacity for understanding and particular skills (focused). For students to get the most of what they are studying, they need to be able to find meaning in the work by seeing its value (engaging), and the content needs to push students and emphasize growth (demanding). For students to be successful, teachers need to use various strategies, including both large- and small-group instruction, modeling, and materials, among other things, to support students, and teachers must define clear criteria for success (scaffolded). These cogs work together to build a differentiated classroom where both students and teachers flourish. In line with principles of middle level education, a differentiated classroom recognizes that students must feel valued and cared for before they can concentrate on academics.

Students' most basic needs for physical and social safety must be met for learning to occur. Safety depends on the creation of classroom community and building norms for students to feel supported and validated. Research in recent decades has focused on student mindset, specifically growth mindset. Carol Dweck (2006) and Jo Boaler (2022) encourage educators to harness the power of the plasticity of the brain by having students shift the way they think about their own abilities and talents to see a pathway toward understanding. This is particularly important in differentiating instruction. If teachers are not adjusting their instruction according to students' readiness for example, some students will be bored as they are not being challenged, while another part of the class will feel stressed and unable to learn because the content feels inaccessible. Gregory and Chapman (2013) explain that approximately one quarter of our students will learn "in spite of us" as they are the students who naturally arrive to school enthusiastic and ready to learn, regardless of what strategies and approaches a teacher might use. Almost a quarter of our students are identified with exceptionalities and need additional resources to support those exceptionalities. The learning of the remaining half of our students is significantly affected by the strategies and approaches toward effective instruction we use.

WHAT DIFFERENTIATION IS . . . AND ISN'T

Teachers, particularly beginning teachers, may feel overwhelmed by the prospect of differentiating instruction to support each student. A common misconception about differentiation is that it means that a teacher needs to have individualized lesson plans for each student. Quite the contrary, it simply means that teachers need to have a range of approaches for instruction so that all students can find a good fit for their needs. Differentiation in many ways aligns with the best practices that are advocated for by leading organizations in each content area. For example, the NSTA (National Science Teacher Association) emphasizes **inquiry-based instruction**, which includes project-based learning and explorations through inquiry-guided activities, which are differentiated-instruction strategies. The NCTM (National Council of Teachers of Mathematics) focuses on problem-based learning where students engage with novel, real-world problems with an emphasis on multiple entry points and multiple solution pathways. The NCSS (National Council for the Social Studies) employs inquiry-based processes as well as data collection and analysis for students to become active problem solvers as members of a global community. The vision of the NCTE (National Council of Teachers of English) is focused on students as critical thinkers, consumers, and creators who work toward making the world a better place. Regardless of content areas, we are advocating for what is already best practice in teaching, and we just need to hone our craft by utilizing these practices well. Following is a definition of what differentiation is and isn't:

Differentiation *is* a philosophy of teaching that is based on implementing effective practice for learning.

It *is not* just a set of quick-fix strategies that can be arbitrarily applied.

Differentiation *is* responsive instruction.

It *is not* an individualized lesson plan for each student.

Differentiation *is* data-informed practice. Teachers analyze evidence of learning and make instructional adjustments as needed.

It *is not* an activity randomly applied *nor* is it necessary every day.

Differentiation *is* a pathway to grade-level standards.

It *is not* a way to "dumb down" curriculum.

Differentiation *is* for *all* learners.

It *is not* only for struggling learners.

Adapted from Doubet & Hockett, 2015

There are several sets of elements to consider when planning for differentiation. One set of elements relates to our driving force—the students and their readiness, interests, and learning profiles. We will explore how each of these interrelates to how we differentiate instruction. The second set of elements relates to what and how we differentiate. We can differentiate the content, the process, or the product. For example, we may differentiate the content, based on student readiness. Perhaps we give a **preassessment** and find varying needs among students. We then adjust some activities so that groups of students are working on the skills they need to move forward. More often, the content stays the same for all students, but we give options for what product students create to prove mastery of that content. These are the strategies we will explore below with general templates and specific classroom examples.

Pause and Reflect: Think back to your middle school experience. Based on this brief introduction, can you identify ways your teachers may have used differentiation strategies? What were those experiences—how did they help you as a learner? How about your peers?

STUDENTS: THE WHO OF DIFFERENTIATION

Readiness

Readiness is about tasks being closely aligned to a student's skill and understanding. For students to learn and grow, we want the tasks they engage in to be just *slightly* out of reach of their *current* skill level and understanding. We then provide scaffolds to help students incrementally reach just a bit higher until they have fully mastered the content. Doubet and Hockett (2015) define readiness as "where a student is in his or her grasp of learning goals at a certain point in time, according to recently gathered formative assessment data that are relevant to those goals" (p. 177). To accurately know your students' readiness and to ensure that your students are getting the content they need when they need it, you should consistently use data collection and monitoring. This requires the intentional use of preassessments. Most often preassessments are like **summative assessments** but with a quite different purpose . . . and that purpose is pattern sniffing. Let's say Ms. Edwards, an eight-grade math teacher, is starting a unit on linear functions. For students to be successful in this unit, they need to successfully identify proportional relationships, identify dependent and independent variables, work with one- and two-step equations, and interpret points on graphs. These are *some* of the prerequisite tasks that students should have mastered in seventh grade.

A solid preassessment assesses subtasks related to each of those prerequisite tasks and some of the grade-level tasks related to those standards. Then, as Ms. Edwards looks at the student responses, she is not assigning a grade or *evaluating* per se. Instead, she is looking for any patterns in gaps students might have (which she can then later target in a small-group lesson during a **center/station** lesson), and she is looking for strengths students may already have for the upcoming unit. Ms. Edwards then designs appropriate tasks for *all* students to meet their current needs. Several strategies that are particularly useful for differentiating based on readiness are **tiered assignments** and **learning contracts** (menus, choice boards, etc.). We will give more detailed examples of those later in this chapter. A brief example will suffice for now. Perhaps, based on observations or previous assignments, Ms. Edwards knows her students need a range of reading materials. She then creates QR codes or has folders with appropriately leveled readings, and she tells each student or group which one to use. Many teachers worry about the potential stigma caused by having students working on different tasks and being labeled as "smart" or "dumb." If not responsibly managed, this certainly can be a problem. A teacher can avoid such a problem if there is a classroom norm that the teacher takes the job seriously to ensure that all students are getting what they need when they need it. And that students see and believe it. Building strong relationships and trust with students is key. If this practice is developed and consistent throughout the year, it is very possible to get students to buy in, particularly if the teacher works to give students specific feedback on their learning. This helps develop a growth mindset in students and has the potential to encourage students' own intrinsic motivation.

Student Interest

Wise teachers know the power of an engaging lesson. For students to be engaged, they need to find meaning in their work. We know that adolescents thrive when given voice and choice in some capacity in their work. We also know that working from an assets-based perspective and tapping into students' strengths can be immensely powerful. Teachers need to invest in getting to know their students so that they know what interests students have and use those interests to engage them meaningfully with content. This can take many forms, and many of them are simple. A simple example is, instead of using whatever generic formulated word problems are in, say, a given mathematics curriculum, to transform those tasks to represent what students already have interest in. It is knowing that Khalil really loves mountain biking and that he particularly likes the Bob Gnarly trail and then using that context to get him to look at the relationship between speed and distance on a graph. That simple change may hook Khalil and Khalil's like-minded buddies just by engaging their personal interests. Similar tailoring can be done in various subjects and to many interests. A more complex plan would be to tailor an entire project of independent investigation to student interests and to align instruction to the standards and learning goals identified by the teacher. In a unit on nonfiction, while the entire class is required to read and utilize skills to comprehend what they read and then create a written product meeting specific writing goals, students could choose *what* they read to then support their writing.

Tomlinson (2017) outlines five specific goals for differentiating by interest:

(1) helping students realize that there is a match between school and their own desires to learn,

(2) demonstrating the interconnectedness of all learning,

(3) using skills or ideas familiar to students as a bridge to ideas or skills less familiar to them,

(4) helping students develop competency and autonomy as learners, and

(5) enhancing student success. (p. 97)

If a teacher designs a unit of study in which students can explore content standards and learning goals through a topic of choice related to their interests, the teacher has checked off all five of these goals. This may feel like a big ask, and no one expects teachers to have this option *all* the time. This is something to aim for in the journey toward becoming a master teacher. Remember that small adjustments make an impact as well. Ultimately, if we are keeping our focus on students and actively thinking about engaging the specific students in front of us, we are on the right track.

Learning Profile

Early work on differentiated instruction put emphasis on learning styles and **multiple intelligences**. What we have found over time is that, while these ideas have some conceptual merit, overgeneralization of learning styles is dangerous as it pigeonholes students into a particular style rather than recognizes that all learners will make connections in a variety of ways. In Chapter 1, we discussed the theme that young adolescents are constructors of their own knowledge. What we know from research is that students learn by actively making connections in working memory, utilizing strategies to connect previously learned knowledge with new knowledge. What varies from individual to individual is what parts of the learning environment the student pays attention to, which is primarily tied to the student's interests or to what teachers can get the student interested in, and the student's prior content knowledge, which is already stored in the student's long-term memory. If we prioritize singular learning "styles," we lower the number of connections that students make in their working memory. That leads to brittle forms of knowledge. If a student thinks that her learning style is "visual," and she only uses visual methods to try to understand things, then she will not be able to make connections when presented with something not visual, thus limiting her capacity as a learner instead of growing and translating that understanding to new situations. Studies have tried to measure learning styles and link them to better learning, but those studies have been unable to do so reliably. Leaning from a **constructivist view of learning**, we capitalize on students experiencing a variety of styles (visual, tactile, auditory, etc.), as this will lead to broader, richer, and more robust learning (Willingham, 2018).

THE WHAT AND THE HOW OF DIFFERENTIATION

Content

When we refer to content, we are referring to what we teach and what we want students to learn. There are two ways to think about differentiating content: "(1) as adapting what we teach or want students to learn or (2) as adapting how we give students access to what we teach or want them to learn" (Tomlinson, 2017, p. 124). When possible, we want the "what" students are learning to remain the same—all students should have access to the same content. But how we give access to that content may change, depending on the individual needs of students. In particular cases, when students have a gap in skills, we may choose to alter what content students engage with. For example, in a unit on integers, we may choose a set of whole-number problems for struggling students to work with while we give advanced learners a set that includes rational numbers. While the objective of learning operations with positive and negative numbers remains the same, some students are progressing toward the objective of operations with rational numbers while other students are solidifying understanding of the basic skill first.

Process

Differentiating the learning process applies to how students make sense of information. When differentiating process, we think about offering a variety of modalities for students to demonstrate their understanding. These modalities should have a range of sophistication and potentially different time spans. There may be a variety of peer-support options built in as well. If a teacher is differentiating process based on readiness, students may all be creating a writing product, but multiple versions of directions are given to students. One version might have more structure and scaffolds in place, like a template; another may have a checklist of what is needed; and a third might include an additional push to meet more rigorous expectations. If a teacher is targeting student interest or learning profiles, the instructional emphasis will be on giving choices of a particular slice of the content. In a science unit on disease, some students may prefer to look at a more historical perspective on bubonic plague while others may be more interested in the COVID-19 pandemic.

Product

Tomlinson (2017) describes three ways of differentiating products, ways for students to demonstrate what they are learning: sense-making activities, **performance tasks/assessments**, and products. Sense-making activities are formative in nature and require students to make, complete, or write something about a snippet of content that may have been presented over a day or two of instruction. The use of exit tickets is an example of this approach. These activities are not to be graded but are data points teachers use to get a pulse on what students know and can do. It is also an opportunity for teachers to give feedback to students to continue their progress toward mastery.

Performance tasks or assessments are more summative in nature (used at the end of or even the midpoint of a unit) and are graded. The expectations at this point are that students have had the opportunity to master the content and that this task allows students to demonstrate their understanding. A product may encompass a large chunk of learning and has almost infinite possibilities for students. Products work best as mechanisms for capitalizing on student interest and enthusiasm to help students find an option that they are hooked on. It is important to make sure that the product has the possibility for demonstrating mastery of the essential knowledge of the unit. Having clear expectations for products is key to success. When you begin working in the realm of products, start simply and offer only two or three main options. Then work to differentiate for individuals, as needed. Eventually (especially if this is a regular practice in your classroom), you may be able to open the door for students to suggest potential projects and fit them into your existing expectations and structures. The basic structure you will need to do this well is to first establish what knowledge, understanding, and skills are to be demonstrated. Then you may establish what expressions are to be utilized (media presentation, written product, etc.), and then, finally, you may determine what support structures students will need to accomplish their creations. To get creative juices flowing, Table 10.1 has just a few ideas of the kinds of products students might develop.

Table 10.1 Examples of Products

Action Verb	Product
Create	A photo essay, cartoons, an art exhibit, a podcast, a multimedia presentation, a dictionary
Design/develop/plan	A product, a website or app, a puppet show, learning centers for peers, a solution to a community issue, a blog, an advertising campaign, a class, a mock trial
Write	A biography, a set of poetry, a new law, a musical, an article, a letter to editor

Strategies for Differentiation

While we clearly argue that differentiation is not a set of random strategies that you implement at ambiguous points, we do want to offer a set of core differentiated-instruction strategies that can be implemented across grade levels and content areas. These intentional strategies can provide a toolkit to help make grade-level content accessible for struggling learners while also stretching and pushing advanced learners. Keep in mind that these strategies, just like differentiated instruction itself, are not one size fits all—they will need to be adapted, based on your comfort with implementation, to your set of students and to your content area.

It is possible at this point to be conceptually on board with this idea but still to feel overwhelmed by the logistics of making differentiation happen. That is okay. Differentiated instruction is an approach, a set of skills that teachers continue to hone as they work toward becoming a master teacher. In the meantime, know that there are many of what Tomlinson refers to as "low prep" differentiation strategies that will help build a journey into differentiation with small steps, as listed in Table 10.2.

There are entire books written on the topic of differentiation, and several of them, referenced at the end of this chapter, are worth a look. For our purposes here, we will introduce a set of tried-and-true core differentiation strategies to start building a toolkit beyond the low-prep tools listed above. In Table 10.3 is a list of **high-prep differentiation strategies**. The ones in bold will be a core set of foundational strategies that we will explore more deeply with classroom examples.

Table 10.2 Low-Prep Differentiation Strategies

Low-Prep Category	Low-Prep Differentiation Strategies
Choice and variation	Choices of reading, variation of collaboration (independent, peer-group work, competition), variation of writing prompts, variation of pacing, etc.
Materials	Materials in first language, materials with depth and breadth to support differing readiness, inclusive materials, etc.
Discussions	Varied complexity in questioning, inviting multiple perspectives, collaborative teacher/student goal setting, small-group sharing like think-pair share.
Reading support	Front-loading of vocabulary, range of materials at varied reading levels, online resources with varied Lexile levels, word maps, story sentence and paragraph frames, podcasts with scripts for reading comprehension, etc.
Miscellaneous strategies	Flexible seating, games and apps for skill mastery, range of media, open-ended activities, minilessons for reteach/extend, variety of options for expressing mastery of content, etc.

Source: Adapted from Tomlinson (2017)

Table 10.3 High-Prep Differentiation Strategies

High-Prep Differentiation Category	High-Prep Differentiation Ideas
Centers/stations	Interest-based centers, differentiated learning centers
Learning contracts	**Menus**, bingo boards, Think-Tac-Toe
In-class tasks and tools	Jigsaws, **RAFTS assignments**, specialty/expert groups, **flexible grouping**, complex instruction/group-worthy tasks, **literature circles**, graphic organizers, **tiered activities, compacting, varied questions, journaling**
Inquiry-based learning approaches	Long-term explorations based on student interest, problem-based learning, project-based learning

Source: Adapted from Tomlinson, 2017

FLEXIBLE GROUPING

To begin, let's think about some consistent models that could be embedded into your teaching routine. One model to consider is the use of **flexible grouping**. Flexible grouping is the intentional pre-planned use of a variety of grouping structures so that students can work with other students who are most like themselves, with other students who are most dissimilar from themselves, and even by themselves at various points within a unit of instruction. These groups are formed based on student readiness, student interest, or a specific approach to learning. The most important attribute of flexible grouping is . . . flexibility. If, for example, students are first placed in homogeneous groups, based on readiness, at the beginning of a unit of instruction, so that the teacher can work specifically with that small group on a particular skill, then, later in the unit, the teacher should utilize a heterogeneous grouping strategy, based on student interest. There are several important reasons for this practice. For one, we do not want to encourage any sort of tracking, where students are organized into groups that are based on leveled ability and have no opportunity to grow out of that group. We also want our students to build community with their *entire* community, so we want them working with different peers along the way. This encourages collaboration and communication among students. We also want students to be able to select their groups and work independently.

CENTER OR STATION TEACHING

High-quality middle level instruction in all content areas should use various modalities and arrangements of instructional segments. Let's start by thinking about a tangible example of contemporary middle school teaching. Long gone are the days of straight rows of desks and fifty-minute lectures. We know that many adolescents will not have the stamina to sit and listen and absorb information this way. Frankly, even adults struggle with that kind of attention stamina. Therefore, we need to explore a variety of arrangements that foster differentiated instructional models. Whole-group instruction is one of the primary ways we instruct, but there are many ways to facilitate this. Whole-group instruction methods include introductions to topics/skills, classroom discussions and sharing of ideas, modeling of ideas, activation of prior knowledge, other pre-assessments that are based on readiness or interest, and wrapping up a lesson. Other methods to mix with whole-group instruction include shared reading in small groups (pairs, triads, or quads), task exploration, inquiry, and collaborative sense making. Individual or personalized activities, with opportunities to practice or apply skills, including independent-inquiry, assessment, homework, and reading skills, are also important. Teacher-to-student conferences provide another arrangement that is helpful for mentoring and troubleshooting students' individual needs or for getting a pulse on what students know through **formative assessments**. Not all these structures must be used on any single day, but teachers should try to think flexibly about how using several methods could provide personalized instruction in a flexible way.

Remember elementary classrooms and parts of the day where small groups were rotating through centers? Sometimes students worked with the teacher, sometimes students were doing a computer activity individually, and, maybe, the rest of the time students were working on a math game with a partner? This structure disappears from classrooms by middle school . . . But look back to those instructional arrangements, and think how beautiful it could be to start a lesson with a short whole-group instruction session—a mini lesson or an activation of prior knowledge—followed by students working through a rotation (not necessarily in the span of one lesson; it might take two or three days). Every student gets either some one-on-one time or small-group time with the teacher, some time to collaborate with peers on a structured activity, and independent time in which they are practicing or working on an independent-inquiry project. When done well, this can all occur seamlessly and simultaneously. Centers, or station teaching, is absolutely appropriate for the middle school classroom.

Let's think of the power this has. In a fifty-minute class that is primarily teacher-led whole-group instruction, what do we often see? The same handful of active participants volunteers to answer questions, and a handful of students is completely disengaged or off task. If we ask ourselves at any given moment what *each* student understands, do we have a deep sense of the individual differences in understanding within our class? But if, at least once a week, teachers have the opportunity to engage with students, either one on one or in small groups, teachers are much more likely to have a strong indication of each of the student's progress, and, if teachers have structured the activities well, students are also having some voice, choice, and autonomy (which as we know from other chapters in this book are a big deal to adolescents). Station teaching is just one of many strategies we can use to differentiate.

LEARNING CONTRACTS, CHOICE BOARDS, AND MENUS

Learning contracts have many names, including choice boards, menus, bingo boards, Think-Tac-Toe, **Layered Curriculum**®, and other creative names. At their core, these options are just that—options. The central ideas are to identify the key content or standards that you want students to demonstrate mastery of and to design choices within a clear structure for students to display their knowledge and understanding. The structure of a menu or a Think-Tac-Toe board is that, while choice is built into the experience, the choices are designed and constrained by the teacher to ensure that students are indeed engaging in the specific content that they need to master. The possibilities for these methods are endless, and the teacher's work is mostly frontloaded

204 CHAPTER 10

so that, during implementation, teachers can work one on one with students and can act as facilitators.

Here we share examples from Amanda Clapp's science classroom. Amanda is a master-level teacher (see her teacher profile in Chapter 1), and menus and contracts are a regular part of her practice. First, we share a menu that is set up with links for students to navigate to activities. In this example, students choose one appetizer that is based on learning vocabulary through two different modalities. In the main dish, students choose two options to explore a variety of problems related to the standards, and then finally comes dessert. In this case, students are doing some summary or application, depending on their menu options. Figure 10.1 shows the structure of this menu and can be used as a template for endless choices.

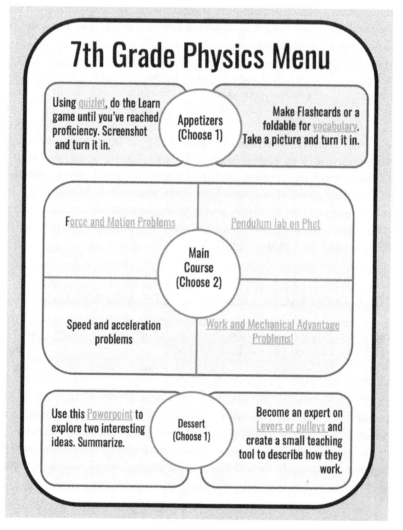

Figure 10.1 7th grade physics menu. Amanda Clapp

DIFFERENTIATING INSTRUCTION FOR ALL LEARNERS 205

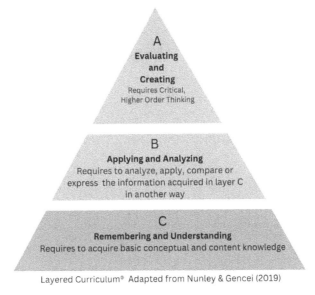

Figure 10.2 *Layers in Layered Curriculum®*. Created by authors

Another example is the use of Layered Curriculum®, a method invented by Kathy Nunley in the 1980s. It uses the basic structure of menu boards. Nunley's model is based on three concepts: choice, **higher-order thinking**, and **student autonomy** and accountability. Three layers of tasks are given, with each layer differing in complexity. Students then choose options at each layer, based on their interests, readiness, or learning approach. Students are accountable for their own learning in this approach. The layers of tasks are organized based on **Bloom's taxonomy** and go from easier to more difficult or, in other words, from more concrete to more abstract. This gives students multiple pathways to achieve the same learning goals in different modalities. Figure 10.2 highlights the layers and associated skills.

Here, we provide another example from Amanda Clapp's classroom. This layered curriculum is an adaptation from Nunley's original structure but with core principles intact. Amanda's unit is on classification of matter for eighth graders. There is a central idea, based on a state standard, and then **I-can statement** objectives for students to explore. The activities are then clustered, and options are given of how many activities from each cluster students should choose. Be mindful that the "clusters" are aligned by content and complexity so that students are choosing things that match similar goals. Figures 10.3 and 10.4 show the entire layered curriculum unit.

Matter Layered Curriculum

8.P.1.1 Classify matter as elements, compounds, or mixtures based on how the atoms are packed together in arrangements.

OBJECTIVE	First Ranking/ Date	Final Ranking/ Date
I can describe the structure of an atom		
I can explain how the atom takes up space and has mass		

3 Layer (Choose any of the options to add up to 50 points)

- ☐ Mini Lecture Wednesday (*Required*). Take notes.   10 pts

- ☐ Matter Inquiry Lab with ONE partner   10 pts

- ☐ Crash Course: https://www.youtube.com/watch?v=ELchwUIIWa8&feature=youtu.be
    - Answer: What is volume? Mass? Weight?   10 pts

- ☐ Read the article about atoms. (http://www.chem4kids.com/files/atom_structure.html)
    - Explain the importance of atoms in a paragraph.   10 pts

- ☐ Diagram the basic atomic structure in a small poster.
    - Label the nucleus, proton, electron, neutron   10 pts

- ☐ Do the study jam here
    http://studyjams.scholastic.com/studyjams/jams/science/matter/atoms.htm
      10 pts

- ☐ Vocabulary Cut and Paste:
    https://middleschoolscienceblog.files.wordpress.com/2015/01/matter-cut-and-paste-vocabulary.pdf   10 pts

- ☐ Vocabulary: Use the Quizlet link to study atom vocabulary https://quizlet.com/_3mtz7s
      10 pts

4 Layer (Choose One)

- ☐ Read "How Many Atoms are in a Person?"
    Respond: What did you notice about the make up of the human body? Write a paragraph describing your questions.

- ☐ Do the tutorial here:
    https://unctv.pbslearningmedia.org/resource/lsps07.sci.phys.matter.theatom/the-atom/#.WaTlQca-L-Y . What new vocabulary do you think is important?

Figure 10.3 Layered Curriculum® Matter Unit Part 1. Amanda Clapp

COMPACTING

Compacting is a process that emphasizes a systemized way for students (and teachers) to build on knowledge, eliminate unnecessary busy work, and focus on meaningful use of time. This is a fantastic way to push students who come to the classroom with an already-deep understanding of content and a need (and desire) to learn more. In this process, three steps occur. First is assessing what a student knows about upcoming content and recognizing what skills or content still needs to be mastered. Second, the teacher identifies which assignments or activities from the upcoming unit that student does and does not need to do, based on the student's current areas of mastery. Then the teacher plans alternative activities for the student, activities that will deepen his or her understanding. This is a great motivator for independence in learners, with the

OBJECTIVE	First Ranking/ Date	Final Ranking/ Date
I can give examples of pure substances		
I can compare compounds and mixtures		
I can compare how atoms behave in solids, liquids, and gases		

3 Layer: Choose 60 points from the following list.

- ☐ Mini Lecture Thursday (Required). Take Notes. — 10 pts
- ☐ Play this game and record your score. Define solid, liquid, and gas.
  https://www.brainpop.com/games/mattersorter/ — 10 pts
- ☐ Follow the directions for this online lab:
  https://phet.colorado.edu/sims/html/states-of-matter/latest/states-of-matter_en.html — 10 pts
- ☐ Study vocabulary using this link: https://quizlet.com/_3mu67j — 10 pts
- ☐ Read the article and list the differences between different mixtures and compounds.
  http://www.ivyroses.com/Chemistry/GCSE/Elements-Mixtures-Compounds.php — 10 pts
- ☐ Use a graphic organizer to compare compounds and mixtures — 10 pts
- ☐ Separating mixtures: Chromatography lab with ONE partner — 10 pts
- ☐ Classifying matter: Inquiry Lab with ONE partner — 10 pts

4 Layer: Choose ONE of the following:

- ☐ Investigate plasma and Bose-Einstein Condensates. Describe them and compare them to solids, liquids, and gases.
- ☐ Make a model that shows the arrangement of atoms in solids, liquids, and gases.

Figure 10.4 Layered Curriculum® Matter Unit Part 2. Amanda Clapp

caveat that those learners need to have strong self-regulation skills to be able to manage their time well.

TIERED ASSIGNMENTS

Tiered assignments are an excellent frequent-use strategy. This strategy can be used in various contexts in simple and complex activities. Tiering is based on student readiness and can be considered a low-floor, high-ceiling approach. What we mean by that is that tasks (or activities like learning contracts, products, **rubrics**, assessments) should be accessible to all learners so that even struggling learners can find success while advanced learners are getting appropriate challenge and push. Tomlinson (2017) recommends beginning the planning for tiering for advanced learners first to establish a rich and robust learning experience. Then **scaffolding** is used to make that content more accessible. Questioning strategies can be powerful here as built-in scaffolds. The goal is to give just enough support so that students can keep making progress and not to give too much support. Thinking remains the responsibility of the student. Effective tiering does not "dumb down" the content—the essential skills and understanding should remain the same. What is flexing here is the complexity of the task. Below we share an example from an eighth-grade math lesson in which students are presented with a task with multiple entry points and solution pathways. The scaffolds are provided through follow-up questions and mini tasks, allowing students to try strategies to continue moving toward a solution. Whole-group discussions are an effective part of tiered assignments. They allow contributions from all students and exposure to the multiple pathways students utilized along the way.

Let's look at an example from a mathematics classroom. Below in Figure 10.5 is a pattern task with multiple entry points and multiple solution pathways. The goal is for students to generalize an expression to model the pattern they see. Look at the scaffolded questions, which provide access and strategies to students while keeping the task open.

Circle Fever

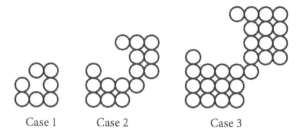

Case 1 Case 2 Case 3

1. How do you see the pattern growing? Where do you see the new circles being added when you move from case 1 to 2? Where do you see the new circles being added when you move from case 2 to 3?

2. What would the 10th case look like?

3. What would the 100th case look like? How many circles would be in the 100th case?

4. How many circles would be in the 0 case? What would it look like?

5. What would the -1 case look like?

6. Model the pattern with a rule or expression?

7. Write a rule for the number of circles in the 100th case?

Inspired by http://www.visualpatterns.org

Figure 10.5 Circle Fever Task. https://www.youcubed.org/

Pause and Reflect: Look at the task given above. Analyze the task to see how it is tiered to meet the needs of advanced and struggling learners. Describe how these diverse needs can be met by this task.

Practice It: Choose either to find a standard in your state-standards document for your content area or to search online for a task or activity that is currently NOT tiered. Work with a partner to adjust the task so that it is tiered, remembering to plan for advanced learners first and then to create scaffolds to make the task accessible for all learners.

VARIED QUESTIONS

We will discuss the importance of discourse practices across many chapters in this book. It bears repeating because it is such a crucial factor in best practices across all content areas and because it is pertinent to differentiating instruction. Through the lens of differentiation, the purpose of asking **varied questions** is to ensure that *all* students in your classroom can contribute to discussions. This means that we alter what we ask based on readiness, interest, and approaches to learning. Let's connect this to the tiered assignment above. Notice that the first question asks students to describe what they see in the picture—this allows even struggling learners who might have a challenging time producing the generalized expression an opportunity to connect and engage with the task. Every student in the classroom can likely come up with *something* that he or she notices, whether or not it is related to the mathematical rigor of the task. Good teachers know how to sequence questions in such a way that students' success in answering a question motivates them to remain engaged and to answer further questions. For example, if a teacher heard small groups discussing the cubes task and noticed that Aleah, a struggling learner, said something about noticing the middle tower growing by one, the teacher, as she starts the whole-group conversation, could ask Aleah directly what she noticed. Aleah then would have something tangible and important to contribute to the conversation. Then, as she asks other questions that work toward the generalization of the task, Aleah also gets access to that higher-level thinking to help her move forward in her understanding of the larger mathematical concept. In addition to asking "floor opener" questions, such as the one the teacher asked Aleah, effective teachers focus also on asking open-ended questions, questions to which there is not one answer in mind. Asking such questions can give students private thinking time or can provide a think-pair-share opportunity. The teacher can then facilitate a whole-group discussion so that all students have time to actively consider the content.

ROLE-AUDIENCE-FORMAT-TOPIC ASSIGNMENTS

Role-Audience-Format-Topic (RAFT) assignments can be utilized as an interest-based or readiness-based activity. In RAFT assignments, students are given various prompts that centralize on the same objectives or skills within a unit of instruction. Students then have an opportunity to assume a particular *role* for a specific *audience*, using a particular *format* on that *topic*. For example, in a science class, students might take on the role of a rice cracker speaking to other rice crackers in the format of a travel guide about the journey through the digestive system. Or students in a history class could take on the role of Abraham Lincoln writing to the Dear Abby audience, using the format of an advice column, about problems he is having with his generals. Using this strategy allows both teachers and students to engage with material in meaningful and creative ways. Below we share an example from Kayleigh's eighth-grade classroom with samples of students' work.

Students are reading *House Arrest* by K. A. Holt. This novel follows the story of a twelve-year-old boy, Timothy, who has been placed under house arrest. While Timothy deals with a difficult family situation, he navigates the challenges of being confined and forms a bond with a quirky neighbor who helps him find his voice using poetry. Figure 10.6 shows a RAFT strategy for students to engage with the content in *House Arrest*.

House Arrest - RAFT Strategy Activity

Role	Audience	Format	Topic
Timothy	Timothy's Mom	Poem	Write an apology poem to your mom about the crime you committed.
Timothy	Timothy's Probation Officer	Journal/Diary Entry	Write a journal entry about the ways you have changed/developed since the crime and writing in the journal.
The Probation Officer, **James**	The Court	Formal Letter/Report	On behalf of Timothy, write an official report on how he has changed since the beginning of his sentence until now.
Timothy's little brother, **Levi**	You choose: Timothy Their mom The court	You choose: Poem Diary Report to the court	Put yourself in Levi's shoes. What does this sacrifice from your brother mean to you? Explain that to the person you choose and write anything that you think Levi would want these people to know.

Figure 10.6 House Arrest RAFT strategy activity. Created by authors

Practice It: With a partner, identify a topic that you think might be interesting as a RAFT assignment. Use the example to then flesh out the entire RAFT task.

LITERATURE CIRCLES

Literature circles are a strategy to differentiate among students, based on their readiness or interests. Do not be fooled into thinking that literature circles are only for the English-language-arts classroom. They can easily be integrated into units in other core-content areas and built into some effective interdisciplinary units. The basic premise of literature circles is that students can choose what they will read from a handful of texts chosen by the teacher. The teacher may encourage students toward a particular choice if the teacher has a sense of how accessible the text will be for particular learners, or the teacher may have students pick a text purely based on interest. In an English-language-arts classroom, there may be more variety in the choice of texts; and, in an interdisciplinary unit, the texts may all be based on a certain theme (such as diseases, to meet eighth-grade science standards). Student groups are then formed, and students begin to read their text, with each student having an assigned job within the group and with students doing teacher-designed tasks to help them engage with the text. Below, in Figure 10.7, Kayleigh provides an example of a calendar for a literature circle. This calendar, available digitally to students, gets highlighted as days are completed and provides a clear vision of when students should be done with reading certain sections. In class literature-circle meetings, students rotate through responsibility-laden positions, such as discussion leader, summarizer, passage analyst, essential connector, and vocabulary enricher. These are just examples of the types of jobs that teachers can include, and these roles can be adapted to the needs of your students. An important aspect of this kind of activity is the use of rubrics to hold students accountable and to make expectations clear. In Figure 10.8, Kayleigh shares her rubrics from a standards-based grading system used at her school for each job.

Planning and structure are key to success in using literature circles as a differentiated activity for students. If you frontload the work, you will have a well-oiled machine in no time.

Literature Circles - House Arrest

			Thursday, Sept. 7th Introduction to Unit	Friday, Sept. 8th NO ELA Incentative Day
Monday, Sept. 11 Read pages 1-24 Job: Discussion Director	Tuesday, Sept. 12 Read pages 25-47 Job: Summarizer	Wednesday, Sept. 13th Read pages 48 - 73 Job: Essential Connector	Thursday, Sept. 14th Read pages 74 -107 Job: Passage Analyst	Friday, Sept. 15 Adventure Center
Monday, Sept. 18 Read pages 108 - 129 Job: Vocab Enricher	Tuesday, Sept. 19th WCU Library Trips	Wednesday, Sept. 20th Read pages 130 - 153 Job:	Thursday, Sept. 21st Read pages 154 - 180 Job:	Friday, Sept. 22nd 8th to Cherokee
Monday, Sept. 25 Read pages 181 - 211 Job:	Tuesday, Sept. 26th Read pages 212 -237 Job:	Wednesday, Sept. 27 Read pages 238 - 260 Job:	Thursday, Sept. 28 Read pages 261 - 283 Job:	Friday, Sept. 29 Read pages 284 - 296 Job: Discussion Questions from the author

Figure 10.7 *Literature Circle Calendar.* Created by authors

Literature Circle Jobs Rubric

	1 Emerging	2 Progressing	3 Meets	4 Exceeds
Discussion Director	The questions are not completed, page numbers are provided, and/or the questions do not make sense to the content.	Less than 5 questions are listed. The questions are "right there" questions in the text. All of the questions are not complete and/or do not make sense to the content.	At least 5 thought-provoking questions are provided. (Why, how, if, what, and who...). The page numbers that inspired the question are listed.	At least 5 thought-provoking questions are provided. (Why, how, if, what, and who...). Page numbers that inspired the question are listed. The correct answer to the question is provided with reasoning.
	1 Emerging	2 Progressing	3 Meets	4 Exceeds
Passage Analyst Rubric	Less than 2 passages are provided with little to no explanation.	2 or fewer passages are provided. The significance of the passage is not included or not clearly explained or a true representation of what is occurring.	Two different passages/text evidence are provided and are clearly cited with quotations and page numbers. The significance of each passage is expressed and connects to the current events within the text.	Two or more different passages/text evidence is provided and is clearly cited with quotations and page numbers. The significance of the passage is expressed and connects to the current events within the text. The explanation tells how the event developed throughout the text.
	1 Emerging	2 Progressing	3 Meets	4 Exceeds
Summarizer Rubric	Identify the main idea.	Identify the main idea and 4 key events.	Identify the main idea and key events with multiple accurate and relevant supporting details within a paragraph format. The summary must include at least 5-8 sentences.	Identify the main idea and key events with multiple accurate and relevant supporting details within a paragraph format. The summary must include at least 5-8 sentences. The paragraph should contain little to no grammatical errors.
	1 Emerging	2 Progressing	3 Meets	4 Exceeds
Essential Connecter Rubric	Less than 2 passages are provided with little to no explanation.	Two or fewer passages are provided. The passages are without correct citations. Responses do not provide a connection to the outside world.	Three different passages/text evidence are provided and are clearly cited with quotations and page numbers. There is a clear connection or comparison to another book, TV show, movie, or personal life event.	Three or more different passages/text evidence are provided and are clearly cited with quotations and page numbers. There is a clear connection or comparison to another book, TV show, movie, or personal life event with an anecdote to explain the reasoning.

Figure 10.8 Literature Circle Job Rubrics near here. Created by authors

JOURNALING

Journaling is another strategy that can be used regularly to support differentiation in your classroom. Just as literature circles do not belong solely in the English-language-arts classroom, nor do journals. In fact, we will use the mathematics classroom as our primary example below. Think back to the big ideas of differentiating based on readiness, interest, and learning profiles, integrated with differentiating content and process. (We are intentionally leaving out product here because, in this case, the product is a journal entry for everyone.) Holly and Meghan (another master teacher—check out her profile in Chapter 1) utilize math journals weekly to connect with their students, encourage growth mindsets, and allow students to have voice and choice in engaging with mathematics tasks and practices. At the start of the year, our initial assignments for journal entries focus on having students share their previous relationship with math (many students have some math trauma in their backgrounds). Through this one-on-one dialogue, we begin to learn more about how students interact with mathematics and then start to create prompts to help students repair that relationship, if repair is needed. Struggling students may repair their relationship with math by choosing engaging tasks in which they can find success, whereas students who clearly need a challenge should be encouraged to select an enrichment option. The teacher may suggest specific tasks to specific students, or she may offer a set of prompts and allow students to choose. There is a natural differentiation built into the use of journals.

Let's look at a specific example where Meghan had all the students work on the same task for their journal. In this example, we will highlight how the same task can be utilized for all students but can be altered with feedback based on readiness, interest, or learning approach. Just like tiering, adjustments can be made to enrich or push students or can be scaffolded to support students who may be struggling. The "locker problem" is a classic math task that can be adjusted for students in a myriad of ways.

The locker problem is as follows (Krulik & Rudnick, 1989):

> The new school has exactly 1000 lockers and exactly 1000 students. On the first day of school, the students meet and agree on a plan: The first student will enter the building and open all the lockers. The second student will then enter the school and close every locker with an even number (2, 4, 6, etc.). The third student will then enter the school and reverse every third locker (3, 6, 9, etc.). That is, if the locker is closed, he or she will open it; if the locker is open, he or she will close it. The fourth student will reverse every fourth locker, and so on until all 1000 students have entered the building and reversed the proper lockers. Which lockers finally remain open? Why? (p. 16)

We have found that students by nature are curious about this task and are motivated to find the answer. But it can also seem daunting to some students. Teachers can provide scaffolds via feedback from an initial journal entry on this task to allow students to first try working with one hundred or fewer lockers instead of one thousand lockers. Or teachers can also provide individual feedback in the journal to encourage a particular strategy, like using a hundreds board to organize thinking or using two color counters to help represent the lockers. This feedback loop can continue (without the pressure of time) until students successfully find the pattern. Other students may work through this task quickly and need extensions for their next journal entries. The locker problem can be connected to other classic novel tasks, like the checkerboard problem, or the counting triangle problem, as shown in Figure 10.9 and Figure 10.10, below. Journals create an authentic way to build community with your students and many ways to differentiate for students, based on readiness, interest, and learner profiles, for any content area.

How many squares are on a standard checkerboard?
(Original Source Unknown)

Figure 10.9 The Checkerboard Problem. Created by authors

214 CHAPTER 10

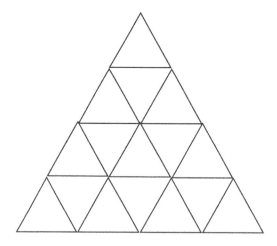

How many triangles are there?
(Original Source Unknown)

Figure 10.10 The Counting Triangles Problem. Created by authors

Practice It: With a small group, choose a content standard and one of the high-prep differentiation strategies. Spend some time creating a plan, a structure, and rubrics, as needed, to implement your strategy.

Conclusion

Teachers spend years honing their skills in differentiating instruction. As we have explored in this chapter, there are many possibilities for creating engaging, accessible, and challenging content for students. Remember, though, when you are a beginning teacher, trying too much too soon will lead to less-than-positive experiences. Focus first on trying some of the low-prep strategies suggested in Table 10.2, and then experiment with just one of the higher-prep tools at a time. This will allow you to focus on setting up strong structures for success, and lessons will have a much better chance of going smoothly.

To summarize, let's revisit our learning outcomes:

1. **Understand the concept of differentiated instruction, and recognize different ways to differentiate instruction, based on product, process, content, or learning environment.** Differentiating instruction is an approach to teaching that is aimed at meeting all students' needs in the classroom. It is not a one-time strategy implementation; nor does it involve having an individual lesson plan for each student. Differentiation is based on student readiness, student interest, and learner profiles, and teachers can differentiate the content (the what) and the process and product (the how) of instruction.

2. **Identify strategies for differentiated instruction (tiered assignments, flexible grouping, etc.).** There are many ways for teachers to use differentiation. Effective teachers find ways to pair creativity with structure. As a beginning teacher, focus first on implementing simple low-prep strategies, like offering choices to students or using flexible seating or differentiated materials. Then work toward using higher-prep strategies, like learning menus, flexible grouping, or literature circles.

3. **Apply differentiated instruction principles: practice lesson-plan design to incorporate strategies (lesson complexity, multiple-pathways-of-mastery demonstration, individual learning goals, etc.).** We have provided several examples of differentiation in this chapter, with a focus on having organized expectations and using rubrics for accountability. If you frontload your planning of differentiated activities, you not only will save time but also will avoid having headaches down the road. See the suggested reading list for more resources on differentiated instructional strategies.

Suggested Readings

Doubet, K. J. (2022). *The flexibly grouped classroom: How to organize learning for equity and growth*. ASCD.

Doubet, K. J., & Hockett, J. A. (2015). *Differentiation in middle and high school: Strategies to engage all learners*. ASCD.

Tomlinson, C. A. (2017). *How to differentiate instruction in academically diverse classrooms*. ASCD.

AMLE Reading Resources

https://www.amle.org/letting-students-succeed-at-their-own-speed/.
https://www.amle.org/differentiating-instruction-for-ells/.
https://www.amle.org/encouraging-students-to-embrace-academic-challenges/.
https://www.amle.org/grading-students-identified-as-special-education-ell-rti-mtss-or-otherwise-in-general-education-classes/.
https://www.amle.org/team-passion-project-the-importance-of-offering-student-choice-in-the-middle-grades/.

References

Bransford, J., Derry, S., Berliner, D., Hammerness, K., & Beckett, K. L. (2005). Theories of learning and their roles in teaching. In Linda Darling-Hammond & John Bransford (Eds.), *Preparing teachers for a changing world: What teachers should learn and be able to do, 40* (p. 87). Jossey-Bass.

Dehaene, S. (2021). *How we learn: Why brains learn better than any machine . . . for now*. Penguin.

Doubet, K. J., & Hockett, J. A. (2015). *Differentiation in middle and high school: Strategies to engage all learners*. ASCD.

Krulik, S., & Rudnick, J. A. (1989). *Problem solving: A handbook for senior high school teachers*. Allyn & Bacon/Logwood Division.

Lappan, G., Fey, J. T., Fitzgerald, W. M., Friel, S. N., & Phillips, E. D. (2004). *Connected Mathematics, say it with symbols: Algebraic reasoning* [Teacher's Edition]. Pearson Prentice Hall. © Michigan State University.

Nunley, K. F., & Gencel, İ. E. (2019). Layered curriculum: principles, planning, implementing and evaluation. *Mersin Üniversitesi Eğitim Fakültesi Dergisi, 15*(2), 349–62.

Tomlinson, C. A. (2003). *Fulfilling the promise of the differentiated classroom: Strategies and tools for responsive teaching*. Association for Supervision and Curriculum Development.

Tomlinson, C. A. (2014). *The differentiated classroom: Responding to the needs of all learners*. ASCD.

Tomlinson, C. A. (2017). *How to differentiate instruction in academically diverse classrooms*. ASCD.

Tomlinson, C. A., & Imbeau, M. B. (2023). *Leading and managing a differentiated classroom*. ASCD.

Willingham, D. T. (2018). Ask the cognitive scientist: Does tailoring instruction to "learning styles" help students learn? *American Educator, 42*(2), 28.

CHAPTER 11

Assessment

Learning Outcomes:

1. Understand the history and evolution of assessment and accountability.

2. Advocate for the use of varied and ongoing assessments, appreciating the diversity in student talents and skills, and tailoring assessments to accommodate individual learning preferences.

3. Recognize the role of grades and the benefits of using rubrics in the assessment process.

Connecting Assessment and Instruction

Assessment and instruction are interconnected components of the teaching and learning process. The data generated through assessments inform instructional decisions, and effective instruction, in turn, influences the outcomes of assessments. Before exploring types and purposes, let's operationally define assessment. Assessment is defined as a process for documenting, in measurable terms, the knowledge, skills, attitudes, and beliefs of the learner (Capraro et al., 2011). It is important to distinguish the subtle difference between assessment and evaluation. While assessment focuses primarily on gathering information and evidence about a student's knowledge and abilities, evaluation is focused on making judgments and interpreting assessment data. Both aspects are important, but the distinction helps us think about our purpose in planning assessments and in providing feedback to students.

THE ERA OF ASSESSMENT AND ACCOUNTABILITY

Since the turn of the twenty-first century, schools have faced intense scrutiny in assessment and accountability. **High-stakes tests** and all the pros and cons that come along with them are a norm in our educational environments. In 2002, President George W. Bush signed into law the No Child Left Behind (NCLB) Act, which increased accountability measures for schools. Based on this act, all schools created accountability plans, used standardized tests to assess students annually in grades three through eight, and participated in the **Nation's Report Card**. Schools were held accountable for meeting a**dequate yearly progress (AYP)** targets, and consequences for underperformance included potential sanctions or restructuring. The period following enactment of the NCLB Act was one of significant pressure for schools, teachers, and students to perform well, and the act's requirements created some stress surrounding the nature of testing in schools. While the goal was to ensure the success of all students, in many ways the systems put in place only highlighted many of the gaps in our educational support for all students. In the next decade, President Obama signed the Every Student Succeeds Act (ESSA) (2015). Unlike its predecessor, the NCLB Act, ESSA offers more flexibility in and local control of what and how schools utilize data. Under ESSA, schools must have annual assessments in English language arts and math in grades three through eight and, once students are in high school, as a measure of student progress and achievement over time. Additionally, science assessments were added to the tests to be administered at least once during each of the following grade spans: grades three to five, grades six to nine, and grades ten to twelve. These are all examples of summative assessments, which we will explore later in the chapter. ESSA also allows flexibility for states to design their own accountability systems; states may select the types of assessment utilized as well as the option of using other indicators, such as student growth. Requirements are likely to continue evolving as the landscape of education adjusts to new policies and political eras.

VARIED AND ONGOING ASSESSMENTS

AMLE advocates for the use of **varied and ongoing assessments** for middle school learners. Using varied assessments celebrates the diverse talents and skills of students and recognizes that students may perform differently, depending on the style of assessment utilized and according to personal preferences and personal strengths. Teachers can utilize classic assessments, like a traditional multiple choice/short-answer test or quiz, but may also include nontraditional assessments, like portfolios, projects, presentations, performance, or discussion-based assessments. By employing a variety of assessment methods, educators can capture the multifaceted nature of student learning, allowing for a more holistic understanding of students' abilities and progress. Ongoing assessment relates to the use of formative assessment (described in a later section) to systematically collect information about student learning throughout instruction. This may occur daily or even at multiple points within a singular lesson. The primary purpose of ongoing assessment is to inform instructional decisions in real time. It helps teachers understand how well students are grasping concepts, identify areas of confusion, and make immediate adjustments to teaching strategies to meet the needs of individual students or the class. This approach of using varied and ongoing assessment fosters a more inclusive and responsive learning environment, recognizing and supporting the unique characteristics and needs of middle school students.

Pause and Reflect: Take a moment to think back to your educational experience. What kinds of assessments did you participate in as a learner? If it has been too long to remember, what kinds of assessments have you seen in your practical school experiences/observations? Which of these felt most effective in terms of showing teachers what you (or students you observed) knew? What is your sense about these assessments being varied and ongoing, in light of the above description?

Diagnostic or Preassessment

Diagnostic assessments, or preassessments, help teachers identify students' current understanding of a set of content and identify any misconceptions students might have regarding it. This can be particularly helpful if a teacher has a sense that the group has a basic grasp of a subject so that the teacher can then alter the instructional plans to better meet the individualized needs of students. For example, if a group of sixth-grade students comes to a class with pretest results showing that they have strong algebraic-reasoning skills, they may not need several lessons on solving one-step equations. Instead, the teacher may differentiate the tasks for students to enrich their current understanding or to target specific needs among students whose preassessment results indicated some learning gaps. Some teachers may utilize a broad preassessment at the beginning of the year or semester to gauge a wide breadth of skills; alternatively, a smaller diagnostic assessment may be utilized prior to the launch of a specific unit. These assessments may be a formal test, an interview or observation, or a self-assessment in which students answer written or oral questions.

Formative Assessment

Formative assessment is an ongoing process of gathering evidence of learning through instruction. In many ways it is like a temperature check—we want to know where our students are in their progress toward mastering a learning outcome, and we want to use that information to guide our next steps in instruction. We also want to utilize the opportunity to give students feedback on their learning progress. As defined by Shepard and colleagues (2005), formative *assessment* is "assessment carried out during the instructional process for the purpose of improving teaching or learning" (p. 275). Concisely, formative assessment is assessment *for* learning while summative assessment (described next) is assessment *of* learning. This distinction is important, as formative assessments should *not* be graded. Their purpose is to give teachers and students feedback. For teachers, it informs the next steps of instruction, and, for students, it gives feedback that allows them to set goals and continue moving forward in their understanding of content. Black and William's (2009) work has identified the following strategies for integrating formative assessment into instruction:

1. Clarifying and sharing learning intentions and criteria for success.
2. Engineering effective classroom discussions and other learning tasks that elicit evidence of student understanding.

3. Providing feedback that moves learners forward.

4. Activating students as instructional resources for one another.

5. Activating students as the owners of their own learning. (p. 8)

A solid formative assessment gives a clear sense of learning outcomes and an opportunity to give students feedback.

While the following is not an exhaustive list by any means, here are some examples of formative-assessment activities:

- Quick quizzes, polls, and exit tickets
  - This is a great strategy for activating prior knowledge or finding out what students have learned from a lesson. These activities can easily be created using technological tools for quick collection of data and for providing instant feedback to students. Common technological tools for this include Kahoot, Mentimeter, Poll Everywhere, Quizlet, Blooket, Quizzez, Desmos, and Formative, to name a few. These activities can be short and specific to gauge student understanding of a particular learning objective or can be more open-ended, depending on the teacher's goal.

- Classroom discussions or debates
  - These assessments are more variable in nature but can be helpful in establishing the collective understanding of the group. Teachers can start with an open-ended prompt and some follow-up probes to see what students contribute. Note patterns or gaps in understanding, and then use that information to make instructional decisions for next steps.

- One-minute papers or reflections
  - This quick assessment tool is designed for students to write something pertaining to the day's lesson. Having a prompt or a structure—such as asking for three things they learned today—is helpful. Or maybe you use an open-ended prompt, saying, "Tell me what you understand about _____" or "How was _____ helpful (or not) in class today?" Students use only a minute to write their responses and turn them in. Teachers could have students put their names on their responses or leave them anonymously, as the primary purpose is providing feedback for driving next instructional decisions for the following day.

- Concept-mapping activities
  - Concept maps are visual representations of a concept. They can take many forms, including a graphic organizer, a flow chart, a Venn diagram, bubble maps, and so on. The aim is for students to be able to link ideas together in some way or to chunk information to help with retention of information.

- Think-pair-share exercises

- A think-pair-share activity is a fantastic way to get students to share their thinking with others. While this process will not necessarily give the teacher information about what all students know, good teachers know how to circulate, and they monitor these quick discussions to notice themes of what students are sharing with each other. A quick implementation of this is to have students start with some private thinking time about a prompt (could be open-ended or something quite specific). Then they pair up with another student and share their thinking with each other. This encourages all students to participate, whereas, in a whole-group discussion only a few students can share their thoughts.
- Peer feedback sessions
  - This activity can be utilized in any content area; one of the most common uses of it may be in a writer's workshop. Peer feedback sessions allow students to see how peers are thinking and working and then to give feedback to help their peers in their work or understanding of a concept. An objective is set (either collectively as a class or between partners), and peers then switch artifacts with a partner. The partner looks at the work independently and then gives feedback through compliments ("positive noticings") about the work and then also gives constructive feedback that may help the partner extend his or her work or thinking.
- Observations of student work or group activities
  - This assessment might be considered the most informal of those on our list, but it is an important one for instruction. Good teachers circulate around the room while students are working on tasks and put their listening skills to effective use. Teachers likely anticipated how students will engage in an activity and are listening for key ideas related to the learning objective. They then use good questioning strategies (see Chapter 9 on pedagogy, for more) to help students toward mastery of the concept. This helps teachers make in-the-moment instructional decisions, based on the needs of the students.
- Partner quizzes
  - Partner quizzes are a terrific way to have students demonstrate their understanding collaboratively. While teachers will not necessarily get individualized feedback on each student's understanding, a partner quiz does give a quick temperature check of how students are progressing without the pressure of formal assessment.
- Self-evaluations
  - Self-evaluations allow teachers to see how students are perceiving their own progress. While this mostly gives teachers perception data, it is helpful to correlate student perceptions to their performance on other assessments. Long-term use of self-evaluations can help students more accurately assess their performance.

222   CHAPTER 11

- Ed-tech games

Picture 11.1   Math class. Photo, Western Carolina University

- We mentioned a ton of these under the quick quizzes/polls but here is an even more expansive (still not exhaustive) list of tech tools: Kahoot, Mentimeter, Poll Everywhere, Quizlet, Blooket, Quizzez, Desmos, BookWidgets, Plickers, Classcraft, Nearpod, EdPuzzle, Socrative, and Formative. Note that some of these may have associated costs (but most have a free version of sorts).

Plan it: While it is likely that you recognized some of the ed-tech tools above, there is hopefully at least one that is new to you. Take some time to look up a few. Play with them. See what their capacities are for using premade things, for creating your own items, and so on. Choose a standard from your state standards, and either find a premade formative assessment that is well aligned to that standard or create a formative assessment from any of the other options listed above. If you are in a class with peers, then trade those formative assessments, and give critical feedback to your peers on how well aligned the assessment is, and share what you will know as a teacher from student responses to that assessment.

Here is one example of a student self-assessment for a seventh-grade science unit:

Summative Assessment

Summative assessment is more of what we typically conceptualize—think test, benchmark, end-of-semester exam. These assessments are more evaluative in nature as they gauge student mastery of learning objectives. These assessments are graded and usually contribute in large part to a student's grade that would be communicated, say, on a report card. Summative assessments, while more formal in nature, do not necessarily have to take the form of a traditional *test* per se. Some culminating assessments can take the form of portfolios, products, performance, or other alternative assessments. These summative assessments are an important piece of the puzzle evaluators face when trying to understand student learning and align it to curriculum standards. Policymakers use the standardized assessments to make comparisons of learning across schools and districts. They use the results in making decisions about changing the curricula or engaging in other types of education reform. Good teachers know that summative assessment is important but that balancing use of formative and summative assessment provides a more comprehensive picture of student proficiency and progress. For classroom-based summative assessment, our focus here, let's explore just a few of the many options teachers can utilize.

The basic, more traditional options include the following:

- Tests and quizzes that may have any combination of
  - Multiple-choice questions
  - Matching items
  - True/false questions
  - Short-answer questions
  - Essays
- Writing assessments, a category that includes a wide range of activities and products, such as
  - Research paper
  - Compare/contrast activity
  - How-to guide
  - Poem
  - Graphic novel
  - Personal essay
  - Brochure
  - Fact sheet or infographic
  - Editorial
  - Proposal
  - Letter
  - Song lyrics
- Presentations or performances
  - Speech
  - Role-playing

- Debate
- Experiment
- Physical models
- Play
- Musical creation
- Exhibit
- Slide-show presentation
* Product
  - Blog
  - Map
  - Sculpture
  - Public service announcement
  - Podcast
* Reflective assessments
  - Journal
  - Literary response
  - Learning log reflection

Good teachers balance the use of assessment types so that students consistently receive feedback about their progress and focus on the concept of assessments as a feedback tool. In the next section, we explore concepts and strategies to prioritize providing feedback to support students' continued progress.

Rubrics and Grades

Grades are an important communication mechanism in communication about learning. An important consideration in engaging in assessment is asking ourselves, "What does it mean to be proficient in this content objective?" Answering this question is potentially more complex than one would think. Good teachers know that grading an assessment should give students reflective feedback on their mastery of that content. In this next section, we will explore conceptual understanding of what grades mean and examine a tool commonly used to provide this feedback, using rubrics.

GRADES

What is the meaning of a **grade** in school? We received them throughout our educational careers—our kindergarten report cards told our parents how we behaved in school, the quality of our handwriting, our progress in reading and mathematics, and so on. At this early stage, the report cards are often written more in the format of **standards-based grading (SBG)**. SBG is a student-centered approach to education that measures students' progress against specific skills and standards, providing transparency about students' strengths in a subject area and giving guidance on the areas in which students' performance needs improvement. Some of us may have been lucky enough to have this continue through our middle and high school experiences, but, for many of us, by the time we reached middle school, our report card looked more like a simple numerical or alphabetical representation of what we know and understand. Our parents would receive either a score of 90 or a B as the communication of what we knew of the content we had covered in class during that quarter. In college, this traditional system persists, with grades often representing just a few tests, administered across the semester, paired with some points for our attendance and participation in class. We will talk much more in depth about the benefits of using SBG in middle school, but, for a moment, let's tease out more traditional systems and think about what a grade really tells us.

A traditional grading system usually uses a singular number or letter to represent the average "score," "grade," or "outcome," to communicate in some capacity the amount of knowledge one demonstrates on some set of assignments or tests. Educators have argued about whether these grades truly represent a student's proficiency level with respect to content or whether it captures something else entirely. Depending on how the grades are collected and what those grades represent, the number or letter could represent a variety of variables. Take for example the idea of a missing assign-

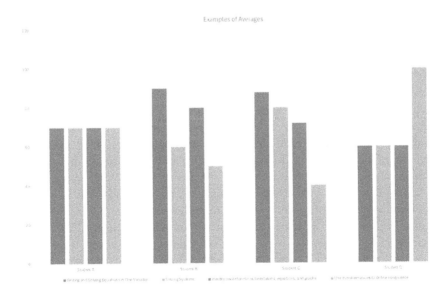

Figure 11.1 Student Averages. Created by authors

ment being recorded as a zero. Does the zero accurately portray the content knowledge of the student or, rather, does it measure compliance (which could mean an array of different things that are not at all academically related)? Rick Wormeli has long advocated for moving away from using averages to communicate grades to students (check out the list of recommended readings at the end of this chapter for more of his expertise). At the core, grades *should* be utilized as a communication system. Grades should communicate to students what they are demonstrating related to proficiency on a content objective. Grades should communicate to the teacher how each individual student is performing as well as give a sense of how the entire class is demonstrating proficiency. And for parents, grades should communicate what *content* students have mastered in school. But let's see what boiling a grade down into a singular average communicates. In the example in Figure 11.1, each student is bringing home a report card with an average of 70. When we look at the performance of each student across several assignments and content objectives, however, we see a very different picture. Student A has performed consistently across all areas, and that average of 70 accurately depicts the student's proficiency of content across the quarter. Student B, however, shows quite a bit more variability across objectives, and what we learn from looking at the individual scores rather than the average is that this student is excelling in algebraic concepts, like solving equations, but needs some targeted interventions in geometric principles of transformations. If we shift away from using a singular average score to represent students' knowledge, we can see a much clearer picture of how students are progressing. So, how do we do that? Enter SBG.

STANDARDS-BASED GRADING

One way to provide transparency in grading and to improve student learning is to utilize **SBG**. SBG is a student-centered approach to education that measures student progress against specific skills and standards, providing transparency about students' strengths in a subject area and identifying areas in which students' performance needs improvement. SBG can help teachers identify areas where students are struggling and where they are thriving and provide feedback to help students improve. This approach to assessment can also help students take ownership of their education and make instruction more relevant. SBG departs from traditional grading systems that rely on letter grades and percentages and, instead, measures students on the mastery of specific learning objectives. This approach not only encourages students to take ownership of their education, but it also provides educators with a more insightful understanding of each student's strengths and areas for growth. One advantage to SBG is that it breaks down large subjects into smaller learning outcomes to help teachers better measure student learning. Instead of assigning a grade to students according to traditional grading scales, SBG measures students against specific skills and standards. This makes it really clear to teachers where students are thriving and where they need help. Another advantage is that SBG can be a way to view student progress based on proficiency levels for identified standards rather than relying on a holistic representation as the sole measure of achievement. Marzana and Heflebower (2011) called this an **omnibus grade**.

SBG is most often contrasted with the more traditional approach to grading and assessment. Instead of using percentages and letter grades, SBG considers evidence of learning and the data it produces in different ways. Perhaps the most important advantage is that students are intrinsically motivated and have ownership of their learning. Students can focus on mastery and understanding in a standards-based classroom without constantly worrying about getting the most points.

Most of the work to implement SBG happens up front—in defining standards and/or benchmarks and creating rubrics. Once the standards are identified and clearly defined, the rubric itself acts as a communication tool, indicating a student's level of performance and providing feedback to help the student work toward success. Most often, the scales are 1–4 or 1–5, and each level is defined on the rubric. Each grading term, teachers document student performance level on each outcome, provide feedback, and even adapt instruction to meet student needs. All learning materials (e.g., assignments, projects, papers, etc.) should be tied to the standards, learning outcomes, or targets that have been identified as items to measure. The key idea is that SBG is meant to be responsive to learning. As students progress, more complex material is covered, and mastery can be achieved. Some students progress immediately while others need more time. Regular feedback, reteaching, and opportunities to reassess are essential to help all students move toward mastery.

RUBRICS

A **rubric** is a scoring guide that outlines specific components of and expectations for student performance on a work product (e.g., assignment, activity, paper, project, etc.). Rubrics are used both by the learner while completing the work and by the teacher when assessing the final product. They are written based on a set of assessment criteria that highlights, for both teachers and students, where the students are on a continuum of understanding. Essentially, rubrics help us document how students understand the standards against which work will be measured. Providing consistency in evaluation of student work is an overarching goal of rubric use. Rubrics are meant to detail scoring criteria in a clear way so that multiple teachers, using the same rubric, would arrive at the same score or grade. Rubrics should be used from the launch to the completion of a student work product. They provide a system to assess specific tasks and are customized to each project so that, as the expected work product becomes more complex, the rubric does as well. Rubrics can be a helpful tool for students, letting them know what is expected of them. It is essential for teachers to clearly state, in understandable language, the expectations for an assignment. Doing so will help students see that learning is about gaining specific skills in academic subjects as well as about learning overall problem-solving and life skills. Of course, rubrics allow students the opportunity to do self-assessment along the way and to reflect on the learning process at the end. There are various kinds of rubrics, and a few have been included here. An **individual rubric** includes a list of requirements or components for any kind of work product (e.g., assignment, activity, paper, project, etc.) and a description of expectations for each. It is utilized by both the student and the teacher. A **project rubric** lists the requirements for the completion of a larger project. Typically, some sort of presentation of the final project is required. The teacher either sets project goals or has students collaborate to set goals and suggest how the work should be evaluated. A project rubric should include components that 1) describe the expected quality of the work and the main idea of the project; 2) accurately summarize (expected) content; and 3) outline how well the presentation is to be designed and delivered. A **team rubric** includes details that allow each team member to know what is expected. This type of rubric should contain descriptions of individual tasks to be completed while the students are working as a team. Consequences for lack of participation should be included.

Designing and Implementing Effective Rubrics

Common rubrics and templates can be helpful to teachers—there are many resources providing them online. In fact, some sites will create a rubric as you input components and descriptions of levels. It is a good idea to avoid using the same checklist of rubric components across multiple classroom activities. Components and descriptions should be altered, even slightly, as traits of and expectations for various work products differ. It is a good idea, however, to utilize learning targets and performance tasks over and over in your classroom. By this, we mean adopting common language to label performance (e.g., using "level 1," "level 2," "level 3," "level 4," and "level 5" or "unsatisfactory," "satisfactory," and "target" across all rubrics). Students feel more confident when they begin work understanding expectations and target performance guidelines.

When making decisions about what traits or components to include in a rubric, a great place to start is with the lesson or unit learning objectives (or outcomes). Spend time thinking about the traits, or learning outcomes, you want the assignment or project to assess. The process of creating a rubric can often help clarify the assignment itself. If the assignment has been well articulated, with clear and specific learning goals in mind, the language for your rubric can come straight from the assignment, as written. Otherwise, try to unpack the assignment, identifying areas that are not articulated clearly. If the learning objectives are too vague, your rubric will be less useful (and your students will have a difficult time understanding your expectations). If your stated objectives are too mechanistic or specific, your rubric will not accurately reflect your grading expectations. Keep in mind that, if the students can't understand the rubric, then we cannot expect it to guide instruction, reflection, and assessment. If the idea is for students to engage in using the rubric, they must understand it. Teachers should ensure that the rubric's language is learning-level appropriate. If you use academic language or concepts, then you'll need time to teach students those meanings and concepts.

The next steps are thinking about the traits identified and figuring out if each trait should be listed separately, with its own scale, or if one scale would work for the entire assignment. A rubric using one scale, often referred to as a **holistic rubric**, would work only for assignments without much complexity. A rubric listing each trait separately, with its own scale, is an **analytic rubric**. It is also necessary to decide if the rubric will lead to a letter-grade scale; a point scale, which may or may not be translated into a grade at the end; or some other scale (e.g., labels, such as "poor," "unsatisfactory," "proficient," "fair," "satisfactory," "target," "excellent," etc.). Teachers should decide what information should be conveyed to students about their grade, and all rubrics should include at least some narrative commentary on performance. Keep in mind that using more detailed scales and point differentiations results in work products taking longer to grade. The most important reminder is to stay consistent with the lesson or unit learning objectives.

Once the target learning objectives have been identified, descriptions of expectations for work must be detailed in every cell of the rubric. Articulating the differences between, say, "level 1" and "level 2" or between "fair" and "target" is particularly helpful for students. Looking over sample student work may also help to identify the various levels of accomplishment. Starting with a description of the ideal work product is a good idea. It will be easier to then describe unacceptable work products and to fill in the levels between ideal and unacceptable work products. If there is no student work from the past to review, think through the steps students will take to complete the assignment, the difficulties they might encounter, and the lower-level (the unexemplary) products students may create.

After the rubric has been used for assessment of an assignment, it is essential to consider whether it accurately reflects grading expectations. Revising the rubric for future use is not only acceptable but also expected. There may be times when rubric alteration is necessary while students are still working; however, substantially altering grading criteria already laid out for students should not be an option. The rubric should be used to give constructive feedback to students, and teachers should consider also distributing the marked-up rubric when student work is returned. Marking up a rubric includes circling or underlining sections that stood out as descriptive of that student's work, adding comments, and more. In other words, the rubric itself can be used to facilitate the process of explaining grades and to provide students with clear instructions about where they should place more effort to improve their learning and their work product. Figure 11.2 provides a template for rubric construction.

Rubric Template

Levels to the Right Components Below	Poor	Below Average	Average	Good	Excellent	Points Earned
	Level 1	Level 2	Level 3	Level 4	Level 5	
	Description of level of work goes in each column of this row					*In this column, input points earned for each component, based on level of work*
Name of each required component goes in each row of this column						

Figure 11.2 Rubric Template. *Note:* A rubric should have rows for each trait or component to be measured. There may be fewer than five levels, but most rubrics have three to five levels of assessment. Additional columns or rows can be added for comments and/or total score. Created by authors

Assessment is a complex construct to understand and implement well. Many, if not most, teacher preparation programs will have entire courses dedicated to the design and implementation of assessments. Our goal in this chapter was to address the big ideas and concepts of assessment rather than to take a deep dive into the logistics and details of assessment. Much of that deep learning will come as we have more opportunities to engage with students in classrooms. Understanding the conceptual basis of good assessment is a key piece in building a philosophy of teaching that best supports adolescents through responsive instruction.

Let's revisit the learning outcomes:

1. **Understand the history and evolution of assessment and accountability:** Since the twenty-first century, assessment and accountability in education have evolved significantly, marked by initiatives like the NCLB (No Child Left Behind) Act and the ESSA (Every Student Succeeds Act), emphasizing standardized testing and school performance targets. These measures aim to ensure student success but have sparked debate over their effectiveness and impact on educational equity.

2. **Advocate for the use of varied and ongoing assessments, appreciating the diversity in student talents and skills, and tailoring assessments to accommodate individual learning preferences:** Utilizing diverse assessment methods, such as portfolios, projects, and ongoing formative assessments, celebrates students' diverse talents and preferences. This approach supports inclusive learning environments by providing personalized feedback and adapting instructional strategies in real time, based on student progress.

3. **Recognize the role of grades and the benefits of using rubrics in the assessment process:** Grades serve as a crucial tool for communicating students' proficiency in attaining learning objectives and should provide clear feedback on students' understanding and performance. Using rubrics enhances this process by outlining specific criteria and expectations, ensuring consistency in assessment, and supporting both students' learning and teachers' instructional decisions.

Suggested Readings

https://www.amle.org/assessment/
https://www.amle.org/formative-and-summative-assessments-in-the-classroom/
https://www.amle.org/formative-assessment-practices-in-successful-middle-level-classrooms/
https://www.amle.org/curriculum-instruction-and-assessment/
Wormeli, R. (2006). Accountability: Teaching through assessment and feedback, not grading. *American secondary education*, 14–27.
Wormeli, R. (2011). Redos and retakes done right. *Educational Leadership, 69*(3), 22–26.

References

Black, P., & Wiliam, D. (2009). Developing the theory of formative assessment. *Educational Assessment, Evaluation and Accountability (formerly: Journal of personnel evaluation in education), 21*, 5-31.

Capraro, R. M., Roe, M. F., Caskey, M. M., Strahan, D., Bishop, P.A., Weiss, C. C., & Swanson, K. W. (2011). *Research summary: Assessment*. Retrieved [Dec 12, 2023] from http://www.amle.org/TabId/270/ArtMID/888/ArticleID/309/Research-Summary-Assessment.aspx.

Marzano, R. J. (2011). Grades that show what students know. *Educational Leadership, 69*(3): 34–39.

CHAPTER 12

Literacy across the Disciplines

Learning Outcomes:

1. Understand how phonemic awareness, phonics, vocabulary, and fluency all support reading comprehension.
2. Recognize how the models of teaching reading and writing work together, and, subsequently, learn how to make good choices when it comes to strategy instruction within the disciplines.
3. Analyze disciplinary literacy in content areas to understand how content knowledge, experiences, and skills link to the ability to read, write, listen, speak, think critically, and perform in a way that is meaningful within the context.
4. Evaluate what it means to know a word, and learn how to increase student word knowledge.
5. Demonstrate how to incorporate evidence-based strategies in support of literacy.

Reading Comprehension

Reading is a complex activity, and successful reading includes multiple interrelated processes. Comprehension, the ability to understand what you are reading, is the goal of reading. In what is often referred to as the five big ideas of reading, four support comprehension: phonemic awareness, phonics, vocabulary, and fluency. In addition to vocabulary and fluent reading of text, reading comprehension requires background knowledge, understanding sentence and text structures, monitoring understanding, and connecting ideas. Before we can dive deeply into instructional choices that lead to comprehension, we need to cover models and concepts around reading and writing. Students need explicit instruction in how to think before, during, and after reading; how to monitor their understanding; and how to help themselves when meaning breaks down. Table 12.1 outlines the big five ideas of beginning reading and writing.

Table 12.1 The Five Big Ideas of Beginning Reading & Writing

Phonemic Awareness	The ability to identify and play with individual sounds in spoken words. Practice blending phonemes prepares students to read words, and practice segmenting phonemes prepares them to spell words.
Phonics	Understanding how letters and groups of letters link to sounds to form letter-sound relationships and spelling patterns. It involves learning letter-sound correspondences and common spelling patterns. Phonics supports decoding and spelling and leads to fluent reading.
Fluency	The ability to read words, phrases, sentences, and stories correctly, with enough speed and expression. When decoding skills become automatic, students can more easily focus their attention on understanding words and text. Fluency is the bridge to comprehension.
Vocabulary	Knowing what words mean and how to say and use them correctly. Many word meanings are learned through reading, but before students can read text on their own, vocabulary can be taught through oral language interactions and reading books aloud.
Comprehension	The ability to understand what you are reading. In addition to vocabulary and fluent reading of text, reading comprehension requires background knowledge, understanding sentence and text structures, monitoring understanding, and connecting ideas.
Writing	The ability to combine marks or signs that represent coherent words and composing text. The formation of letters to express words and ideas in print, in a way that renders language visible.

Source: National Center on Improving Literacy

> The point of reading is to understand. Word recognition is crucial and cannot be minimized. But for reading to be fully realized, there must be a relentless focus on comprehension, not as a mere collection of ingredients but as a series of chemical reactions. The chemistry of reading comprehension requires building background knowledge (not just activating it), motivation (not just the hope that it will emerge), analytic thinking, and persistence to move forward when the text gets hard (Fisher, Frey, & Lapp, 2022, p. 8).

MODELS OF READING

The Simple View of Reading

Gough and Tunmer (1986) identified the two most important abilities that result in reading comprehension according to their simple view of reading model: the ability to decode the words and the ability to comprehend the language of the text. Decoding, or recognizing words, refers to the accuracy and automaticity with which the words are read and is the foundation for reading comprehension. Language comprehension is the ability to understand spoken language through the use of various linguistic processes (Moats & Tolman, 2019). Both decoding and language-comprehension abilities are necessary for reading, and both must be strong. Strength in one area cannot compensate for a deficit in the other area.

Scarborough's Reading Rope

Conceptualized by Scarborough (2001), the model of the reading rope breaks down the word-recognition and language-comprehension domains emphasized in the simple view of reading model into specific skill areas. The illustration of the rope in Figure 12.1 provides understanding that there are three skill areas that make up word recognition; the areas include phonological awareness, decoding (and spelling), and sight word recognition. These three areas form the foundation of reading comprehension and automaticity, as these skills are critical for skilled reading. The top of the rope, the language-comprehension domain, includes skills that are necessary for comprehension of spoken language, which supports readers becoming more strategic as they develop these skills.

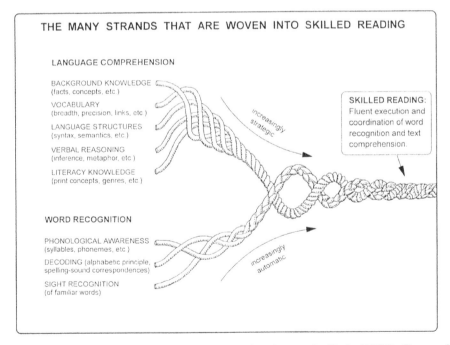

Figure 12.1 Scarborough's Reading Rope. Scarborough, H. S. (2001). Connecting early language and literacy to later reading (dis)abilities: Evidence, theory, and practice. In S. Neuman & D. Dickinson (Eds.), Handbook for research in early literacy (pp. 97-110). New York: Guilford Press. Permission obtained from Guilford Press via CCC Marketplace.

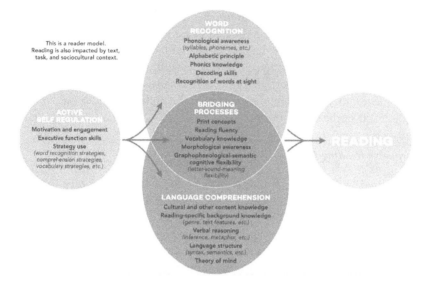

Figure 12.2 The Active View of Reading. Duke, N. K., & Cartwright, K. B. (2021). The science of reading progresses: Communicating advances beyond the Simple View of Reading. Reading Research Quarterly, 56(S1), S25-S44. https://ila.onlinelibrary.wiley.com/doi/full/10.1002/rrq.411 is an open access article under the terms of the Creative Commons Attribution-NonCommercial-NoDerivs License, which permits use and distribution in any medium, provided the original work is properly cited, the use is non-commercial and no modifications or adaptations are made.

The Active View of Reading

This is a reader model in which reading is also impacted by text, task, and sociocultural context. In other words, this model views reading as a multidimensional process that involves the reader's active meaning-making. Duke and Cartwright (2021) combined the simple view of reading with the results of more recent research. The active view of reading, as shown in Figure 12.2, suggests that reading depends on active self-regulation, which allows for language comprehension and word recognition. Self-regulation of reading involves using neurocognitive skills to plan, organize, remember, strategize, and attend to how to read a text.

The Four-Part Processing Model

This model for word recognition (Seidenberg & McClelland, 1989) is a simplified model that illustrates how the brain reads or recognizes words. It illustrates that there are four cognitive processes that are active in the reading brain.

- Phonological processes enable our work with the speech-sound system of our own language and other languages.
- Orthographic processes enable us to recognize and recall written language symbols.

- Meaning (or semantic) processes help us interpret word meanings in and out of context.
- Context processors interact with and support the meaning-processing system to help us comprehend text.

Ehri's Phases of Word Reading

This model identifies five phases of reading-skills development. These phases help us understand how children grow and develop on their path to proficient reading. Phonemic awareness, phonics skills, and reading behaviors are identified at each level. Ehri's phases help explain how words become "sight words" to beginning readers through **orthographic mapping**. The phases are as follows: prealphabetic, partial alphabetic, full alphabetic, consolidated alphabetic, and the automatic alphabetic.

- Prealphabetic phase. This phase is characterized by a reader's limited understanding of the alphabetic principle. In other words, the reader is not yet knowledgeable about the alphabet.
- Partial alphabetic phase. Readers begin to connect letters with sounds, but only partially. The reader is weak at decoding and reading by analogy because both of these strategies rely on stronger skills with the alphabetic principle. The reader can recognize and use letter-sound relationships but is not yet proficient and often makes mistakes.
- Full alphabetic phase. Many developing readers enter this phase by late kindergarten or early first grade. Most readers remain in this phase much longer than in the previous phases. Readers have a good understanding of the alphabetic principle and attend to each letter in a given word. Readers in this phase can decode words by applying their knowledge of letter-sound relationships and blending those sounds together to form words.
- Consolidated alphabetic phase. In this phase, readers become more automatic and fluent in their word-recognition skills and more efficient at decoding unknown words. Readers develop a large bank of sight vocabulary and no longer need to decode word by word while reading. Larger chunks of text are recognized, including word families, syllables, and roots. Readers use all of these for more efficient decoding rather than relying on individual phonemes.
- Automatic alphabetic phase. This stage is characterized by proficient readers, who can recognize and comprehend words quickly and effortlessly. At this stage, readers have developed a strong sight vocabulary, have a deep understanding of word structures, and can make connections between words with similar spellings and meanings. Unfamiliar words are decoded with automaticity, and readers can focus entirely on meaning. Most proficient adolescent readers have reached the automatic phase.

Structured Literacy

Structured literacy refers to a specific way of teaching students how to read. This method has been shown to support all students, regardless of their background or skill level. This approach is defined by four parameters and is based on the Orton-Gillingham method.

- Explicit. The concepts and skills being introduced to students are directly taught and practiced. We should not assume that students acquire literacy concepts through exposure alone.

- Systematic and cumulative. Each concept taught should build on the previous concept learned. Skills should be presented in a way that progresses from simple to complex.

- Hands-on, engaging, and multimodal. Students learn best when they are engaged and active in the learning process. This method combines listening, speaking, reading, and writing, which in turn develops a student's language-comprehension skills and fosters multimodal learning. The goal is to cultivate language-comprehension skills by allowing students to experience learning in a more interactive and engaged way.

- Diagnostic and responsive. We must be responsive to the needs of individual students, must continuously assess progress, and must adjust teaching accordingly. When teachers introduce new concepts, they should adapt the pacing of instruction, the mode of presentation, and students' opportunities for practice according to students' individual skill levels and understanding, ensuring students who need more time and guidance get that support.

Writing Rope

The literature related to literacy instruction tends to focus on reading, but we know that writing is just as important for students' literacy achievement. Joan Sedita (2019) created the writing rope model with Scarborough's reading rope model in mind, as shown in Figure 12.3. According to the writing rope model, substantial attention focuses on the components of reading while writing is often referred to as one (albeit large) skill. This model demonstrates the components necessary for skilled writing. The same metaphor—one of a rope—is used to illustrate the various strands that contribute to fluent, skilled writing. Of course, many of the skills that support writing also support reading comprehension.

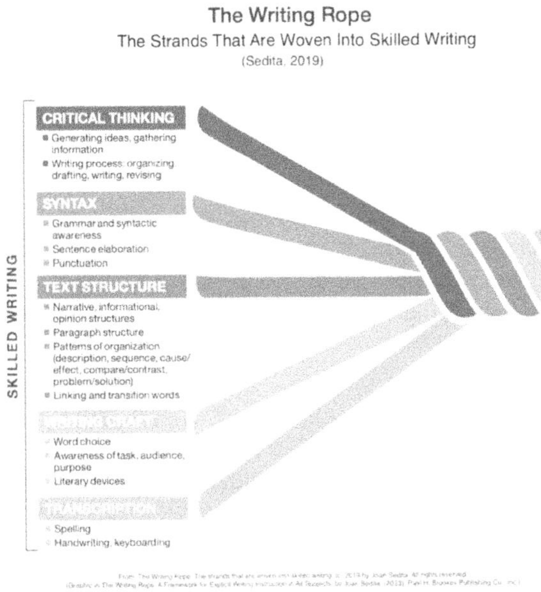

The Writing Rope
The Strands That Are Woven Into Skilled Writing
(Sedita, 2019)

CRITICAL THINKING
- Generating ideas, gathering information
- Writing process: organizing, drafting, writing, revising

SYNTAX
- Grammar and syntactic awareness
- Sentence elaboration
- Punctuation

TEXT STRUCTURE
- Narrative, informational, opinion structures
- Paragraph structure
- Patterns of organization (description, sequence, cause/effect, compare/contrast, problem/solution)
- Linking and transition words

- Word choice
- Awareness of task, audience, purpose
- Literary devices

- Spelling
- Handwriting, keyboarding

SKILLED WRITING

Figure 12.3 The Writing Rope. Sedita, J. (2019). The Writing Rope. Rowley, MA, Keys to Literacy. Reprinted with permission from Joan Sedita All rights reserved.

HOW THE MODELS WORK TOGETHER

It is important for teachers to think hard about the skills they teach, asking how students will use these skills in reading and writing. We must remember that reading and writing are communication processes. Writers think about their audiences and what they need to tell readers to communicate effectively. There is value in having readers think about authors and authors' perspectives. If we involve our students in reading and responding to each other's texts, the quality of their writing often improves. Of course, the combined use of reading and writing helps us accomplish academic goals, such as studying or learning from text and composing synthesis papers (think lab reports or summary reports). The What Works Clearinghouse includes an IES Practice Guide on improving reading comprehension in the early grades (K–2), but the underlying principles apply to us middle grades teachers as well (Shanahan et al., 2010). It is essential to teach students how to use comprehension strategies and how to identify and use a text's organizational structures as well as to guide students through focused, high-quality discussions about texts. This means that our selection of texts must be purposeful and that we establish an engaging and motivating context in which to teach reading comprehension. Students need explicit instruction in how to think before, during, and after reading. This instruction should include how to monitor their understanding and how to help themselves when meaning breaks down (Duke, Ward, & Pearson, 2021). Even if students know how to read and can do so fluently, this is very often still true in the middle grades. Comprehension strategies to teach include activating prior knowledge, predicting, questioning, visualizing, monitoring (includes clarifying or fixing up), drawing inferences, and summarizing/retelling (Shanahan et al., 2010).

Before we think about strategy instruction, it is important to consider the variety of reasons why adolescents may struggle with text. Their difficulties may be insufficient vocabulary knowledge, lack of general knowledge of topics and text structures, not knowing what to do when comprehension breaks down, or poor proficiency in monitoring their own reading comprehension. Most recent literacy initiatives target younger readers and attempt to instill basic decoding and comprehension skills, but struggling adolescent readers in our schools face more complex and persistent challenges. Supporting these readers as they grapple with the highly specific demands of texts written for different content areas will help prepare them for the world outside of school, encourage personal growth, and open up opportunities for future education and employment.

STRATEGY INSTRUCTION

A 2014 study from The Iris Center about middle school struggling readers revealed that 47 percent had difficulty with word identification. Of the 47 percent, nearly all of them also struggled with fluency and/or comprehension and 84 percent struggled with comprehension either in isolation or in combination with other reading skills. Many students were floundering not only in reading comprehension but also in other areas, at basic levels. Knowing this means we must be thoughtful in our selection of strategies. Strategies are not the same as the comprehension skills that are typically listed in core reading programs; nor are they teaching activities. Instead, strategies are mental actions that are intentionally engaged in during reading and that improve reading comprehension. These are the deliberate efforts made by a reader to better understand or remember what is being read. It is essential for teachers to understand that strategies are not instructional activities, such as completing worksheets, which rarely include instruction in what students should actively do in their heads to improve comprehension. Strategies are also not exercises aimed at giving students practice with skills, such as sequencing or drawing conclusions, but that lack explicit instruction in how to think while reading. Teachers need to become familiar with what the strategy is meant to do and why (before using it). They must ask themselves, "What skills is this strategy meant to support?" and "What content should be known?" For example, if the goal is to build vocabulary, a strategy meant to support fluency is unlikely to yield the desired result. It is important for us to remember that readers must know something about the content in order to use a strategy effectively.

READING CONNECTIONS

While early reading focuses on learning that letters make sounds and that words carry meaning, reading quickly develops to a point where the message taken from text depends on what the reader brings to it. In the Carnegie Report for New York's Council on Advancing Adolescent Literacy, Lee and Spratley (2010) describe this phenomenon, saying that "the ability to comprehend written texts is not a static or fixed ability, but rather one that involves a dynamic relationship between the demands of texts and prior knowledge and goals of the reader" (p. 3). Therefore, electricians reading a journal article that describes the concepts of voltage and current will take more information away from the text than would novices because of their knowledge and experience. Both generic and more discipline-specific strategies support students as they attempt to comprehend complex text. While the generic strategies pertain across content areas, discipline-specific ones must be tailored to match the demands of the content area. Both types of strategies and knowledge must be applied to the comprehension and evaluation of textbooks; journal and magazine articles; historically situated primary documents; full-length books; newspaper articles; book chapters; and multimedia and digital texts.

Literacy within the Disciplines

WHAT IS DISCIPLINARY LITERACY?

Literacy, defined as the ability to read, write, listen, speak, think critically, and perform in different ways and for different purposes, begins to develop early and becomes increasingly important as students pursue specialized fields of study in high school and beyond. Disciplinary literacy is defined as the confluence of content knowledge, experiences, and skills, merged with the ability to read, write, listen, speak, think critically, and perform in a way that is meaningful within the context of a given field. These abilities are important in *all* courses and subjects. There is a need to broaden this effort and to include all disciplines and every educator in every grade level, from kindergarten through twelfth grade. Efforts to build literacy must begin as soon as children have access to formal education and must continue intentionally as college and career readiness goals advance for all children.

Table 12.2 Generic versus Discipline-Specific Reading Strategies

Generic Reading Strategies	Discipline-Specific Reading Strategies
Monitor comprehension	Build prior knowledge
Pre-read	Build specialized vocabulary
Set goals	Learn to deconstruct complex sentences
Think about what one already knows	Use knowledge of text structures and genres to predict main and subordinate ideas
Ask questions	
Make predictions	Map graphic (and mathematical) representations against explanations in the text
Test predictions against the text	Pose discipline relevant questions
	Compare claims and propositions across texts
Re-read	Use norms for reasoning within the discipline (i.e. what counts as evidence) to evaluate claims
Summarize	

Source: Lee & Spratley, 2010

WHY IS DISCIPLINARY LITERACY IMPORTANT?

Workforce trends tell us that some kind of postsecondary education, whether it be vocational training or apprenticeship or a higher education, is necessary. Success depends on our ability to comprehend and produce the kinds of complex texts found in all disciplines (in whatever form, including printed materials, digital materials, how-to manuals, guidance documents, lab summaries, traditional textbooks, etc.). Therefore, the economic future of our state as well as of our students and their success as productive citizens and critical thinkers link to disciplinary literacy. Textbooks, articles, manuals, and historical primary-source documents create specialized challenges for learners. These texts often include abstracts, figures, tables, diagrams, and specialized vocabulary. The ideas examined in such texts are complex and build across paragraphs, requiring focus and strategic processing. To comprehend and produce this type of text, students must be immersed in the language and thinking processes of that discipline and they must be supported by an expert guide, their teacher (Lee & Spratley, 2010). A focus at the elementary and middle school levels on foundational reading, when expanded to include engaging experiences connected to informational texts, vocabulary, and writing for content-specific purposes, builds background knowledge and skills in each discipline. This increases opportunities for success as students approach more rigorous content in those disciplines (Alliance for Excellent Education, 2011). Reading, writing, speaking, listening, and critical thinking must be integrated into each discipline across all grades so that all students gradually build knowledge and skills toward college and career readiness. The message is that literacy is integral to attainment of content knowledge and that content is essential background knowledge for literacy development. This interdependent relationship exists in all disciplines.

Pause and Reflect: How would you define literacy in your discipline? What does deeper learning look like in your discipline? What about rigor? If you had to name the most important skill students need (in your discipline), what would that be? How does it compare to skills they may need in other subjects?

No one is asking you to be a reading teacher, but ensuring that all students read, write, think, and learn should be at the core of all instruction. Disciplinary literacy is about how to read in a discipline. It is about asking questions, such as "What does a mathematician do?" and "What about a scientist?" For the most part,

- reading in science is about inquiry;
- reading in math includes noticing patterns and relationships as well as understanding through visuals or abstract representations; and
- reading in social studies largely focuses on context and perspective as well as the examination and interpretation of primary-source documents.

Academic learning begins in early childhood and develops across all disciplines. Each discipline has its own specific vocabulary, text types, and ways of communicating. Children begin learning these context- and content-specific differences early in life and continue through high school and beyond. School offers all students opportunities to develop the ability to, for example, think like a scientist, write like a historian, and solve problems like a mathematician. Table 12.3 shows examples of how disciplinary professionals read. As students' literacy skills develop, educators gradually place increasing amounts of responsibility for reading, writing, listening, speaking, and critical thinking on students through guided supports in both individual and collaborative learning experiences.

Content knowledge is strengthened when educators integrate discipline-specific literacy into teaching and learning. Educators help students recognize and understand the nuances of a discipline by using strategies that "make their thinking visible." They promote classroom reading, writing, listening, speaking, and critical thinking using authentic materials that support the development of content-specific knowledge. They guide students through these complex texts by using strategies that develop conceptual understanding of language and set expectations for relevant application of skills. These literacy practices deepen students' content knowledge, strategies, and skills so that their learning transfers from the classroom to real-world situations.

The literacy skills of reading, writing, listening, speaking, and critical thinking improve when content-rich learning experiences motivate and engage students. Educators who foster disciplinary literacy develop experiences that integrate rigorous content with relevant collaborative and creative literacy processes to motivate and engage students. Setting high expectations, they structure routines and supports that empower students to take charge of their own learning. When students work in teams to research

Table 12.3 How Disciplinary Professionals Read

Scientists	Mathematicians	Historians
• assume an objective stance • search for answers to relevant questions • evaluate quality and quantity of evidence • look for data- or evidence-based outcomes • pay attention to details and numbers • chart, illustrate, and graph data and conclusions • ask "Why?" more than "What?"	• use information read as pieces of a puzzle to be solved • make meaning out of symbols and abstract ideas • ask questions as they read • look for patterns and relationships • identify what the problem is asking rather than reading only for information • make note of confusions • apply previous learned concepts • look for what is missing	• interpret primary and secondary sources, scrutinizing for bias • compare and contrast events, accounts, documents, and visuals (e.g., photographs) • create narratives from existing information • use knowledge of the present to make sense of the past and vice versa • think sequentially to piece together timelines • make inferences and determine what is important from what is just interesting • differentiate fact from conflicting accounts and perspectives • determine meanings of words within context

Source: Lent, R. C. (2016)

science and mathematics concepts in the development of an invention or a graphic-arts design or when they collaboratively build a blog that explains their recent marketing venture, they use specific literacy skills and strategies to solidify learning. Students need these opportunities over time to develop the precise and complex reading, writing, listening, speaking, and critical-thinking skills demanded in today's careers. Students demonstrate their content knowledge through reading, writing, listening, and speaking as part of a content-literate community.

Students who are literate in a particular discipline can successfully read in, write in, and speak about that discipline and can listen to and think critically about communications in that community. Performance tasks that allow students to present the complexity of a content area in a way that is meaningful to the field become authentic approaches to assessing mastery within a discipline. Such tasks empower students to discover the real-world connections across disciplines and to actively participate in communities of discipline-literate peers. These performance tasks should become integral to assessment of student learning.

To become college and career ready, students must grapple with more complicated works whose significance extends across genres, cultures, and time. Such works offer insight and serve as models for students' own thinking and writing. Through wide and deep reading of literature and literary nonfiction of steadily increasing difficulty, students gain a treasure trove of literary and cultural knowledge, references, and images; the ability to evaluate complex arguments; and the capacity to prevail over the challenges posed by complex texts.

Making writing connections is important, and emphasis should be placed on three types of writing: narrative, informational, and logical argument. Writing that presents a logical argument is especially appropriate to discipline-specific work since the nature of credible evidence differs across content areas. The ability to consider multiple perspectives, assess the validity of claims, and present a point of view is required in argumentative writing. These thinking and communication skills are critical to future readiness (for, e.g., postsecondary education/college, workforce training, and career development). Research on writing to learn, rather than only for assessment, has a significant impact on content learning. Studies have found that writing to learn was equally effective for all content areas (social studies, math, and science) and at every grade, from fourth through twelfth.

For students, writing is a key means of making and defending claims, illustrating what they know about a subject, and conveying what they have experienced, imagined, felt, and thought. To be college- and career-ready writers, students must take the task, their purpose, and their audience into careful consideration, choosing words, information, structures, and formats deliberately. They need to know how to combine elements of different kinds of writing. One example would be using narrative strategies within an argument and using explanation within a narrative to produce complex writing. Students need to be able to use digital resources strategically when creating, refining, and collaborating on writing. And they have to become adept at gathering information, evaluating sources, and citing material accurately, reporting findings from their research and analysis of sources in a clear and convincing manner. Flexibility, concentration, and fluency are required to produce high-quality first drafts, just as the capacity to revisit a piece of writing and make improvements to it over multiple drafts, when circumstances encourage or require it, is essential.

When a social-studies teacher guides students in taking on the perspective of a person from a specific historical era, he or she might ask students to write a first-person narrative from that perspective. Students can be successful at this task only after engaging in research into that era (including investigation of primary-source documents) to discover the personal beliefs of the historical person. Digging into the personal experiences, ideas, and events involved in the era should help a student to visualize life in that period. These tasks help students develop a rich understanding of the era and embed language from that era into writing that they create.

SPEAKING, LISTENING, AND LANGUAGE CONNECTIONS

Having the ability to share ideas and orally communicate with credibility in a specific academic discourse empowers students and allows access to specialized groups. Teachers need to prioritize these skills so that students are at ease as they enter situations connected to a specific content area and are more likely to continue learning in that discipline. As expertise develops, students feel more comfortable applying knowledge and skills while speaking and listening in a specific discipline.

Language and literacy develop progressively over time; many call this process a "staircase of literacy demands." The conceptual understanding of functions in math may begin to develop in elementary school in its simplest form. As students' understanding of this concept develops over the years, students will use the word *function* in a meaningful way, when speaking and writing, to describe this concept. When educators explicitly connect a math term to its application and repeatedly expose students to the concept connected to the term, a specialized language becomes second nature to students in the math classroom. Students must have extensive vocabularies, built through reading and explicit instruction, embedded in the context of content learning. This enables them to comprehend complex texts, engage in purposeful writing, and communicate effectively within a discipline. Skills in determining or clarifying the meaning of words and phrases encountered, choosing flexibly from an array of strategies, and seeing an individual word as part of a network of other words that, for example, have similar **denotations** but different **connotations** allow students to access information and support their own learning.

LITERACY IN MULTIPLE LANGUAGES

In the current setting of increasing economic, security, cross-cultural, and global demands, the significance of literacy in more than one language has grown. Students who think, read, write, and communicate in multiple languages are an asset to our own country and can more easily interact and compete in the world at large. English learners in our classrooms face significant challenges as they add a new language and work to grasp content at the same rate as their English-speaking peers. Researchers have found that a focus on academic literacy is crucial for English learners' success in school. In their description of academic literacy, they include reading, writing, and oral discourse that

- varies from subject to subject;
- requires knowledge of multiple genres of text and purposes for text use and text media;
- is influenced by students' literacies in contexts that are outside of school; and
- is influenced by students' personal, social, and cultural experiences.

The needs of English learners are addressed when we embed disciplinary literacy strategies into our subject-area teaching. These high-impact strategies and skills allow English learners and all students to more readily access content knowledge and connect it to the prior knowledge they bring to the classroom. When educators take the initiative to understand and embed these strategies and skills, they offer additional opportunities for success to all of our students.

Pause and Reflect: How do teachers step back from presenting content and begin to infuse literacy skills into every class, every day, so that students can produce and not just memorize information? Teachers must be free to employ the tools, texts, and principles of their discipline to give students opportunities to use and apply knowledge. Having such freedom, in most middle and high schools, is a big order. Your role as the teacher is to help students learn how to use the knowledge they are learning as a tool to participate in work within the discipline you teach.

Promoting Comprehension through Read-Alouds, Shared Readings, Close Reading, and Think-Alouds

The first three of these techniques provide opportunities to model comprehension through think-alouds. It is important to think about the focus of your class—text selection is key.

READ-ALOUDS

In this technique, the teacher selects a text or passage to read (out loud) to a small or large group of students. The purpose is to focus the content of the text.

Pause and Reflect: What are some elements to consider when planning for read-alouds?

SHARED READING

In this technique, a text or passage is jointly read by the teacher and a student. The text is chosen because of its content and as a way to draw attention to a feature or comprehension strategy.

Pause and Reflect: What are some examples of comprehension strategies that are suitable for shared reading? What are some guidelines on how to successfully implement a shared reading?

CLOSE READING

This technique is used with complex texts. Students read the selection repeatedly and discuss it at length while the teacher uses text-dependent questions to draw students back to the text. Close reading is an important comprehension tool because it encourages students to read and reread a text in order to understand it and to draw logical inferences from it. Using short, but relevant, text selections, close reading asks students to focus on what is explicitly stated by the author, to make inferences from the key details presented, and to support conclusions and inferences with evidence that is directly in the text.

Pause and Reflect: How do you distinguish lessons incorporating close reading from those incorporating the other two techniques?

THINK-ALOUDS

Think-alouds refers to a process in which teachers share their thinking with students. They model thinking while reading, and students should follow along in their minds and even interject when their own thinking becomes visible. There are five basic steps to follow:

1. Select to read aloud passages that contain points of difficulty, ambiguities, contradictions, or unknown words.

2. While orally reading and modeling thinking aloud, have students follow silently and listen to how trouble spots are thought through.

3. Have students work with partners to practice think-alouds by taking turns reading short, carefully prepared passages and sharing thoughts.

4. Have students practice independently—while you monitor the strategies they use—reflecting on the predictions they made, the mental images they formed, or the analogies they recognized.

5. Integrate practice with other lessons (to encourage transfer), and provide occasional demonstrations of how, why, and when to use think-alouds.

   Teachers should be sure that students are

- developing hypotheses by making predictions;
- developing images by describing pictures forming in their heads from the information being read;

- linking new information with prior knowledge by sharing analogies;
- monitoring comprehension by verbalizing a confusing point; and
- regulating comprehension by demonstrating strategies.

Planning and preparing for use of any of these techniques should include practice and rereading. Lessons will go more smoothly when you (the teacher) know and understand the text deeply. All these techniques are meant to deepen students' interactions with texts, which must be carefully selected. Careful preparation and practicing in advance can be helpful for you as the teacher.

Evidence-Based Practices

PROMPTING CONNECTIONS TO PRIOR KNOWLEDGE

Students learn new ideas by reference to ideas they already know (Bransford, Brown, & Cocking, 2000). Teachers should prompt students to activate important prior knowledge and explicitly connect it to new ideas—this is how we learn new ideas. We learn more efficiently and effectively when prompted to "retrieve" information from long-term memory, information that we can use to process our new learning (Deans for Impact, 2015, 2023). Students who do not make successful connections to prior knowledge are less likely to understand new ideas. Teachers should make instructional choices that prompt students to make connections to relevant knowledge they already have. Students have lots of prior knowledge at their disposal, but, if teachers do not purposefully activate students' prior knowledge, students may not know what is most useful to help them make sense of new information. Because new learning builds on prior knowledge in a way relating to how the prior knowledge is organized (in **schema**), learning gaps are exacerbated for students who may not encounter informal opportunities to learn about concepts outside of school. By making the organization of ideas visible and prompting students to think about those connections among prior and new learning, teachers can help all students sharpen schema and process new information. In practice, this means each lesson includes the following:

- relevant prior knowledge that is important and specific;
- a structure of and relationships among concepts (i.e., schema) that are sufficiently explicit that students see the deep structure; and
- prompts that allow all learners to activate prior knowledge.

Teachers should *avoid* engaging in the following practices:

- Brain dump. Doing a brain dump includes using unstructured prompts in applying strategies like the know-want to know-learn strategy, according to which students are simply asked, "What do you know about X?" This strategy does not target specific-enough knowledge to ensure students are thinking about the most relevant material. For example, a science teacher wants students to understand how the process of photosynthesis stores energy. A typical prompt might include the following: "Take three minutes to jot down every fact you can think of related to photosynthesis." A more effective way to prompt students to recall that the food energy that plants contain comes from sunlight would be to ask students to write a response to the following questions: "What do plants eat?" and "How do they grow and fuel themselves to make fruits and seeds and new leaves?"

- Superficial skim. When teachers use prompts that elicit only surface-level knowledge, without elaboration, or a list of isolated concepts or one-word answers, they are doing a superficial skim. For example, a social-studies teacher has students read and discuss the thesis of Martin Luther King Jr.'s *Letter from the Birmingham Jail*; its thesis is that sometimes civil disobedience is an appropriate response to injustice. At the start of the next lesson, the teacher might ask simply, "Let's recall information about MLK Jr. What was the name of the text we read yesterday?" This question elicits only surface-level knowledge. An effective alternative would be to have students do a card sort in which they organize a variety of terms into categories and explain their thinking to other students. A few terms could be *segregate, tension, justice, injustice, mutuality, provincial, deplore, futility, impunity, legitimate, provocation*, and *status quo*.

- Taking hands. Taking means engaging only a few students, which results in only some students receiving opportunities to activate their prior knowledge. A common question when taking hands might be something like, "What effect does the greenhouse effect have on the earth's surface temperature? I see four hands . . . X, what do you think?" Only the selected student may answer. A more effective approach would be for the teacher to offer directions on the prompt: "Turn and talk to your neighbor about . . ." or "Take two minutes to write or illustrate in your notes . . ."

- Tangential personal connections. When a teacher focuses on less relevant connections that do not help students call up prior academic knowledge to learn new content, the teacher is focusing on tangential personal connections. For example, a teacher says, "Turn and talk to your neighbor. What are linear equations? Why are they important?" A more effective prompt would be to ask, "Tell your neighbor how you identify a linear equation. Have your neighbor tell you what a nonlinear equation is. Ask your neighbor how he or she knows."

DRAWING ATTENTION TO MEANING

As we learned in Chapter 1 from the model of the mind and the science of learning (Deans for Impact, 2015, 2023), we can learn only what we pay attention to, and our attention is finite. Teachers should focus student attention on the most important content of the lesson, and each part of the lesson must be aligned to the big idea. All students miss out when they waste instructional time thinking about less relevant material, and the tasks teachers ask of students directly reflect what they think students are capable of. When students are repeatedly offered lessons that do not align to grade-level learning goals, the missed grade-level learning opportunities compound over time and fuel inequitable outcomes. Students who are prompted to think about grade-level content can build on their knowledge when they hit more advanced topics, while their peers who were denied those opportunities struggle. In practice, this means the following:

- Each lesson has a learning goal that is clear, achievable, and on grade-level.
- Each lesson component focuses attention on the most important content.
- All learners are thinking about the meaning of content in relation to the learning goal.

Teachers should *avoid* the following:

- Activity-driven planning. Such planning focuses on engagement only—using games, centers, and group work to engage students—rather than also focusing on designing instruction to assist students in attaining the learning goal. For example, in a lesson about how animals adapt to their environment, key knowledge to be learned may be that giraffes have long necks and tongues that allow them to eat leaves from tall trees without competing with other animals; or the thick fur of a polar bear keeps it warm. A teacher using activity-driven planning may ask students to construct a habitat. These students may thinking mostly about the materials needed to build the habitat or about how to construct a long neck on a cardboard giraffe. A more effective alternative would be to have students illustrate a habitat but spend most of class time writing or explaining how the animal's features adapted to fit its regional habitat.

- Differentiation overload. When instruction is based on the learning-styles myth or is designed in a way that struggling students do not experience meaningful learning that is aligned to the objective of the lesson, the instruction reflects differentiation overload. The idea of learning styles is a myth because there is no scientific evidence to support it. The myth is based on the idea that people are either visual, auditory, or kinesthetic learners and that their preferred learning style is related to their sensory perception. However, research suggests that some students may perform better when taught in a different modality than their self-identified learning style. Additionally, most studies of learning styles use a methodology that applies multiple styles to all learners, making it difficult to isolate learning style from teaching method. In a classroom, this might look, for example, like giving "visual learners" a word sort about animals adapting to habitats. A more impactful option would be to plan for students to encounter multiple modalities of learning about animals and their habitats.

- Unambitious content. Using unambitious content refers to using content that is inappropriate for the grade level. Students end up missing opportunities to build knowledge and skills that successive grade levels build upon. In a typical scenario involving unambitious content, students might be asked to make a bullet list of facts about the Emancipation Proclamation but are never asked to synthesize learning and are assessed only on the number of facts they write down. A more impactful instructional choice would be to ask students to evaluate the reasons the Emancipation Proclamation was issued in September of 1862. Next, students would examine primary- and secondary-source documents to answer a series of inquiry questions.

- Mile-wide, inch-deep content. Such instruction attempts to include in a lesson too many objectives for a single lesson, which results in superficial learning and students who are not sure where to focus. An example would be a lesson on common representations of Native Americans in the United States as well as how they are represented in today's society with their actual customs, traditions, and way of life, even as students are learning about each tribe for the first time. More effective instruction could instead focus on key features of each Native American tribe as a focus for comparing and contrasting tribes. Future lessons could cover representations in today's society.

PROMPTING FOR EFFORTFUL THINKING

Teacher's questions and tasks should require students to engage in effortful thinking, which is the core of learning (Deans for Impact, 2015, 2023). How hard we think about something influences how well we learn it. Teachers can prompt deeper, "effortful" thinking with elaborative questions and tasks that cue thinking about relationships between ideas. These prompts often start with "how" or "why." Effortful prompts help teachers check for understanding, but their core purpose is to promote learning, so students encode more deeply and durably into long-term memory. In practice, this means teachers should do the following in each lesson:

- Prompt students to analyze, justify, and explain ideas to be remembered.

- Space effortful prompts, and prioritize and structure instructional time so students have time to process.

- Offer prompts to all, not just some, students.

    Teachers should *avoid* using the following:

- Checking-the-box questions. A teacher who uses questions to get through a lesson and who moves on as soon as a student provides an answer is using checking-the-box questions. This strategy typically looks like a teacher reading an excerpt from a text and stating, for instance, "This is an example of . . ." and then asking, "What part of the story's structure is this?" or "How does this impact temperature?" As soon as a student says an appropriate response, the teacher moves on to the next excerpt. A more effective approach would be saying, "Take a moment and write down your thoughts" and then asking, for instance, "What part of the story's structure did we just read? How do you know?" Another example would be instructing students to "Take a moment and write down your thoughts," then asking, "What are some factors that impact ocean temperature? How do you know?"

- One-word-answer questions. Such questions start with who, what, when, or where, but not why or how. Students do need to think deeply to recall a short answer. When teaching about how to solve for the slope, a teacher might ask, "What is the y-coordinate of slope intercept form?" A more productive scenario would be something like this: "To solve this equation, explain to your neighbor where you start and why." After listening to responses, a teacher might prompt further by asking, "What do we need to do next to solve this equation? How do you know?"

- Teacher bowtie. When a teacher answers his or her own questions or rephrases student responses in ways that cue the answer, the teacher is using a teacher bowtie. Not all students can think deeply and process their ideas in this scenario. A common example would be a teacher asking, "What part of the animal cell is this (referring to an image)?" After a student answers, the teacher might respond, "Correct. This is the . . . part of the cell because . . ." A more impactful approach would be to follow-up by asking another question, such as "How do you know?" and then instructing students to "Tell your neighbor why animal cells do not have walls" (this allows animal cells to change more in size and shape than plant cells can).

- Dressing up questions. This practice may seem to encourage effortful learning but does not engage students in deep processing. Dressed up questions shift students away from the key idea. Examples include "What did you do next?" and "Who else noticed something?" They may also include recall questions disguised with higher-order verbs: "Create a list of . . ." In a lesson on functions, for example, a dressed up question would be the teacher asking a student whether a relation is a function or not. A more effective approach would be to ask, "How did you know the relation was a function?" Other effective questions include the following: "When is a relation also a function?"; "How do you evaluate functions using function notation?"; and "How do you identify the domain and range of a relation or function?"

USING EXAMPLES AND NONEXAMPLES

Teachers prompt students to connect and distinguish varied examples and contrasting *nonexamples* (Deans for Impact, 2015, 2023). A nonexample is the opposite of an example; an example provides an instance of similarity, whereas a nonexample provides an instance of contrast. We need both to refine our mental models of a concept in long-term memory. Varied examples help a learner define the most important parts of a concept so they are not fooled by distracting factors that might cause them to undergeneralize about key ideas. Nonexamples help students attend to the boundaries of a concept and avoid overgeneralizing about key ideas. Because new learning builds on prior knowledge and builds on it according to how that knowledge is organized in long-term memory (i.e., schema), learning gaps are exacerbated if we do not support students in developing nuanced schema about ideas. For students who may not encounter informal opportunities to learn about the concepts outside of school, these chances to refine schema are especially important. Prompting students to articulate the connections and differences among examples helps them tune into the deep structure so they build accurate schema. By thinking deeply about the connections, students are more likely to store the ideas in durable ways and to be able to draw on the ideas more easily in the future. In practice, this means each lesson includes the following:

- Varied examples that draw student attention to the deep features of a concept
- Nonexamples to draw student attention to the boundaries of a concept
- Prompts to get students to explain connections and differences among examples and nonexamples

Teachers should *avoid* using the following:

- Missing pieces. Having missing pieces means students do not have the necessary pieces to build schema because a teacher has failed to provide examples, nonexamples, or opportunities to make connections between the two. A teacher might say, "Something is *soluble* in water if its molecules dissolve in it. So, with that in mind, today we're exploring how we can conduct electric current through certain liquids." Instead, the teacher could say, "Something is *soluble* in water if its molecules dissolve in it. For example, salt is soluble in water, but oil is not. How might they be different in their composition to make that be true?"

- Unplanned examples. When a teacher does not intentionally select examples and nonexamples ahead of time and, therefore, comes up with something in the moment that may be confusing or misleading for students, the teacher is using unplanned examples. In a lesson where students seem confused about the meaning of *soluble*, the teacher might say, "You know, like salt is soluble, but flour is insoluble." And a student might say, "But flour does kind of disappear in water and just makes it cloudy, what do you mean?" Instead, the teacher has planned in advance and says "Think about salt and sand. If I stir a little bit of salt into a glass of water, it disappears and doesn't come back. That's soluble. If I add sand, once I stop stirring it all settles to the bottom. That's insoluble."

- Familiarity bias. When a teacher selects examples with which students are already familiar, they do not have opportunities to broaden schemas due to their familiarity bias. This might look like the teacher giving examples only from common household items, like sugar, salt, oil, and vinegar. Instead, the teacher might augment household examples with discussion of how different medicines have different solubilities and are taken up at different rates in the body. Students then get to see how medical science is influenced by the concept.

- Treating all examples as equal. When a teacher does not intervene to contradict or clarify student-generated examples or nonexamples that do not fit or that are not relevant, the teacher implicitly treats all examples as being equal. In this scenario, students miss out on receiving feedback to help them correct their developing schema. In this scenario, a student learning about linear and nonlinear equations might say, "I like constants. They are always changing." "Mmhmm," says the teacher and moves on. Instead, the teacher could say, "Let's take a moment with that. What does the word 'constant' mean?" Students would likely talk about the meaning as being unchanging, remaining the same, or something similar. Then the teacher could go on to say, "An equation is a statement in which the values of two mathematical expressions are equal. These statements consist of constants and variables. Constants are values that never change. Variables like y or x represent unknown numerical values."

QUESTIONING DURING INSTRUCTION AND STRATEGIES THAT PROMPT THINKING

Questioning during instruction is one of the most effective ways to engage students, keep them on task, and get them to think more deeply about content. The key to developing an effective questioning technique when discussing readings is to prepare questions in advance. Additionally, questions should be tied to learning tasks that are familiar so that they are a natural part of the lesson (rather than a "quiz" of knowledge at the end). Teachers use questions to

- motivate and interest students,
- stimulate thinking,
- pace and orient cognitive processing,
- check for understanding,
- increase student involvement,
- build communication skills, and
- draw out prior knowledge related to a topic.

At the *beginning* of a lesson, questioning can activate schema. *During* the presentation, or developmental phase, of the lesson, questioning serves several purposes. The first would be to focus on what material is most important. Others might be to find out if students are comprehending the presentation or to allow for direct student participation. At the *end* of a lesson, questioning may be used to evaluate student knowledge or to allow students to share their knowledge of a topic with the class. There are two overall types of questions: low-level (require only mental recall to be answered) and high-level (require thought to be answered). Teachers should also consider developing both convergent and divergent questions. Convergent questions require students to search for a single answer to the question posed. There is only one single correct response. Divergent questions cause students to explore different possible acceptable answers. Many possible answers are appropriate, and examples are shown in Table 12.4.

Table 12.4 Convergent and Divergent Questions

Low-Level Convergent **Questions** basic recall/attention to detail	**High-Level** Convergent **Questions** problem solving/using clues/analysis
What is 5 x 9?	Identify each of the following as a screw or a wedge: a) nail, b) fork, c) ax, d) needle, and e) winding staircase.
Low-Level Divergent **Questions** recall/attention to detail	**High-Level** Divergent **Questions** recall/analysis/evaluation/observation
What is an example of an inclined plane?	What is your favorite period of American history and why?
	Name a famous person you admire and tell why you look up to him or her.

A few important reminders for teachers:

- Incorporate adequate wait time. Wait time is when a teacher deliberately pauses to allow students time to think, write, engage. This is especially important to do while asking questions. We tend to jump right to the answer and not allow students time to think. You might count silently to enforce wait time. Or another strategy would be to have students first jot down a few thoughts and then engage in discussion of the answer.

- Plan to redirect questions. This practice encourages participation if your student is not responding or allows your student to correct himself or herself if the student said an incorrect answer. If the conversation stops, you can use a redirecting question to get it on track. Do this by asking, "Can you think of another way to think about this?"; "How is your answer different from . . .?"; "Let's figure out what information we need to answer the question"; or "That is a solid book definition, but how can we define that in our own words?"

- Prompt and probe. Think of prompts as little reminders; think of probes as ways to get students to say more about the topic. Prompt by saying, "You haven't mentioned . . ." Keep in mind that your goal is to remind, cue, or tell them what you would like them to talk about. Probes might include who, what, when, where, and how follow-ups. Another way to probe is to ask students to elaborate on a response: "Would you elaborate on that?" or "Can you give me more detail?"

- Use a framework, such as Bloom's taxonomy or Costa's levels-of-thinking-and-questioning model (Bloom, 1956; Costa, 1985, p. 125–37), to ramp up the quality of your questions for students. Table 12.5 highlights examples and strategies to help with implementation. For students to better understand the content being presented in the content areas, it is important for them to learn to think critically and to ask higher levels of questions. By asking higher levels of questions, students deepen their knowledge and create connections to the material being presented, which in turn prepares them for the inquiry that occurs in lessons. Teachers should be familiar with Costa's or Bloom's levels of questioning to assist them in formulating and identifying higher levels of questions. Bloom's taxonomy is a hierarchical ordering of cognitive skills that can help teachers and students, while Costa's levels of thinking is a way to create questions that apply the levels-of-thinking-and-questioning model of cognition in three levels.

Table 12.5 Bloom's Taxonomy and Costa's Levels of Questioning

Bloom's Taxonomy			
Level	**Verbs**		
Knowledge questions encourage students to recall information in the form in which they learned it.	Name List Identify Acquire Label	Locate Quote Record Repeat	
Comprehension is the ability to grasp the material's meaning, and comprehension questions encourage students to communicate an idea or concept in a new or different form.	Describe Estimate Reorganize Retell Simplify Translate	Explain Classify Determine Define Compare	
Application questions encourage students to apply ideas or skills to new situations or use knowledge to solve a problem.	Relate Apply Collect Convert Demonstrate Graph	Predict Transfer Relate Prove Modify Discover	
Analysis questions require students to break something down or take it apart to uncover its characteristics.	Dissect Analyze Deduce Outline Take apart	Illustrate Examine Diagram Differentiate Categorize	
Synthesis questions encourage students to bring things together and think about them in original or inventive ways.	Build Arrange Develop Predict	Present Produce Rewrite Invent	
Evaluation questions require students to judge something by determining a standard or comparing it to a standard.	Rank Argue Relate Measure	Judge Justify Critique Discriminate	

(Continued)

Table 12.5 (Continued)

Costa's Levels of Questioning			
Level	Definition	Sample Verbs	Sample Questions/ Prompts
Gathering and recalling information	These questions can be answered with yes, no, or specific information found in written material, lectures, movies, etc. A person can point to the information, read it, or physically see it.	Define, describe, identify, list, name, observe, recite, scan	
Making sense of gathered information	These questions require students to expand what they already know by using facts, details, or clues.	Analyze, compare, contrast, group, infer, sequence, synthesize	What would happen to you if . . . ?
Applying and evaluating information	These questions require students to reflect on their thinking and to be able to respond with a personal opinion that is supported by facts. The student makes a value judgment or wonders about something. There is no right or wrong answer.	Apply a principle, evaluate, hypothesize, imagine, judge, predict, speculate	Speculate about whether life could exist on other planets in other solar systems.
Examples in Subject Areas			
Subject	Level 1	Level 2	Level 3
Language Arts	What information is provided? Locate in the story where . . . When did the event take place? Point to the . . .	Would you have done the same thing as . . . ? What occurs when . . . ? Compare and contrast . . . to	Predict what will happen to . . . as . . . is changed. Write a new ending to the story (event). Describe the events that might occur if . . . .

(*Continued*)

Table 12.5 (Continued)

	Examples in Subject Areas		
Subject	**Level 1**	**Level 2**	**Level 3**
	List the . . . Where did . . . ? What is . . . ? Who was/were . . . ? Illustrate the part of the story that . . . Make a map of . . . What is the origin of the word . . . ? What events led to . . . ?	What other ways could . . . be interpreted? What is the main idea of the story (event)? What information supports your explanation? What was the message in this piece (event)? Give me an example of . . . . Describe in your own words what . . . means. What does . . . suggest about . . .'s character? What is the author trying to prove? What evidence does he/she present?	Add something new on your own that was not in the story. Rewrite the . . . from your point of view. What do you think will happen to . . . ? Why? What is most compelling to you in this . . . ? Why? Could this story have really happened? Why or why not? How would you solve this problem in your life?
Math	What information is provided? What are you being asked to find? What formula would you use in this problem? What does . . . mean? What is the formula for . . . ? List the . . . Explain the concept of . . . Give me an example of . . . Describe in your own words what . . . means.	What additional information is needed to solve this problem? Can you see other relationships that will help you find this information? How can you put your data in graphic form? What occurs when . . . ? Does it make sense to . . . ? Why or why not?	Predict what will happen to . . . as . . . is changed. Using a math principle, how can we find . . . ? Describe the events that might occur if . . . . How can you tell if your answer is reasonable? What would happen to . . . if . . . (a variable) were increased/decreased? How would repeated trials affect your data?

(Continued)

Table 12.5 (Continued)

	Examples in Subject Areas		
Subject	**Level 1**	**Level 2**	**Level 3**
	What mathematical concepts does this problem connect to? Draw a diagram of	How else could you account for . . . ? Explain how you calculate . . . . What equation can you write to solve the word problem?	
Social Studies	What information is provided? What are you being asked to find? When did the event take place? Point to the . . . . List the . . . . Name the . . . . Where did . . . ? Who was/were . . . ? Make a map of	What would happen to you if . . . ? Can you see other relationships that will help you find this information? Would you have done the same thing as . . . ? What occurs when . . . ? If you were there, would you . . . ? How would you solve this problem in your life? Compare and contrast . . . to . . . . What other ways could . . . be interpreted? What things would you have used to . . . ? What information supports your explanation? Give me an example of	Predict what will happen to . . . as . . . is changed. What would it be like to live . . . ? Describe the events that might occur if . . . . What would the world be like if . . . ? How can you tell if your analysis is reasonable? What do you think will happen to . . . ? Why? What significance is this event in the global perspective? What is most compelling to you in this . . . ? Why? Do you feel . . . is ethical? Why or why not?

(Continued)

Table 12.5 (Continued)

	Examples in Subject Areas		
Subject	**Level 1**	**Level 2**	**Level 3**
Science	What information is provided? What are you being asked to find? What formula would you use in this problem? What does . . . mean? What is the formula for . . . ? List the . . . . Where did . . . ? Describe in your own words what . . . means. What science concepts does this problem connect to? Draw a diagram of . . . . Illustrate how . . . works.	What additional information is needed to solve this problem? Can you see other relationships that will help you find this information? How can you put your data in graphic form? How would you change your procedures to get better results? What method would you use to . . . ? Compare and contrast . . . to . . . . Which errors most affected your results? What were some sources of variability? How do your conclusions support your hypothesis? How else could you account for . . . ? Give me an example of	Design a lab experiment to show . . . . Predict what will happen to . . . as . . . is changed. Using a science principle, how can we find . . . . Describe the events that might occur if . . . . Design a scenario for . . . . What would happen to . . . if . . . (a variable) were increased/decreased? How would repeated trials affect your data?

READING STRATEGIES THAT INCORPORATE QUESTIONING

The **survey-question-read-reasoning (SQRR) technique** encourages metacognitive behaviors from students. SQRR is a technique that asks students to do the following:

1. *Survey* the problem. Read the question sentence first.
2. *Question* yourself. "What is this asking me to find?" This provides a purpose for reading the problem word by word.
3. *Read* the problem aloud in its entirety, and explain how you determine which information is key and which information is extraneous. If appropriate, draw a sketch and label it using the key information. Ask, "What is the correct process to solve this problem?" Work the problem.
4. Check your *reasoning*. Ask, "What process did I use? Why did I choose that process? Was my reasoning correct?"

An alternative approach to reading a verbal problem in math would be for the teacher to use a series of steps to guide students through the written language of the problem:

1. Read the problem quickly to obtain a general understanding of it. Visualize the problem. Do not be concerned with the numbers.
2. Examine the problem again. Identify the question you are asked to answer. This question usually comes at the end of the problem, but it may occur anywhere in the problem.
3. Read the problem again to identify the information given.
4. Analyze the problem to see how the information is related. Identify any missing information and any unnecessary information.
5. Compute the answer.
6. Examine your answer. Label the parts of the solution to correspond with the question that the problem asks you to answer. Is your answer sensible?

Questioning the author (QtA) is a strategy that engages students actively with a text. Rather than reading and taking information from a text, the QtA strategy encourages students to ask questions of the author and the text. Through forming their questions, students learn more about the text. Kucan and Beck (1997) identified specific steps you should follow when using the questioning-the-author strategy in a lesson. This strategy is best suited for nonfiction texts and will probably work best in language arts, social studies, or science. The steps are as follows:

1. Select a passage that both is interesting and can spur a good conversation.
2. Decide appropriate stopping points where you think your students need to obtain a greater understanding.
3. Create queries or questions for each stopping point.
4. Ask, "What is the author trying to say?"
5. Ask, "Why do you think the author used the following phrase?"
6. Ask, "Does this make sense to you?"
7. Display a short passage to your students along with one or two queries you have designed ahead of time.
8. Model for your students how to think through the queries.
9. Ask students to read and work through the queries you have prepared for their readings.

ReQuest is a strategy that allows students to read with a partner to ask and answer questions in the text; the goal is to build on prior knowledge and vocabulary through discussion.

The **question-answer relationship (QAR) model** provides students with four types of questions and a system for thinking about where the answer might be, based on the type of question. The power of the QAR model lies in it requiring teachers to explicitly instruct students to identify what type of question is being asked and to consider, therefore, what resources are required to answer the question. The types of questions are 1) *right there* (answers can easily be found in the text); 2) *think and search* (answers require a bit of thinking and searching); 3) *author and you* (questions are based on information found in the text but ask the reader to relate the question to his or her own experience—that is, the answer does not lie directly in the text, but the student must have read it in order to answer the question); and 4) *on your own* (the questions do not require students to have read the passage—the reader relies on background and prior knowledge to answer).

Text-dependent questions require that students use the information from the text in their thinking and use the information (i.e., cite the evidence) in their response. These questions might not focus only on "right there" information, as they may require students to have read the text in order to form their responses. The goal is to have students think deeply and critically about texts so that their responses are stronger and based on evidence.

Vocabulary Development across the Curriculum

Students must know what words mean and have opportunities to use words in their various forms. Knowledge of vocabulary is highly related to the ability to comprehend complex text and achieve overall academic success (Carlo et al., 2004; Cunningham

& Stanovich, 1997; Hirsch, 2006; Nagy, Berninger, Abbott, Vaughn, & Vermeulen, 2003). Adolescents encounter ten thousand or more new words per year and are expected to learn three thousand new meanings per year just to keep up. Most of these words are specific to the content areas, and many are low-frequency, complex, **multisyllabic words** (Moats, 2014; Nagy et al., 2006). It is essential that teachers know how to provide explicit vocabulary instruction for all students.

Word recognition is the ability to effectively and efficiently decode words and is necessary for reading comprehension (Boardman et al., 2008; Nagy, Berninger, & Abbott, 2006; Scammacca et al., 2007; Wharton-McDonald & Swiger, 2009). Approximately one third of middle school struggling readers have difficulty at the basic word level as well as with comprehension (Brasseur-Hock, Hock, Kieffer, Biancarosa, & Deshler, 2011; Paulesu et al., 2001; Scammacca et al., 2013; Vaughn et al., 2010). Struggling adolescent readers may be able to read single-syllable words but must be taught strategies to decode multisyllabic words, which are common in complex texts (Archer, Gleason, & Vachon, 2003). To do this well, students must be taught explicit strategies to decode unknown words (Biancarosa & Snow, 2004; Pearson & Gallagher, 1983). Teachers who use explicit instruction explain the strategy, model the process, provide guided practice with scaffolding, and require independent application of the strategy. Decoding, analogizing, and predicting are three strategies students can learn to apply while reading unfamiliar words (Ehri, 2014). Students use a decoding strategy by taking the letters and blending them into phonemes to pronounce the word. If the word is familiar, students can decode it and then check to see if the word makes sense in context. Analogizing is a useful strategy for readers who have many words stored in memory, as they can recognize familiar patterns and figure out similar words, such as *motivate*, *motivation*, and *motivator*. Students apply the predicting strategy to read words by using context cues to anticipate an unfamiliar word and then by matching the pronunciation with the spelling to make sure that the sounds fit the letters (Ehri, 2014).

By the time students enter the sixth grade, they should know the most common consonant and vowel sounds and orthographic patterns, irregular words, multisyllabic words, and the most common prefixes and suffixes. In sixth and seventh grades, students learn more complex forms or words and should be prepared to tackle such complex words as *isosceles*, *isotherm*, *phenotype*, *psychology*, and *geography*. **Word study** interventions that address concepts that relate semantic connections and morphology have significant positive effects on student reading achievement (Moats, 2006; Scammacca et al., 2007). A word sort is a list of vocabulary terms that is sorted into groups, based on word structure. There are two types of word sorts, closed word sorts and open word sorts. To do a closed word sort, the teacher gives the students a list of words and the categories to which they belong.

There are numerous possibilities for using word sorts in the middle school classroom. In language arts, a teacher might want to develop students' morphological analysis. An idea for a closed word sort, as shown in Table 12.6, would be to provide a list of words and the categories to which they belong. In this example, students would

Table 12.6 Example of a Word Sort (Closed)

Base Words		Prefixes
Responsible	Operable	Ir
Rational	Numerable	In
Regular	Tolerable	Im
Refutable	Credible	Il
Material	Secure	
Mortal	Sane	
Mobile	Active	
Mature	Legible	
Practical	Logical	
Balanced	Legal	
Possible	Literate	
Effectual		

group words: irresponsible, irrational, inoperable, intolerable, illegal, illiterate, and so forth.

Word sorts can also be a useful tool in math class to help students understand relationships between concepts and solve more complex problems. In an open word sort, the teacher would not provide prompts, and students would work at figuring out categories and word placements by themselves. The snip and sort is an example of a closed sort in which a piece of paper is divided into three columns with the labels *one solution, no solution,* and *infinite solutions* or *many solutions*. Then students cut out slips of paper with linear equations in one variable to sort into the three columns.

EXPLICIT VOCABULARY INSTRUCTION

Vocabulary is knowledge of word meanings, and it supports comprehension (Carlo et al., 2004; Cunningham & Stanovich, 1997; Hirsch, 2006; Nagy, Berninger, Abbott, Vaughn, & Vermeulen, 2003). The ability to read with comprehension helps to ensure success in school. However, approximately 70 percent of students in middle and high school experience difficulties with vocabulary and reading comprehension (Biancarosa & Snow, 2004). Schools need to implement strategies to raise the level of vocabulary across content areas. All students, including those with disabilities, English-language learners, and accelerated learners, benefit from increasing their vocabulary. Teachers in all content areas have multiple opportunities to involve students in engaging and productive vocabulary learning (Baumann, Kame'enui, & Ash, 2003). Students must know what words mean and have opportunities to use words in their various forms. Researchers have found that it takes between twelve and seventeen exposures to a word before students learn it (Ausubel & Youssef, 1965; McKeown, Beck, Omanson, & Pople, 1985). This reiterates our earlier point that it is essential for teachers to know how to provide explicit vocabulary instruction for all students. The evidence supporting explicit instruction of vocabulary is abundant. Archer and Hughes (2011) summarized the research:

- Students experience growth in vocabulary when they receive explicit, engaging vocabulary instruction (Tomesen & Aarnoutse, 1998; White, Graves, & Slater, 1990).
- When students are intentionally taught target words, their comprehension of text containing those words improves (McKeown et al., 1985; Stahl & Fairbanks, 1986).
- Most new words learned are the result of wide reading and explicit instruction on vocabulary words.
- Explicit vocabulary instruction is particularly critical for struggling readers who may not read widely and have difficulty using context to determine word meanings (Beck, McKeown, & Kucan, 2002).
- A vocabulary instructional routine is helpful for both teachers and students. Archer and Hughes (2011) developed a routine that teachers can follow. The routine consists of four steps with options that may be selected, depending upon the word taught, the context, and student needs: 1) introduce the word (i.e., pronunciation, decoding, and modeling); 2) introduce the meaning of the word (options include providing a basic, uncomplicated explanation); 3) guide students in analyzing the meaningful parts of the word; and 4) have students determine the essential traits embedded in the definition. Additionally, teachers should assist English-language learners or emergent bilinguals in recognizing **cognates**, should illustrate with examples, and should check for understanding.

VOCABULARY INSTRUCTION IN ACTION

Vocabulary frames are helpful when teaching terms with concise definitions and concepts with elaborate definitions. Such frames should be used before, during, and after reading to help students gain deep understanding of the most important concepts necessary to understand a topic (Ellis, 2013). Online tools, beneficial for all students, are especially convenient for teachers and students (see creately.com, readwritethink.org, responsiveclassroom.org, or thinkport.org, and search for graphic organizers).

Some tools, such as Frayer diagrams, as shown in Figure 12.4 (Frayer, Frederick, & Klausmeier, 1969), create visual and verbal word associations to help students learn new words. This technique requires students to define target vocabulary and apply their knowledge by generating examples and nonexamples, giving characteristics, and/or drawing a picture to illustrate the meaning of the word. It is used before reading to activate background knowledge, during reading to monitor vocabulary, or after reading to assess vocabulary. This strategy supports students' acquisition of new words and use of resource materials by providing students with a structure requiring them to examine words for their definitions and characteristics and to provide examples and nonexamples. Word learning requires multiple exposures to the word within meaningful contexts. In order to implement this strategy with fidelity, first select a word from a self-contained passage of text and establish with students the purpose of the strategy. Next, provide students with a blank copy or show them how to draw one.

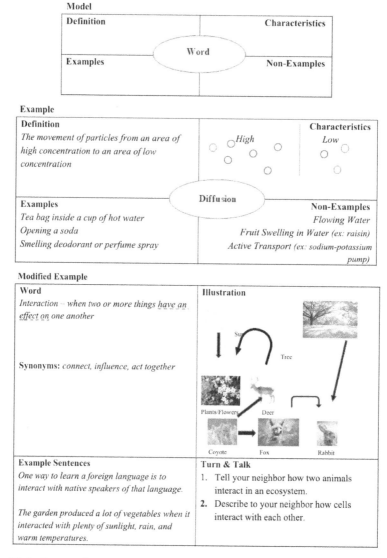

Figure 12.4 Frayer diagram model.

Use a think-aloud as you model the process of applying the Frayer model to analyze the word and determine its meaning. Students will write the selected word along with characteristics of the selected word. Support students along the way through thinking aloud, demonstrating, modeling, or questioning (e.g., **scaffold**). Students will write examples and nonexamples of the selected word. Last, students will write a definition for the selected word in their own words. You will continue to scaffold, as needed, especially when first implementing the strategy. Students can check the meaning of the word against a dictionary definition, context from text, or other sources. It should be said that these models and their variations should be used for challenging or more abstract words and concepts. You would not take the time to engage in this way for all content terms.

USE OF GRAPHIC ORGANIZERS

Activities that allow students to learn the in-depth meanings of words and manipulate the words in context are effective. Word webs, word lines, **semantic mapping**, and **word maps** are useful graphic organizers that support all students, including those with disabilities, as they learn the meaning of words (Dexter & Hughes, 2011; Heimlich & Pittelman, 1986; Novak, 1993; Reutebuch, Ciullo, & Vaughn, 2013; Schwartz & Raphael, 1985). Three examples are verbal and visual word associations, semantic maps, and vocabulary frames. Semantic or concept maps are graphic organizers that graphically represent concepts and can also highlight examples and nonexamples, including ones familiar to students and those from the texts they are reading. Table 12.7 shows various examples and templates of semantic maps. Semantic feature mapping is defined as listing features related to a word or concept. Such a map is commonly built using interconnected circles and charts. This strategy helps students map out how words and concepts are related to each other and can lead to the development of deeper understanding beyond labeling. The completed feature map can be used as a tool for studying and writing about the concepts.

Pause and Reflect: After reviewing the following examples, create a semantic feature map of your own.

List-group-label is a semantic map strategy that helps students improve their vocabulary and categorization skills and learn to organize concepts. This strategy helps students organize new concepts in relation to previously learned concepts through grouping and labeling words. Table 12.8 highlights an example.

Concept circles (Vacca & Vacca, 1999) were originally developed as a way to support student vocabulary development in language arts. A circle was divided into four or more sections, with a smaller circle drawn in the middle of the graphic. Students place key words from a text they have read in the outside sections (one per section). After discussing how the words relate to one another, the students decide on the concept that all of the words in outside sections support and write that word in the middle circle. This process enables students to deepen their understanding of vocabulary and to enhance their reading skills. Over the years, concept circles have been used for vocabulary development in many subject areas. Figure 12.5 shows concept circles of two math concepts.

Story mapping, as shown in Table 12.9, is a graphic organizer that helps students learn the elements of a narrative, story, or event.

A **problem-and-solution outline** is a graphic representation that depicts a problem, attempted solutions, and the result, or outcomes associated with the attempted solutions. It works equally well with narrative or informational texts to display the central problem in a story or the problem-and-solution text pattern. When first using this strategy, try a familiar story, such as *Goldilocks and the Three Bears*.

Table 12.7 Semantic Feature Maps

Template Model

	→ Features → Terms				

Geographic Features of Landforms

	Contains Water	Has Vegetation	Has Animal Life	Is Above Sea Level	Is Below Sea Level
Delta	+	+	+	+	+
Plateau	+	+	+	+	
Tundra	+	+	+	+	–
Mesa	+	+	+	+	–

Vertebrates

	Backbone	Cold-Blooded	Warm-Blooded	Gills	Lungs	Smooth Skin	Scales	Feathers	Fur or Hair	Produces Milk
Fish	X	X		X			X			
Amphibian	X	X		X	X	X				
Reptile	X	X			X		X			
Bird	X		X		X			X		
Mammal	X		X		X				X	X

Classifying Polygons*

Shapes	Parallel Lines	Perpendicular Lines	Right Angle(s)	Obtuse Angle(s)	All Sides Equal	Two Equal Sides	Number of Sides	Concave	Convex
1									
2									
3									
4									

*This one is a concept sort. Students would have manipulatives and document their features.

CHAPTER 12

Table 12.8 List-Group-Label on Measurement

Student-Generated List of Terms:		
Weight	Pound	Time
Foot	Circumference	Kilogram
Tape measure	Radius	Length
Scale	Quart	Thermometer
Age	Yard	Temperature
Cup	Meter	Ruler
Height	Mile	Perimeter
	Distance	Width

Categories:

Units of Measure	Things You Measure	Tools for Measurement
Foot	Weight	Tape Measure
Pound	Age	Scale
Yard	Height	Cup
Quart	Circumference	Ruler
Meter	Area	Thermometer
Mile	Distance	
	Time	
	Length	
	Width	

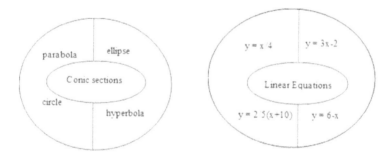

Figure 12.5 Concept circles.

Table 12.9 Story Mapping—History Frame

Title of Event:	Participants/Key Players:
Problem or Goal:	Where:
	Where:

↓

Key Episodes or Events:	Resolution or Outcome:

↓

Themes/Lessons—So What?

Table 12.10 Problem-and-Solution Outline

Problem	Who has the problem?	
	What was the problem?	
	Why was it a problem?	
Solutions	**Attempted Solutions**	**Outcomes**
	End Result	

Making and Taking Notes across the Curriculum

Note-taking is a generic literacy skill that has strong evidence for its effectiveness across disciplines. Students must learn to take notes and then learn how to study from them. Note-taking teaches students not only to pay attention but also what to pay attention to. This valuable tool also teaches students, as they read textbooks and articles, to evaluate the importance of information and the relationship between different pieces of information. Finally, note-taking is a valuable way to organize information into a format to serve a purpose. Teachers should keep in mind that there is a difference between note-taking and note making. Note-taking is the practice of writing notes during direct instruction or discussion, while note making is the practice of recording notes from printed materials or other sources to which students can return again and again. The products may look quite similar, but the *process* of taking the notes differs. Note-taking serves both process and product functions. The process is recording the notes, and the product is reading the notes later. While taking notes, students must pay attention to the information as they write. The product should be useful for studying later. In other words, it really is not the taking of notes that improves students' learning; it is the study opportunities the notes provide. There are a variety of effective tools for note making:

- Cornell Notes include recording key ideas into columns with a summary at the bottom.

- A mind map or concept map is a way to show relationships between words and concepts. An arrow connecting two words shows that those words are related in some way. Words can be grouped together with a circle or box.

- Infographics are visual representations of data, usually images such as charts or diagrams used to represent information or data.

- Outline frameworks should be used when the information is dense and/or the vocabular is unfamiliar. To utilize this tool, write points in an organized manner, based on space indentation. Major points are placed farthest to the left and more specific details are indented farther to the right. The level of importance of information is indicated by distance away from the left margin. This method emphasizes content as well as relationships within the material. Outlines also reduce the time needed for editing and allow for easy reviewing. Making accurate, understandable outlines does require thinking in depth about the content.

- Directed note-taking activity (DNA) is a formal structure that includes self-questioning and direct instruction. The process begins by having students use only one side of their paper to take notes. A sheet of paper can be folded, or a line drawn, to create a two-inch column on the left, which becomes the margin. During instruction, students take notes on important details. Later, students will write key terms or concepts in the margin (which could later be covered while studying). This technique activates self-questioning and helps build students' metacognitive abilities by making students think about what they mean as they write the notes, key terms, and concepts.

Cornell Notes		Mind Map/Concept Map
Main Ideas Key Questions Major Terms or Concepts	Definitions Dates People Places Diagrams	
Summary:		
Outline Framework		

I. xxx
  A. xxx
    1. xxx
    2. xxx
    3. xxx
II. xxx
  A. xxx
  B. xxx
    1. xxx
    2. xxx		

Figure 12.6 Notetaking Tools.

Final Thoughts

In this chapter we explored practices related to disciplinary literacy and the overarching goal of reading, which is to understand or comprehend what is being read. It is important for middle grades teachers to have a strong conceptual understanding of the five big ideas of reading (i.e., phonemic awareness, phonics, fluency, vocabulary, and comprehension) as well as writing. The bottom line is that reading is a complex activity, and successful reading includes multiple interrelated processes. We know that students need explicit instruction in how to think before, during, and after reading; how to monitor their understanding; and how to help themselves when meaning breaks down. As teachers, we must be thoughtful in our selection of strategies as they must stimulate intentional mental actions during reading that improve reading comprehension.

Disciplinary literacy—the confluence of content knowledge, experiences, and skills merged with the ability to read, write, listen, speak, think critically, and perform in a way that is meaningful within the context of a given field—is important in *all* courses and subjects. Together, we explored a multiplicity of evidence-based strategies to build reading comprehension and disciplinary literacy. Some can be utilized before, during, and after reading; some are intended to build vocabulary; some are for use across several content areas, whereas others are better used in one area; and some relate to note-taking while learning.

To summarize, let's revisit our learning outcomes:

- **Understand how phonemic awareness, phonics, vocabulary, and fluency all support reading comprehension.** Reading comprehension is the ability to understand what you read. These four interrelated processes work together to create the overall reading experience. As students learn to read, they must develop skills in each of these areas to become successful readers.

- **Recognize how the models of teaching reading and writing work together and, subsequently, learn how to make good choices when it comes to strategy instruction within the disciplines.** These models shape educators' beliefs and guide how to plan classroom instruction and intervention. A basic understanding of these models is important since they can guide our decisions about which instructional practices are most effective. We can eliminate instructional practices that lack evidence and waste instructional time. Finally, these models provide insight into why a reader or writer may be struggling so that teachers can work together to target specific assessment and intervention supports.

- **Analyze disciplinary literacy in content areas to understand how content knowledge, experiences, and skills link to the ability to read, write, listen, speak, think critically, and perform in a way that is meaningful within the context.** Disciplinary literacy is the confluence of content knowledge, experiences, and skills merged with the ability to read, write, listen, speak, think critically, and perform in a way that is meaningful within the context of a given field. These abilities are important in *all* courses and subjects, and students' future success as productive citizens and critical thinkers link to disciplinary literacy. A focus at the elementary- and middle-school level on foundational reading, when expanded to include engaging experiences connected to informational texts, vocabulary, and writing for content-specific purposes, builds background knowledge and skills in each discipline. Reading, writing, speaking, listening, and critical thinking must be integrated into each discipline across all grades so that all students gradually build knowledge and skills toward college and career readiness. Literacy is integral to attainment of content knowledge, and content is essential background knowledge for literacy development.

- **Evaluate what it means to know a word, and learn how to increase student word knowledge.** Students must know what words mean and have opportunities to use words in their various forms. Knowledge of vocabulary is highly related to the ability to comprehend complex text and achieve overall academic success. It is essential that teachers know how to provide explicit vocabulary instruction for all students. Teachers in all content areas have multiple opportunities to involve students in engaging and productive vocabulary learning.

- **Demonstrate how to incorporate evidence-based strategies in support of literacy.** Evidence-based strategies are practices that are based on research and professional knowledge and that help students with reading and writing. These strategies can help all students, including those with learning difficulties, and can lead to greater student achievement. This chapter included a wide variety of strategies, explanations, and content-specific examples. You should be able to construct additional examples in practice.

References

Alliance for Excellent Education. (2011, November). *The high cost of high school dropouts: What the nation pays for inadequate high schools.* https://all4ed.org/wp-content/uploads/2013/06/HighCost.pdf.

Archer, A. L., Gleason, M. M., & Vachon, V. L. (2003). Decoding and fluency: Foundation skills for struggling older readers. *Learning Disabilities Quarterly, 26*(2), 89–101. https://doi.org/10.2307/1593592.

Archer, A., & Hughes, C. (2011). *Explicit instruction: Effective and efficient teaching.* Guilford.

Ausubel, D. P., & Youssef, M. (1965). The effect of spaced repetition on meaningful retention. *Journal of General Psychology, 73*, 147–50. https://doi.org/10.1080/00221309.1965.9711263.

Baumann, J. F., Kame'enui, E. J., & Ash, G. (2003). Research on vocabulary instruction: Voltaire redux. In J. Flood, D. Lapp, J. R. Squire, & J. J. Hensen (Eds.), *Handbook of research on teaching the English language arts*, 2nd ed. (pp. 752–85). Lawrence Erlbaum.

Beck, I. L, McKeown, M. G., & Kucan, L. (2002). *Bringing words to life: Robust vocabulary instruction.* Guilford.

Biancarosa, G., & Snow, C. E. (2004). *Reading next: A vision for action and research in middle and high school literacy: A report to Carnegie Corporation of New York.* Alliance for Excellent Education.

Bloom, B. S. (1956) *Taxonomy of educational objectives, handbook: The cognitive domain.* David McKay, New York.

Boardman, A. G., Roberts, G., Vaughn, S., Wexler, J., Murray, C. S., & Kosanovich, M. (2008). *Effective instruction for adolescent struggling readers: A practice brief.* Portsmouth, NH: RMC Research Corporation, Center on Instruction.

Bransford, J. D., Brown, A. L., & Cocking, R. R. (2000). *How people learn: Brain, mind, experience, and school.* National Academy Press.

Brasseur-Hock, I., Hock, M., Kieffer, M., Biancarosa, G., & Deshler, D. (2011). Adolescent struggling readers in urban schools: Results of a latent class analysis. *Learning and Individual Differences, 21*, 438–52. https://doi.org/10.1016/j.lindif.2011.01.008.

Carlo, M. S., August, D., McLaughlin, B., Snow, C. E., Dressler, C., & Lippman, D. (2004). Closing the gap: Addressing the vocabulary needs of English language learners in bilingual and mainstream classrooms. *Reading Research Quarterly, 39*, 188–215. https://doi.org/10.1598/rrq.39.2.3.

Costa, A. L. (1985). *Developing minds: A resource book for teaching thinking.* Alexandria, VA: Association for Supervision and Curriculum Development.

Cunningham, A. E., Perry, K. E., Stanovich, K. E., & Stanovich, P. J. (2004). Disciplinary knowledge of K–3 teachers and their knowledge calibration in the domain of early literacy. *Annals of Dyslexia, 54*(1), 139–67. https://doi.org/10.1007/s11881-004-0007-y.

Cunningham, A. E., & Stanovich, K. E. (1997). Early reading acquisition and its relation to reading experience and ability 10 years later. *Developmental Psychology, 33*, 943–45. https://doi.org/10.1037//0012-1649.33.6.934.

Deans for Impact. (2023). *Instructional modules overview.* Austin, TX: Deans for Impact.

Deans for Impact. (2015). *The science of learning.* Austin, TX: Deans for Impact.

Dexter, D. D., Park, Y. J., & Hughes, C. A. (2011). A meta-analytic review of graphic organizers and science instruction for adolescents with learning disabilities: Implications for the intermediate and secondary science classroom. *Learning Disabilities Research & Practice, 26*(4), 204–13.

Duke, N. K., & Cartwright, K. B. (2021). The science of reading progresses: Communicating advances beyond the Simple View of Reading. *Reading Research Quarterly, 56*(S1), S25–S44. https://ila.onlinelibrary.wiley.com/doi/full/10.1002/rrq.411

Duke, N. K., Ward, A. E., & Pearson, P. D. (2021, May). The science of reading comprehension instruction. *The Reading Teacher, 74*(6): 663–72.

Ehri, L. C. (1995). Phases of development in learning to read words by sight. *Journal of Research in Reading, 18*(2), 116–25. https://doi.org/10.1111/j.1467-9817.1995.tb00077.x

Ellis, E. (2013). *Makes sense strategies.* http://www.graphicorganizers.com

Ehri, L. C. (2014). Orthographic mapping in the acquisition of reading, spelling memory, and vocabulary learning. *Scientific Studies of Reading, 18*, 5–12. https://doi.org/10.1080/10888438.2013.819356

Fisher, D., Frey, N., & Lapp, D. K. (2022). *Teaching reading: A playbook for developing skilled readers through word recognition and language comprehension.* Corwin Publishers.

Frayer, D., Frederick, W. C., & Klausmeier, H. J. (1969). *A schema for testing the level of cognitive mastery.* Madison, WI: Wisconsin Center for Education.

Gough, P. B., & Tunmer, W. E. (1986). Decoding, reading, and reading disability. *RASE: Remedial & Special Education, 7*(1), 6–10. https://doi.org/10.1177/074193258600700104.

Heimlich, J. E., & Pittelman, S. D. (1986). *Semantic mapping: Classroom application.* Newark, DE: International Reading Association.

Hirsch, E. (2006). Building knowledge. *American Educator, 30*(1), 8–51.

Kucan, L., & Beck, I. (1997). Thinking aloud and reading comprehension research: Inquiry, instruction, and social interaction. *Review of Educational Research, 67*(3):271–99. https://doi.org/10.2307/1170566.

Lee, C. D., Spratley, A. (2010). *Reading in the disciplines: The challenges of adolescent literacy.* New York, NY: Carnegie Corporation of New York.

Lent, R. C. (2016). *This is disciplinary literacy: Reading, writing, thinking, and doing ... content area by content area.* Corwin Publishers.

McAndrews, S. L. (2020). *Literacy assessment and metacognitive strategies: A resource to inform instruction, PreK–12.* Guilford.

McKeown, M. G., Beck, I. L., Omanson, R. C., & Pople, M. T. (1985). Some effects of the nature and frequency of vocabulary instruction on the knowledge and use of words. *Reading Research Quarterly, 20*(5), 522–35. https://doi.org/10.2307/747940.

Moats, L. C. (2006). How spelling supports reading and why it is more regular and predictable than you may think. *American Educator, 29*(4), 42–43.

Moats, L. C. & Tolman, C. A. (2019). *LETRS* (3rd ed.). Voyager Sopris Learning.

Moats, L. (2014, April 3). When older kids can't read [Webinar]. In *Voyager Sopris Learning.* www.voyagersopris.com

Nagy, W. E., Berninger, V., & Abbott, R. (2006). Contributions of morphology beyond phonology to literacy outcomes of upper elementary and middle school students. *Journal of Educational Psychology, 98*(1). https://doi.org/10.1037/0022-0663.98.1.134.

Nagy, W. E., Berninger, V., Abbott, R., Vaughan, K., & Vermeulen, K. (2003). Relationship of morphology and other language skills to literacy skills in at-risk second-grade readers and at-risk fourth-grade writers. *Journal of Educational Psychology, 95*(4), 730–42. https://doi.org/10.1037/0022-0663.95.4.730.

Novak, J. D. (1993). How do we learn our lesson? Taking students through the process. *Science Teacher, 60*(3), 50–55.

Paulesu, E., Demonet, J. F., Fazio, F., McCrory, E., Chanoine, V., & Brunswick, N. (2001). Dyslexia: Cultural diversity and biological unity. *Science, 291*, 2165–67. https://doi.org/10.1016/s1053-8119(01)91927-5.

Pearson, P. D., & Gallagher, M. C. (1983). The instruction of reading comprehension. *Contemporary Educational Psychology, 8*(3), 317–44. https://doi.org/10.1016/0361-476x(83)90019-x.

Reutebuch, C. K., Ciullo, S., & Vaughn, S. R. (2013). Graphic organizers for the adolescent learner in content-area, secondary inclusive classrooms. In R. Boon & V. G. Spencer (Eds.), *Reading comprehension strategies to promote adolescent literacy in the content-areas for the inclusive classroom* (pp. 65–78). Brookes.

Scarborough, H. S. (2001). Connecting early language and literacy to later reading (dis)abilities: Evidence, theory, and practice. In S. Neuman & D. Dickinson (Eds.), *Handbook for research in early literacy* (pp. 97–110). Guilford Press.

Scammacca, N., Roberts, G., Vaughn, S., Edmonds, M., Wexler, J., Reutebuch, C. K., & Torgesen, J. K. (2007). *Interventions for adolescent struggling readers: A meta-analysis with implications for practice.* Portsmouth, NH: RMC Research Corporation, Center on Instruction.

Scammacca, N., Roberts, G., Vaughn, S., & Stuebing, K. (2013). A meta-analysis of interventions for struggling readers in grades 4–12: 1980–2011. *Journal of Learning Disabilities.* Advance online publication. https://doi.org/10.1177/0022219413504995.

Schwartz, R. M., & Raphael, T. E. (1985). Concept of definition: A key to improving students' vocabulary. *The Reading Teacher, 39,* 198–203.

Shanahan, T., Callison, K., Carriere, C., Duke, N. K., Pearson, P. D., Schatschneider, C., & Torgesen, J. (2010). *Improving reading comprehension in kindergarten through 3rd grade: A practice guide* (NCEE 2010-4038). Washington, DC: National Center for Education Evaluation and Regional Assistance, Institute of Education Sciences, U.S. Department of Education. whatworks.ed.gov/publications/practiceguides.

Stahl, S. A., & Fairbanks, M. M. (1986). The effects of vocabulary instruction: A model-based meta-analysis. *Review of Educational Research, 56,* 72–110. https://doi.org/10.2307/1170287.

The IRIS Center. (2014). *Secondary reading instruction (part 2): Deepening middle school content-area learning with vocabulary and comprehension strategies.* https://iris.peabody.vanderbilt.edu/module/sec-rdng2/.

Tomesen, M., & Aarnoutse, C. (1998). Effects of an instructional programme for deriving word meanings. *Educational Studies, 24*(1), 107–28.

Vacca, R. T., & Vacca, J. L. (1999). *Content area reading: Literacy and learning across the curriculum.* Longman.

Vaughn, S., Denton, C., & Fletcher, J. (2010). Why intensive interventions are necessary for students with severe reading difficulties. *Psychology in the Schools, 47*(5), 432–44. doi:10.1002/pits.20481

Vaughn, S., Gersten, R., Dimino, J., Taylor, M. J., Newman-Gonchar, R., Krowka, S., Kieffer, M. J., McKeown, M., Reed, D., Sanchez, M., St. Martin, K., Wexler, J., Morgan, S., Yañez, A., & Jayanthi, M. (2022). *Providing Reading Interventions for Students in Grades 4–9* (WWC 2022007). Washington, DC: National Center for Education Evaluation and Regional Assistance (NCEE), Institute of Education Sciences, U.S. Department of Education. https://whatworks.ed.gov/.

Wharton-McDonald, R., & Swiger, S. (2009). Developing higher order comprehension in the middle grades. In S. E. Israel & G. G. Duffy (Eds.), *Handbook of research on reading comprehension* (pp. 510–30). Routledge.

White, T. G., Graves, M. F., & Slater, W. H. (1990). Growth of reading vocabulary in diverse elementary schools: Decoding and word meaning. *Journal of Educational Psychology, 82,* 281–90. doi:10.1037/0022-0663.82.2.281.

CHAPTER 13

Classroom Dynamics
STRATEGIES FOR EFFECTIVE DISCIPLINE AND CLASSROOM MANAGEMENT

Learning Outcomes:

1. Understand and apply principles of culturally responsive discipline practices.
2. Identify and understand structures and principles of commonly utilized discipline policies (such as positive behavioral interventions and supports and restorative discipline) in middle schools.
3. Apply basic principles of classroom management, including rules, routines, and procedures.
4. Understand the connection of families to school policies.

Classroom Management Basics

Classroom management is perpetually discussed in preservice education programs. It is often the aspect of teaching that candidates feel the most unprepared for and anxious about as they leave their programs. There are many reasons for this.

- It doesn't matter how much teachers read about strategies for and suggestions about how to run a classroom effectively—the reality is that classroom management is often learned in the moment.
- Preparing candidates for classroom management is difficult because policies vary widely among districts, schools, and teams.
- There are individual differences among teachers, and, much as teenagers must navigate adolescent identity development, teachers must develop their teacher identity.
- Much of what we notice as *good* classroom management at times seems invisible. We know it when we see it, but it is sometimes hard to articulate what teachers do to make things effective or ineffective.

In this chapter, we will zoom in on specific aspects of management. First and foremost, we want to explore principles of culturally relevant and responsive practice as they relate to classroom and behavior management. Many of the strategies and systems traditionally utilized in schools are no longer effective or productive in our increasingly diverse schools. Second, we want to explore the commonly used systems currently seen in middle schools. Such programs include **positive behavior intervention support (PBIS) systems** and the increasingly prevalent **restorative discipline**. Third, we want to investigate the practical details of setting up a classroom that feels authentic to teachers, students, and families. Finally, we will focus on setting up a climate of safety in classrooms and discuss how to address "big" behaviors when they inevitably occur.

Pause and Reflect: Before we get started, take a moment and jot down a list of words you associate with the term classroom management. As we continue through the chapter, we will revisit this list and see if anything changes in your mind. What words would you add, and what needs to be deleted from your list—and why?

As we explore the creation of healthy classroom environments in this chapter, it is important to define several key concepts that we will grapple with along the way. These terms need to be clear in our minds as we navigate where we personally stand in terms of classroom management and **discipline** practices. Classroom management has historically meant the creation of a productive and "orderly" environment. When we think of classroom management, we are often thinking of how we address "bad" behavior or disruptions to class. Personal definitions of what productive and orderly mean will vary widely by person, and therefore it is helpful to think of classroom management as existing on a continuum, with a more rigid discipline-, and teacher-centered approach on one end and a more student-centered and flexible approach on the other end. There are lots of places to land in between these two, and we will highlight the pros and cons of various positions.

The individual teacher's personality and preferences will have a significant impact on how the teacher enacts classroom management. Some teachers deem an orderly and quiet environment to reflect "good" management, while other teachers embrace an organized chaos that may exhibit as a much louder and more active albeit still productive and engaged environment. The definitions below will help you explore your own approaches to and preferences for options on the classroom-management spectrum.

Culturally Responsive Discipline Practices

We reference culturally relevant practices in many ways in this text. In Chapter 8, we explore the seminal definitions and make connections to teaching practice. There is much to unpack when it comes to **culturally responsive discipline** policies because our schools historically have not addressed these issues well. In Chapter 5, we mention that even early versions of our guiding document in middle level education have a strong Eurocentric emphasis that has not aged well in terms of serving our diverse populations. Other policies in past decades have also negatively impacted school climates, and there are current strong pushes toward making changes in school-wide discipline policies. There is a wealth of research indicating the ineffectiveness of traditional discipline policies—particularly that of exclusionary **punishments** (like suspensions and expulsions) and links of those practices to the school-to-prison pipeline. Many schools have shifted toward using PBSS and restorative practices as a more equitable and culturally responsive approach. These systems put more emphasis on logical **consequences** and **restitution**. When President Bill Clinton passed the Safe Schools Act and the Gun-Free Schools Act in 1994, there was a wave of implementation of **zero-tolerance policies** in schools across the United States (such policies already existed in many places throughout the '70s and '80s, as part of the war on drugs). These policies were aimed at egregious, violent, and gun-related incidents; unfortunately, however, those zero-tolerance policies also were applied to more ambiguous and innocuous infractions and, ultimately, landed a lot of students in the courtroom—and, eventually, some students in prison. Data from the US Department of Education spotlight significant disparities in application of discipline policies between members of the mainstream community and members of marginalized communities. Figure 13.1 highlights these data, showing that Black boys and girls, when compared to their peers, are disproportionally

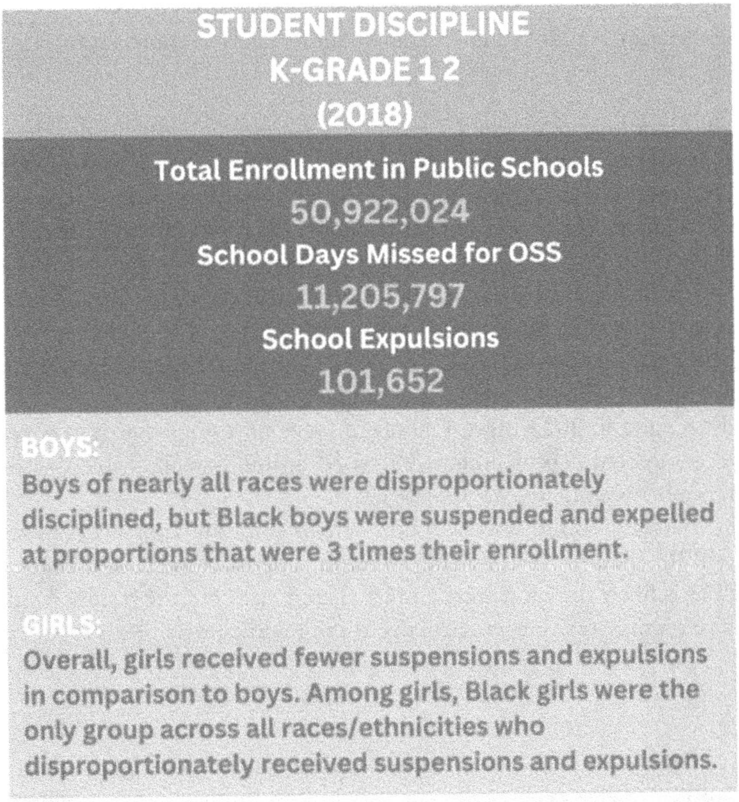

STUDENT DISCIPLINE
K-GRADE 12
(2018)

Total Enrollment in Public Schools
50,922,024

School Days Missed for OSS
11,205,797

School Expulsions
101,652

BOYS:
Boys of nearly all races were disproportionately disciplined, but Black boys were suspended and expelled at proportions that were 3 times their enrollment.

GIRLS:
Overall, girls received fewer suspensions and expulsions in comparison to boys. Among girls, Black girls were the only group across all races/ethnicities who disproportionately received suspensions and expulsions.

Figure 13.1 School Discipline K-12. SOURCE: U.S. Department of Education, Oce for Civil Rights, 2017-18 Civil Rights Data Collection, released October 2020, updated May 2021, available at https://ocrdata.ed.gov

Table 13.1 Punishment-Based versus Responsive Discipline

Punishment-Based Discipline	Responsive Discipline
Use of exclusionary measures that are punitive in nature	Focuses on restorative measures that are inclusive and supportive in nature
Emphasis is control, compliance, and power	Relies on relationships and responsiveness
Does not treat the root of the behavior—is focused on penalties for bad behavior	Focuses on finding root of behavior and teaching student to manage and on growth mindset
Done to	Done with
Reactive	Proactive, responsive
May lead to feelings of shame and/or guilt	Maintains dignity of student
Deficit oriented	Asset oriented
Adult oriented	Student oriented

Source: Adapted from Office of Safe and Supportive Schools Technical Assistance Center Collaborative (2023)

disciplined. Black boys represent 7.7 percent of student enrollment, but their rates of in-school suspension, out-of-school suspension, and expulsion are approximately 20 percent, 25 percent, and 26 percent, respectively. To think of these data in another way, Black students lost 61 days of instruction per every 100 students enrolled due to out-of-school suspensions, while their white peers lost 14 days per 100 students enrolled. Additionally, students with disabilities lost 41 days per 100 students enrolled compared to 19 days lost for students without disabilities.

As these inequities persist, researchers, educators, and the US Department of Education have pushed schools to rethink discipline. A publication from the US Department of Education in 2023 urged schools to focus on using what it calls ***responsive discipline***, as opposed to **punishment-based discipline** systems. Table 13.1 delineates the difference between these two approaches.

In the following sections, we will outline two common approaches to responsive discipline: PBIS (positive behavior intervention support) systems and restorative discipline. PBIS is likely the most widely utilized approach, but the restorative-discipline movement is gaining traction, particularly at the middle level.

Equity

In terms of **equity**, we revisit once again the importance of using culturally relevant and responsive pedagogies to ensure that we address implicit biases, embrace all cultures in our classrooms with validation and affirmation of all cultures, and ensure that we are not forcing arbitrary compliance to the dominant cultural practices in school. PBIS requires input from and collaboration among school personnel, families, and students. Teachers must have high expectations for *all* students.

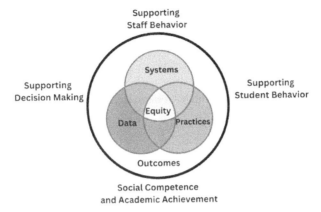

Figure 13.2 Interrelated Elements of PBIS. Created by authors

Systems

The term *systems* refers to organizational structures. Consider how teams are structured and how teachers are supported through training and/or coaching. The systems help ensure the implementation fidelity and effectively collect and use data for outcomes.

Data

Data-based decision-making is a crucial component of PBIS implementation. Data collection relies on using categories, such as **universal screening** and student outcomes. Universal screeners are utilized to help identify which students need additional support (also a pertinent component of MTSS), then student outcomes, which, when focused on behavior, may include office discipline referrals or other tracking of discipline data, suspensions, school climate data (which may be reported by staff, families, or students), attendance, and academic outcomes.

Outcomes

The primary goal of PBIS is to improve **outcomes** by utilizing a network of supports, from students, to students' families, to educators. These outcomes may be behavioral in focus—having fewer office discipline referrals or achieving overall improvement in school climate—or the outcomes may be related to academic or social-emotional goals.

Practices

Teachers implement school- and classroom-based practices to support the PBIS implementation and focus on positive school climate and to support students. These practices are a critical component of the structure and comprise of interventions and strategies supported by research to help students meet their goals. For most school-wide implementations, a matrix is used. It is organized by key rules or principles with clear outlines of expectations for students as they move throughout their day.

These matrices vary widely by school (or classroom) but typically should include the following:

- three to five behavioral expectations, which are usually tied to an acronym (PRIDE, LEAD, PAWS, CARE, etc.). Each letter represents an expectation, such as personal responsibility, respect, integrity, determination, excellence, and so on.
- Each column represents the context in which students show those behaviors: classroom, hallway, arrival/dismissal, bus, lunchroom, restroom, and so on. Keep these as short and simple as possible so as not to have too many expectations.
- Each cell then articulates observable student behaviors, using positively framed language.

Pause and Reflect: In Figure 13.3, we provide an example of a PBIS matrix from one middle school. Look at it either individually or with a partner. Looking at the criteria above, assess how well you think this matrix meets (or does not) meet the mark. Is there anything you would change to be more student friendly? More culturally responsive? Justify your choices with a peer.

	Entering Room	Individual Work	Group Work	Exiting Room
Positivity	Line up in your lane Enter the correct door	Be independent Problem-solve	Work together Listen to advice, try all ideas Stay on task	Listen to instruction Say something nice Have Self Control
Respect	Enter at appropriate time	Don't distract others Work quietly	Everyone does his/her part Listen to others	Clean up work space Push in your chair
Integrity	Be ready to learn Take ownership of directions	Do your own work Be efficient Use technology as expected	Be patient with your team Everyone contributes to the group	Be responsible for your own materials
Dedication	Be on time Make smart seating choices	Persevere through challenges Try your best	Do your work well Hold each other accountable	Clean your space Keep the room neat
Excellence	Be prepared for class Computer is charged	Ask for help Give the extra effort	Share your ideas Be a team leader	Straighten the room Exit quietly

Figure 13.3 Example of PBIS Matrix. Created by authors

POSITIVE BEHAVIORAL INTERVENTIONS AND SUPPORTS INCENTIVES

Many schools utilize PBIS incentives to motivate students to utilize structured expectations. While there are strong arguments against the use of extrinsically motivated rewards, it is still a very effective way to get students to buy into the system and then utilize it consistently. Will it work for all students? Not a chance. But many schools have found success with most students through an incentivized system. Once again, how these systems work will vary by school and by team. Here we share the successful structure that our school has utilized to help students stay on track. We first collect several types of data by rating how well each student has been engaged in class each week, noting missing assignments, proficiency on standards, attendance, discipline referrals, and so on. In weekly MTSS meetings, teachers debrief and discuss students' individual needs, setting up conferences with students and or working toward more targeted interventions if needed. The school's schedule has built-in afternoons when students who earn the privilege can participate in a school-wide incentive program. Sometimes it is an extended recess with snow cones; sometimes it is a trip to the pool or bowling alley. For students to qualify for incentives they must have no missing work, no office referrals, and no more than two unexcused absences for the four-and-a-half-week period. Students who are ineligible for the incentive stay with teachers in the classroom, usually working towards completing missing work or doing some sort of service to the school. A standing structure that teachers utilize is giving students tickets throughout the day. Students earn tickets in academic and nonacademic ways. Students might be given tickets for sharing their thinking in a class discussion, for helpfully pitching in to clean up after a science lab, or for being kind to another peer. Teachers sprinkle the use of tickets across the population all day, ensuring they notice as many positive acts as possible. Students can spend their tickets in the school store weekly. The store is run by the student government association and involves significant student input. The student government association members run the store once a week during homeroom time, and they collect input from students to see what to stock in the store. The association treasurer even collects data on what students are buying (or not buying) in the store so that the association can make informed decisions on next purchases. The student investment in this process is key.

Restorative-Discipline Practices

A restorative-discipline approach focuses on restitution to repair harm rather than on a punitive approach. There are several key components to an effective restorative system. First is **accountability**. Individuals are held accountable for their actions by encouraging those responsible for harm to take ownership over their behavior and the impact of that behavior on others. The central goal is to restore the well-being and relationships of all parties, which is often accomplished with the use of dialogue. Open and honest communication among the affected individuals is a core component. Such communication includes structured dialogues or conferences where all parties can express concerns, feelings, and needs. Restorative discipline aims to build empathy and understanding by having individuals consider the perspectives and experiences of others. This often helps students identify and understand the root cause of the misconduct. A problem-solving approach is utilized to collaboratively identify solutions and prevention strategies so that future misconduct and conflict may be avoided or minimized. This may include developing action plans to address issues systematically. While restorative discipline is reactive to specific instances, it is proactive by actively teaching individuals conflict-resolution and communication skills.

The primary difference between more traditional discipline-related practices and restorative practices is that more traditional discipline systems rely on punishment to deter misconduct. Restorative discipline instead seeks to address the root causes of behavior, to repair harm, and to promote personal growth and community cohesion. It is a more student-centered and holistic approach to addressing conflict, and it encourages students to take responsibility and to invest in the school community.

Here we share some experiences of the use of restorative practices from a first-year teacher, Amy Wilt, who works at a middle school in central North Carolina.

> The restorative practices that my school focuses on specifically is **restorative circles** within the context of MTSS. Restorative circles are a form of restorative practice where everyone is seated in a circle, and there is one person mediating a conversation for the group. The mediator is always the first to speak and gives prompts to the circle in the form of questions. The circle utilizes a talking piece, which is an object that can be held that holds some sort of significance. This piece means that the person holding it is the only person who can speak at that time. This is significant because it creates a space where everyone's voice can be heard. Circles have many different contexts, including community building, where we ask questions that are surface level, and do activities to engage students in building relationships and teamwork. We also utilize these types of community building circles at all our staff meetings and PLCs (professional learning communities) as openers to connect with each other and build a strong academic community amongst professionals. There are also circles where the mediator, or the person leading the conversation, runs a dialogue between two specific parties when there has been harm done. Examples of these such events include bullying, fighting, or just general unkindness towards each other. During these circles, the job of the mediator is to bring questions to the circle to help with the healing process while also working to build relationships between the two parties. We also do circles for rebuilding community on a larger scale when there has been harm done within our community.

One example of this from something I personally experienced was when we had a specific group of kids on my team that were making harmful comments while in class. This incident escalated over the course of a couple of weeks before we chose to take action as a whole team using a restorative circle. My team and I chose to do a team wide restorative circle with all our 110 kids. Along with our dean of culture, and other admin, we produced a circle that would give students the opportunity to voice how this incident made them feel, as well as creating a space for how we as a community can move on from this. How this looked is that we all ran the same circle at the same time with our respective homerooms. The circle began with an opener where students brought in their own talking piece, or something significant to them, and placed it in the center of the circle. We went around the circle, and one at a time placed our talking pieces in the circle. After this, we asked our students if one person would like to share about their talking piece, and we could use it for class. For my class, the student whose talking piece we used picked up a small bear and told us about how they got it from their parents after they had a successful year in school. We used this talking piece for the rest of the circle. After this opener, we began with the first prompt of "An incident has occurred within our community that has been harmful, how did this incident make you feel?" Following this prompt, we moved on to prompts, such as "What does it mean to interrupt harmful behavior?"; "What does it mean to be a bystander?"; and "How does it make you feel when someone stands up for you?" During these prompts, we mediated the conversation making sure that everyone had the chance to be heard and felt supported and safe. Following this, we did a closing activity where every student held a piece of string. Starting with the mediator, everyone went around the circle and said "I am here for you, and I support you" to the person to their right. Following this, they tied their piece of string to that of the person next to them. After everyone in the circle had the chance to participate in this, we all collectively placed the string, that was now tied into a complete circle, into the center to become part of the center piece of the circle. Following this circle, my team and I have noticed a new sense of closeness amongst our students. Many students have begun to check in with students who were on the receiving end of some of the harm, and a lot of the behavior from this situation has shifted.

This is just one example of how we have used restorative circles this school year to repair harm that has been done to our community. I have truly enjoyed being a part of a community that uses restorative practices. I believe they are so beneficial to students and staff members alike. They have helped to build a strong community within our school where staff members and students alike feel as though they are empowered and have a voice. I strongly recommend using restorative circles within any classroom context as it creates a space where everyone is on even ground and can share their thoughts and feelings. My strongest advice for someone beginning restorative circles, especially new teachers, would be to take it slow, and begin with setting expectations. The expectations that we have in our circles in my classroom is that we respect the talking piece (meaning that there is one voice at a time), that we can take lessons of what we learn from the circle, but stories always stay in (this creates a safe space where students may feel more comfortable sharing), and that we ALWAYS have the right to "pass" the talking piece. What this means is that just the act of students physically holding the talking piece is empowering them, however, some students may not feel comfortable at first, or for the first few times they participate in a circle. However, they should always have a choice for their voice to be heard (by holding the talking piece), and they should always have the right to pass it to the next person without talking if they choose. Along with this, it is important to always be kind to yourself when you are practicing restorative practices. Sometimes we mess up because we are human, and we are still learning all the time, so it is important that if you mess up within restorative practice, you are kind to yourself and repair the damage if any was done, then you try again!

Pause and Reflect: Look at Amy's experience with restorative practices as a first-year teacher, and then reflect back on our description of restorative practices in schools. What strengths do you see in this model? What challenges do you see? How do you think restorative practices can blend with PBIS models?

Look back to the list of words you made to associate with classroom management. After reading these first sections of the chapter, what would you add? What would you change?

Creating Classroom Communities: Relationships, Rules, and Routines

RELATIONSHIPS

It is evident in this text that relationships are at the core of building classroom communities, and it is no surprise that this is impactful when it comes to classroom management. Long gone are the days when teachers are told to "not smile until Christmas" to demand respect and exert control over the classroom. Think back to the previous section about culturally responsive discipline, and we can easily see all the potential negative ramifications of this approach. For a classroom to run smoothly, routines, rules, and procedures should be established so that expectations of students *and* adults are clear. Before those can work well, relationships must be built for students to trust and buy into the classroom community. We will explore ways to establish this community, keeping in mind that the individual personalities of teachers and students will largely define the nature of the classroom community. Below, Holly shares an experience of building a relationship with a challenging student.

> I'd like to share an example of the importance of relationship building by reintroducing Brooklyn, a feisty and somewhat troubled eighth grader who you met in Chapter 7. Brooklyn joined our school community in the middle of seventh grade. She had not had great success in other schools, and her file was filled with suspensions and a trail of social services calls due to her turbulent home life. I had only observed Brooklyn as an outsider passing through the school building, and I only noticed Brooklyn based on loud outbursts in class or the hallway or a series of curses as she stomped to the restroom shouting how terrible this place was and how awful all the teachers were for anyone who would listen. Some days Brooklyn would be dressed to the nines with trendy and slinky outfits, full eyeliner, and shimmery eyelids. Other days she would be in pajama pants with an oversized sweatshirt that seemingly swallowed her whole. She clearly didn't like to be approached by strangers, and I knew attempting to build a relationship with her was going to be challenging. I ended up covering the math classes for a week while the primary math teacher was out sick, and I got to see Brooklyn in the class-

room firsthand. As the instructional liaison for the school, I aim to know all the students by name and most barely seemed phased by me taking over the math teaching and calling on them to engage in discussion as they were used to my presence in the building. Brooklyn, however, seemed unamused that I even knew her name: "you don't know me . . . and I certainly don't know you" was one of the first utterances I heard from her. She was sitting slumped down in her chair with her hoodie pulled up over her head and her arms tightly wrapped across her body. As I talked with others in her group, she began goading me by dropping inappropriate snippets about what she had done that weekend, asking me if I had ever been drunk before, calling another teacher a bitch, etc. She seemed to be testing whether I would blow up at her, remove her from the setting, or punish her in some other way. Instead, while I got the rest of her group moving forward on the task, I simply asked her a mathematical question and to my surprise, she answered with a thoughtful response. I gave a positive reinforcement saying, "I like how you thought about that connection, now what about . . ." And I walked away from the group to work with another. Of course, as I left the table, I heard her mutter something about "that bitch," referring to me, but once again, in that moment, I chose not to address it. The comments she was making were clearly oriented towards getting attention, but the only attention I could give would be negative, which wasn't going to help me at that moment. It was clear that I was in for a long road of gradual trust building with this student. So, knowing that I would be working much more closely with Brooklyn as an eighth grader (the math teacher and I co-teach eighth grade for the first month of school), I started inserting myself more into her nonacademic life. Brooklyn and I could not have come from more different backgrounds. I grew up in a privileged middle-class home with supportive and loving parents, every need met, and a wealth of resources (I have an ACES score of 0). Brooklyn's ACES score is nearly off the charts with a background of instability, abuse in the home, exposure (and participation with) drugs, etc. To her my life was a foreign concept and her distrust that I could possibly know or understand her was palpable. And to me, her resilience simultaneously impressed me and broke my heart as truly I don't have full capacity to understand her, but I wanted to support her. I began showing up in the building before school started for the day and first, I would just take my laptop and sit near her and work but would take small opportunities to ask about things in her life and start up conversations. She liked my style of dress, and we would discuss shoes ("How do you walk in those heels?" she would ask me every day), my affinity for soft clothing like velvet, and then would discuss makeup and jewelry choices. She had chosen one weekend to pierce her own ears and they were irritated and fighting infection. After a brief conversation about the hypoallergenic earrings, I wore from a set I purchased I returned the next day with a pair for her. I said, "No pressure if you hate them, I just thought they might be helpful to put in and let your ears heal a little. I hope you like them." And then I just walked away. The next morning, I noticed she had them in and I simply looked at her, pointed to my own ears and said, "They look great." And the shift in our dynamic was palpable. And it was simple . . . I talked to her about nonmath things, I listened to her, and I connected with her. And she was infinitely more responsive to me academically in class. Now, was it all rainbows and butterflies? No—she had multiple outbursts towards me, most definitely has called me a bitch, but we continued to work on building trust. She knew she would be held accountable for her behavior and unfortunately had multiple more suspensions throughout the year, but I (and her other teachers) knew not to take things personally when she would shout how evil we were and how this school sucks. We believe that by loving the child incessantly we may have created the healthiest and most stable school year she has ever had.

Relationships MATTER. And they are foundational for all the other things we put into place, which we will dig into next.

RULES ABOUT RULES

There are several key considerations when creating the rules that will govern the classroom. In middle and secondary classrooms, there is often more emphasis on using a **democratic approach** to building rules, as this gives students voice and investment into the chosen rules. Things to consider are whether these rules are for this classroom alone or for use by a whole team or the whole school. These are conversations to have with other stakeholders prior to the start of school to ensure everyone is on the same page and using the same protocols if needed. It is common to have students engage in a group discussion about what norms in the classroom help them feel successful, regardless of whether the rules that are agreed on will apply to a class, a team, or an entire school. What does the class look like, feel like, sound like? Facilitating this conversation will help students articulate what is important to them and what they are willing to uphold and invested in upholding. The idea of giving up this "control" to the students can be unnerving, but we have done this exercise with many groups of students over the years, and, ultimately, we end up deciding on essentially the same rules every year, with slight variations in the wording.

Whether teachers decide to do this collaboratively with students or not, here are a few rules about rules.

- Rules need to be clearly stated and specific.

- Rules should be stated in positive framing language so that they feel supportive rather than punitive in nature.

- Rules should be things that feel important to uphold. If there is a rule about not chewing gum but the teacher does not actually care that much about gum chewing, she is likely not to consistently enforce that rule and then mixed messages are sent to students about whether rules matter.

- While rules should be specific, too much specificity should be avoided, as it can make a rule seem arbitrary and isolated.

- Rules should be limited to a maximum of six. It is cognitively too demanding to try to remember more than that, and we want our students to recall every rule at a moment's notice.

In Figure 13.4 we share several sets of classroom rules.

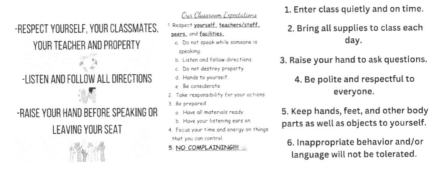

Figure 13.4 Examples of classroom rules. Created by authors

Pause and Reflect: Take a moment and look over our "rules about rules," and then look at the three examples. Do you think each set meets the criteria? Why or why not? Justify your thoughts with a peer.

Plan It: Think about the examples above, and think about how you might want to build your rules. Think about these two ways. First, if you were solely responsible for creating the rules, what would your rules be? Think mindfully about the following characteristics of your rules: how many rules (maximum of six), positively framed, specific, and meaningful. Now, brainstorm how you would facilitate this conversation with students to end up with a set of rules that are very close to your established set. Script a conversation with the class about what a successful classroom looks like, feels like, sounds like. As you script, write down anticipated student responses to those prompts. Then analyze those potential responses for themes, and see how closely those norms match your list of rules.

ROUTINES AND PROCEDURES

Routines, or **procedures**, are an essential part of a well-functioning classroom. Rick Smith and Grace Dearborn describe routines and procedures as the train tracks and the content as the train (2016). Having well-established routines in the classroom allows maximum instructional time to be spent on content exploration. One of us reflected recently on a graduate-school experience of watching videos of mathematics instruction. One of the tasks was to track the amount of time spent on academic tasks. Consistently, classrooms that had strong routines and procedures typically had more time on spent on academic tasks than did those that had less structure; less routinized classrooms lost instructional time due to things like transitioning to groups or turning in homework. Establishing routines takes time; however, a large investment of instructional time, especially when made during the first few weeks of school, will buy heaps of time back later in the year, as things are working smoothly.

So, what routines and procedures need to be established? Well, likely a lot of them. They will not all be taught at once, and they will all need a lot of practice to become second nature for students. Teachers need to think through routines for time before class, during class, and at the end of class and for special situations, like fire drills and field trips. Below is *short* list of the kinds of routines one might need:

- Before class
  - Entering the classroom
  - Warmup/bellringer procedure
  - Turning in of homework
  - Coming back from being absent
- During class
  - Getting the whole group's attention
  - Distributing/collecting materials
  - Restroom protocols
  - Asking for help (during whole-group, small-group, independent-work sessions)
  - Leaving the room (calls home, nurse or counselor visits, lockers)
  - Sharpening/borrowing pencils or getting other classroom tools, like calculators
  - Use of technology (computers, tablets, listening to music)
  - Cooperative-learning group norms
- End of class
  - Formative assessments—exit tickets
  - Classroom cleanup
  - Homework protocols
  - Exiting the room
  - Special circumstances
  - Norms related to library, bus, off-campus field trips
  - Fire drills (or other safety protocols)

This list could be extended but we would be here all day. Some of the first things to think of when culling this list and/or brainstorming other routines are thinking about what routines will be school or team based and making sure *everyone* is on the same page and consistent with those routines. Then think about personal preferences. We all have certain thresholds when it comes to things like cleanliness and organization, and everyone likes to do things differently. Think about nonnegotiable items, and implement those routines first. For example, if the idea of a student sharpening a pencil in the middle of instruction is like fingernails on a chalkboard to you, ensure that there is a routine for students to be able to borrow a pencil or wait until an appropriate time. Some teachers like to have toolkits at each group table, equipped with backup pencils and other tools to minimize movement in the classroom. Other teachers have things in a central place and have students get their notebooks, pencils, calculators, and so forth as they transition into the room and only then. Some teachers do not mind if students get tools at any point if they are not disruptive. One teacher at our school has students line up at the entrance door to be greeted and to receive initial instructions before entering the room each day. Holly describes below several of the strategies she has used over the years in her teaching.

> I gave out cards (from this resource https://makemathmoments.com/random-cards/) at the beginning of class each day. The cards indicated how students would be grouped. This helped keep groups random and heterogenous and allowed for a personal greeting and eye contact with each student before class began. Some years I utilized music or a timer to help all of us in transition. Students knew not to come up to me during class transitions—they had jobs to do getting their materials for class while I was taking attendance or handing papers back etc. By the time the song ended we were all set and ready to focus on the warm-up activity. I knew in my early years in teaching that I needed students to put papers into the box created for each class because I worried that I would put it down somewhere and lose it. I also remember my dog ate a student's homework one time, and I hated admitting to a student that his paper was lost. To ensure my students were always prepared, I had [a] bunch of pencils in a mug on my desk and students were welcome to borrow one, but they had to leave collateral, so they'd remember to return it (it was often a shoe which in retrospect was probably not the best smelling or safest choice, but it was effective). Something I had read from Harry Wong many years ago was always in the back of my mind—that it should be the students who are doing most of the work. If I am exhausted at the end of the day because I have been running around handling all the little things, I am not doing it right—utilize students' capabilities to help the system run smoothly. They enjoy being trusted to be helpful, and it will save immense amounts of time and energy.

Pause and Reflect: When our college students write their first teaching autobiography, the routines and procedures they want to have in their classrooms tend to be the things they write about. They envision this environment, and they think creatively about how our space is going to be special or better than any learning environment they have been in. Take a moment, and look at the list of potentially needed routines. Highlight the ones that feel most pertinent to you. Then take a few moments to add to the list—what are your personal quirks that will require a particular routine or procedure?

Herein lies the crux of making routines . . . well . . . routine. Routines must be modeled. And they must be practiced. Again. And again. And again. Here, Holly shares reflections from her first year of teaching.

> When I first began my teaching career, I had planned all my organizational procedures and routines, and I had told my students what to do in each situation throughout the first week of school. And then I was irritated when none of those things were still happening by week three. I had made several errors here. I assumed that just telling my students the procedures was sufficient—they are thirteen after all, not six. I had assumed modeling and making them practice would insult their intelligence. I also assumed that hearing it just once was enough. How wrong I was. The second semester of my first year I tried again—we came back from winter break, and I reintroduced the routines and procedures—but this time I showed them exactly what I needed. And then I had them practice it several times. And we did that for several weeks. It is monotonous and painful to practice so often, but it matters. By March things were running smoothly, but I also remodeled and repracticed things after long weekends or spring break.

The phrase *practice makes permanence* has real impact here—we need students to actively put those routines into place, using regular reminders before it becomes second nature. When reminders are needed it may be as simple as saying, "Who can remind us of what our process is for transitioning to lunch?" Put the responsibility on the students to explicitly state what is needed. It will pay off in the long term.

Practice It: During class, get into small groups of at least four. Each of you should pick a routine or procedure that you want to model. Script out exactly how you would model the routine and how you would facilitate students in practicing that routine. Focus on the feedback you give students in your debriefing after practicing: for example, "I noticed . . ."; "What could we do more efficiently?"; and so on. Then practice at least once more with a group, debriefing to solidify understanding.

SILENT SIGNAL

One more tangible example for us to explore is the use of signals as procedures in classrooms. There are various purposes of using and ways to use signals to streamline processes during instructional time. One teacher on our team uses sign language to have students indicate to her if they need to get water, go to the bathroom, or ask a question. She keeps her eyes moving and can give permission nonverbally (with a nod or a wave) to the student without disrupting the flow of the lesson at all. The use of sign-language communication is also effective during whole-group discussions. Students sign when they have a comment or a question or if they agree with another student. This allows the teacher to seamlessly orchestrate the discussion in meaningful ways without off-task disruptions.

The other procedure we want to emphasize here is the use of a **silent signal**. When teachers need to get everyone's attention quickly, the use of a silent signal is effective and efficient. It eliminates the need for teachers to raise their voices and helps ease transitions from meeting in individual or small groups back to meeting as a whole group. One thing to note when deciding on a silent signal is that it must work for the individual teacher. Many of the things we are about to list are silly and goofy and work only for a teacher who is comfortable with them. Others are simple, straightforward, and effective. The effectiveness of each method, however, is drastically impacted by the consistency with which it is used. If a teacher models and practices a silent signal for the first two weeks of school but does not utilize it regularly for another month—well, good luck! Kayleigh and Holly's approaches to silent signaling are very different from each other's, but both are equally effective. Kayleigh's protocol is to say, "Give me five," and then she counts down. By the time she says one, she expects students to be quiet and giving her their full attention. Holly's protocol is more playful but still effective.

> I mostly use my silent signal to transition from small groups back to whole groups. I simply say, quite loudly, "Stop," and students would reply "Collaborate and listen" (quintessential pop culture reference from the 1990s. Look it up). It is one of those songs that seems to persist across generations and while completely silly, it brought me a sense of joy and because it was funny, my students responded gleefully and efficiently.

Some teachers use clapping rhythms or do the "If you can hear me, clap once; if you can hear me, clap twice . . ." method. One year, one of our interns would say "Macaroni and cheese," and students would reply, "Everybody freeze." For several years, our school used a school-wide signal that was based on our mascot—the Catamount. We would say, "Paws up," and all students were to be silent and make little paws with their hands. It truly does not matter what signal is chosen: choose something, and be consistent with it. One piece of feedback we give interns all the time is that they begin talking before they have everyone's attention. The (consistent) use of a silent signal helps hold everyone accountable to being quiet and ready to listen when needed.

Teacher Presence and Persona

The teacher persona is made up of how we set up our classroom and how we communicate, both verbally and nonverbally, with students. Much of our communication is nonverbal. Our posture and facial expressions communicate clear messages to students. Holly remembers when an intern expressed in her journal that she was feeling like students were not responding well to her and that she was struggling to keep them engaged.

At the next observation I tried to take notes of what might be causing my intern's struggles. I first noticed that she mostly sat at the table in the front of the room with her shoulders slightly slumped as she did example problems. While it was not that long ago, this classroom still used an overhead projector so while she was facing the students, she was sitting low, and I could barely see her in the back of the room. I noticed that when she stood, she stayed glued near the front white board and as she asked questions of the students, she leaned against the board with her arms crossed. Several messages were sent to me in these moments—she is bored, she is grumpy, so why would I care about what she is asking me to do?

Pause and Reflect: Next time you go to class, take observational notes about the body language of your instructor and yourself and your peers. What do you notice? How does the instructor move about the room? How does this impact your engagement with the class? At the end of class, you and your classmates and instructor should respectfully debrief what you have noticed.

Having a commanding presence is key to successful classroom management. Do not misunderstand—we do not mean commanding in a domineering sense. We mean to present ourselves in a way that shows confidence, investment, and ownership in the community. We also must assume a friendly and approachable posture that lets students know we want them there and want to engage with them meaningfully.

Picture 13.1

VERBAL COMMUNICATION

How we talk to students will establish the rhythm of our classrooms. We want to ensure we have clear and firm expectations and boundaries while also setting up an open and inclusive environment where students feel comfortable sharing their thinking. We want to be mindful of the words we choose to use and even more mindful of the tone we use to convey them. A final note on language, and we know this one will feel uncomfortable for some: reconsider the use of the word *please*. Many of us were likely trained throughout life to make polite requests using the "magic word." But, when setting up a firm, friendly but I-mean-business kind of environment, it is important that we make statements rather than questions or requests. It is not "Devon, will you *please* sit down," it is, "Devon, sit down."\

Practice It: Get with a partner. Each partner is responsible for reading one of the two sentences below. Read the sentence first with an excited tone. Read it again with a bored tone. Read it a third time with an angry tone. Reflect after the three readings what feelings and reactions you had in response to each reading. Discuss why these different tones, though used with the same words, make such a difference to your response.

Sentence one: Go on, try it.
Sentence two: Really, [insert name].

To make this more explicit, let's take a note from the **Responsive Classroom**® approach to think about how we use language to support students. Responsive Classroom® is an educational approach that is focused on creating positive and inclusive classrooms where social and emotional learning is intertwined with academic instruction. At its core are relationship building, student autonomy, and community building. The emphasis is student-centered, and the program gives advice on how we engage with students to foster positive classroom communities. In its model, three types of teacher language are highlighted to connect with and reach students in positive and meaningful ways. First, they describe the use of ***envisioning language***, which focuses on creation of positive mental images showing students how successful they can be. This is done by asking students to think about what they will need to be successful with something, or it is done by creating a visual for students to help them keep their eyes on the prize, saying, for example, "Imagine that . . . " or "I hope that . . . ." The second kind of teacher language the program encourages is ***reinforcing language***. In this style of language, the emphasis is on explicitly noticing positives about what students are doing socially and academically so that they are encouraged to continue those behaviors. This is an asset-based approach that focuses on students' strengths. Remember that this applies to more than just behavior; it applies to academics as well. Think about the feedback given on an assignment—instead of a generic "nice work," the phrasing could be more concrete and specific about what was done well. A teacher might say, "I noticed that you utilized your grammar conventions well in this paper"; "I see that you organized your steps for solving equations to help you keep track of where you were"; or, simply, "I noticed that . . .." These statements have a clear purpose—to make actions and behaviors visible and to stimulate active reflection on those behaviors. The last of the types of language that Responsive Classroom® focuses on is *reminding language*. This is how we model and build capacity for self-regulation. Behaviors must be taught, and this is one way to do that. Once again, the focus is put on the students; they must articulate what should be happening. It gives students an opportunity to take responsibility and gives them, yet again, a moment to reflect on their behaviors. Examples of reminding language might include, "Show us how we transition from lunch back to class" or "Remind everyone of our three group norms when we work in small groups." These statements and questions get students to be explicit about how they should be doing the classroom's regular routines and procedures. Notice that, among all three types of language, there is no deficit language and no negative tone. Everything is stated in a positive fashion to put the focus on what we *do* want to see happening. This approach puts a lot of responsibility on the students; the teacher facilitates the learning process to keep students more engaged and accountable.

PHYSICAL SPACE

Many teachers dream about the physical instructional space—there are Pinterest boards full of ideas of how to set up the classroom. Some teachers will begin teaching in schools that have already invested in **flexible seating** choices, and their classrooms may have easily maneuverable tables, chairs, wobble stools, and café tables. Others will enter a bare-bones situation and will spend weekends sewing and attaching cushions to milk crates. Old desks may be large and covered in old chewing gum, and Amazon wish lists may be full of string lights or lamps—anything to avoid bright overhead fluorescents. We are incredibly lucky in our school to have modern furniture that was chosen to provide flexible seating choices. One of our teacher's first classroom had a mixture of wobble stools and chairs, yoga mats, and pillows; students thus had the option to find comfortable places on the floor to read. Around the perimeter of the room, there was a string of LED lights that could change color, depending on the class mood. The teachers could move tables, depending on whether students would be working in small groups, with partners, or on their own. The essence of this room was calm. Another teacher was not so lucky with her first classroom. This room had more than thirty large desks (and yes, old chewing gum). In this situation, creativity was key. One strategy was to organize the desks into two nested U-shapes. The teacher's use of a tablet that would project to a screen gave the teacher a sense of proximity with all students at any given time. The teacher organized desks into groups of three or four to facilitate group work. When organizing classroom furniture, important considerations include whether all students see the board; whether the teacher can easily move through the groups; and how accessible tools or manipulatives are. Experiment and try lots of structures to find what feels most productive.

Traditional Classroom Arrangements

Flexible Seating Arrangements

Picture 13.2 Classroom Designs. Created by authors

CONSISTENCY

Consistency is at the core of any well-functioning system. In the realm of classroom management, it is also one of the most familiar pitfalls where beginning teachers struggle. Middle school students can be persuasive, persistent, and downright pains at times. For some adolescents, a good power struggle or argument is their idea of a good time. Sometimes it is a test—will the teacher actually follow through on his word? Sometimes it is a battle of wills "if I keep going, I will wear her down." Holding one's ground is a crucial part of being consistent. Rules have been created and posted; routines and procedures have been modeled and practiced—now it is time to follow through. Smith and Dearborn (2016) describe holding ground as an invisible quality and define it as the ability and willingness to be firm while still being friendly.

Practice It: For this exercise, we pull from Smith and Dearborn (2016) an activity they use in workshops to highlight how quickly emotions can impact interactions with students. For this exercise, one partner is the teacher and the other partner is the student. If you are the student in this activity, your job is to be persuasive and persistent and use any compelling argument possible to get permission to leave the room. If you are the teacher, your job is to hold your ground so that the student cannot leave the room. Set a timer for ninety seconds. At the end of ninety seconds, if you are the teacher, you are going to limit your responses to, "No" or "I understand; the answer is no." Continue for another thirty seconds or so. Then debrief. If you played the teacher, share what emotions and feelings you had and celebrate any successes you found (Activity adapted from Smith and Dearborn (2016). Conscious Classroom Management, p.68.)

COMMUNICATING WITH FAMILIES

Families are vital stakeholders in a student's well-being and educational success. Establishing an authentic partnership between schools and families can be challenging, but it is necessary to establish a system of support for students. It is important to reach out to families to inform them of decisions being made on their student's behalf and to include them in those decision-making processes. This allows for more consistency between home and school and provides students with a predictable and supportive circle of support.

CLIMATE OF SAFETY

Students who feel safe and supported in their learning environment are more likely to show up for school and be an active part of the learning community. Building a climate of safety relies on many aspects within a school: the facilities and resources, the inclusivity of all students, the investment in and connection of students, staff, and families. We know from research that positive school climates have positive impacts on things like attendance, achievement, and retention of students.

Addressing Big Behaviors

We always hope that the proactive preventative practices we utilize in classroom management will keep our classrooms running like well-oiled machines. This will primarily be the case with consistent modeling, relationship building, and explicit teaching of self-regulation strategies. However, behaviors can escalate and, occasionally, "big behaviors" will occur. Students exhibiting these behaviors are often in what we call a state of dysregulation. They are either in fight or flight mode, in which they are hyperaroused and may be agitated or reactive, or they are in freeze mode, in which they completely shut down. When students are in a state of dysregulation, we may see behaviors such as fights, emotional meltdowns that cause disturbances, or something even more egregious. There are four phases of such disturbances: prevention, escalation, crisis, and recovery/restoration.

The prevention phase encompasses the periods when our normal proactive measures (rules, routines, and procedures, as outlined in previous sections) effectually reduce the risk for or prevent a disturbance. During this phase, students are still in a regulated state; the typical strategies of redirecting students, reminding them of classroom norms, and modeling positive behaviors are effective. However, despite use of preventive measures, something may cause students' emotions to become dysregulated; at that point, the escalation phase begins. During the escalation phase, students may or may not be in a regulated state. They may exhibit slight agitation, or they may be quickly accelerating into a dysregulated state. Here, teachers need to utilize a range of strategies to remain calm and to attempt to calm the student. Students may also reach the crisis phase; it is important to note here that students' progression through these phases is not necessarily linear, and students may go directly to this phase. In the crisis phase, teachers must rely on school-based protocols to keep all students safe, and teachers need to employ strategies to keep themselves calm, cool, and collected. The final stage in de-escalation is to recover and restore. Here, teachers focus on welcoming students back into the learning environment and reintegrating them into the community. Table 13.2 outlines what students and teachers are doing at each phase, with examples of language to utilize at each phase.

PRACTICAL APPLICATIONS

Our goal is to provide a safe learning environment for all our students in a culturally responsive and equitable fashion. Sometimes students need to be removed from the classroom setting, if only for a few minutes, to maintain the integrity of the learning environment for others. In this section, we will share a few cases of handling "big behaviors," with an emphasis on the reflective practices of good teachers. In some cases, we will see that the teachers handled things seamlessly—and that, ultimately, there was a good outcome for all. Other cases may have not gone as well, but the teacher's reflection afterward can help us hone our skills in responding to students.

Before we delve into those cases, let us think about the basics. Remember that we can control only ourselves and our own behaviors. Remember also that, at times, self-control can be helpful in diffusing situations. Keeping our voices calm and controlled is key. The phrase "be the calm in the storm" comes to mind. Be observant. Try to capture as much detail as possible of any potential triggers that may have instigated the issue. Listen. Show empathy and kindness, and be nonjudgmental as students share their perspective. Give choice. Teachers control what the choices are, but, oftentimes, having a choice gives the student a sense of autonomy and control, which may help de-escalate the situation. Give space and time. Sometimes a few minutes without discussing the situation gives the student a chance to calm down. Use some of the re-set strategies discussed in Chapter 7, such as deep breathing, push against the wall, etc. Ask if the student can articulate what he or she needs in the moment.

There may be moments when we do not keep it together. We may lose our cool and yell. One of us can identify at least three instances of slamming the classroom door so hard the building shook (effective for getting attention but not recommended). When these moments happen, it is important to hold ourselves accountable—apologize when needed, regroup, reflect, and move forward. We must give ourselves grace as we navigate hard situations, and reflecting on how we handled situations helps us continue to harness our de-escalation skills and become better and more supportive teachers.

Table 13.2 **Phases of De-Escalation**

	Prevention	Escalation	Crisis	Recovery & Restoration
What the brain is doing	Regulated	Regulated OR dysregulated	Dysregulated	Regulated
What students are doing	Business as usual—perhaps occasional minor behavior challenges, easily redirected	Student may be slightly agitated or may have reached an accelerated point of agitation	Student is in need of support to regulate emotion and/or behavior	Student is calm and able to reenter classroom environment
What teachers are doing	Business as usual—relationship building, implementation of practiced routines and procedures, modeling, and implementation of coping strategies for calmness	Utilize responsive strategies, such as offer choice, use redirection, prompt student about norms, provide space, model and practice self-regulation for student	Focus on maintaining safety for all students; remain calm; use few words; utilize preestablished crisis protocol	Debrief with student (may be a restorative conversation); keep track of data; debrief as class if applicable/appropriate; reintegrate student into classroom activities

Source: Adapted from Strickland-Cohen, M. K., et al. (2022)

Practice It: In this next section, we ask you to become problem solvers and reflective practitioners. We will present various situations that include significant behaviors that may not be easily addressed by our classroom routines and protocols. Read the case introductions, then, either individually or in pairs, brainstorm how you would handle the situation. Then read our descriptions of what happened, with reflections from the teacher, and think about how the teacher responded and what you might do differently and why.

Scenario 1

Holly shares an experience with a seventh-grade student.

The Situation

Luke was a student with a short temper. I learned on the first day of school he liked to argue, push back, and was volatile with his emotions when frustrated. I can think back to an instance when he got very frustrated during a competitive review game and what felt like out of nowhere, he slammed his computer on the desk, uttered a litany of profanities, and then picked up the computer and threw it towards my face.

Pause and Reflect: Brainstorm with your partner—what would you do in this situation?

What Happened

Luckily, I was able to deflect the computer and Chrome books are remarkably resilient. I was taken off guard by the outburst and had several loud feelings rumbling inside of me in response. But I knew that would not de-escalate the situation. Instead, I employed the powers of nonverbal communication mustering up my best "teacher look" and pointing towards the door that I expected him to exit. I did not say a word. I just held my ground and pointed until he started walking that way. He was still riled and slammed a few desks on his way out, but he exited the room while I quickly texted our enrichment coordinator across the hall to intercept him and have him wait in the office. My first focus was getting the rest of the students back to engaging in the game, and I was able to leave my intern with the class to keep rolling (I recognize that [having] another adult is not always possible and [the situation] would need to be handled differently if not for her presence). I purposefully waited a few minutes before I went to retrieve the student; he and I both needed a moment to calm down. As I walked towards the office, I thought of what needed to be communicated: a) He needed to be heard, and I needed to listen, b) I needed to communicate why the outburst was problematic, and c) we needed to find a better way for him to process his frustrations. I walked in, and while he had calmed down some, it was also clear that he was still agitated. I said to him, can you tell me exactly what made you feel frustrated? He told me that he did not feel like the process of how I was taking people's answers was fair and that he felt he was not able to contribute even though he knew all the answers. I nodded along as I listened to him, tamping down my own defensive thoughts as he continued to berate my game and my process. I had to remind myself that ultimately it was not about me. Once he had said his piece, I responded that I was sorry that this had been so frustrating. I said, but it is never okay to throw things at me or anyone else and that we needed to figure out a different way for him to express himself. I invited him to brainstorm other ways the game would feel fairer for him, and that while I made no promises, I would take his ideas into consideration for next time. I asked if he was ready to re-join his peers or if he needed more time. He came back to join us, sullen, but calm.

Reflection

Unfortunately, Luke and I had many more instances like this one, and it took both of us continually frustrating each other before I realized we needed a plan and that my imposing one upon him was not going to be effective. After another outburst, both of us near tears, we finally sat down for a heart-to-heart conversation. We expressed honestly what each of us was doing to trigger the other. We found that much of the source of his frustration was when I challenged his thinking. He had always been so naturally successful with math, and he was finally reaching a point where I was challenging him. My teaching style is to give students many strategies to solve something, and he would get overwhelmed and overstimulated. Sometimes students would contribute ideas that did not match his thinking; he would assume everyone else was wrong—usually with a loud outburst of frustration. We produced a system that either of us was able to say at any moment—"I need a breather," and walk away from each other, we would revisit after we both felt calmer. I would go back to him and ask what strategy felt most natural to him and spend a few minutes with him just on that strategy. Finding the root of his frustration was epically helpful, and we miraculously made it through the year without any additional large-scale meltdowns (for either of us).

Pause and Reflect: Analyze what happened with Holly's reflection. What is your perception of how she handled this situation? What might you do differently?

Scenario 2

Morgan has been teaching for seven years and has a variety of teaching experiences, including teaching fourth grade and middle and high school social studies in Costa Rica, serving one year as a Native American mentor and AVID elective teacher at a local high school, and working for two-and-a-half years as an affective-needs special-education teacher at a local middle school. Affective-needs teachers work with students diagnosed with a significant emotional disability (SED). The affective-needs program was a self-contained classroom with eleven students. In these next two cases, Morgan shares her experience of some "big behaviors" she encountered.

The Context

While working as a special education teacher with students diagnosed with social and emotional disorders, I experienced many big behaviors. There were many times when my school and I responded appropriately and just as many times that we did not respond in the best way. When you are in these situations, fight, flight, or freeze can take over. It can be difficult to remain regulated when everyone around you has flipped their lid.

One day I was out of the classroom for less than twenty minutes, leaving my paraprofessional in charge. As I returned, I heard the screams of my student Kamron. Kamron immediately starts screaming my name and begging for help. My principal and a local police officer were holding him against the wall. Kamron continued to fight the two men, and they eventually forced him on the ground to handcuff him and take him to the police car. At this point, I did not know what was going on and I followed them. As Kamron was being walked to the police car, he was screaming things such as, "F- you, get the f- off me . . . You don't know what it is like for both your f-ing parents to be dead . . . Miss Morgan, help me, save me." A group of students was walking into the building from P.E. class, and Kamron started screaming at them, "What the f- are you looking at? F- you." Kamron eventually gets into the police car, and he is beating on the window saying, "Please help me, Miss Morgan. I don't want to go to jail." The police officer drives away and I enter the school to see what happened and went to comfort another upset student. It turns out that Kamron stole a pair of scissors from my desk (the only pair in the room to help ensure safety) and tried to stab another student with them. The other student defended himself and threatened Kamron as he was approaching him. Multiple students in the classroom tried to stop Kamron from stabbing the student.

Pause and Reflect: Hopefully, teachers encounter such situations rarely, if ever. Take the time to think—what would you do? What do you think is the most appropriate course of action?

What Happened

My paraprofessional assistant called administration and they came to assist. The paraprofessional encouraged administration to use their Crisis Prevention Institute training to get the scissors from the student. In the assistant's mind, the administration did not react quickly enough, and she approached the student and grabbed the scissors out of his hand. They evacuated everyone except the student from the classroom, and the police were called.

Fast forward to me walking into the classroom. There is one student curled up in the corner sobbing, another yelling in anger, and my assistant looking stunned. I told her that I would talk to the administration. She said, "no you are not—I am going to go take a break." I tell the yelling student to go to our classroom balcony and ask the other students if they are okay. They all said yes. I approached the sobbing student who told me that watching the violence took him back to the violence he used to watch his mom receive from her boyfriends. He told me that he was scared and wanted to go home. I ended up taking him to the room beside my classroom, put a blanket on him, turned the lights out, and let him call his mom.

Reflection

This situation included positive and negative responses. The assistant calling administration immediately gave a positive response. The administration stepping in but not working to take the scissors out [of] the student's hand could go either way. Some would argue that they were protecting their personal safety, and some would argue that they were not protecting other students. It is hard to know how you would react in such a high intensity moment. Maybe they should have evacuated everyone out of the room as soon as they saw what was going on. My assistant grabbing the scissors from the student was an act of bravery and could have put herself in danger. Again, you could argue either way on how that was handled. The aggressive treatment of the student by the administration and police officer is something that has scarred me for years. Was it appropriate for them to push him to the ground even though he was unarmed and no longer a threat? I do not know. Did I handle it well when I followed this student, who tried to harm another, and support[ed] him while he was being arrested? Was it appropriate to comfort him in a high stress situation that he caused? My gut and heart say yes. When a student acts this way, there are significant emotional/mental as a response to difficult situations happening in their life. They do not have the necessary coping skills to manage their anger, and they have been shown that this is how you respond when angry. I should have considered the trauma that my assistant experienced and offered a break or let them go home. I appreciated her putting me in my place and telling me that she was going to take a break. I can confidently say that I responded appropriately to the student who was sobbing in the corner. I showed them love, support, compassion and did all that I could to ensure that the student felt safe. At the end of it all, the student did not have charges pressed against them, and they were not expelled from school. It was determined that these behaviors were a manifestation of their disability. If you ask teachers in my school, many say that the student should have a harsher consequence. Does the child have a right to come back to school after those actions? I believe that the student deserved to come back to school, and I believe that they needed to come back with significant support and therapy.

Pause and Reflect: Look closely at the events and Morgan's reflection. What resonates with you? Compare Morgan's response to your brainstorming of how you would have handled it—any similarities or differences?

Scenario 3

Morgan shares another instance of big behaviors from her teaching experience.

Context

One of my Affective Needs students had a love hate relationship with me. When she was happy, I was the best person on the planet. When she was angry, I was the worst person on the planet. This student, Shona, was known for resolving conflict through fighting. I cannot remember what happened to start the incident, but Shona was furious with me. She ended up walking out of the classroom, I followed her, and she verbally let me know she was angry and needed space. She went into the counselor's office and yelled to the counselor about me. I walked into the office and said, "Shona is mad at me, and she doesn't need to be." I started to walk away, and the student followed me. She got so close to my face that I could feel the spit on my cheek as she was yelling at me. She was screaming, "You want to f-ing fight? I am going to punch you in the f-ing face you f-ing bitch."

Pause and Reflect: Brainstorm with your partner—what would you do in this situation?

What Happened

She was saying "You want to f-ing fight? I am going to punch you in the f-ing face you f-ing bitch" repeatedly in my face and I just looked away from her during this time. I remember sitting there and thinking, "Stay calm, stay calm." An administrator ended up getting in between us and walking the student away from me. After about an hour apart from each other, we had a restorative conversation.

Reflection

Reflecting on this situation, I did not respond appropriately to this situation. When Shona walked out of the classroom, I should have called the administration and let them know she left without permission. I should not have followed her to prove my point. This did nothing but fuel the fire. I needed to stop at that moment and recognized that I was dysregulated. I certainly should not have walked into the counseling office because she asked me for space, and I did not give it to her. I knew that she did not have the coping skills to deal with me at that moment and yet I chose to follow. My choosing to follow increased her anger and ended with her threatening me and screaming in my face. I am not justifying any of her actions, but I had the choice to not engage. I had the choice to take a breath and recognize that she was angry. I am thankful that she did not punch me in the face and grateful that we were able to resolve the situation at the end of the day. This was certainly a lesson in listening to a student when they say that they need space.

Pause and Reflect: Analyze what happened in Morgan's experience. What is your perception of how she handled this situation? What might you do differently?

School Codes of Conduct

As we mentioned previously, some of these big behaviors will instantly head into the realm of the school code of conduct. In each case above, administration was appropriately called in for reinforcement. Once in the hands of an administrator, the code of conduct provides a framework for assessing behaviors and assigning consequences. Most schools have moved away from those zero-tolerance policies that were not culturally responsive in nature, but most policies do still include in-school and out-of-school suspensions. Here we share language from a school code of conduct to orient readers to the progression of consequences for behaviors addressed outside the classroom.

In the following example of a school code of conduct, its general philosophy is stated, so that stakeholders understand that a positive and proactive approach should be taken before students reach any exclusionary consequences. It states,

GENERAL DISCIPLINE PHILOSOPHY

> We believe good discipline is essential to good learning; each student has the right to be free from distractions caused by others' inappropriate behavior. We believe this can be established using the principles of a democratic community and restorative justice. A democratic community approach to classroom management involves attention to relationships with and among learners and an intentional effort to create a climate of mutual caring and respect; a positive view of learners, including their inclination toward and motivation for learning and their responsiveness to kind and respectful treatment, consideration of each learner and his/her subsequent behavior within the social context of the classroom.
>
> Day to day practices that generate community in the democratic classroom involve learners, teachers, and school personnel getting to know each other; involve learners setting mutually agreed upon classroom expectations for behavior, and teachers and peers support learners in meeting expectations through teaching expectations, reminding, redirecting, and re-teaching expectations as needed.
>
> Regular classroom and school meetings are designed to foster school community involvement. Through problem-solving and sharing experiences, students learn and practice social skills such as listening to and responding positively to each other, showing empathy, and generating solutions to problems. Class meetings involve the following:

- share acknowledgment and appreciation for positive behaviors that sustain and enhance the learning community.

- acknowledge and generate solutions for problems and concerns that affect the learning community. Solutions are ideas generated by students that support learners in the community and work to resolve and prevent problems from reoccurring. The focus is on solutions rather than consequences or punishment.

- students share their life experiences.

- students plan classroom experiences such as field trips and service-learning opportunities. For problems that interfere with the learning community and the health and well-being of individual students beyond that which can be handled through class meetings or staff/student conferences, staff will work to identify early warning signs of problems that interfere with learning and the functioning of the learning community, safety, health, and well-being of students. Staff will develop personalized growth plans to prevent problems from escalating and/or remediate problematic behavior.

> When individuals in the learning community display disrespectful, hurtful, or harmful behavior to their peers or the community at large, the teacher and student work together to identify appropriate restitution to make amends.
>
> The following standards of student behavior are intended to mirror, when appropriate, the partner school district's policy. While students are enrolled in a school run by the university, students are expected to follow many of the expected behavior norms of its partner school district and its host school. Food services and daily transportation will be provided by the district partner and students are expected to follow all rules and regulations when utilizing those services.
>
> We expect our students to behave in a socially acceptable and responsible manner and believe there must exist a climate conducive to learning and respect for oneself, other people, and property for a school to meet student needs satisfactorily. Staff will maintain a positive behavior support system to model and encourage constructive methods of correcting and managing student behavior. When possible, we will engage and involve resources from the university, public school system, and community resources and organizations to identify and correct root problems of behavior and disruption of the educational process. It is a goal of our school to have students in school as much as possible and avoid drop-outs, suspensions, and expulsions.
>
> Every student has the right to learn, and every teacher the right to teach. The following guidelines were developed to ensure this situation is present throughout the school.

- Students will show respect and courtesy toward all staff members. Students will also follow any lawful directive from a staff member. Students must give their names when asked by a staff member (including secretary, custodian, teacher aide, bus driver).

- Students will not participate in, encourage, or instigate fighting at any school function. Participants in and instigators of fights will be subject to disciplinary action and may be referred to law enforcement for charges.

- Students will not use or display profanity or vulgar language.

- Students will not abuse or misuse school property or equipment.

- Students will not threaten, coerce, or intimidate, either singly or in groups, any other students, or staff members in any manner.

- A student shall not possess, handle, or transmit any object that reasonably can be considered a weapon on school grounds, school transportation, or any school function.

- Unnecessary noise or loud talking in halls, cafeteria, etc., will not be tolerated.

- Students will be in assigned places, with necessary materials, on time.

- Disruptive behavior will not be tolerated on campus.

- No student will possess, use, sell, or be under the influence of any drugs or alcohol at school, at any school function, or on any school transportation.

- Students shall not possess or use tobacco products, nicotine products, or any type of personal vaporizer (vape pen, e-cig, etc.) at school, on school-affiliated transportation, or as a participant in any school-sponsored activity.

- Students will refrain from inappropriate displays of affection.

- Students will wear appropriate dress as described in the dress code section of this handbook.

- Students may not carry nor have in their possession beepers, walkie-talkies, video cameras, or laser lights. These items may be confiscated by the administration and returned only to a parent or guardian.

- Phones should not be visible or used during the school day unless authorized by a staff member. Students are encouraged to store their phone in their backpack or locker during school hours.

- Appropriate behavior is expected at school-wide assemblies and all extracurricular activities.

Then the student code of conduct states the following:

> As stated in the general discipline philosophy, focus is placed on building community through democratic classroom and restorative justice practices. While this document is intended to provide notice to students and parents of general expectations for behavior and consequences for misconduct, it must be understood that discretion is used in dealing with a wide range in age and maturity of students, and that consideration must be given to the

seriousness of the infraction(s) when determining the severity of the consequences. The principal or designee may reduce or increase the penalty when there is a finding of mitigating circumstances, except in cases where law or policy requires suspension.

Table 13.3 shows the progression of consequences for this code of conduct.

Pause and Reflect: Use a web browser to find a second example of a code of conduct from a school district. Read it carefully. What similarities and differences do you notice between the foregoing code and the code you have obtained? Are there key features in these codes that seem like they will impact you directly as a teacher in connection with your classroom discipline policy?

This chapter has many big ideas and practical applications. They become more pertinent and applicable as teachers have more in-school practicum experiences but also prepare teachers for what is utilized in most contemporary classrooms.

To summarize, let's revisit our learning outcomes:

1. **Understand and apply principles of culturally responsive discipline practices.** We need to be mindful of the antiquated practices that do not serve our diverse populations. It is important to address any biases we may have and ensure the use of inclusive practices that celebrate the cultures of our students.

2. **Identify and understand structures and principles of commonly utilized discipline policies in middle schools (such as PBIS and restorative discipline).** PBIS systems are a multitiered approach to promote positive behavior and improve the overall social and emotional climate. It is designed to prevent and address challenging behaviors in individuals, especially children and students, by providing a framework that encourages and reinforces positive actions. PBIS systems utilize rewards and incentives for students and are usually centered around a matrix of positively stated behavior statements. Restorative discipline is an approach to managing and addressing conflicts, misconduct, and behavioral issues that focuses on repairing harm, fostering accountability, and restoring relationships rather than solely punishing or excluding individuals who engage in wrongdoing. A common component of restorative discipline is the use of restorative circles aimed at student ownership of behavior and repairing harm.

3. **Apply basic principles of classroom management, including rules, routines, and procedures.** Consistent routines and procedures build the foundation for a smoothly running classroom. Routines and procedures take modeling and practice to build consistency for students. Rules should be few, positively framed, and used equitably to hold all students accountable.

4. **Understand the connection of families to school policies.** Families are key stakeholders in the educational success of students. Two-way communication strategies should be employed to involve families with the systems utilized in school to create a strong and predictable network of support for students.

Table 13.3 Code of Conduct Consequences

Category 1 Offenses	First Offense	Second Offense	Third or Subsequent Offense
Engaging in inappropriate bus behavior	Warning, seat assignment, and parent contact	One-day bus suspension with parent contact	Two-day bus suspension with parent contact *Fourth offense: five-day bus suspension with parent contact *Fifth offense: bus suspension for the remainder of the year
Engaging in unauthorized use of cell phones, headphones, audio devices, lasers, or any other electronic, magnifying or communicating devices, trading cards, and toys (the school is not responsible for confiscated items)	Written or verbal warning	Required to store item in locker	Confiscate and hold for parent picks up; or require student to store item in locker

Category 2 Offenses	First Offense	Second Offense	Third or Subsequent Offense
Engaging in inappropriate display of affection	Staff-student conference	Staff-student conference	One-day in-school suspension (ISS)
Engaging in dishonesty, defined as making false statements (written or verbal)	Staff-student conference	Staff-student conference	One-day ISS
Cheating, including the actual giving or receiving of any unauthorized assistance or the actual giving or receiving of an unfair advantage on any form of academic work	Staff-student conference, no credit will be given for the work	Staff-student conference, no credit will be given for the work	One-day ISS, no credit will be given for the work
Plagiarizing, including the copying of the language, structure, idea, and/or thought of another and representing it as one's own original work	No credit will be given for the work	No credit will be given for the work	One-day ISS, no credit will be given for the work
Engaging in theft*	Staff-student conference, restitution	One-day ISS, restitution	One-day out-of-school suspension (OSS), restitution
Skipping class or being in an unauthorized area	Staff-student conference	One-day ISS	One-day ISS

(Continued)

Table 13.3 (Continued)

Category 2 Offenses	First Offense	Second Offense	Third or Subsequent Offense
Failing to comply with directions of a school authority	Parent conference	One-day ISS	One-day OSS (four or more occurrences may lead to as many as five days of OSS, at the school's discretion)
Inappropriately using the Internet	Staff-student conference	Parent conference	One-day ISS, may lose device privilege
Engaging in horseplay, rough play, or inappropriate physical contact	Staff-student conference	Staff-student conference	One-day ISS
Teasing, name calling, bullying, or using inappropriate language	Staff-student conference	Parent conference	One-day ISS (four or more occurrences may lead to as many as five days of OSS, at the school's discretion)

Category 3 Offenses	First Offense	Second Offense	Third or Subsequent Offense
Any violations of Category 3 offenses automatically result in parent-student-staff conferences			
Leaving school grounds without authorization (law enforcement may be notified, as appropriate)	One-day ISS	Two-day ISS	One-day OSS
Engaging in defiant or disruptive conduct, cursing (using vulgar, abusive, or demeaning language), choosing deliberately to disrupt class by disruptive actions or provoking others (disorderly conduct by disrupting, disturbing, interfering with the teaching of students or otherwise disrupting or disturbing the peace; this offense, if legally charged, is a violation of GS 14-33(a), a class-2 misdemeanor)	Two-day ISS	One-day OSS	Three-day OSS (four or more occurrences may lead to as many as five days of OSS)

(Continued)

Table 13.3 (Continued)

Category 3 Offenses	First Offense	Second Offense	Third or Subsequent Offense
Possessing or distributing literature or illustrations that significantly disrupt the educational process, or that are obscene, pornographic, or unlawful, immoral, indecent, lewd, or disreputable or behavior of an overly sexual nature in the school setting	One-day OSS	Two-day OSS	Three-day OSS
Failing to observe established safety rules, standards, and regulations in any school building, school vehicle, or on the school grounds at any time, at any school-related activity, including an athletic event or at any time when the student is subject to the supervision of school personnel, including during school trips; such violations of safety standards include but are not limited to being in restricted or unauthorized areas without permission, failing to follow school procedures, and failing to follow lawful directions of a teacher or another school authority	One-day ISS	One-day OSS	Three-day OSS
Using tobacco products: students are prohibited from possessing or using any tobacco product(s), nicotine products, or personal vaporizers (e-cigs, vape pens, etc.), regardless of nicotine content, lighters or matches in any school building, in any school vehicle, or on the school grounds at any time, at any school-related activity, including athletic events, at any time when students are subject to the supervision of school personnel, including during school trips	One-day OSS and confiscation of product or item	Two-days OSS and confiscation of product or item	Three-day OSS and confiscation of product or item

(Continued)

Table 13.3 (Continued)

Category 3 Offenses	First Offense	Second Offense	Third or Subsequent Offense
Engaging in theft of or damage to school property: students are prohibited from stealing or attempting to steal school or private property and/or from knowingly having stolen property; students are prohibited from damaging or attempting to damage any school property or private property at any time.	Restitution, one-day OSS	Restitution and three-day OSS	Restitution and five-day OSS

Category 4 Offenses	First Offense	Second Offense	Third Offense
Playing abusive or dangerous tricks or otherwise subjecting another student to personal indignity	Three-day OSS	Five-day OSS	Ten-day OSS
Striking another student	One-day OSS	Three-day OSS	Five-day OSS
A student attacking an employee, an adult volunteer, or another student, which attack does not result in serious injury but which is intended to cause or reasonably could cause serious injury	From five-day OSS up to expulsion		
A student attacking another person, whereby the victim suffers obvious severe or aggravated bodily injury, such as broken bones, loss of teeth, possible internal injuries, laceration requiring stitches, loss of consciousness, significant bruising or pain, or the victim requires hospitalization or treatment at a hospital emergency room as a result of the attack	From ten-day OSS up to expulsion		

(Continued)

Table 13.3 (Continued)

Category 4 Offenses	First Offense	Second Offense	Third Offense
Engaging in prohibited activity relating to drugs or alcohol: unauthorized or illegal drugs and alcohol are a threat to safe and orderly schools and will not be tolerated; students are prohibited from possessing, using, transmitting, selling, or being under the influence of any illegal substance or any alcoholic beverage, malt beverage, or fortified wine; or other intoxicating liquor; narcotic drugs; hallucinogenic drugs; amphetamines; barbiturates; marijuana or any other controlled substance; any chemicals or products with the intention of bringing about a state of exhilaration or euphoria or of otherwise altering students' mood or behavior; students also are prohibited from possessing, using, transmitting, or selling drug paraphernalia or counterfeit (fake) drugs	From a minimum of a five-day OSS to notification of law enforcement to expulsion		
Harassing others (includes sexual harassment): students are prohibited from engaging in or encouraging any form of harassment against students, employees, or any other individuals on school grounds or at school-related functions; harassment is unwanted, unwelcomed, and uninvited behavior (profane or vulgar language intended to abuse, threaten, or harass another person) that demeans, threatens, or offends the victim and results in a hostile environment for the victim; the hostile environment can be created through pervasive or persistent misbehavior or a single incident, if sufficiently severe; the principal or the principal's designee will investigate the matter and may impose disciplinary sanctions on the harassing student in accordance with disciplinary policies	Investigation and, if warranted, a three-day OSS	Investigation and, if warranted, a five-day OSS	Investigation and, if warranted, a ten-day OSS

(Continued)

Table 13.3 (Continued)

Category 4 Offenses	First Offense	Second Offense	Third Offense
Accessing or possessing pornography in any form and on any device	From a three- to ten-day OSS up to suspension or expulsion and notification of law enforcement	From a three- to ten-day OSS up to suspension or expulsion and notification of law enforcement	From a three- to ten-day OSS up to suspension or expulsion and notification of law enforcement
Breaking and entering into school buildings or buses or severely damaging school property	From ten-day OSS, notification of law enforcement, and restitution up to expulsion		
Category 5 Offenses			
Making threats, defined as a student communicating a bomb threat, communicating a threat that endangers the lives of students and/or staff, or perpetrating a threatening hoax	Ten-day suspension and a mental health assessment will be required before an alternative placement is considered; law enforcement will be contacted, and charges will be filed		
Engaging in prohibited behavior involving weapons and weapon-like items: students are prohibited from possessing, handling, or transmitting any weapon or any instrument that reasonably looks like a weapon or could be used as a weapon on any school property, including vehicles;. weapons include but are not limited to all of the following: any firearm or destructive device, including a gun, pistol, or rifle; explosives, including a bomb, grenade, or mine; knife, including a pocket knife, bowie knife, switchblade, dirk or dagger; slingshot or slung shot; leaded cane; blackjack; metal knuckles; BB gun; air rifle or air pistol; stun gun or other electric-shock weapon; icepick; any sharp-pointed or -edged instrument except unaltered nail files and clips and tools used solely for preparation of food, instruction, and maintenance; this behavior is in violation of GS 14-269.2(d), Misdemeanor Possession of Weapon on Educational Property, a class-1 misdemeanor	Short- to long-term suspension; if the suspension is longer than ten days, the principal will determine the length of the suspension based upon a documented review of the student's culpability, the student's dangerousness, and the harm caused by the student; any student who brings a firearm or powerful explosive onto school property shall be given a 365-day suspension unless the director of the school recommends and approves a modification		

Resources and Recommended Readings

Gardner, T. W. (2016). *Discipline over punishment: Successes and struggles with restorative justice in schools*. Rowman & Littlefield.

Maynard, N., Weinstein, B. (2016) Hacking School Discipline: 9 Ways to Create a Culture of Empathy and Responsibility Using Restorative Justice (Hack Learning Series). Times 10 Publications.

Milner IV, H. R., Cunningham, H. B., DeLille-O'Connor, L., & Kestenberg, E. G. (2018). *"These kids are out of control": Why we must reimagine "classroom management" for equity*. Corwin Press.

Pinto, L. E. (2013). *From discipline to culturally responsive engagement: 45 classroom management strategies*. Corwin Press.

Smith, R., Dearborn, G. (2016). *Conscious classroom management: Unlocking the secrets of great teaching*. Conscious Teaching LLC.

Websites

https://www.pbis.org/tools/all-tools#data-based-decision-making

https://www.pbis.org/

https://makemathmoments.com/random-cards/

https://www.responsiveclassroom.org/

AMLE Resources

Amle. "Reimagining school discipline: It takes all of us" https://www.amle.org/reimagining-school-discipline-it-takes-all-of-us/

Dearborn, G. "Compassionate discipline: Dealing with difficult students" https://www.amle.org/compassionate-discipline-dealing-with-difficult-students/

Roberts, T. L. "You can smile! Classroom management tips" https://www.amle.org/you-can-smile-classroom-management-tips/

References

Gardner, T. W. (2016). *Discipline over punishment: Successes and struggles with restorative justice in schools*. Rowman & Littlefield.

Office of Safe and Supportive Schools Technical Assistance Center Collaborative. (2023). Creating and sustaining discipline policies that support students' social, emotional, and academic well-being and success. Strategies for school and district leaders. [Fact sheet]. https://t4pacenter.ed.gov/SupportiveSchools

Pinto, L. E. (2013). *From discipline to culturally responsive engagement: 45 classroom management strategies*. Corwin Press.

Smith, R., Dearborn, G. (2016). *Conscious classroom management: Unlocking the secrets of great teaching*. Conscious Teaching LLC.

Strickland-Cohen, M. K., Newson, A., Meyer, K., Putnam, R., Kern, L., Meyer, B. C., & Flammini, A. (2022). Strategies for de-escalating student behavior in the classroom. Center on Positive Behavioral Interventions and Supports. https://www.responsiveclassroom.org/

The Catamount School. Parent and student handbook. https://www.wcu.edu/_files/learn/TCS-Handbook.pdf

CHAPTER 14

Philosophy and History of Middle Level Schools

Learning Outcomes:

1. Describe the history of middle level schools.

2. Identify the attributes and characteristics of an effective middle school.

3. Ascertain major accomplishments or developments that can be attributed to the middle school movement.

4. Examine ways of working in contexts that don't implement the middle school concept.

A Brief History

In this textbook, we have explored many topics that are related to the specific needs of adolescents. As we discussed in the introductory chapter, our work is situated within the elements and characteristics of the effective middle school, as outlined by AMLE. But these elements and characteristics are built on previous work in the field. The notion of advocating for the necessary goal of strengthening academics and responding to the needs of students in the middle grades is not new. Literature in the twentieth century highlights advocacy for improved schooling for young adolescents. Throughout the middle school movement of the 1960s, we see lingering concern for the quality of schooling for young adolescents. And the final years of the century included pleas for schools that are "academically excellent, developmentally responsive, and socially equitable" (National Forum to Accelerate Middle-Grades Reform, 1998). Doesn't sound too different from the calls for action these days, right? Looking back and, perhaps more importantly, looking into a mirror will be necessary for continued progress. As we share some key moments in the evolution of middle schools, we reflect on what has changed and what has remained consistent through time.

GROWTH AND RATIONALE OF THE MIDDLE SCHOOL

In 1909, for the first time, a separate school organization was created to bridge the gap between elementary and high school. These separate schools, commonly known as junior highs, typically became miniature versions of high schools. With inadequate teacher preparation, the classrooms were teacher- and textbook-centered, and the students were left with unmet needs. Hundreds of middle schools opened in the late 1960s and early 1970s, and the middle school movement was in full swing. By the 1990s there were approximately fifteen-thousand middle schools across the United States. These special schools "in the middle" were intended to have programs with strategies and innovations focused on the unique needs of students between the ages of ten and fourteen and the transitions from one phase of education to the next. Middle schools strive to be unique schools, offering students a structure and programming that differs from those of elementary and high schools. Consider them transitional schools, designed to allow students to move from elementary through middle and on to high school in a way that is smooth and successful. We use the term *middle school* to distinguish it from **junior high** or *upper elementary* and to describe a school that is designed to be responsive to young adolescents' developmental needs (see Table 14.1). While middle schools typically include some combination of grades five through nine, grade-level organization is less essential than the idea of being responsive to and meeting the developmental needs of students.

We recognize that looking at dense historical documents can be daunting. That said, we want to highlight a few critical historical pieces that frame our current practices in middle level education. We will also ask for some participation along the way to unveil what elements have stood the test of time and where there have been updates and advances in our ways of thinking.

Pause and Reflect: The following sections will share snippets of landmark documents, outlining calls for action to improve schooling at the middle level. As you read, your job is to take notes of the timing of each set of recommendations and sniff for patterns: What similarities are there? Are there any fundamental differences you notice?

ALEXANDER'S *THE EMERGENT MIDDLE SCHOOL* (1968)

William Alexander, one of the founding fathers of the middle school concept and the first to use the term *middle school*, published *The Emergent Middle School* in 1968. In this text, he proposed several specific aims for the middle school concept:

1. To serve the educational needs of the "in-between-agers" (older children, preadolescents, early adolescents) in a school bridging the elementary school for childhood and the high school for adolescence.

2. To provide optimum individualization of curriculum and instruction for a population characterized by great variability.

3. In relation to the foregoing aims to plan, implement, evaluate, and modify, in a continuing curriculum development program, a curriculum which includes provision for: (a) a planned sequence of concepts in the general education areas; (b) major emphasis on the interest and skills for continued learning; (c) a balanced program of **exploratory experiences** and other activities and services for personal development; and (d) appropriate attention to the development of values.

4. To promote continuous progress through and smooth articulation between the several phases and levels of the total educational program.

5. To facilitate the optimum use of personnel and facilities available for continuing improvement of schooling. (Alexandar, 1968, p. 19)

Table 14.1 Key Differences between Junior High and Middle School

Junior High	Middle School
Academics at the center of learning	Students at the center of learning with academic learning, exploration, and intervention based on student needs and interest
Emphasis on cognitive development	Emphasis on both cognitive and affective development as well as on social and emotional learning (SEL)
Organizes teachers in subject-based departments	Organizes teachers and students in teams, which are often interdisciplinary
Focus on academic rigor and preparing students to manage assignments and expectations	Focus on collaborative and project-based learning as well as on developing students' social and emotional skills, all of which lead to academic success
Provides academic-focused classes and electives	Provides academic, exploratory, interdisciplinary, and project-based classes
Traditional instruction dominates, with the teacher at the center	Experiential and student-centered approaches to instruction
Classes offered in brief segments, typically six to eight class periods per day	Flexible scheduling allows for classes to be built around student needs, often in blocks of time; students may not have every subject each day
Provides academic classes	Provides academic, exploratory, and intervention- or enrichment-based classes
Offers study hall and/or homeroom	Offers advisory classes and teams of teachers and students so that opportunities exist for relationship-building, mentoring, and guidance
Classrooms arranged randomly or by subject or grade level	Team classrooms placed in close proximity to each other

Source: Adapted from Association for Middle Level Schools, 2012; Carnegie Council on Adolescent Development, 1989; Jackson & Davis, 2000; Powell, 2015

Carnegie Corporation's *Turning Points: Preparing American Youth for the 21st Century (1989)*

Fast forward to the 1980s, when the Carnegie Corporation published *Turning Points: Preparing American Youth for the 21st Century* and established an associated task force, which created a list of recommendations to improve middle grades education.

These suggestions are aimed at creating adolescents with specific characteristics that the task force identified as those adolescents would have, had they been well served by middle grades schools. The task force concluded that an effective human being will be intellectually reflective, headed toward a lifetime of meaningful work, a good citizen, caring and ethical, and healthy. The task force suggested doing the following to create such effective persons:

1. Create small communities for learning where stable, close, mutually respectful relationships with adults and peers are considered fundamental for intellectual development and personal growth. The key elements of these communities are schools within schools or houses, students and teachers grouped together as teams, and small group advisories that ensure that every student is known well by at least one adult.

2. Teach a core academic program that results in students who are literate, including in the sciences, and who know how to think critically, lead a healthy life, behave ethically, and assume the responsibilities of citizenship in a pluralistic society. Youth service to promote values for citizenship is an essential part of the core academic program.

3. Ensure success for all students through elimination of tracking by achievement level and promotion of cooperative learning, flexibility in arranging instructional time, and adequate resources (time, space, equipment, and materials) for teachers.

4. Empower teachers and administrators to make decisions about the experiences of middle grade students through creative control by teachers over the instructional program linked to greater responsibilities for students' performance, governance committees that assist the principal in designing and coordinating school-wide programs, and autonomy and leadership within sub-schools or houses to create environments tailored to enhance the intellectual and emotional development of all youth.

5. Staff middle grade schools with teachers who are expert at teaching young adolescents and who have been specially prepared for assignment to the middle grades.

6. Improve academic performance through fostering the health and fitness of young adolescents, by providing a health coordinator in every middle grade school, access to health care and counseling services, and a health-promoting school environment.

7. Reengage families in the education of young adolescents by giving families meaningful roles in school governance, communicating with families about the school

program and student's progress, and offering families opportunities to support the learning process at home and at the school.

8. Connect schools with communities, which together share responsibility for each middle grade student's success, through identifying service opportunities in the community, establishing partnerships and collaborations to ensure students' access to health and social services, and using community resources to enrich the instructional program and opportunities for constructive after-school activities.

(Carnegie Council on Adolescent Development, 1989, p. 8–9)
Jackson et al.'s *Turning Points 2000: Educating Adolescents
in the 21st Century* (2000)

Another twenty years later, an update was made to the original *Turning Points*. The central focus of these recommendations is to ensure student success but there are also a few changes in these new recommendations. Compare the following with the previous report.

1. Teach a curriculum grounded in rigorous, public academic standards for what students should know and be able to do, relevant to the concerns of adolescents and based on how students learn best. Considerations of both excellence and equity should guide every decision regarding what will be taught. Curriculum should be based on content standards and organized around concepts and principles. A mix of assessment methods should allow students to demonstrate what they know and what they can do.

2. Use instructional methods designed to prepare all students to achieve higher standards and become lifelong learners. To be effective, instruction should mesh with three other aspects of teaching and learning: the standards and resulting curriculum outlining what students should learn; the assessments students will use to demonstrate their knowledge and skills; and the needs, interests, and learning styles of the students themselves. Classes should include students of diverse needs, achievement levels, interests, and learning styles, and instruction should be differentiated to take advantage of the diversity, not ignore it.

3. Staff middle grades schools with teachers who are expert at teaching young adolescents, and engage teachers in ongoing, targeted professional development opportunities. Schools should hire staff specifically trained for the middle grades and should provide mentors and "induction" to teachers new to the profession or the school. Schools should also engage teachers in ongoing professional development—driven by results, based on standards, and embedded in their daily work—that yields improvements in student learning. A facilitator, either full- or part-time, should coordinate professional development opportunities.

4. Organize relationships for learning to create a climate of intellectual development and a caring community of shared educational purpose. Large schools should be divided into smaller learning communities, with teams of teachers and students as the underlying organizational structure. To ensure strong teams, schools must

pay attention to the nature and quality of interactions among teachers and student team members, ensuring that teams continually concentrate their efforts on achieving high standards for both teaching and learning. Schools should also attend to critical elements affecting team success, such as team size, composition, time for planning, and continuity.

5. Govern democratically, through direct or representative participation by all school staff members, the adults who know the students best. All decisions should focus relentlessly on attaining the goal of success for every student and should be based on data drawn from various sources. Schools should be proactive, not reactive, in their efforts to ensure every student's success, using a "living" school improvement plan to direct actions in both the short and the long term.

6. Provide a safe and healthy school environment as part of improving academic performance and developing caring and ethical citizens. Healthy lifestyles and academic success are tightly interwoven—improvement in one leads to improvement in the other, both directly and indirectly. Positive intergroup relations are essential to a safe and healthy school. Middle grades schools, in partnership with the community, should support physical and mental health and fitness by providing a safe, caring, and healthy environment, health education, and access to health services.

7. Involve parents and communities in supporting student learning and healthy development. Schools and families must collaborate to establish continuity (for example, similarly high expectations) and communication between home and school; to monitor and support students' schoolwork and academic progress; to create opportunities outside the school for safe, engaging exploration; and to improve the school itself through parent and community involvement onsite. Schools and communities should forge connections to provide needed services to students, offer career exploration opportunities, expand learning beyond regular school hours and outside school walls, and advocate for the school improvements critical to ensuring success for every student.

(Jackson & Davis, 2000, pp. 23–24)

The Association for Middle Level Education's *The Successful Middle School: This We Believe (2021)* A major professional organization, AMLE (the Association for Middle Level Education), formally the National Middle School Association, is recognized as the voice promoting the well-being and education of young adolescents. AMLE believes the true middle school has been planned and organized to address the developmental and cultural needs of students of ages ten to fourteen, generally including grades five through eight. Its major position paper, **The Successful Middle School: This We Believe**, now in its fifth edition, has become the acknowledged standard that middle schools aspire to meet. Although the middle school movement represents "an educational success story unparalleled in our history" (Lounsbury, 1997, p. xi), advocates for the middle school concept or philosophy have faced challenges in sharing that story. Historically, education for young adolescents (ages ten to fifteen) has occupied a shadowland in the world of federal and state legislation and policy. Schooling for students in grades five through nine is too often overlooked, underserved, and under-resourced while policy and resources flow to the "bookends" of education P–16," with high school and college on one end and early learning on the other (Andres, 2010).

It is crucial to implement multiple elements of middle grades reform and maintain those elements over time to realize positive outcomes for students (Association for Middle Level Education, 2012).

> A learning environment is very complex, and young adolescents' academic success is highly dependent upon physical, intellectual, moral, physiological, and social-emotional factors—all inexorably intertwined. Flexible structures and a shared vision are important, but without a challenging curriculum, varied learning approaches, and programs for health and wellness, among other essential components, the middle grades school will likely function with diminished capacity and fail to achieve its tremendous potential (p. 1).

In the introduction to our text, we shared the attributes and characteristics of the successful middle school. We have referenced these throughout the text as they were pertinent to ideas we have shared. Figure 14.1 restates the five attributes and sixteen characteristics of successful middle schools, as defined by AMLE.

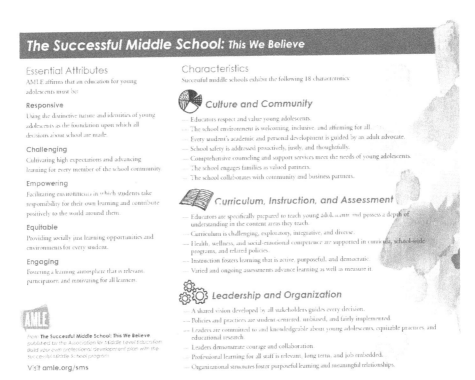

Figure 14.1 Successful schools for young adolescents. Reprinted with Permission AMLE (2021)

The sixteen characteristics are described here in slightly more detail.

- Curriculum, Instruction, and Assessment

  - *Value Young Adolescents.* **Educators value young adolescents and are prepared to teach them.** Effective middle grades educators make a conscious choice to work with young adolescents and advocate for them. They understand the developmental uniqueness of this age group, the appropriate curriculum, effective learning and assessment strategies, and their importance as models.

  - *Active Learning.* **Students and teachers are engaged in active, purposeful learning.** Instructional practices place students at the center of the learning process. As they develop the ability to hypothesize, to organize information into useful and meaningful constructs, and to grasp long-term cause and effect relationships, students are ready and able to play a major role in their own learning and education.

  - *Challenging Curriculum.* **Curriculum is challenging, exploratory, integrative, and relevant.** Curriculum embraces every planned aspect of a school's educational program. An effective middle level curriculum is distinguished by learning activities that appeal to young adolescents, is exploratory and challenging, and incorporates student-generated questions and concerns.

  - *Multiple Learning Approaches.* Educators use multiple learning and teaching approaches. Teaching and learning approaches should accommodate the diverse skills, abilities, and prior knowledge of young adolescents; cultivate multiple intelligences; draw upon students' individual learning styles; and utilize digital tools. When learning experiences capitalize on students' cultural, experiential, and personal backgrounds, new concepts are built on knowledge students already possess.

  - *Varied Assessments.* **Varied and ongoing assessments advance learning as well as measure it.** Continuous, authentic, and appropriate assessment measures, including both formative and summative ones, provide evidence about every student's learning progress. Such information helps students, teachers, and family members select immediate learning goals and plan further education.

- Leadership and Organization

  - *Shared Vision.* **A shared vision developed by all stakeholders guides every decision.** When a shared vision and mission statement become operational, middle level educators pursue appropriate practices in developing a challenging academic program; they develop criteria to guide decisions and a process to make changes.

  - *Committed Leaders.* **Leaders are committed to and knowledgeable about this age group, educational research, and best practices.** Courageous, collaborative middle level leaders understand young adolescents, their society, and their theory of middle level education. Such leaders understand the nuances of teaming, student advocacy, exploration, and assessment as components of a larger program.

  - *Courageous and Collaborative Leaders.* **Leaders demonstrate courage and collaboration.** Leaders understand that successful schools committed to the long-term implementation of the middle school concept must be collaborative enterprises. The principal, working collaboratively with a leadership team, focuses on building a learning community that places top priority on the education and healthy development of every student, teacher, and staff member.

- *Professional Development.* **Ongoing professional development reflects best educational practices.** Professional development is a continuing activity in middle level schools where teachers take advantage of every opportunity to work with colleagues to improve their students'' learning experiences.

- *Organizational Structures.* Organizational structures foster purposeful learning and meaningful relationships. The ways schools organize teachers and groups, and schedule students has a significant impact on the learning environment. Interdisciplinary teams, common planning time, block scheduling, and elimination of tracking are related conditions that contribute to improved achievement.

- Culture and Community

  - *School Environment.* **The school environment is inviting, safe, inclusive, and supportive of all.** A successful school for young adolescents is an inviting, supportive, and safe place, a joyful community that promotes in-depth learning and enhances students' physical and emotional wellbeing.

  - *Adult Advocate.* **Every student's academic and personal development is guided by an adult advocate.** Academic success and personal growth increase markedly when young adolescents' affective needs are met. Each student must have one adult to support that student's academic and personal development.

  - *Guidance Services.* **Comprehensive guidance and support services meet the needs of young adolescents.** Both teachers and specialized professionals are readily available to offer the assistance many students need in negotiating their lives in and out of school.

  - *Health and Wellness.* **Health and wellness are supported in curricula, school-wide programs, and related policies.** Abundant opportunities are available for students to develop and maintain healthy minds and bodies and to understand their personal growth through health-related programs, policies, and curricula.

  - *Family Involvement.* **The school actively involves families in the education of their children.** Schools and families must work together to provide the best possible learning for every young adolescent. Schools take the initiative in involving and educating families.

  - *Community and Business.* **The school includes community and business partners.** Genuine community involvement is a fundamental component of successful schools for young adolescents. Such schools seek appropriate partnerships with businesses, social service agencies, and other organizations whose purposes are consistent with the school's mission.

Pause and Reflect: You have now looked at recommendations from the 1960s, 1980s, 2000, and 2021. What do you note as similarities among all these charges for middle school education? What has changed over time? Which of these elements do you see in classrooms you have observed (or experienced as a learner)? If you have already read the previous chapters, where can you make connections to that content? Create a graphic organizer or mind map to represent your thinking.

The Contemporary Middle School

School organization and curricular offerings in middle schools typically offer a block schedule with longer, more exploratory classes, whereas junior-high students have a six- to eight-period schedule, with shorter classes that typically do not allow time for application of knowledge, practice of skills, or engagement of students. These middle years, between elementary and high school, are filled with growth, opportunities, and challenges in physical, intellectual, emotional, and social development. Success in school between the ages of eight and fourteen tends to be a significant predictor of future academic engagement. A critical focus of the middle school learning environment is developing social, emotional, organizational, and interpersonal skills in students. Exploring a variety of subjects and electives and enrichment opportunities are key to building knowledge and confidence in abilities. Overall, middle schools are student-centered, with classes offered in longer chunks of time (referred to as blocks) and divided by general subject areas, exploration, and enrichment. Students typically spend an entire school year, except for their time in elective or enrichment classes, with the same team of content teachers, allowing for more engagement, depth, and creativity in their learning. Middle school teachers work collaboratively in interdisciplinary teams that plan curriculum, which often includes a strong cross-curricular or PBL (project-based learning) approach.

Pause and Reflect: Think back to your experience during this time of life. What kind of school did you attend? If that memory is too far away, notice what kind of school you have visited or observed in. Was it a middle school? How were the teachers and students organized for learning—by content areas, on teams, or in some other way? Did the school more closely resemble an elementary or a high school? If you had to label your school, would you call it traditional or innovative? Why? Take some private thinking time first, and then find a partner to talk to about your reflections.

ACCOMPLISHMENTS AND DEVELOPMENTS ATTRIBUTED TO THE MIDDLE SCHOOL MOVEMENT

A considerable body of research supports the middle school concept, and successful implementation of the characteristics of effective middle schools has been shown to impact student well-being and academic achievement (Anfara, Andrews, Hough, Mertens, Mizelle, & White, 2003; Backes, Ralston, & Ingwalson, 1999; Balfanz,

Ruby, & Mac Iver, 2002; Danielson, 2002; Elmore, 2000; Epstein & Mac Iver, 1990; Flowers, Mertens, & Mulhall, 1999; Furney, Haaszi, Clarke/Keefe, & Hartnett, 2003; Garza, 2001; McEwin & Greene, 2011; Mertens & Flowers, 2006; Mertens, Flowers, & Mulhall, 2002). School policies and programs reflect advocacy as an obligation of middle level schools. There are many developments that could and should be attributed to the middle school movement:

Early adolescence has gained recognition as a distinct developmental period. There has been wide acceptance of the position or belief that young people, roughly between the ages of ten and fifteen, comprise a definable and particular group whose members warrant educational experiences specifically designed for them. The older perception that early adolescence is a difficult and unproductive stage of life has fortunately gone by the board.

A three-tiered organization of public education has been established. The old elementary–secondary pattern has given way throughout the nation to an elementary–middle school–high school pattern. Local, state, and federal school policies and data-collecting systems now reflect these three levels.

Teacher preparation and licensure increasingly recognize the middle level. Slowly but surely, states have come to recognize the middle level with a distinctive verification or at least an endorsement of the qualifications one needs to have for teaching young adolescents. Teacher-education institutions, in turn, are providing appropriate preparation programs to fulfill these requirements.

The concept of teaming has become firmly established. Teaching was long conducted either in essentially self-contained classrooms or in departmentalized situations. This practice has given way to *teaming*, particularly in middle schools; teams of teachers cooperate with one another in teaching the students they have in common. Teaming, strongly supported by teachers, has become the majority practice in middle level schools and seems likely to become nearly universal, with the more effective teaching as partners or in smaller teams becoming more common.

Advisory programs consist of small groups of students meeting regularly with a teacher or staff member during a dedicated class period. Such programs ensure every student is well known by an adult.

The place, value, and use of collaboration among those engaged in the teaching-learning enterprise have been well established. While advanced considerably by interdisciplinary teaming, the concept and practice of collaboration has properly taken root in all areas of education, such as administration where the whole concept of leadership has undergone a change.

The active engagement of young adolescents in their education has become an accepted and desired practice. Soliciting and acting on student voice in helping to determine what and how to study, as promoted by the middle school movement, is seen as a valid way to both improve student achievement while also effectively meeting other equally important noncognitive goals. As a result, a gradual shift from traditional teacher-centered classrooms to more student-centered classrooms is underway in most middle level schools. Table 14.2 highlights a short (not exhaustive) list of developmentally appropriate strategies and practices in middle school that we have explored across multiple chapters.

Table 14.2 Exemplars of Developmentally Appropriate Strategies and Practices in Middle Schools

Social Emotional Learning

Project-based learning, an instructional approach whereby students learn by actively engaging in real-world and personally meaningful projects.

Student-led conferences, which put learners in the position of being responsible for their own education.

Curriculum integration, a major step beyond interdisciplinary instruction, centers on a major problem or issue, rather than on one or more subjects, and develops critical thinking, problem-solving, and the interpersonal skills and attitudes required to function as an effective team member.

Service learning, interwoven into academics, has come into its own as a curriculum component in the middle grades.

Looping and multiage teaming have brought back the old pattern of keeping students and teachers together for more than one school year. The long-term student–teacher relationships achieved in multiyear situations make it possible to fulfill the goals of middle level education more adequately than does the standard practice of changing teachers every year. These relationships are particularly valuable in the education of young adolescents, who are undergoing extensive physical, social, emotional, and intellectual changes during this period and who profit immensely, academically and otherwise, from the continuing association with caring adults who know them and their families well.

WORKING WITHIN CONSTRAINTS

Our work in this text has presented what we and others in the field recognize as best practices within the middle school concept. We are also aware that reality and expectations do not always align. Many teachers will work in schools that feel disconnected from the research and theory they learned in their teacher-preparation programs and the content within this text. While we cannot address all concerns here, we want to address some of the most common disconnects teachers might encounter.

School Lacks Interdisciplinary Teams or Does Not Use Interdisciplinary/Integrative Teaching

Finding a single colleague to work with is one way to mediate this concern. This process begins by asking what that colleague is teaching in his or her class. Then, in our classes, we make connections to that content. While we may not come up with a plan to be on the same page, day by day, as we would within an interdisciplinary unit, we would still make connections between our content areas. For example, sixth graders study Egyptians as well as Greek and Roman gods in social studies. In English language arts, students read fables and analyze fiction and nonfiction texts. In science, students study astronomy and other concepts about space. In math, they study fractions, which Egyptians used. Without spending time planning an interdisciplinary unit, knowing ways that the content of each discipline relates to our own content allows students to make these connections.

School Lacks an Advisory Program

Without an advisory program, caring for students' social and emotional needs is still feasible. While, ideally, an advisory program provides a small-group setting and a specific adult advocate for each student, the goal of this is to build relationships and support students in learning how to "do" school and how to function socially in school. Homeroom is an excellent time to introduce advisory content in small samples. We have taken attendance with warm-up questions that focus on emotion. A homeroom teacher might ask students, "What color symbolizes your mood and how you are feeling today?" or "What unique adjective describes how you feel today?" Students can often reflect on their "vibe." These two questions alone allow us, as teachers, to discuss how identifying exactly what emotion we are feeling empowers us to get to the root of our conflicts. Introducing a mantra or quote of the day also offers time for teachers to discuss small life issues. For example, when we notice that eighth graders are nervous about the transition into high school, we may introduce an affirmation like, "The current chapters of our life may feel comfortable and safe, but, in our next chapter, we may discover happiness in the changes we encounter in our lives." If the school doesn't have homeroom either, this kind of activity can be shortened even more to be some very brief introduction to class that only takes a minute or two. This could be a greeting or a quick prompt, for example. Lastly, although very much not least, there is the power of standing at your classroom door. Some of the best student-teacher relationships are formed with students we compliment and banter with in hallways. Students desire to feel loved, safe, and like someone believes in them. Smiling at them, saying "I'm glad you're here," and telling them about the shows we watch or music we listen to can create bonds.

School Lacks an Exploratory Program

Adjusting a school-wide schedule to include an exploratory program is not always necessary. Implementing a genius hour or a passion project into our classes has been one uncomplicated option. For thirty minutes to an hour each week, with parameters, we allow students to practice, study, and create products and projects tailored to their interests. An alternative option is for teachers to pick a single topic or activity to engage in each week. One week, teachers could all practice free coding programs with kids. The next week, students could participate in a script read-aloud and then write their own scripts. If the school schedule is somewhat flexible, teachers can discuss implementing a "club day" with their administrators, providing a consistent time that is built into the schedule for clubs to meet, and each teacher could lead one of the programs.

School Schedule Is Not Flexible

If the school schedule is set and opportunities to change the entire structure of a day are not present, teachers can still control how time is utilized within the four walls of their classrooms. If the constraint is that there are only fifty-minute periods, a teacher might think about how time can be utilized more flexibly across the week during those periods so that direct instruction is used on some days, followed by several days that are focused on discovery, and so that one day is always used, say, for practice or writing workshop or labs.

Pause and Reflect: Based on schools you visited or your school experience as a student, what parts of the middle school concept did you witness? Which pieces were missing, and how do you think your experience would (or wouldn't) change if they had been in place?

To summarize, let's revisit our learning outcomes:

- **Explain the history of middle level schools.** In 1909, for the first time, a separate school organization was created to bridge the gap between elementary and high school. These in-between schools were called junior highs, and, due to inadequate preparation of teachers and administrators to meet the unique needs of young adolescents, instruction was teacher- and textbook-centered, mirroring instruction in high schools of the time, which left students with unmet needs. The middle school movement of the 1960s created exponential growth of schools that were intended to have programs implementing strategies and innovations focused on the unique needs of students between the ages of ten and fourteen. In 1998, the **National Forum to Accelerate Middle-Grades Reform** called for middle schools that were academically excellent, developmentally responsive, and socially equitable; similar calls are made today. Decades of research supports the middle school concept, and successful implementation of the characteristics of effective middle schools has been shown to impact student well-being and academic achievement. Today, three separate levels of school—with one in the middle—is the most common grade configuration. The landscape of American public education has vastly changed. Due to a global pandemic, public schools in the United States entered remote learning, with online instruction and hybrid delivery of content and assessments for long periods of time. Additionally, there have been other significant educational reforms and movements within public education, and these have renewed our interest in the backgrounds, languages, and cultures of our learners. We have realized just how important it is that teacher preparation puts the learner and learning at the center. These efforts and the shift in focus must include culturally and developmentally responsive and sustaining instruction and a commitment to equity, diversity, access, and inclusion.

- **Identify the attributes and characteristics of an effective middle level school.** An effective middle school offers students a structure and programming that differ from those in other levels of school and that are designed to be responsive to the developmental needs of young adolescents, who are typically in some combination of grades five through nine. An education for young adolescents must be developmentally responsive, challenging, empowering, and equitable. When this is true, students are at the center of academic learning, exploration, and intervention, and these activities are appropriate for meeting their needs and relating to their interests.

Effective middle schools are built around sixteen characteristics that can be grouped into three categories: 1) curriculum, instruction, and assessment; 2) leadership and organization; and 3) culture and community.

- **Ascertain major accomplishments or developments that can be attributed to the middle school movement.** There is now wide acceptance of young adolescence as a distinct period of development in the lifespan. A three-tiered organization of schools exists, and teacher licensure has increasingly recognized the middle level over the years. Concepts like interdisciplinary teaming, advisory programs, collaborative planning and learning, and engagement of the young adolescent learner originated as part of the middle school movement and now are frequently used in practice.

- **Examine ways of working in contexts that don't implement the middle school concept.** Not all middle schools will implement the true middle school concept. If teachers want to implement structures, such as interdisciplinary units, advisory concepts, or flexible scheduling, they may need to think creatively within what they can control. Using the basic principles of these ideas, teachers can plan interdisciplinary units with a single colleague or they can use their own knowledge of what other teachers are teaching to align a unit in their classrooms to match.

References

Andrews, P. G. (2013). Middle grades education: Emerging from the shadows. In P. G. Andrews (Ed.), *Research to guide practice in middle grades education* (pp. 1–7). Westerville, OH: Association for Middle Level Education. (Reprinted from *Yes, middle schools are often overlooked* by P. G. Andrews. Retrieved from http://education.nationaljournal.com.)

Anfara, V. A., & Lipka, R. P. (2003). Relating the middle school concept to student achievement. *Middle School Journal, 35*(1), 24–32.

Anfara Jr., V. A., Andrews, P. G., Hough, D. L., Mertens, S. B., Mizelle, N. B., & White, G. P. (2003). Research and resources in support of *This We Believe*. Westerville, OH: National Middle School Association.

Association for Middle Level Education. (2012). *This we believe in action: Implementing successful middle level schools*. Westerville, OH: Author.

Backes, J., Ralston, A., & Ingwalson, G. (1999). Middle level reform: The impact on student achievement. *Research in Middle Level Education Quarterly, 22*(3), 43–57.

Balfanz, R., Ruby, A., & Mac Iver, D. (2002). Essential components and next steps for comprehensive wholeschool reform in high poverty middle schools. In S. Stringfield & D. Land (Eds.), *Educating at-risk students: One hundred-first yearbook of the National Society for the Study of Education: Part II* (pp. 128–47). University of Chicago Press.

Bishop, P. A., & Harrison, L. M. (2021). *The successful middle school: This we believe, 5th edition*. Westerville, OH: Author.

Carnegie Council on Adolescent Development. (1989). *Turning Points: Preparing American youth for the 21st century* (pp. 37–70). Washington, DC: Author.

Danielson, C. (2002). *Enhancing student achievement: A framework for school improvement*. Alexandria, VA: Association for Supervision and Curriculum Development.

Dickson, T. S. (Ed.). (2001). *Reinventing the middle school*. Routledge Falmer.

Elmore, R. (2000). Leadership for effective middle school practice. *Phi Delta Kappan, 82*(4), 291-92.

Epstein, J. L., & Mac Iver, D. J. (1990). *Education in the middle grades: Overview of national practices and trends.* Columbus, OH: National Middle School Association.

Flowers, N., Mertens, S. B., & Mulhall, P. (1999). The impact of teaching: Five research-based outcomes of teaming. *Middle School Journal, 31*(2), 57–60.

Furney, K. S., Hasazi, S. B., Clark/Keefe, K., & Hartnett, J. (2003). A longitudinal analysis of shifting policy landscapes in special education and general education reform. *Exceptional Children, 70*(1), 81-94.

Garza, I. M. (2001). A comparison between alternate block and traditional scheduling on student achievement and selected variables at middle school campuses in selected education service centers in Texas. *Dissertation Abstracts International, 62*(04), 1369. (UMI No. 3011709).

Flowers, N., Mertens, S. B., & Mulhall, P. (1999). The impact of teaching: Five research-based outcomes of teaming. *Middle School Journal, 31*(2), 57-60.

Jackson, A. W., & Davis, G. A. (2000). *Turning points 2000: Educating young adolescents in the 21st century.* New York, NY: Carnegie Corporation of New York.

Lee, V., Smith, J. (2000). School size in Chicago elementary schools: Effects on teachers' attitudes and students' achievement. *American Educational Research Journal, 36*(1), 3-31.

Lee, V., & Smith, J. (1993). Effects of school restructuring on the achievement and engagement of middle-grades students. *Sociology of Education, 66*(3), 164-87.

McEwin, C. K., & Greene, M. W. (2011). *The status of programs and practices in America's middle schools: Results from two national studies.* Westerville, OH: Association for Middle Level Education.

Mertens, S. B., & Flowers, N. (2006). Middle Start's impact on comprehensive middle school reform. *Middle Grades Research Journal, 1*(1), 1-26.

Mertens, S. B., & Flowers, N. (2003). Middle school practices improve student achievement in high poverty schools. *Middle School Journal, 35*(1), 33-43.

Mertens, S. B., Flowers, N., & Mulhall, P. (2002). The relationship between middle-grades teacher certification and teaching practices. In V. A. Anfara Jr., & S. L. Stacki (Eds.), *Middle school curriculum, instruction, and assessment* (pp. 119-38). Information Age Publishing.

National Forum to Accelerate Middle-Grades Reform. (1998). Vision statement. Newton, MA: Education Development Center.

National Middle School Association. (2010). *This we believe: Keys to educating young adolescents.* Westerville, OH: Author.

Powell, S.D. (2015). *Introduction to middle level education* (3rd ed.). Upper Saddle River, NJ: Pearson.

Springer, M. A. (2009). Seeing the future of middle level education requires a mirror rather than a crystal ball. *Middle School Journal, 50*(5), 32-36.

Sweetland, S. R., & Hoy, W. K. (2000). School characteristics and education outcomes: Toward an organizational model of student achievement in middle schools. *Educational Administration Quarterly, 36*(5), 703-29.

Wormeli, R. (n.d.). *Middle school, not junior high.* Retrieved June 23, 2023, from https://www.amle.org/middle-school-not-junior-high/.

CHAPTER 15

Middle School Organization and Structure

Learning Outcomes:

1. Articulate structures of time in middle school settings.

2. Describe structures of place and practice used to make informed decisions when grouping students for instruction.

3. Identify structures of curriculum, programming, and partnerships in support of learning.

4. Identify essential school partnerships and the structures that support building healthy and safe schools.

Structures of Time

A developmentally responsive middle school is one in which the organizational structure is built around the students it serves (NMSA, 2010; AMLE, 2012; Bishop & Harrison, 2020). This structure encompasses team teaching and how these teachers use the instructional considerations and limitations and the time allotted. Traditional **departmentalized schedules** are characterized by a fixed number of daily periods of the same length, with delivery of instruction that is teacher-centered and guided by departmental procedures (Hackmann & Valentine, 1998). Meehan (1973) indicated that **traditional scheduling** makes it difficult to offer instructional experiences that are active and engaging, such as lab activities, field trips, and collaborative or PBL (project-based learning). In contrast, flexible block scheduling permits the flexibility to schedule what is important to an interdisciplinary team and a school community. Two of the most common forms of **block scheduling** are the **alternate-day block schedule** and the **flexible block schedule**. The alternate-day block schedule may be adapted to meet the needs of schools that offer six or eight courses. In these schools, half of the classes meet in double instructional blocks (i.e., ninety minutes) one day, while the remaining classes meet in double blocks the next day. Some schools have students meet in all six or eight classes one day each week for shorter periods of time. The primary purpose of using flexible block scheduling for young adolescent learners is to support a range of integrated activities. According to this model, typically two to five teachers implement interdisciplinary and/or PBL. In these curricular strategies, instead of incorporating content from only one subject, learning segments are organized around academic themes or problems and questions of interest to the students. This model may promote inquiry about students' areas of interest, such as mental health and wellness, school violence, local environmental issues, and social issues.

The concept of flexible block scheduling is rooted in concerns about creating sufficient time to immerse students in the learning experience. Flexible block scheduling is a vehicle to help implement the recommendations of several professional associations, recommendations that call for interdisciplinary teams, grouping of students, and **common planning time** (Association for Middle Level Education, 2012 & 2022; Carnegie Council on Adolescent Development, 1989; Jackson & Davis, 2000). Using block scheduling and organizing interdisciplinary teams are both prevalent ways to restructure middle level schools. Although teaching in interdisciplinary teams is recommended as the best practice, to be an interdisciplinary team, the team teachers do not have to be scheduled to teach at the same time. Flexible block scheduling, however, requires that the teachers involved are, in fact, teaching at the same time, and it has become a hallmark feature of middle level education. The practice of block scheduling is to assign a group of students (maybe as many as 100 to 120) to a team of teachers with a chunk of time in which two to four class periods of forty-five to sixty minutes each can be organized. This team is typically responsible for instruction in math, science, social studies, and language arts. The goal is to establish a sort of school within a school, which nurtures a close relationship between students and teachers.

It is also important to differentiate between the block-scheduling model commonly used in high schools from that which is recommended and used in middle schools. The high school block schedule typically includes a four-period day in which blocks are approximately ninety minutes, and students take a mix of core and elective courses in one semester to earn a full year of credit. Effective middle school schedules, however, are based on the philosophy that schools should be flexible and responsive to student learning and social-emotional needs. A flexible and responsive schedule supports blocks of instructional time; appropriate planning time for teachers; advisory time; flexibility for special schedules, intervention, and enrichment; and time for both elective and core subjects. Instruction is **student-centered**, teachers are empowered to make curricular and instructional decisions, and students benefit from time for in-depth investigation and the development of critical-thinking skills.

Middle school teachers should become proficient with instructional strategies that are compatible with flexible block scheduling. As students are presented with varying blocks of time in which to learn, accommodations in curriculum and pedagogical strategies as well as a shift toward students taking more responsibility for their own learning are needed for flexible block scheduling to become effective (Salvaterra and Adams, 1995). Such scheduling also provides a unique opportunity to individually address diverse learning abilities without **tracking** students into classes by perceived ability group.

The most important scheduling consideration is to provide a structure in which both students and teachers can achieve the school's mission. In some school settings, the implementation of a completely flexible schedule can be challenging. Resources for effectively implementing common planning time and arranging for the proximity of classrooms are often limited. Curriculum design may and ability grouping does reduce the opportunity for the same set of teachers to create a "school within a school" for a common set of students. The interdisciplinary schedule provides middle school teachers with the freedom and flexibility to design instruction that is most responsive to the needs of the young adolescent. The research evidence is clear that a flexible block schedule to support integrated team teaching is the most beneficial to high-quality adolescent learning (George & Alexander, 2003).

Schedules are key to support the professional collaboration needed for interdisciplinary instruction. Therefore, common planning periods must be clearly defined and should be incorporated within the school day for teachers. Although core and exploratory or elective teams traditionally meet as separate groups, it is possible to create time during the day for interactive planning. Since common planning time is an integral part of the teachers' school day, guidelines are needed for the effective use of this time. To promote the relationship between planning and delivery of instruction, teachers must regularly assess their use of common planning time.

As a transitional school between elementary school and high school—transitional in student and teacher organization, curriculum, and instruction—the middle school makes use of scheduling techniques that are a happy medium between these two levels. At least until the upper grades, elementary schools often employ a **self-contained** classroom approach, with individual classroom teachers controlling decisions about time in the subject areas. High school time is typically divided among departments, which deliver curriculum and instruction. These departments are based on subject-area expertise, and each teacher has an allocated block (or blocks) of time, often called periods; blocks or periods are of equal length. Because of the number of teachers and blocks or periods, time is controlled by a bell, which is not conducive to flexibility. High schools today are a mix of traditional, often relatively short, class periods or blocks.

Time and schedules are typically a function of student and teacher organization into teams at the middle school level. Since this involves multiple teachers working together in a variety of ways, according to curricular and student needs, the schedule is not as externally controlled as in the high school. And, since multiple teachers are working with common students, no one individual makes all the time and other decisions. As a result, scheduling is a function of the entire team, with decision-making turned over to the teachers/teams, in partnership with their administrators, to create flexibility and structure for themselves and their students. Table 15.1 illustrates the character of these three organizational structures (George & Alexander, 2003).

Table 15.1 Organization of Time in Schools

Elementary School	Middle School	High School

EXAMPLES OF SCHOOL SCHEDULES

The first example schedule (Table 15.2) is characterized by interdisciplinary team organization (two teachers at each grade level), an advisory program, and an extended block for exploratory experiences.

The second sample schedule (Table 15.3) uses a common, more traditional rotation. The schedule changes quarterly (every twelve weeks), and the students experience the day in shorter academic blocks, lunch, and exploratory classes. Each quarter, teams begin the day in a content class that has extra time built-in for advisory and homeroom. Teachers have team and individual planning time at various points during the school day while students are in health and physical-education classes or an exploratory class. The schedule is structured so that, in the fall, sixth graders have academics first, which is helpful to their initial transition and orientation to the middle school and its program. As the year progresses, sixth graders begin to experience the range of the schedule.

Table 15.2 Sample Schedule One

Sixth Grade	Seventh Grade	Eighth Grade
Advisor/advisee period 8:00–8:20 am		
Physical-education & exploratory classes (team planning) 8:30–9:55 am	Core-content-area classes 8:30–11:30 am	Core-content-area classes 8:30–10:05 am
Core-content-area classes 10:05 am–12:30 pm		Physical-education & exploratory classes (team planning) 10:05–11:40 am
	Lunch 11:30–11:55 am	Lunch 11:40 am–12:05 pm
Lunch 12:30–12:55 pm	Core-content-area classes 11:55 am–1:00 pm	Core-content-area classes 12:05–2:35 pm
Core-content-area classes 1:00–2:35 pm	Physical-education & exploratory classes (team planning) 1:00–2:35 pm	
Home base/wrap-up 2:35–2:45 pm		
Escort students to car pickup or bus 2:45 pm Planning and lunch for exploratory and physical-education teachers 11:40 am–1:00 pm		

Table 15.3 Sample Schedule Two

	Grade	\multicolumn{7}{c}{Period}
		1	2	3	4	5	6	7
Fall	6th	Math	ELA	Science	Lunch	Social studies	Exploratory (planning)	Exploratory (planning)
	7th	ELA	Math	Lunch	Social studies	Exploratory (planning)	Science	Exploratory (planning)
	8th	Science	Exploratory (planning)	Math	Exploratory (planning)	Lunch	Social studies	ELA
	HPE & Exploratory	(Planning)	8th HPE	Lunch	8th Exploratory	7th HPE	6th Exploratory	6th HPE 7th Exploratory
Winter	Grade	1	2	3	4	5	6	7
	6th	ELA	Math	Lunch	Exploratory (planning)	Science	Social studies	Exploratory (planning)
	7th	Math	ELA	Science	Lunch	Exploratory (planning)	Exploratory (planning)	Social studies
	8th	Science	Exploratory (planning)	ELA	Social studies	Lunch	Math	Exploratory (planning)
	HPE & Exploratory	(Planning)	8th HPE	Lunch	6th Exploratory	7th HPE	7th Exploratory	6th HPE 8th Exploratory
Spring	Grade	1	2	3	4	5	6	7
	6th	Science	Math	Social studies	Lunch	ELA	Exploratory (planning)	Exploratory (planning)
	7th	ELA	Science	Lunch	Math	Exploratory (planning)	Social studies	Social studies
	8th	Math	Exploratory (planning)	ELA	Exploratory (planning)	Lunch	Science	Social studies
	HPE & Exploratory	(Planning)	8th HPE	Lunch	8th Exploratory	7th HPE	6th Exploratory	6th HPE 7th Exploratory

ELA = English-Language Arts & HPE = Health & Physical Education

Practice It: In a small group, choose one of the options below, and plan a flexible time schedule to accomplish the objectives described.

Option One: You are a member of a new four-person interdisciplinary team at the seventh-grade level. You and your teammates have responsibility for teaching the core four subjects to one hundred students daily (mathematics, social studies, science, and language arts). This is your first day together as a team during preplanning workdays (the first three days of your contract before students arrive). As a team, you need to decide how you will arrange your base schedule—the normal daily schedule that will serve as a starting point for doing other flexible alterations. You have a total block of time from 8 a.m. to 1:20 p.m. daily, including lunch, but not including common or individual planning time. Create a base schedule that will accommodate an equality of time among the subjects and an equality of workload/responsibilities among team members.

Option Two: You are a member of a two-person eighth-grade interdisciplinary core team (teaching math, science, social studies, and language arts) that is preparing to implement PBL. Students will define a project theme and important questions, but your teacher team will plan for PBL time within each of the core four subjects. You have sixty students on the team and a total block of time (referred to as your block schedule) from 8:15 to 11:30 a.m., daily, not including lunch or common or individual planning time. Create a schedule for five days that would accomplish the goal of content coverage and PBL time without giving priority to any one area.

Structures of Place and Practice

GROUPING STUDENTS FOR INSTRUCTION

Effective middle school teachers know that one group combination or size rarely fits all, so they use flexible grouping, based on informed decisions. It is essential to think about whether the current student organization is the only possibility for learning. With each lesson, teachers should consider whether students may have more success in independent or small-group learning scenarios. Not all student needs may be met with one type of grouping or with the same activity. Many structures and factors can be considered for flexible grouping: whole class, partners, teams, small groups, one-on-one tutoring (between students or with an adult), centers for learning, or by readiness, interest, and learner profile. All groups should be engaged in developmentally appropriate and respectful tasks.

Being flexible when grouping students for instruction is considered a data-driven teaching practice in which a teacher puts students into groups to work together for only as long as is needed for them to develop an identified skill or to complete a learning activity. The groups can be **heterogeneous** or **homogeneous**. Groups makeup should change often, based on the learning objective and student needs or interests.

REGROUPING FOR INSTRUCTION

Interdisciplinary teams or individual teachers may group or regroup students for instruction. The core-subject-area teachers typically remain the same, and student engagement, academic progress, and interests are monitored and discussed in team meetings. Flexible grouping is an effective strategy for creating an inclusive classroom culture that recognizes learner variability. Research has shown that all students in classrooms that employ flexible grouping show academic gains (Bates, 2013; Boyer, 2014; Burris & Welner, 2005; Castle, Baker Deniz, & Tortora, 2005; Steenbergen-Hu, Makel, & Olszewski-Kuilius, 2016). Teachers should use data to put students into small groups for instruction, those groups should change frequently in response to the desired outcome and student needs, and teachers should remember that students can be grouped homogenously or heterogeneously. The end goal, of course, is to see an increase in student engagement, support of student social and emotional wellness, and accelerated learning and skill development.

Looping

The practice of **looping** typically includes a three-year cycle (although as few as two years may be considered looping). During a cycle, students remain together with their teacher, sometimes for their entire middle school experience. The practice allows teachers to get to know individual students well while building relationships with them and, often, their families or support groups. Time is saved at the beginning of the second year as there is no need to spend time getting to know the students or learning procedures—the work of the class can begin immediately. There is evidence that looping can also lead to improved student behavior, attitude, voice, and even self-esteem, all due to in-depth interactions and relationship with the teacher (Lounsbury, Tarbet-Carson, & Andrews, 2013). Although this grouping strategy does limit the number of teachers that students experience, which may enhance students' feelings of trepidation over changing teachers, the positive outcomes outweigh this or other concerns.

Meet Lillian: Lillian is an expressive eighth grader with impressive artistic skills. Lillian demonstrates a wide range of emotions throughout their typical day. They is a nonbinary student who has sought out a community that is supportive of their individuality. Like many middle school students on the pathway to self-discovery, Lillian seeks attention from students and teachers alike as they searches for a sense of belonging. Their academic journey has been stagnant, and they has not demonstrated much growth in core classes. For much of the year, they exhibited task-avoidant behaviors and was often distracted by their artwork or peers. One of the solutions to success for Lillian, that they also requested, was sitting close to the front of the room or alone as well as the use of earbuds with music to help them focus.

Pause and Reflect: How might Lillian benefit from looping? In other words, what specific benefits might Lillian gain from having teachers who know them academically and socially for longer periods of time?

INTERDISCIPLINARY TEAMING

An interdisciplinary team consists of two or more content teachers and the students they teach. According to a research summary by Mertens and Flowers (2004),

> Team teachers plan, coordinate, and evaluate curriculum and instruction across academic areas. Teams cultivate meaningful and regular communication with families. Teams often share the same schedule and the same area of the building. For teachers, teams provide a collaborative and supportive work group. For students, teams offer stable relationships with teachers and peers (Jackson & Davis, 2000). Seventy-nine percent of principals in middle level schools report that they had teams in 2000, up from 57% in 1992 (Valentine, Clark, Hackman, & Petzko, 2002).

The most widely recognized principles for organizing successful teams include keeping them small (in the number of teachers and students), providing sufficient individual and common planning time for teachers, allowing teams to design the daily schedule, assigning teams to their own area of the building (with team members in close proximity to each other), and allowing teams to work together for multiple years (Erb & Stevenson, 1999). Characteristics of effective teams include the following (George & Alexander, 2003):

1. Student-centered focus.
2. Strong commitment to academic achievement.
3. Collaborative policies and accountability systems.
4. Strong sense of team community.
5. Regular communication with parents.
6. A proactive approach.
7. Teachers who work professionally and collaboratively.

A prerequisite for effective interdisciplinary instruction is professional collaboration. Concept-based instruction that meets students' needs can occur when teachers can collaborate during the school day in interdisciplinary or multidisciplinary teams. Middle schools must provide common planning time for teachers within the schedule of the day to promote the collaboration necessary to develop relationships and address content, concepts, and skills within interdisciplinary instruction.

Inclusion and Co-Teaching

AMLE calls for middle schools to provide an environment that is welcoming, inclusive, and affirming for all (2012). Inclusion must be fundamental to the shared vision and mission of the school and must include a pledge to embrace, value, and educate a diverse range of learners. Diversity enhances the school community, creating a learning environment that reflects the world around us, while inclusion fosters opportunity for the entire school community to thrive. In an inclusive school, students', parents', teachers', and community members' voices are heard and valued. A school that values listening and understanding has administrators and teachers who are willing to engage in critical conversations that might be uncomfortable but that should not invoke fear. The classroom is one small component of the larger school, and representation matters and permeates throughout the school. According to the foremost researcher in the field, co-teaching is a "service-delivery mechanism as a means for providing specially designed instruction to which students with disabilities are entitled while ensuring access to general curriculum in the least restrictive environment with the provision of supplementary aids and services" (Friend, 2007). Co-teaching allows students with disabilities to be equitably served in an inclusive classroom. The method involves two or more teachers, typically one with content licensure and the other with licensure in special education. These teachers are equal contributors to planning and instruction rather than one serving only as support. Co-teaching occurs most often in a shared classroom or workspace in which both teachers have "responsibility and accountability for a single group of students." Co-taught classes are interactive, with high levels of engagement, if teachers have professional preparation to grow their skill and comfort level. It is important for teachers and their teams to clearly outline roles and responsibilities.

Multitiered Systems of Supports and Positive Behavioral Interventions and Supports

Two programmatic structures that guide current practice in schools today are MTSS (multitiered system of supports) and PBIS (positive behavioral interventions and supports). MTSS is a proactive and preventive framework that many schools use to give targeted support to struggling students. This framework integrates data and instruction to maximize student achievement and support students' social, emotional, and behavioral needs from a strengths-based perspective. MTSS is more of an umbrella framework to encompass data on the whole child (e.g., including academic and social-emotional behavior). It is also a mechanism that drives system-level resources to sustainably meet the needs of all students and accelerate learning for all. MTSS brings about cohesion to the work and best practices that are already happening so that those efforts are no longer happening in isolation. Within the framework, we are effectively working and communicating with all stakeholders to provide a unified support system and a means to equity.

MTSS and PBIS are related but are not the same thing. MTSS typically includes three tiers of support: universal, targeted, and intensive. The goal is to ensure that all students receive the support they need to succeed academically and behaviorally. In contrast, PBIS is a specific behavior-management approach that is often used as part of an MTSS framework. PBIS focuses on promoting positive behavior by teaching and reinforcing appropriate behavior rather than only punishing negative behavior. PBIS includes the use of specific strategies and interventions, such as establishing clear expectations for behavior; providing positive feedback and reinforcement; and using data to monitor and adjust interventions, as needed. Chapter 6 provided more on MTSS.

Structures of Curriculum and Programming

AMLE advocates for using challenging, relevant curriculum, with a strong basis in core subjects, for significant segments of each school day (AMLE, 2012; Bishop & Harrison, 2020). Developing curriculum, instruction, and assessment that meet the developmental and learning needs of young adolescents is challenging—especially because teachers and their administration must meet state and federal standards and must balance effective instructional practice with high-stakes assessments.

ADVISORY PROGRAMS

Widely promoted to strengthen connectedness, **advisory programs** are configurations in which an adult advisor meets regularly during the school day with a group of students to provide academic and social-emotional mentorship and support, to create personalization within the school, and to facilitate a small peer community of learners (Shulkind & Foote, 2009). The underlying goal of most advisory programs is to provide each student with consistent support and guidance from a member of the school staff. This adult advocates for a group of students and facilitates the group's daily activities, which may include implementation of a curriculum, facilitation of a discussion, and sharing of school information. One of the major benefits of having an advisory program is the creation of positive relationships. These programs also help build a sense of community in schools, and studies have shown that students' educational success is based on academic and social support (Burkhardt, 1999). In addition to improving the academic performance of students, advisors can also help students plan for their future academic careers, and advisory class can serve as a time for discussion about future goals and aspirations and assist students in making decisions that will help them achieve their goals. Teachers and school staff work hard to make a difference in the lives of students, and the advisory program provides them with extra opportunities to get to know students well and help them in a substantial and meaningful way.

Practice It: Your job is to set up an organizational structure for an advisory period. Respond to the following areas:

a) Students: Set the teacher-student ratio and grouping strategy.

b) Schedule: Address time allotment and regularity of meetings.

c) Vision: Describe your overall goal or goals for the course along with your supporting rationale for them.

d) Plan: Outline a typical week in your advisory class. Use Table 15.4 as a template for your design. Include at least three distinct types of activities you plan to implement during this week. Give a rationale for choosing each activity. Activities could relate to the personal, instructional, or school concerns of students and to exploratory and career education.

MIDDLE SCHOOL ORGANIZATION AND STRUCTURE

Table 15.4 Template for an Advisory Program

Monday	Tuesday	Wednesday	Thursday	Friday

Here is one example if needed:

a) **Students:** Teacher-student ratio and grouping strategy

   The tecratio will be 1:15 and students will be heterogeneously grouped

b) **Schedule:** Time allotment and regularity of meetings

   We will meet three days a week, on Mondays, Wednesdays, and Fridays, for an hour

c) **Vision:** Your overall goal or goals for the course along with supporting rationale for them

   The goal will be to learn overall wellness by teaching students various ways to incorporate aspects of healthful living into the students' lives

d) **Plan:**

   Monday: Hygiene is part of taking care of overall wellness, and, unfortunately, some students are not taught this at home. Activity: The teacher will show an image of rotten teeth and read a description of disease that can be formed from not brushing. Then a dental hygienist will come in and teach the children how to properly brush their teeth.

   Wednesday: Nutrition and sleep is something that many students lack, especially in today's fast-paced society. Today we will write down what we have eaten in the last twenty-four hours, then we will discuss it. We will learn how to make healthy nutrition choices and that being sleep deprived is detrimental to our health. Today we will go to the home economics room to make some healthy snacks as a class. (Cut up fruits and veggies.)

   Friday: Exercise is something that many Americans lack due to insufficient time. Today we will teach children that exercise is vital to our health. We will discuss many ways exercise can be fun. Then we will play some physically active games, like kickball.

EXPLORATORY AND ENRICHMENT PROGRAMS

An *exploratory* and *enriching* curriculum directly responds to the probing nature of young adolescents. Rather than being a specific category, exploration and enrichment are more of an approach to all curriculum and instruction. According to one of the latest in AMLE's *This We Believe* series (2019), these experiences broaden student views of themselves and the world; help students discover their interests and aptitudes; assist students with career exploration and decisions about their futures; contribute to the development of well-rounded, self-sufficient citizens; and open doors to new ideas and areas to investigate (Beane, 1993, 1997; Brodhagen, 1995; Nesin & Brazee, 2013; Springer, 1994, 2006, 2013).

Exploration develops self-esteem and celebrates uniqueness, and having time to explore positively impacts self-esteem by allowing pursuit of personal interests; providing time to explore is a sign that we value students and their interests. AMLE recommends that,

> middle schools supplement the core curriculum with strong elective and enrichment offerings. Electives help students identify and pursue interests outside of core academic subjects and allow them to develop a sense of career interests. These courses reveal student strengths and provide outlets for different peer interactions than students may experience in their academic classes. Middle schools should also schedule time for advisory periods to promote connectedness among students and between students and teachers. Notably, a higher percentage of high achieving schools in the AMLE's national middle school surveys reported weekly advisory periods (65 percent), compared to the randomly selected schools (53 percent). Based on this finding, the authors of the report recommend that all middle schools schedule advisory periods at least twice each week. (2019)

Minimally, exploratory classes allow students to investigate a variety of courses to determine what interests them for future study. Students may explore courses that allow them to try something new, to be challenged further, or even to find something that they may want to specialize in during high school. Traditional exploratory classes (often called electives) include everything from music to art or band. Contemporary options vary widely and may include foreign language, STEM-based topics, drama, writing, technology, physical activity/exercise pursuits like yoga, family and consumer sciences, and so much more.

Practice It: If you were a teacher in a school with a functioning exploratory program, what kind of exploratory course experience would you design for students? Assuming you have at least fifteen to twenty class meetings, develop a description that includes the following:

- Title
- Content areas involved
- Two learning goals (e.g., what students will learn and how they will demonstrate that learning)
- Brief descriptions of two planned learning activities

SCHOOL AND COMMUNITY PARTNERSHIPS IN SUPPORT OF LEARNING

Positive parental engagement is critical for student success in schools, and finding ways to bring the community into school at all levels and in various ways is valuable for everyone (e.g., students, teachers, parents, and the community). When students see themselves as learners who are creating something for a purpose bigger than the classroom or just one teacher, they develop strong community connections. The goal is for the community to see middle school students as valued members of their communities and as people who can make a positive impact.

Structures of Health and Safety

Students' health, nutrition, and safety have a significant impact on their education, and we must learn to work together to create a way to meet nonacademic needs of students and their families. Safe schools, healthy nutrition, and physical activity are all critical to improving academic and social outcomes for students. School safety requires a framework composed of technology, training, education, and community engagement to meet the needs of the whole child. With a system of holistic safety and wellness in place, schools are in a better position to promote the long-term development and success of young adolescents. Every student deserves a strong education in a healthy and safe learning environment. Because of the COVID-19 pandemic, we have learned that it is more important than ever for schools and communities to prioritize the health and safety of students, staff, and families. Students can safely learn and thrive inside their classrooms with the assistance of teachers and school leaders who can provide support and deliver on the promise of an excellent and equitable education for every child.

The quality and character of school life, accruing from patterns of experience of school life and reflecting norms, goals, values, interpersonal relationships, teaching and learning practices, and organizational structures, is what we refer to as **school climate**. A positive school climate is linked to better academic performance, higher graduation rates, a decreased incidence of violence, and increased teacher retention (Tennessee Department of Education, n.d.).

Unwanted, aggressive behavior that involves a real or perceived imbalance of power is **bullying**. The behavior is repeated, or has the potential to be repeated, over time. Bullying may be physical or emotional, and bullies may use access to embarrassing or otherwise harmful information or even their own popularity to control or harm others.

Cyber-bullying is a form of bullying that takes place using technology, including devices and equipment, such as cell phones, computers, and tablets, as well as communication tools like social media, text messages, chat, and websites. Examples may include mean or threatening text messages or emails; rumors, pictures, or videos sent by email or posted on social websites; and fake profiles or pictures.

Any unwelcome conduct against a student that is based on the student being a member of protected class under federal civil-rights laws; that is severe, pervasive, or persistent; and that creates a hostile environment that interferes with or limits the student's ability to participate in or benefit from services, activities, or opportunities offered by a school is **harassment**.

One or more of the following criteria must be met for the conduct to constitute harassment:

- An act that is directed at one or more students and that is received as harmful or embarrassing;

- An act that is directed at one or more students; an act that substantially interferes with educational opportunities, benefits, or programs of one or more students;

- An act that substantially affects the ability of a student to participate in or benefit from the school district's educational programs or activities by placing the student in reasonable fear of physical harm or by causing emotional distress;

- An act that is based on a student's actual or perceived distinguishing characteristics that suggest the student is a member of a protected class or is based on an association with another person who has or is perceived to have any such distinguishing characteristics;

- An act that, repeated over time, is severe, persistent, and pervasive; an act that causes mental duress or psychological trauma to the victim.

COMPREHENSIVE SCHOOL HEALTH PLAN

The health and well-being of children and youth must be a fundamental value of society. Urgent health and social problems have underscored the need for collaboration among families, schools, agencies, communities, and governments in taking a comprehensive approach to school-based health promotion. Experience and research evidence suggest that a **comprehensive school health plan** can improve the health-related knowledge, attitudes, and behaviors of students. Other major determinants of health, such as genetics, the health-care delivery system, and socioeconomic, cultural, and environmental factors, require a multifaceted approach to the maintenance and improvement of health status. A comprehensive approach to improving students' health includes providing a broad continuum of activities and services, in schools or in the surrounding communities, to enable young adolescents to enhance their health, develop to their fullest potential, and establish productive and satisfying relationships in their present and future lives. The goals of a comprehensive approach are to promote health and wellness; prevent specific diseases, disorders, and injury; prevent high-risk social behaviors; intervene to assist children and youth who are in need or at risk; help support those who are already exhibiting special health-care needs; and promote positive health- and safety-related behaviors. Attainment of these goals requires using an integrated approach that coordinates multiple programs and provides multiple strategies. Professional staff development is necessary to effectively address specific health-related issues. A comprehensive school health program focuses on promoting behaviors that contribute to the health, safety, and well-being of students, staff, and families while assuring a supportive and healthy environment that nurtures academic growth and development.

RESTORATIVE DISCIPLINE

A prevention-oriented approach that fosters consensus-based decisions to resolve school conflicts, such as bullying, truancy, and disruptive behavior, is recommended for middle schools. This approach focuses not only on rule-breaking and discipline but also on changing the entire school culture. Also called positive discipline, responsive classroom, or empowerment, restorative discipline focuses on fostering a sense of community within classrooms to prevent conflict and on reacting to misconduct by encouraging students to accept responsibility and rebuild relationships. Restorative-discipline strategies provide an alternative approach to traditional classroom-management and student-discipline models that are typically more punitive. Under traditional models, a student might be detained by a school resource officer (commonly referred to as an SRO) and might face in-school or out-of-school suspension (ISS or OSS) for a physical altercation with another student. With this approach, the student might instead participate in a teacher- or student-led peer mediation session to discuss the fight and might be required to do a task that is helpful to the school community. These practices have grown in recognition in recent years due to an increasing understanding of the negative effects of policies that rely on suspensions and expulsions, particularly for students of color and those with disabilities, who are punished in disproportionate numbers in our schools. Students who are suspended are at higher risk for poor attendance, dropping out of high school, and involvement in juvenile and adult justice systems (Kirsch, 2022).

MENTAL-HEALTH AND WELLNESS PROGRAMS

According to the National Association of Secondary School Principals (NASSP, 2023, p. 1),

> a U.S. Surgeon General report indicates that one in five children and adolescents will face a significant mental health condition during their school years. Mental health disorders affecting children and adolescents can range from attention deficit hyperactivity disorder (ADHD) to autism, depression, eating disorders, schizophrenia, and others. Students suffering from these conditions face significant barriers to learning and are less likely to graduate from high school. Key responsibilities of school leaders regarding this issue include creating a safe and nurturing school environment, supporting the physical and mental health of children, fostering their social and emotional well-being, and being prepared to address teen suicide through effective communication and support. As leaders work to meet these responsibilities, they face an array of challenges related to mental health.

These challenges include their limited capacity to address mental-health issues; disinvestment in school-based **mental-health and wellness programs**; stigma surrounding mental-health issues; and death by suicide (which is the third leading cause of death in young adolescents, ten to fourteen years of age). NASSP (2023) believes that these challenges

> underscore the need for comprehensive mental health support services and prevention programs to build the capacity of schools as they help each student reach his or her maximum potential. The value of significant investments in school-based mental health programs is the right thing to do, and its efficacy is also borne out by prevailing research and data. As a 2017 research review in the Harvard Review of Psychiatry asserted, there is growing evidence supporting the effectiveness of mental health programs in schools and their ability to reach many children. (p. 1)

SCHOOL SAFETY AND CRISIS PLANNING

Schools are well-organized systems that function with great efficiency under normal conditions. During a crisis, however, when schools face unusual demands, they must maintain day-to-day operations while also adapting to unexpected and unpredictable influences. Teachers, staff, and students will be personally affected by the crisis, and, therefore, it is exceedingly difficult for a school to organize an effective crisis-intervention response and still maintain the required long-range perspective. School faculty and staff members may underestimate the full impact of the crisis or feel overwhelmed by the extent and magnitude of it. For schools to effectively address the many issues that typically arise during a crisis, having a preplanned, systematic organizational model to direct decisions is essential. To be effective, a school's crisis-response model must anticipate the results of a crisis and identify the ways it will affect individuals and the community. This includes identifying and preparing for the typical reactions of young people of all ages. In addition, the model must identify and plan how to use the broad range of skills and knowledge represented by those on the school crisis-response team, including those of collaborating professionals, such as mental-health care providers and those working in the juvenile-justice field. Finally, the crisis-response model must anticipate the future needs of the school population and develop plans to meet those needs. A school crisis-response plan must address three general areas: safety and security; dissemination of accurate information to school crisis-response team members, school staff, students, parents/guardians, and, when appropriate, the public; and the emotional and psychological needs of all parties.

Pause and Reflect: Which practices would have impacted your own academic or social success and why? Did your middle level school employ a traditional model of discipline management or restorative justice/positive discipline? How do you know?

To summarize, let's revisit our learning outcomes:

1. **Articulate structures of time in middle school settings.** A developmentally responsive middle school is one in which the organizational structure is built

around the students it serves. This structure encompasses team teaching and how these teachers use the instructional considerations and limitations and the time allotted. Traditional departmentalized schedules include a fixed number of class periods with teacher-centered and departmentalized instruction delivery. In contrast, flexible block scheduling permits the flexibility to schedule what is important to an interdisciplinary team and a school community. Two of the most common forms of block scheduling are the alternate-day plan and the flexible block.

2. **Describe structures of place and practice used to make informed decisions when grouping students for instruction.** Effective middle school teachers utilize flexible grouping that is based on informed decisions. They must consider whether students may have more success in independent or small-group learning scenarios. Not all student needs may be met with one type of grouping or with the same activity. Many structures and factors can be considered for flexible grouping: whole class, partners, teams, small groups, one-on-one tutoring (between students or with an adult), centers for learning, or by readiness, interest, and learner profile. All groups should be engaged in developmentally appropriate and respectful tasks. Other important structures of place and practice include grouping for instruction, looping, interdisciplinary teaming, and inclusion and co-teaching.

3. **Identify structures of curriculum, programming, and partnerships in support of learning.** AMLE advocates for using challenging, relevant curriculum with a strong basis in core subjects for significant segments of each school day. Developing curriculum, instruction and assessment that meet the developmental and learning needs of young adolescents is challenging—especially because teachers and their administration must meet state and federal standards and balance effective instructional practice with high-stakes assessments. Two important structures of curriculum covered in this chapter include advisory and exploratory programs. Forming partnerships in support of learning is critical for student success in schools, and finding ways to bring the community into school at all levels and in various ways is valuable for everyone (e.g., students, teachers, parents, and the community).

4. **Identify essential school partnerships and the structures that support building healthy and safe schools.** Positive parental engagement is critical for student success in schools, and finding ways to bring the community into school at all levels and in many ways is valuable for everyone (e.g., students, teachers, parents, and the community). When students see themselves as learners who are creating something for a purpose bigger than the classroom or just one teacher, they develop strong community connections. The goal is for the community to see middle school students as valued members of their communities and as people who can make a positive impact. Examples of structures of health and safety include a comprehensive school health plan, restorative discipline, mental-health and wellness programming, and school safety and crisis planning.

References

Association for Middle Level Education. (2012). *This we believe in action: Implementing successful middle level schools.* Westerville, OH: Author.

Association for Middle Level Education. (2019). Curriculum, instruction, and assessment. https://www.amle.org/curriculum-instruction-and-assessment/

Bates, C. C. (2013). Flexible grouping during literacy centers: A model for differentiating instruction. *YC Young Children, 68*(2), 30–33.

Beane, J. (1990). *A middle school curriculum: From rhetoric to reality.* Columbus, OH: National Middle School Association.

Beane, J. A. (1993). *A middle school curriculum: From rhetoric to reality* (2nd ed.). Westerville, OH: National Middle School Association.

Beane, J. A. (1997). *Curriculum integration: Designing the core of democratic education.* New York, NY: Teachers College Press.

Bishop, P. A., & Harrison, L. M. (2020). *The successful middle school: This we believe* (5th ed.). Westerville, OH: Author.

Boyer, M. S. (2014). *A case study on a flexible grouping approach to reading instruction.* ProQuest. (2019). Search.proquest.com. https://search.proquest.com/openview/1b11ba1a17534f9f70dc248d511e5db5/1?p q-origsite=gscholar&cbl=18750&diss=y

Brodhagen, B. L. (1995). The situation made us special. In M. W. Apple & J. A. Beane (Eds.), *Democratic schools* (pp. 83–100). Alexandria, VA: Association for Supervision and Curriculum Development.

Burkhardt, R. M. (1999). Advisory: Advocacy for every student. *Middle School Journal, 30*(3), 51–54.

Burris, C. C., & Welner, K. G. (2005). Closing the achievement gap by detracking. *Phi Delta Kappan, 86*(8), 594–8.

Carnegie Council on Adolescent Development. (1989). *Turning Points: Preparing American Youth for the 21st Century* (pp. 37–70). Washington, DC: Author.

Castle, S., Baker Deniz, C., & Tortora, M. (2005). Flexible grouping and student learning in a high-needs school. *Education and Urban Society, 37*(2), 139–50.

Erb, T. O., & Stevenson, C. (1999). From faith to facts: Turning Points in action—What difference does teaming make? *Middle School Journal, 30*(3), 47–50.

Friend, M. (2007). *Co-teaching defined.* http://www.marilynfriend.com/basics.htm

George, P. S., & Alexander, W. M. (2003). *The exemplary middle school* (3rd ed.). Belmont, CA: Thomson/Wadsworth Learning.

Hackmann, D. G., Valentine, J. W. (1998). Designing an effective middle level schedule. *Middle School Journal, 29*(5), 3–13.

Jackson, A. W., & Davis, G. A. (2000). *Turning points 2000: Educating young adolescents in the 21st century.* New York, NY: Carnegie Corporation of New York.

Lounsbury, J., Tarbet-Carson, S., & Andrews, G. (2013). Looping and multiage grouping: Providing long-term student-teacher relationships—and time. In *Research to Guide Practice in Middle Grades Education*, edited by P. Gayle Andrews. Westerville, OH: AMLE.

Kirsch, N. (2022). *Restorative practices for school discipline, explained.* https://www.future-ed.org/restorative-practices-for-school-discipline-explained/

Meehan, M. L. (1973). What about team teaching? *Educational Leadership, 30*(8), 717–20.

Mertens, S. B., & Flowers, N. (2004). *Research summary: Interdisciplinary teaming.* http://www.nmsa.org/ResearchSummaries/Summary21/tabid/250/Default.aspx

National Association of Secondary School Principals. (2023). *Mental health in middle level and high schools*. https://www.nassp.org/mental-health-in-middle-level-and-high-schools

National Middle School Association. (1995). *This we believe*. Columbus, OH: Author.

National Middle School Association. (2010). *This we believe: Keys to educating young adolescents*. Westerville, OH: Author.

Nesin, G., & Brazee, E. (2013). Developmentally responsive middle grades schools: Needed now more than ever. In P.G. Andrews (Ed.), *Research to guide practice in middle grades education* (pp. 469–93). Westerville, OH: Association for Middle Level Education.

Salvaterra, M., Adams, D. (1995). Departing from tradition: Two schools' stories. *Educational Leadership*, 53(3), 32–35.

Shulkind, S. B. & Foote, J. (2009). Creating a culture of connectedness through middle school advisory programs. *Middle School Journal*, 41(1), 20–27.

Springer, M. A. (1994). *Watershed: A successful voyage into integrated learning*. Westerville, OH: National Middle School Association.

Springer, M. A. (2006). *Soundings: A democratic student-centered education*. Westerville, OH: National Middle School Association.

Springer, M. A. (2013). Charting the course of curriculum integration. In P. G. Andrews (Ed.), *Research to guide practice in middle grades education* (pp. 187–215). Westerville, OH: Association for Middle Level Education.

Steenbergen-Hu, S., Makel, M. C., & Olszewski-Kuilius, P. (2016). What one hundred years of research says about the effects of ability grouping and acceleration on K–12 students' academic achievement: Findings of two second-order meta-analyses. *Review of Educational Research*, 86(4), 849–99.

Tennessee Department of Education. (n.d.). School Climate: Improving Academic Outcomes through Enhanced Conditions for Learning. https://www.tn.gov/content/tn/education/districts/health-and-safety/school-climate.html

Glossary

504 plan: A plan developed to ensure that a child who has a disability that is identified under the law and who is attending an elementary or secondary educational institution receives accommodations that will ensure the child's academic success and access to the learning environment.

Accountability: Encouraging individuals who are responsible for causing harm to take ownership of their behavior and its impact on others.

ADHD (attention deficit hyperactivity disorder): A neurodevelopmental disorder characterized by difficulties with attention, impulsivity, and hyperactivity.

Adequate yearly progress (AYP): A measurement defined by the No Child Left Behind Act that assesses whether schools and districts are making enough progress in student achievement each year.

Adolescents: Young people in the transitional stage of development between childhood and adulthood, typically ranging from ages ten to nineteen.

Adult advocate: An adult who supports and guides a student's academic and personal development within the school environment.

Advance organizers: Tools used to introduce and provide a framework for new information, helping students to organize and structure their thoughts before engaging with the material.

Adverse childhood experiences (ACEs): Potentially traumatic events occurring in childhood, such as abuse, neglect, and household dysfunction, which can have long-term impacts on health and behavior.

Advisory program: A school program in which each student is assigned to a teacher advisor who provides academic and personal support and helps in planning and goal setting.

Affective filter: A term used by Stephen Krashen to describe the complex of negative emotional and motivational factors that may interfere with the reception and processing of comprehensive input. A low affective filter facilitates risk-taking in language learning, while a high affective filter inhibits language acquisition.

Affective objectives: Objectives focused on students' attitudes, appreciations, and relationships.

Alternate-day block schedule: A scheduling system where half of the classes meet in extended periods (e.g., ninety minutes) one day, while the remaining classes meet in extended periods the next day. Some schools also include one day each week where all classes meet for shorter periods.

Alternative teaching (co-teaching model): A co-teaching model where one teacher instructs most of the class while the other works with a smaller group for remediation, enrichment, or assessment.

AMLE (Association for Middle Level Education): An organization dedicated to improving the educational experiences of young adolescents by supporting middle level educators through advocacy, research, and resources.

Amygdala: A region of the brain involved in emotion regulation, risk assessment, and the processing of fear.

Anxiety disorders: Mental-health conditions characterized by excessive fear or worry, affecting many adolescents.

Assessment: The process of evaluating students' understanding and proficiency through various methods like quizzes, projects, and exams.

Asset-based language: Language that highlights the strengths, abilities, and potential of individuals rather than focusing on their weaknesses or problems.

Assimilation: The process by which a person or a group's language and/or culture come to resemble those of another group, often leading to a loss of original cultural identity.

Association for Middle Level Education (AMLE): A professional organization dedicated to promoting the education and well-being of young adolescents, formerly known as the National Middle School Association.

Authoritarian-Democratic parenting: A child-centered parenting style characterized by high expectations of children with guidance and support.

Autobiographical memory: Memory that is specific to personal life events and identities, often tied to personal experiences.

Backward design: An approach to lesson planning that starts with identifying desired learning goals, then determining acceptable evidence of learning, and, finally, planning learning experiences and instruction.

Biculturalism: The ability to understand and function within two different cultural contexts, often the dominant culture and one's own minority culture.

Block scheduling: An arrangement of the school day into larger blocks of time (e.g., ninety minutes) instead of shorter periods (e.g., forty-five minutes). This allows for more in-depth teaching and learning activities.

Bloom's taxonomy: A hierarchical model used to classify educational learning objectives into levels of complexity and specificity, ranging from lower-order skills, like remembering, to higher-order skills, like creating.

Body image: An individual's perception of and feelings about his or her own body, which can be influenced by social, cultural, and psychological factors.

Body neutrality: An approach that focuses on appreciating what the body can do rather than on how it appears, promoting a healthy relationship with one's body without emphasizing physical looks.

Body positivity: A social movement advocating for the acceptance of all body types and challenging societal standards of beauty.

Building and bridging: Refers to the instructional strategies that connect students' home cultures and languages to the school culture and language, facilitating academic success and cultural integration.

Bullying: Unwanted, aggressive behavior that involves a real or perceived imbalance of power, repeated or potentially repeated over time; bullying may be physical or emotional.

Carnegie Corporation: An organization that published influential reports on improving middle grades education, such as *Turning Points* in 1989 and its updated version in 2000.

CDC (Centers for Disease Control and Prevention): The national public-health institute in the United States, responsible for controlling and preventing disease, injury, and disability.

Centers/stations: Rotational instructional methods in which students engage in different activities, often including small-group, individual, and teacher-led tasks.

Cerebellum: The part of the brain that controls motor functions, balance, and coordination.

Challenging curriculum: Curriculum designed to be exploratory, integrative, relevant, and appealing to young adolescents, encouraging higher levels of engagement and learning.

Chunking: A strategy to extend the capacity of working memory by grouping smaller units of information into larger, more manageable units.

Cohort differences: Differences in development that arise from the historical and social context in which individuals are raised, such as the influence of technology or educational practices.

Co-teaching: A service-delivery mechanism involving two or more teachers, typically one with licensure in a content area and another with special-education licensure, who are equal contributors to planning and instruction within an inclusive classroom.

Cognates: Words in two languages that share a similar meaning, spelling, and pronunciation.

Cognitive objectives: Objectives that focus on understandings, awarenesses, and insights, typically involving information recall, conceptual understanding, and problem-solving.

Collaboration: The process wherein two or more people work together toward a common goal, sharing responsibility, decision-making, and accountability. In education, it often refers to the partnership between general- and special-education teachers to support all students.

Collaborative for Academic, Social, and Emotional Learning (CASEL): An organization that provides a framework for integrating social and emotional learning into education systems.

Collaborative summarizing: A strategy that helps students develop oracy and make use of purposeful dialogue to create a common product through negotiation and summary writing in groups.

Common planning time: A scheduled period during the school day when teachers of the same team or department meet to plan, discuss, and coordinate curriculum and instruction.

Compacting: A method where teachers assess students' prior knowledge and skills to eliminate redundant work, allowing advanced students to engage in more challenging activities that deepen their understanding.

Comprehensible input: The teacher speaks in such a way that students can understand what is being said even when they do not know or understand all the words being stated.

Comprehensive school health plan: A broad continuum of activities and services that take place in schools and their surrounding communities to enhance health, develop potential, and establish productive and satisfying relationships in present and future lives.

Connotation: The meanings, suggestions, or associations implied by a word.

Consequence: A result of an action.

Constructivist view of learning: An educational philosophy according to which learners construct their own understanding and knowledge of the world through experiences and reflecting on those experiences.

Content standards: Benchmarks that define what students should know and be able to do at each grade level within a specific content area.

Cooperative learning: A strategy that uses partner and group formations to foster sharing responsibility for academic tasks and building social skills through collaboration.

Corpus callosum: A bundle of nerve fibers connecting the left and right hemispheres of the brain, facilitating communication between them.

Cross-curricular opportunities: Opportunities for integrating multiple subjects or disciplines within a single unit or lesson plan to enhance learning.

Cultural differences: The variations among people in developmental experiences and outcomes that result from individuals' varying cultural backgrounds, values, and practices.

Cultural identity: One's sense of identity with or feeling of belonging to a group, based on culture, including traditions, language, religion, and social norms.

Culturally relevant pedagogy: A theoretical model that addresses student achievement, while helping students accept and affirm their cultural identity and develop critical perspectives that challenge inequities perpetuated by schools and other institutions.

Culturally responsive discipline: Approaches to discipline that consider cultural backgrounds and aim to address inequities in traditional discipline policies.

Culturally responsive teaching competencies: Core competencies that facilitate self-appraisal, goal setting, and critical conversations among educators, focusing on promoting engagement and achievement by connecting curriculum to students' daily lives, cultural backgrounds, and concerns.

Culturally responsive teaching: An educational approach that integrates students' cultural backgrounds into classroom instruction to promote engagement, achievement, and empowerment.

Culturally sustaining pedagogy: Pedagogy that seeks to perpetuate linguistic, literary, and cultural pluralism as part of the democratic project of schooling, supporting students in preserving their cultural and linguistic heritage while providing access to dominant cultural norms.

Curiosity: The desire to learn and understand more about the physical and intellectual environment. While general curiosity may appear to decline from childhood to adolescence, early adolescents often find new ways to explore familiar environments.

Cyber-bullying: Bullying that takes place using technology, including devices like cell phones, computers, or tablets, and using communication tools, such as social media, text messages, chat, and websites.

Data-based decision-making: The process of using data to identify which students need additional support and to track outcomes related to behavior and academic performance.

Debrief circles: A strategy to facilitate reflection and discussion among students about their experiences or lessons, encouraging engagement and deeper understanding.

Deep learning: Achieving a thorough understanding of new information through meaningful connections and elaboration, making it easier to remember and apply.

Deficit monitor: A term describing the subconscious predisposition toward biased or deficit-based thinking about others, requiring awareness to make conscious choices to be responsive rather than deficit-oriented.

Democratic approach: In the context of classroom rules, this refers to involving students in the process of creating the rules to increase their sense of ownership and responsibility.

Denotation: A word's direct and explicit meaning.

Departmentalized schedule: A traditional school schedule whereby students have a fixed number of periods each day, each dedicated to a different subject, with instruction typically being teacher-centered and guided by departmental procedures.

Developmentalists: Researchers and theorists who study human development across the lifespan, focusing on the changes that occur from birth to old age.

Developmentally responsive: An approach in middle level education that addresses the physical, intellectual, moral, physiological, and social-emotional needs of young adolescents.

Diagnostic assessment: A type of test used before instruction begins to identify students' strengths and weaknesses, helping teachers to tailor teaching to students' needs.

Differentiated instruction: A teaching approach that tailors instruction to meet individual students' needs. It involves varying the content, process, and product, based on students' readiness, interests, and learning profiles.

Differentiation: A teaching approach that involves creating a range of learning experiences to meet the diverse needs of students.

Direct instruction: A teaching model that emphasizes well-developed, carefully planned lessons that are designed to create small learning increments and to provide clear instruction to eliminate misinterpretations.

Discipline: Teaching students to behave in ways that result in success behaviorally, socially, and academically.

Dissociation: A mental process of disconnecting from one's thoughts, feelings, or sense of identity, often as a response to trauma.

Diversity: Differences among individuals and groups, including in race, ethnicity, culture, language, gender, religion, sexual orientation, socio-economic status, family lifestyle, and dynamics.

Domains of development: Specific areas of development, such as cognitive, social, emotional, and physical growth, which are often studied separately but are interconnected in practice.

Early adolescence: The phase of adolescence between ten and fourteen years of age, marked by significant developmental changes in various areas, including the physical, cognitive, social, and emotional domains.

Emotional regulation: The ability to monitor, evaluate, and modify emotional reactions in various contexts to achieve positive outcomes.

Empowerment: Providing students with voice, choice, and responsibility in their education to build their capacity and engagement.

Engaged: Keeping students engaged means keeping them active in their learning by sparking their natural curiosity and providing opportunities for exploration.

English learners: Students whose first language is not English and who are learning English while also learning content in school. English learners are identified using the state-approved English-language–proficiency assessment and a body of evidence as needing language support to achieve standards in grade-level content in English.

Envisioning language: Language that helps students create positive mental images of success and encourages them to think about what they need to achieve their goals.

Episodic memory: Stores personal experiences with strong sensory qualities and includes vivid "flashbulb" memories.

Equality: Ensuring equality means ensuring individuals and groups are given the same resources or have the exact same opportunities, regardless of their circumstances.

Equitable: Refers to creating socially just and inclusive environments where all students can reach their potential through differentiated learning experiences.

Equity: Ensuring equity means ensuring fairness and inclusion in educational practices, particularly in behavior management, to address implicit biases and to validate all cultures.

Ethnic identity: A component of identity development that includes a sense of belonging to an ethnic group and the attitudes and feelings associated with that group membership.

Eurocentric: A viewpoint that emphasizes Western culture and values over those of other cultures, often leading to biased curricula and practices in education.

Executive functioning: A set of cognitive processes that include working memory, flexible thinking, and self-control and that are crucial for planning, decision-making, and regulating behavior.

Experiential learning: A strategy whereby students learn through hands-on experiences, investigations, experiments, problem-solving, and reflecting on their learning.

Exploratory experiences: Activities and programs in middle schools that allow students to explore different interests and potential career paths.

Flexible block schedule: A scheduling system that allows for varying lengths of instructional time to support a range of integrated activities, often implemented by interdisciplinary teams to promote PBL (project-based learning) and student inquiry.

Flexible grouping: A data-driven teaching practice in which teachers group students, based on specific skills or learning activities, allowing groups to change frequently in response to desired outcomes and student needs or interests.

Flexible seating: Classroom seating arrangements that can be easily moved and adjusted to accommodate different teaching methods and student needs (it is facilitated by having available various types of chairs, tables, and desks).

Formative assessments: Ongoing assessments, such as exit tickets, conducted during the learning process to provide feedback to students and teachers about student progress.

Free and appropriate public education (FAPE): Students with disabilities have a legal right to a FAPE. This right is guaranteed by the Individuals with Disabilities Education Act (IDEA), ensuring that students with disabilities receive necessary education and services without cost to the family.

Frontal cortex: The part of the brain involved in decision-making, problem-solving, and impulse control. It is one of the last areas to mature during adolescence.

Functional behavior assessment (FBA): An approach to understanding the purpose or reasons behind a student's challenging behavior; educators observe and analyze patterns and use them to develop effective intervention strategies.

Gender and sexual identity: Gender identity is one's personal sense of one's own gender. One may conceive of oneself as male, female, a blend of both, or neither, which can correlate with or differ from one's sex assigned at birth. Sexual identity refers to to whom one is attracted sexually and/or romantically.

General-education teacher: The teacher responsible for delivering the general curriculum to all students, often working in collaboration with a special-education teacher in a co-teaching setup.

Gifted students: Students who demonstrate exceptional levels of aptitude or competence in one or more areas, requiring different educational programs or services beyond those provided by the standard school curriculum.

Grade: A letter or number given to a student, based on the student's performance in a class, reflecting the student's overall understanding and skills.

Growth mindset: The belief that abilities and intelligence can be developed with effort and persistence. Having this mindset encourages students to see challenges as opportunities for growth.

Guided practice: Part of the direct-instruction model whereby teachers gradually release students to work more collaboratively and independently while monitoring and providing feedback to students.

Harassment: Unwelcome conduct that is based on a student being a member (or being perceived to be a member) of a protected class under federal civil-rights laws. To constitute harassment, the behavior must be severe, pervasive, or persistent, creating a hostile environment that interferes with the student's ability to participate in or benefit from school services and activities.

Harter's multifaceted view of self-competencies: A perspective theorizing that adolescents evaluate themselves in seven domains: academics, physical appearance, behavioral conduct, relationships with close friends, romantic appeal, job performance, and athletics.

Health and wellness programs/curriculum: School initiatives that promote healthy lifestyles and physical and mental well-being among students.

Heritage: Refers to the complexities and intangibles passed down through family, community, and cultural traditions that shape individual and collective identities.

Heterogeneous grouping: Arranging students based on their differences or to ensure a diversity of skills and abilities within each group.

High-prep differentiation strategies: More complex and time-intensive strategies for varying instruction, such as learning contracts, tiered activities, and PBL (project-based learning).

Higher-order thinking: Cognitive processes that involve analysis, evaluation, synthesis, and creativity, going beyond basic recall of facts.

High-stakes test: A test with significant consequences for students, teachers, or schools, such as determining promotion to the next grade or graduation.

Holland's themes: A framework for understanding individual differences in interests, categorized into six themes: realistic, investigative, artistic, social, entrepreneurial, and conventional. These themes help explain the educational and occupational choices people make.

Homogeneous grouping: Arranging students in groups based on academic achievement levels.

Hyperarousal: A state of heightened alertness and reactivity, often displayed as irritability, aggression, or difficulty in concentrating.

Hypervigilance: Constantly being on high alert, which can result in tension and an exaggerated response to perceived threats.

I-can statements: Clear, student-friendly statements that outline what students should be able to accomplish after a lesson or unit.

Identity development: The process through which adolescents explore and form their personal identities, influenced by their experiences and interactions in the educational environment.

Identity statuses (Marcia's theory): Four categories that describe different states of identity development: 1) identity diffusion: a lack of clear identity and confusion about personal direction; 2) foreclosure: adopting an identity, based on external influences, without personal exploration; 3) moratorium: active exploration of different identities without a final commitment; 4) identity achievement: having a clear and confident sense of identity following exploration.

Identifying similarities and differences: An instructional strategy whereby students analyze and compare information on a particular topic or idea and then generalize, demonstrating a deeper understanding.

Inclusive practices: Educational strategies and approaches that ensure all students, regardless of their abilities or backgrounds, participate fully in classroom and school activities.

Indirect instruction: A student-centered approach that focuses on active engagement and discovery, including inquiry-based, problem-based, and PBL (project-based learning).

Individual differences: The unique variations among individuals in their developmental trajectories, influenced by genetic, environmental, and experiential factors.

Individualized education program (IEP): A legally binding document developed for each public-school child who is eligible for special education. It outlines the child's specific learning needs, the services the school will provide, and how progress will be measured.

Individual rubric: A tool used to assess a student's work, based on specific criteria, often including different levels of performance.

Inductive reasoning: The cognitive process of making broad generalizations or principles from a body of observations.

Inquiry-based learning: An instructional method wherein students learn by engaging in investigation and exploration, often driven by their questions and interests.

Instructional objectives: Specific, measurable, short-term, observable student behaviors that match the intended results of instruction.

Instructional strategies: Methods used to achieve learning outcomes, chosen based on their support for student learning, feedback, assessment opportunities, and accessibility for all students.

Interdisciplinary team: Consists of two or more content teachers and the students they teach, promoting collaboration, planning, and evaluation of curriculum and instruction across academic areas and fostering meaningful communication with families.

Interdisciplinary units: Educational units that integrate content and skills from multiple subject areas, providing a more holistic learning experience.

Interest: We can engage students in learning in meaningful ways when we incorporate their interests into instruction.

Journals: A strategy used across various subjects to support differentiation. It involves students writing regularly to reflect on their learning, express their understanding, and connect with the content on a personal level. Journals help teachers gauge students' readiness, interests, and learning profiles so that they can tailor instruction accordingly.

Junior high: This traditional school model for grades seven through nine focused on academic rigor and preparing students for high school.

Language structure: Refers to the complex and arbitrary relationships between sounds and meanings in spoken languages and between gestures and meanings in sign languages.

Layered Curriculum®: An instructional approach that was developed by Kathy Nunley in the 1980s and that uses a menu board structure to provide students with choices in their learning. It emphasizes higher-order thinking, student autonomy, and accountability, with tasks organized in three layers of increasing complexity, based on Bloom's taxonomy.

Learner profile: Any factor that affects a student's learning, such as family situation, learning preferences, talents, cultural background, languages spoken at home, economic stability, technology access, grade-level changes, and reading proficiency.

Learning contracts: Agreements between a teacher and a student, outlining what the student will learn and how the student will demonstrate his or her learning. These can include menus, choice boards, or Think-Tac-Toe activities.

Learning goals: Desired results or outcomes that teachers want students to achieve by the end of a lesson, unit, or course.

Learning needs: Refers to the ways students learn best and most efficiently. Addressing these needs involves employing various strategies and supports to facilitate effective learning.

Learning outcomes: The specific, measurable achievements students should accomplish because of instruction.

Least restrictive environment (LRE): A principle within IDEA that states that students with disabilities should be educated with their nondisabled peers to the greatest extent appropriate.

Lesson planning: The process of outlining the instructional strategies, activities, and assessments for a specific lesson.

LGBTQIA+: An acronym that stands for lesbian, gay, bisexual, transgender, queer or questioning, intersex, asexual, and other sexual and gender identities.

Literature circles: A student-centered reading activity in which small groups read and discuss different texts, often chosen based on students' interest or readiness. Each student in the group has a specific role, and the activity is supported by structured tasks and rubrics.

Long-term memory: The storage of information over an extended period, which can be facilitated by effective processing in working memory.

Looping: The practice of keeping a group of students with the same teacher for multiple years, allowing teachers to develop deep relationships with students and their families, leading to improved student behavior, attitudes, and academic performance.

Low-prep differentiation strategies: Simple, quick-to-implement strategies for varying instruction to meet students' needs, such as offering choices in reading materials or collaboration methods.

Mental-health and wellness programs: Programs aimed at addressing the significant mental-health conditions faced by students, including ADHD, autism, depression, and eating disorders, with a focus on creating a safe, nurturing environment and providing comprehensive support services.

Metacognition: Awareness and understanding of one's own thought processes. Includes knowing how to strategically learn and recognizing one's own knowledge limits.

Middle school: An educational stage that serves as a transition between elementary and high school, typically including grades six through eight, focusing on addressing young adolescents' developmental needs.

Mindfulness: A mental practice that involves maintaining a moment-by-moment awareness of thoughts, feelings, bodily sensations, and the surrounding environment, often through breathing exercises and guided meditation.

Modeling: An instructional technique whereby the teacher demonstrates a concept or process in detail; often used to help students understand new material by providing clear examples.

Motivation: The internal drive or desire to engage in activities and achieve goals, which influences learning and development.

MTSS (multitiered system of supports): A proactive and preventive framework integrating data and instruction to maximize student achievement and support social, emotional, and behavioral needs, aiming for cohesive and equitable student support.

Multisyllabic words: Words with more than one and usually more than three syllables.

Multiple intelligences: A theory that suggests people have different kinds of intelligences, such as linguistic, logical-mathematical, musical, spatial, bodily-kinesthetic, interpersonal, intrapersonal, and naturalistic intelligences.

Myelination: The process by which myelin, a fatty substance, forms a sheath around nerve fibers, increasing the speed and efficiency of electrical signal transmission.

National Forum to Accelerate Middle-Grades Reform: An organization that advocates for academically excellent, developmentally responsive, and socially equitable middle schools.

National standards: Educational standards developed at the national level that outline what students should know and be able to do in various content areas.

Nation's Report Card: An assessment report, also known as the National Assessment of Educational Progress (NAEP), that provides a snapshot of student achievement across the United States.

Nervous system: The complex network of nerves and cells that transmit signals among different parts of the body, including the brain and spinal cord. It controls various bodily functions and plays a crucial role in the body's response to stress.

Nonbinary: A gender identity that does not fit within the traditional categories of male and female.

Nonlinguistic representations: Strategies that use nonverbal tools, such as visuals and graphic organizers, to support understanding and memory.

One teach, one assist (co-teaching model): A co-teaching model whereby one teacher leads instruction while the other provides support to individual students, as needed.

One teach, one observe (co-teaching model): A co-teaching model whereby one teacher instructs while the other observes specific student behaviors or learning processes to inform future instruction.

Oracy: The ability to express oneself fluently and grammatically in speech, an important skill for demonstrating knowledge and engaging in meaningful communication.

Orienting attention: An automatic response to new, uncertain, or surprising stimuli in the environment; important for survival and learning.

Outcomes: Goals related to behavior, academic performance, or social-emotional development that PBIS (positive behavioral interventions and supports) aims to achieve through its framework.

Pacing guide: A document that provides a timeline for teaching specific content and skills within a school year.

Parallel teaching (co-teaching model): A co-teaching model whereby teachers split the class and simultaneously teach the same content to smaller groups.

PBIS (positive behavioral interventions and supports): A behavior management approach focusing on promoting positive behavior by teaching and reinforcing appropriate behavior rather than punishing negative behavior; often used within an MTSS (multitiered system of supports) framework.

Peer pressure: The influence exerted by a peer group in encouraging a person to change his or her attitudes, values, or behaviors to conform to group norms.

Peer relationships: Interactions and bonds between individuals of similar age, often playing a significant role in social and emotional development during adolescence.

Performance tasks/assessments: Summative tasks that require students to demonstrate their understanding of a unit or large portion of content.

Pre-assessment: An assessment given before new learning begins to determine students' prior knowledge and readiness for the content.

Problem-based learning: A student-centered instructional model focused on investigating and exploring specific problems or scenarios with real-world connections.

Procedural memory: Related to skills, such as motor skills, and how to perform tasks. Practice with focused attention and feedback is crucial to developing this type of memory.

Procedures: Established methods and steps for carrying out classroom activities and routines to ensure a smooth and efficient learning environment.

Project-Based Learning (PBL): An instructional model involving extended processes and interdisciplinary projects that integrate multiple content areas, often resulting in a larger product or longer investigation.

Protocols for discussing: Structured guidelines for facilitating discussions; used to ensure that all students participate and contribute meaningfully.

Protocols for responding: Specific rules or procedures for how students should respond during discussions or activities to promote effective communication.

Psychomotor objectives: Objectives related to the development of specific physical skills, such as using tools or performing physical tasks.

Puberty: The stage of development when adolescents reach sexual maturity and become capable of reproduction. It involves physical changes, such as breast development, pubic-hair growth, and the start of menstrual cycles in females and the maturation of the penis and testicles, pubic-hair growth, and voice changes in males.

Punishment: a punitive penalty that is administered as retribution for an offense.

Punishment-based discipline: Discipline systems relying on punitive measures and exclusion to deter misconduct.

GLOSSARY

Racial identity: How individuals identify with and perceive their race; often influenced by societal perceptions and personal experiences.

RAFT (role, audience, format, and topic) assignments: This strategy allows students to explore content creatively by assuming different perspectives and writing for various audiences and formats. It's useful for differentiating instruction based on interests or readiness.

Readiness: Refers to how prepared students are for more complex lessons. Readiness allows them to experience increasingly challenging tasks as their proficiency develops, focusing on task nature rather than workload quantity.

Reinforcing effort and providing recognition: A strategy whereby teachers promote a growth mindset by acknowledging students' efforts with specific feedback and praise to motivate persistence in learning.

Reinforcing language: The emphasis of this language style is explicitly noticing positives about what students are doing socially and academically so that they are encouraged to continue engaging in those behaviors.

Relationship skills: To be able to establish and maintain healthy and rewarding relationships, students must develop relationship skills in the areas of communication, cooperation, conflict resolution, and seeking help when needed.

Reminding language: Teachers use reminding language to gives students the opportunity to take responsibility and modify behavior.

Resilience: The capacity to adapt successfully to adversity; involves systems working together to support recovery and positive outcomes.

Resiliency zone: A state of well-being in which individuals can effectively handle life's stressors. In this zone, individuals may experience emotions, such as anger or sadness, but they are not overwhelmed by them. They can easily calm themselves and continue functioning despite fluctuations in their emotional state.

Responsible decision-making: Making choices based on ethical standards, safety, social norms, the realistic evaluation of consequences, and the well-being of self and others.

Responsive Classroom®: An educational approach that integrates social-emotional learning with academic instruction, emphasizing relationship building, student autonomy, and community building.

Responsive discipline: Discipline systems focusing on finding the root of behavior, teaching students to manage it, and promoting growth, often involving restorative measures.

Responsiveness: The principle of meeting students where they are and using practical strategies to advance their understanding.

Restitution: The responsibility of students to repair harm caused by their actions.

Restorative circles: A form of restorative practice wherein everyone sits in a circle and a mediator facilitates a conversation using a talking piece to ensure every voice is heard.

Restorative discipline: An approach focusing on repairing harm, fostering accountability, and restoring relationships instead of solely punishing or excluding individuals.

Restorative practices: Methods of building and maintaining relationships in a school community, focusing on healing and repairing harm through inclusive dialogue and mutual agreement.

Retellings for situational appropriateness: Activities where students practice retelling stories or information in contextually appropriate ways, enhancing their language skills.

Risky behaviors: Actions that can potentially expose individuals to harm or significant risk, often observed among adolescents, including sexual activity, substance use, and rule-breaking behaviors.

Role-playing for situational appropriateness: An instructional strategy wherein students act out scenarios to practice using language and behavior that is appropriate for different situations.

Routines: Regular, repeated procedures or practices followed in the classroom to manage daily activities and transitions smoothly.

Rubric: A scoring guide used to evaluate the quality of students' constructed responses. Rubrics typically include criteria and levels of performance.

Safe spaces: Designated areas within schools where students can go to feel secure, calm down, and utilize strategies to manage their emotions and behaviors effectively.

Schema: Mental models or representations that are a collection of knowledge previously gained and that affect how new information is processed.

School climate: The quality and character of school life, based on patterns of experience reflecting norms, goals, values, interpersonal relationships, teaching practices, and organizational structures; linked to academic performance and overall school success.

Scope and sequence: A framework that outlines the content to be taught (scope) and the order in which it will be taught (sequence).

Selective attention: The ability of learners to focus on goal-directed aspects of the environment, which becomes more controlled and refined with age.

Self-assessments: Evaluations that individuals make about their own abilities and competencies in various domains, such as academics, physical appearance, and social relationships.

Self-awareness: Recognizing one's emotions, values, strengths, and limitations and also understanding the influence of these factors on one's behavior.

Self-contained classroom: An elementary school setting where one teacher instructs the same group of students in multiple subjects throughout the day.

Self-directed learning: A form of learning wherein individuals take the initiative to diagnose their learning needs, formulate learning goals, identify resources for learning, select and implement learning strategies, and evaluate learning outcomes. It requires high levels of self-regulation and intrinsic motivation.

Self-efficacy: The belief in one's own ability to succeed in specific situations or accomplish a task, which plays a crucial role in how goals, tasks, and challenges are approached.

Self-management: The ability to regulate emotions, thoughts, and behaviors effectively in different situations, including managing stress and achieving personal goals.

Self-regulation: A complex set of mental processes that involve utilizing strategies or behaviors to achieve goals. It includes the ability to manage one's emotions, behaviors, and thoughts in pursuit of long-term goals. Self-regulated students are active participants in their own learning, employing metacognitive, motivational, and behavioral strategies to reach their objectives.

Semantic map: A strategy for graphically representing concepts.

Semantic memory: Holds propositional knowledge, including facts, concepts, and strategies; central to subjects like math, English, social sciences, and history.

Sentence frames: Structures for writing and speaking in which words have been removed from a sentence. Students then complete the sentence by filling in the removed words to practice and build on language skills, such as academic vocabulary.

Sequential memory: The ability to recall information in a specific order; essential for tasks like reading and problem-solving; often impacted by trauma.

Setting objectives and providing feedback: Strategies that focus on transparency of learning goals for students and giving explicit, constructive feedback to help them progress in understanding content.

Sexual fluidity: The concept that sexual orientation can change over time and is not fixed, allowing for a range of attractions and experiences.

Sexual orientation: The type of sexual, romantic, or emotional attraction one feels for others, often categorized as heterosexual, homosexual, bisexual, and so on.

Shared vision: A common understanding and agreement among all stakeholders in a school community regarding the goals and mission of the school.

Silent signal: A nonverbal signal, such as a hand gesture or clapping rhythm, used by teachers to quickly gain students' attention without disrupting the flow of the lesson.

Social and emotional learning (SEL): The process of acquiring and applying knowledge, skills, and attitudes to develop emotional intelligence, manage emotions, and achieve personal and collective goals, fostering empathy, maintaining healthy relationships, and making responsible decisions in education and life.

Social awareness: The ability to empathize with others, understand social norms for behavior, and recognize resources and supports available in the community.

Social belonging: The feeling of being connected to and accepted by a group, which is a significant aspect of social development during adolescence.

Social justice: Teaching and practices aimed at addressing and correcting unjustified power differences in society, providing all students with learning opportunities regardless of their gender, race, ethnicity, or first language.

Special-education teacher: A teacher who is specialized in working with students with disabilities, providing SDI (specially designed instruction), and collaborating with general-education teachers to support diverse learning needs.

Specially designed instruction (SDI): Instruction tailored to meet the unique needs of students with disabilities, based on their present level of academic and functional performance and related to their individualized education program (IEP) goals.

Standards: Benchmarks that define the knowledge and skills students should acquire at each grade level within a content area.

Standards-based grading (SBG): A grading system that assesses students based on their understanding of specific learning standards rather than comparing them to each other.

Station teaching (co-teaching model): A co-teaching model according to which teachers divide content and students. Each teacher instructs part of the content to a portion of the students, who then rotate to the other station(s).

Student autonomy: The degree to which students have control over their own learning process, making choices about what and how they learn.

Student learning outcomes (SLOs): Specific, measurable achievements that students are expected to reach because of instruction.

Student-centered: An educational approach whereby teaching is tailored to the interests, abilities, and learning styles of students, encouraging them to take an active role in their learning.

Summarizing and note-taking: Strategies requiring students to organize or condense information to aid comprehension and retention.

Summative assessment: An assessment given at the end of a unit or course to evaluate student learning against defined objectives.

Systemic racism: Forms of racism that are embedded in the policies and practices of social and political institutions, which can result in the exclusion or promotion of designated groups.

Team teaching (co-teaching model): A co-teaching model wherein both teachers deliver instruction together in a coordinated and interactive manner.

The Successful Middle School: This We Believe: A major position paper by AMLE, outlining the attributes and characteristics of successful middle schools.

Tiered Assignments: Tasks designed at varying levels of difficulty to meet students where they are in their understanding and to challenge them appropriately.

Total physical response (TPR): A language-learning approach based on the relationship between language and its physical representation or execution. TPR emphasizes the use of physical activity for increasing meaningful learning opportunities and language retention. A TPR lesson involves a detailed series of consecutive actions, accompanied by a series of commands or instructions given by the teacher. Students respond by listening and performing the appropriate actions.

Tracking: A method used by schools to group students according to their perceived abilities, IQs, or achievement levels. Students are placed in high, middle, or low tracks to provide them with a level of curriculum and instruction that is appropriate to their needs. The practice of tracking began in the 1930s and has been the subject of intense controversy for decades.

Traditional scheduling: A school schedule characterized by a fixed number of periods of equal length each day, with a teacher-centered approach to instruction.

Transgender and Nongender-conforming youth: Adolescents whose gender identity differs from the sex to which they were assigned at birth; they often experience unique stresses during puberty.

Trauma-informed practices: Approaches in education and other fields that recognize and respond to the impact of traumatic stress on individuals, emphasizing safety, trust, and empowerment.

Turning points: Influential reports, published by the Carnegie Corporation in 1989 and 2000, providing recommendations for improving middle grades education.

Twice Exceptional (2e): Students who are gifted and also have a learning disability or other special needs, requiring specialized instructional strategies to support both their advanced abilities and their challenges.

Unit plan: Organization and sequencing of content, activities, and assessments for a specific unit of instruction.

Universal design for learning (UDL): An educational framework that guides the development of flexible learning environments and learning spaces that can accommodate individual learning differences. It emphasizes the use of multiple means of engagement, representation, and expression.

Universal screening: Tools used to identify students needing additional support within the PBIS (positive behavioral interventions and supports) framework.

Varied and ongoing assessment: A range of different methods and continuous evaluations used to monitor and support student learning throughout the school year.

Varied questions: A strategy in differentiated instruction whereby questions are tailored to students' readiness, interests, and learning approaches. This helps all students contribute to discussions and engage with the content meaningfully.

Voice and choice: Educational practices that allow students to have input into and make choices about their learning activities. This increases engagement and motivation by giving students a sense of ownership and control over their learning.

Webb's depth of knowledge (DOK): A framework for designing cognitively demanding tasks, focusing on recall/reproduce, skill/concept, strategic thinking, and extending thinking.

William Alexander: A pioneer in the middle school movement who introduced the concept of middle schools in his work *The Emergent Middle School* in 1968.

Word map: A visual representation of a definition. This type of mapping is often applied to reading instruction.

Working memory: The part of memory where attended information is processed and connected to existing knowledge; it has limited capacity and is crucial for learning.

Yearly plan: The mapping of content and skills to be taught over an academic year, ensuring coverage of all required standards.

Youth Risk Behavior Survey (YRBS): A national survey, conducted by the CDC, that monitors health-related behaviors, including physical activity and sedentary behaviors, in youth.

Zero-tolerance policies: Strict policies that apply severe punishment for infractions without consideration of individual circumstances, historically leading to significant disparities in school discipline.

Index

Aaron (pseudonym), 18–19, 76, 88–89, 91
abstract concepts, 37
abstract thinking skills, 77, 97
academic identity, 55
accessibility, 147
accountability, 217, 357; co-teaching and, 118; in Layered Curriculum, 205; for microaggressions, 84; NCLB and, 218; restorative discipline and, 285; rubric for, 215
ACEs. *See* adverse childhood experiences
action verbs, in lesson planning, 176
active learning, 328
The Active View of Reading, 236, *236*
activity driven planning, 250
adequate yearly progress (AYP), 218, 357
ADHD. *See* attention deficit hyperactivity disorder
adolescent brain, research on, 47–48
adolescents, 75, 328, 331, 357; asset-based language for, 22; empowerment of, 3; knowledge bases of, 25–26; obesity of, 45. *See also* early adolescence
adult advocate, 35, 329, 346, 357
adult height, 23
advance organizers, 357
adverse childhood experiences (ACEs), 122, 134, 357
Advisory Program Examples and Resources, *92*

advisory programs, 132, 331, 335, 340, 347, 357; exploratory curriculum in, 348; identity development and, 89; mentors in, 346; SEL in, 49, 117, 127, 333; social development in, 90, 91; Template for, *347*; trauma-informed practice and, 131, 134
advocacy, 91, 138, 150, 321, 331
affective filter, 156, 358
affective-needs teachers, 304–5
Alexander, William, 322–23, 376
Alignment of AMLE Characteristics with Book Chapters, *4*
alternate-day block schedule, 337, 353, 358
alternative teaching (co-teaching model), 105, 111, 358
AMLE. *See* Association for Middle Level Education
amygdala, 47, 61, 126, 358
analogizing, 263
analytic rubric, 228
anxiety, 50, 132; affective filter relation to, 156; classroom management and, 279; expressive language relation to, 123; mindfulness relation to, 130; from school shootings, 35–36; sensory needs and, 129
anxiety disorders, 50, 358
Archer, A., 264–65
asexuality, 76, 87
assessment, 67–68, 168, 230, 325, 358; compacting relation to, 206; culturally

responsive teaching relation to, 161; of enduring understanding, 174; evaluation compared to, 217; feedback from, 180; one-minute papers for, 220; PLCs relation to, 172; rubric for, 229; self-, 30–31, 73, 227, 372; summative, 219, 222–24, 374; tiered assignments and, 207

asset-based language, 22, 358

assets-based perspective, 197

Assignment example connection with ELA and Science Earth PBL, *182*

assimilation, 80, 358

Association for Middle Level Education (AMLE), 2, 3, 326–27, 344, 358; exploratory curriculum and, 348; middle grades curriculum and, 165, 166, 346, 353; varied and ongoing assessment and, 218

attachment theory, 32

attendance, 140, 161, 351

attention, 5, 369, 372; curiosity relation to, 7–8; differentiated instruction and, 202; executive function relation to, 60, 73; focus of, 249; mindfulness relation to, 130; negative, 289; sleep relation to, 10

attention deficit hyperactivity disorder (ADHD), 60, 351, 357

attention lapses, 123

author and you questions, 262

authoritarian-autocratic parenting, 32

authoritarian-democratic parenting, 30–31, 358

autism, 117, 129, 351

autobiographical memory, 6, 26, 358

automatic alphabetic phase, 237

avoidance behaviors, 70

AYP. *See* adequate yearly progress

backward design, 358; learning activities in, 174–75; in lesson planning, 173

Barron, Tammy L., 14, *14*

basic needs, 10

Beck, I. L., 261

behavioral expectations, 284

behavior management, 113, 146, 280; MTSS and, 117–19; PBIS and, 116, 311. *See also* classroom management

belonging, 77, 374; community relation to, 89; differentiated instruction relation to, 194

Benefits and Frequencies of Each Model, *106–7*

Bennett, V. K., 51–52

bias, 141, 142, 282, 311; familiarity, 253; segregation and, 151

biculturalism, 80, 359

bidirectional conversation, 186

big behaviors, 280, 300–301, 304–6, 307

bilateral coordination, emotional regulation and, 130

Black, indigenous, and other people of color (BIPOC), 144–45

Black, P., 219–20

Blakemore, S. J., 31

block scheduling, 330, 335, 337–38, 353, 359, 364

Bloom, Benjamin, 184

Bloom's taxonomy, 179, *179*, 184, *185*, 186, 359; Layered Curriculum relation to, 205; questions and, 255–56, *256–60*; Question Stems for, *187*

Boaler, Jo, 194

body image, 359; LGBTQIA+ relation to, 46; puberty relation to, 43–44; young adult literature about, 154

body language, 296

body neutrality, 46, 359

body positivity, 46, 359

book-banning laws, 153

boundaries, expectations and, 297

braces, 43

brain dump, 248–49

brainstem, in Hand Model of the Brain, 126

Brinegar, K., 80, 89

Brooklyn (pseudonym), 18, 124, 132, 288–90

building and bridging, 156, 359

bullying, 349–50, 359, 362

Busey, C. L., 81

Bush, George W., 218

business partners, 329

Cade (pseudonym), 19; checklists of, 72, *72*; executive function and, 59, 60–61, 65; interventions for, 71, 73

Caldwell, Martha, 89–90

career exploration, 348
Carnegie Corporation, 324–25, 359
Carnegie Report for New York's Council on Advancing Adolescent Literacy, 240
Cartwright, K. B., 236
CASEL. *See* Collaborative for Academic, Social, and Emotional Learning
Caskey, M., 80, 89
Catamount School, 17
Centers for Disease Control and Prevention (CDC), 49, 52, 84–85, 359
centers/stations, 197, 359
cerebellum, 47, 359
cerebral cortex, in Hand Model of the Brain, 126
challenging curriculum, 3, 194, 359
Chamberlain, K., 80–81
Characteristics of Successful Middle Schools, 2
Checkerboard Problem, *213*
checking-the-box questions, 251
checklists, 72, *72*; for executive function, 71; for gender-inclusive environments, 91
chosen names, in learning management systems, 91
chunking, 5, 359
Chunking a Standard, *177*
Circle Fever Task, *208*
citizen science, 8
citizenship, 324, 326
civic competence, 146
Clapp, Amanda, 8, 15, *15*, 168, 204, 205
classroom contracts, 146
classroom debates, 220
classroom designs, 298, *299*
classroom discourse, 123; DOK relation to, 185; middle grades curriculum for, 165
classroom management, 180, 279–80, 351; commanding presence for, 296; consistency in, 299–300; democratic approach in, 308
classroom rules, 290–91, *291*, 299
class transitions, 293
cleanliness, 293
Cleary, T. J., 64, 65
climate of safety, 300
Clinton, Bill, 281
close reading, 247

clubs, 90; culturally responsive teaching in, 152; identity development and, 89
Code of Conduct Consequences, *312–17*
cognates, 265, 360
cognitive capabilities, 7; executive function relation to, 60; homework relation to, 66; myelination relation to, 47
cognitive dissonance, 89–90
cognitive objectives, 176, 360
cognitive psychology, 3
cohort differences, 23, 360
collaboration, *61*, *81*, 360; in cooperative learning, 183; in culturally responsive teaching, 142; on goals, 228; IDEA relation to, 101; IEP relation to, 102; with interdisciplinary team, 331, 339, 344; mutuality and, 128; in restorative discipline, 286; for well-being, 350. *See also* co-teaching
Collaborative for Academic, Social, and Emotional Learning (CASEL), 124, 134, 360
Collaborative Summarizing, 156–57, 360
colorincolorado.org, 160
commanding presence, for classroom management, 296
common planning time, 338, 360
communication, 144, 158, 172, 239; in culturally responsive teaching, 142–43; disciplinary literacy and, 244; with families, 300, 311, 326; grades as, 224, 226, 230; in math classes, 145; in MTSS, 345; nonverbal, 295, 303; in restorative discipline, 285–86; tone of, 297
community, 297; in advisory programs, 131; belonging relation to, 89; culture relation to, 155–56; democratic approach to, 310; differentiated instruction relation to, 194; flexible grouping relation to, 202; in general discipline philosophy, 308–9; identity development relation to, 76; journals relation to, 213; math classes relation to, 145; relationships in, 288, 324, 325–26; restorative circles relation to, 286–87
community partners, 329, 349, 353
compacting, 206, 207, 360
comprehensible input, 156, 360
comprehensive school health plan, 350, 360

concept circles, 267, *270*
concept map, 220, 272
conceptual learning, 150
conflict-resolution skills, 33
connotation, 245, 360
consequence, 281, 360
consistency, 295; in classroom management, 299–300; of modeling, 67
consolidated alphabetic phase, 237
constructivist view of learning, 198, 361
content standards, 168, 361
context processors, 237
continuity, 326
contraception, 51
convergent questions, 254, *255*
cooperative learning, 324, 361; collaboration in, 183; direct instruction relation to, 181
coordination, 47
coping strategies, 126, 128
Cornell Lab of Ornithology, Feederwatch project, 8
Cornell Notes, 272
corpus callosum, 47, 361
Costa's levels-of-thinking-and-questioning model, 255–56, *256–60*
co-teaching, 99–100, 358, 360, 369, 370; accountability and, 118; Benefits and Frequencies of Each Model, *106–7*; disabilities relation to, 345; in English language arts, 104, 105, 109; one teach, one assist, 105, 111–12; parallel, 105, 109, 370; relationships in, 112–13; SDI and, 102–3; Six Models for, *104*; station teaching, 105, 110–11, 114, 203, 374; team teaching, 105, 344, 375
Counting Cubes Task, *189*
Counting Triangles Problem, *214*
country project, 146–47
COVID-19 pandemic, 51, 349
creativity: in differentiated instruction, 215; for flexible seating, 298; middle grades curriculum for, 165, 166
Crisis Prevention Institute, 305
crisis-response model, 352
critical thinking: disciplinary literacy and, 242–43; high-level questions for, 186; middle grades curriculum for, 165, 166
CRMT. *See* culturally relevant mathematics teaching

cross-curricular opportunities, 168, 361
crosswalk process, in lesson planning, 172
cultural differences, 23, 361
cultural identity, 76, *96*, 361
cultural inequities, 94
culturally relevant mathematics teaching (CRMT), 145
culturally relevant pedagogy, 139, 361
culturally responsive discipline, 139, 280–81, 288, 311, 361
culturally responsive teaching, 139–41, 152, 157, 160, 361; for classroom management, 280; communication in, 142–43; in math classes, 145, 161; in social studies classes, 143–44, 146, 161
Culturally Responsive Teaching (New America), 140–41
culturally responsive teaching competencies, 141, 153, 160, 361
culturally sustaining pedagogy, 150, 161, 361
cultural norms, 139
cultural responsiveness, 156
culture, community relation to, 155–56
curiosity, 361; attention relation to, 7–8; differentiated instruction relation to, 193–94; environmental novelty relation to, 28–29; environments relation to, 35, 37; in experiential learning, 182; exploratory curriculum for, 166; pornography relation to, 52; in preschool years, 24
curriculum resources, diversity in, 150–51
cyber-bullying, 349, 362

data-based decision-making, 283, 362
data collection, 114; assessment for, 217; differentiated instruction relation to, 196; for interventions, 172; for progress monitoring, 115, 116
Dawson, P., 67–68, 69
dead names, 89, 91
Dearborn, Grace, 291, 299
debrief circles, 159, 362
decision-making, 26–27, 339; data-based, 283, 362; emotions relation to, 126; middle grades curriculum for, 165, 166; responsible, 125, 134, 371
declarative memory, 25–26

deep learning, 5, 362
deep processing, 7, 252
de-escalation, 300–301, *302*, 303, 304
defiant behavior, 50
deficiency model, 145
deficit-based labels, 139, 155
deficit monitor, 155, 362
Dehaene, Stanislas, 7–10
dehydroepiandrosterone (DHEA), 45
democratic approach, 362; in classroom management, 308; for classroom rules, 290–91; to community, 310
denotation, 245, 362
departmentalized schedule, 337, 362
depression, 50, 130
developmentalists, 21, 362
developmentally responsive, 2–3, 362
developmental psychology, 21
DHEA. *See* dehydroepiandrosterone
diagnostic assessment, 219, 362
differentiated instruction, 201, 214–15, 362; attention and, 202; journals in, 212–13; lesson planning relation to, 195; literature circles and, 210–11; motivation relation to, 194; multiple intelligences relation to, 198; performance tasks/assessments relation to, 199–200; readiness relation to, 193–94, 196–97, 199; station teaching and, 203; varied questions in, 209
differentiation, 175, 362
differentiation overload, 250
Dion (pseudonym), 18, 41, 53, 54
directed note-taking activity (DNA), 272
direct instruction, 181, 362; in backward design, 175; DNA and, 272; in English language arts, 180
disabilities, 99, 282, 304–6; alternative teaching relation to, 111; co-teaching relation to, 345; IEP for, 102, 118; young adult literature about, 153
disciplinary literacy, 241, 242–46, 273–74
discipline, 362; culturally responsive, 139, 280–81, 288, 311, 361; for fighting, 310; responsive, 282; restorative, 280, 285–88, 311, 351, 372
discipline-specific strategies, for reading comprehension, 241
discrimination, 142

discussing, protocols for, 370
discussion prompts, evaluation and, 159–60
dissociation, 123, 363
distraction, 5, 19, 59, 112
divergent questions, 254, *255*
diversity, 90, 137–38, 167, 363; culturally responsive teaching and, 140, 160; culturally sustaining pedagogy and, 161; in curriculum resources, 150–51; in environments, 35, 37–38; inclusion and, 344–45
divorce, 32
DNA. *See* directed note-taking activity
DOK. *See* Webb's depth of knowledge
Dollar Street, 151
domains of development, 22–23, 363
"Don't Say Gay" bill, 87
Doubet, K. J., 195–96
dressed up questions, 252
drugs, 52, 53
Duke, N. K., 236
Durlak, J. A., 124–25
Dweck, Carol, 9, 194
dysregulation, 300–301, 307

EAHCA. *See* Education of All Handicapped Children Act
early adolescence, 22, 24, 33, 37, 363; curiosity in, 28; environments relation to, 34–35; life experience in, 23; second languages in, 8
early college, 73
eating disorders, 45, 46, 351
e-cigarettes, 52, 53
ed-tech games, 222
educational reforms, 334
Education of All Handicapped Children Act (EAHCA), 101–2
effortful learning, 251–52
Ehri's Phases of Word Reading, 237
8th grade Geology Unit Overview, *170*
8th graders in cafeteria, *79*
electives, 152, 348. *See also* exploratory curriculum
elementary schools, 322, 339
Ellerbrock, C. R., 3, 151
ELs. *See* English learners
The Emergent Middle School (Alexander), 322–23

Emma (pseudonym), 63
emotional regulation, 60, 62–63, 129, 363; amygdala relation to, 47; bilateral coordination and, 130. *See also* social and emotional learning
emotions, 333; in classroom management, 299–300; decision-making relation to, 126; puberty and, 128
empathy, 63, 125
empowerment, 3, 363
enduring understanding, 174
engaged, 3, 194, 363
engagement, 146; activity-driven planning and, 250; with big behaviors, 307; block scheduling for, 330
English language arts, 218; alternative teaching in, 111; content standards in, 168; co-teaching in, 104, 105, 109; culturally responsive teaching in, 144, 161; direct instruction in, 180; interdisciplinary team in, 332; lesson planning in, 171; literature circles in, 211; MTSS relation to, 117; PBL in, 182; SBG in, 147; scripted questions for, 190
English learners (ELs), 155, 158, 160, 363; cognates and, 265; Collaborative Summarizing relation to, 157; culturally responsive teaching for, 161; literacy of, 245–46
environmental novelty, 28–29
environments, 8, 327; classroom management and, 280; in culturally responsive teaching, 142; diversity in, 35, 37–38; early adolescence relation to, 34–35; gender-inclusive, 91; hormone-behavior manifestation relation to, 48; identity development relation to, 89; identity resolution relation to, 30; inclusive, 3, 100; interests relation to, 198; mental health relation to, 49; mindfulness relation to, 130; organizational structures relation to, 329; psychological development relation to, 95, 97; restrictive, 101; risky behaviors relation to, 49; student autonomy relation to, 65; well-being relation to, 56
envisioning language, 297, 363
episodic memory, 6, 363

equality, 137–38, 363
equitable, 3, 363
equity, 137–38, 282, 325, 363; culturally responsive teaching and, 140, 160; shared authority and, 150
Erikson, E. H., 24, 76
Espelage, D. L., 86
ESSA. *See* Every Student Succeeds Act
essays, graphic organizer for, 111
ethnic identity, 363; Organizations and Resources for, *96*; self-esteem relation to, 80
Eurocentric, 80–81, 280, 363
evaluation: assessment compared to, 217; discussion prompts and, 159–60; summative assessment for, 222–23
Every Student Succeeds Act (ESSA), 218, 230
evidence-based strategies, 274
exceptionalities, 195
exclusionary punishment, 280–81
executive function, 25–26, 37, 59, 61, 364; frontal cortex relation to, 47; goals relation to, 60, 69; graphic organizer for, 64; interventions for, 68–71; self-regulation and, 19, 65, 67, 73
Exemplars of Developmentally Appropriate Strategies and Practices in Middle Schools, *332*
expectations, 81, 200; behavioral, 284; boundaries and, 297; in classroom contracts, 146; in culturally responsive teaching, 142; in general discipline philosophy, 308; of parents, 83; PBIS and, 285; for restorative circles, 287; in rubric, 227, 228, 229; self-regulation relation to, 64–65
experiential learning, 180, 182, 190, 364
experiments: with gender identity, 88–89; in self-expression, 77, 97
exploration activities, 340; in math classes, 188; in science classes, 149–50
exploratory curriculum, 166, 327, 330, 333, 348
exploratory experiences, 323, 364
expressive language, anxiety relation to, 123
extension activities, 109
extracurricular activities, 17
extrinsic motivation, 60–61, 285

facilitation: of questions, 188; of whole-class discussion, 190
familiarity bias, 253
families, 329; advocacy for, 138; communication with, 300, 311, 326; culturally responsive teaching relation to, 142; peer relationships relation to, 78; relationships with, 343; school governance relation to, 324–25
family traditions, 152
FAPE. *See* free and appropriate public education
FBA. *See* functional behavior assessment
feedback, 70–71; from assessment, 180; formative assessments and, 219–20; for objectives, 184; peer, 221; reinforcing language in, 297–98; rubric and, 224, 229, 230
Feederwatch project, of Cornell Lab of Ornithology, 8
field trips, 309, 337
fighting, 307, 310, 351
Finnan, C., 89
The Five Big Ideas of Beginning Reading & Writing, 233, *234*
504 plan, 99–100, 357
flashbulb memories, 6
flexible block schedule, 335, 337–38, 353, 364
flexible grouping, 202, 342, 343, 353, 364
flexible seating, 298, 364
Flint, Michigan, 150
Florida, 52, 87
Flowers, N., 344
fluency, 158, 240, 244–45
focus, 19; of attention, 249; mental health relation to, 132; mindfulness for, 65
foods classes, 152
Formative, 110
formative assessments, 218, 222, 364; feedback relation to, 219–20; teacher-to-student conferences and, 202–3
forward design, in lesson planning, 173
foster-care placement, 18, 124
foundational reading, 242
Frayer diagrams, 265, *266*
free and appropriate public education (FAPE), 364; EAHCA relation to, 102; IDEA relation to, 101

free and reduced lunch, 126
frontal cortex, 47, 364
frontal lobe, 61, 128
full alphabetic phase, 237
functional behavior assessment (FBA), 112, 364

Gainer, J., 81
Galván, A., 48
gapminder.com, 151
Gardner, T. W., 60
Gay, Geneva, 139, 140
gender identity, 76, 84–85, *86*, 364; experiments with, 88–89; pronouns relation to, 86
gender-inclusive environments, 91
Gender Spectrum, 91
general discipline philosophy, 308–9
general-education classrooms, 99
general-education teacher, 364; co-teaching relation to, 112; EAHCA relation to, 101; modeling by, 105; UDL relation to, 103
Generation Alpha, 48
Generation Z, 51
Generic *versus* Discipline-Specific Reading Strategies, *241*
genius hour, 333
geography, 152
gifted students, 101, 364
Gigi (pseudonym), 17, 33–34
global citizens, 90, 147
global self-worth, 30
goals, 173, 367; in advisory programs, 346; in backward design, 174; for behavior management, 117–18; collaboration on, 228; executive function relation to, 60, 69; grade-level learning, 250; in lesson planning, 190; in middle grades curriculum, 175; for SEL, 127; self-regulation relation to, 64, 73; shared, 34; transparency of, 184
Gotcha, 130
Gough, P. B., 234–35
government-controlled utilities, 150
grade-level learning goals, 250
grades, 224, 225, 226, 230, 365. *See also* standards-based grading
gradual-release model, 180

graduation rates, 140, 161, 349
graphic novels, 153
graphic organizer, 64, 147, *148–49*; for Collaborative Summarizing, 156–57; direct instruction relation to, 181; in English language arts, 190; for essays, 111; for nonlinguistic representations, 183; for word learning, 267
grounding exercises, 130–31
group discussions, 158, 290
growth hormone, 45
growth mindset, 9, 17, 365; in advisory programs, 131; journals for, 212; mindfulness and, 129; motivation for, 183; self-awareness and, 125
growth spurts, 42
Guare, R., 67–68, 69
guidance counselors, 90, 131, 329
guided practice, 180, 365
Gun Free Schools Act, 281

Hand Model of the Brain, 126, *127*
harassment, 86, 349–50, 365
Harter's multifaceted view of self-competencies, 30, 365
health and wellness programs/curriculum, 46, 324, 329, 349, 350–51, 353, 365
health coordinators, 324
healthy habits, 46
Henderson, Bruce, 14, *14*
heritage, 155–56, 365
heterogeneous grouping, 202, 342, 365
Hickey, Meghan, 68
higher-order thinking, 365; in Layered Curriculum, 205; varied questions relation to, 209
high-interest texts, in libraries, 153
high-level questions, 186
high-prep differentiation strategies, 201, *201*, 214, 215, 365
high schools, 2, 322, 338, 339
high-stakes test, 217–18, 365
hippocampus, in Hand Model of the Brain, 126
HIV education, 52, *53*
Hockett, J. A., 195–96
holistic rubric, 228
Holland's themes, 29, 365
Holt, K. A., 210

home economics, 152
home groups, 158
home language, 138
homeroom, 333
homework: intention in, 183; self-regulation relation to, 65–66
homogeneous grouping, 342, 365
homosexual activity, 52
hookup culture, 52
hormone-behavior manifestation, 48
hormones, 45
House Arrest (Holt), 210, *210*
How Disciplinary Professionals Read, *243*
How We Learn (Dehaene), 7
Hughes, C., 264–65
hyperarousal, 123, 365
hypervigilance, 123, 366
hypotheses, 184

I-can statements, 67, 205, 366
IDEA. *See* Individuals with Disabilities Education Act
IDEIA. *See* Individual with Disabilities Education Improvement Act
identifying similarities and differences, 366
identity achievement, 30
identity confusion, 30
identity development, 29–30, 81, 83, 279, 366; environments relation to, 89; peer relationships relation to, 76, 78, 82; racial, 80; safe spaces for, 97; SEL and, 90
identity diffusion, 29
identity resolution, 30, 32
identity statuses, 29–30, 366
IEP. *See* individualized education program
IES Practice Guide, 239
ignorance, 36
incentive programs, 285
inclusion: culturally responsive teaching and, 140, 160; diversity and, 344–45
inclusion teacher, 113
inclusive education, 102
inclusive environments, 3, 100
inclusive practices, 101, 311, 366
independence, 41, 206
indirect instruction, 181, 366
individual differences, 22, 366
individual interests, 29

individualized education program (IEP), 99–100, 366; for disabilities, 102, 118; inventive plan in, 117
individual rubric, 227, 366
Individuals with Disabilities Education Act (IDEA), 99, 101
Individual with Disabilities Education Improvement Act (IDEIA), 103
individuation, 32, 33
inductive reasoning, 160, 366
inequities, 94, 138
infancy, 24
infographics, 272
Inhelder, B., 25
initiate, response, evaluate (IRE), 186
inquiry-based instruction, 195
inquiry-based learning, 366
in-school suspension, 82, 282
instructional objectives, 175–76, 177–78, 179–80, 366
instructional strategies, 10–11, 183–84, 366; in backward design, 174; intention in, 180; for SLOs, 190
integrative curriculum, 166
intellectual challenge, 35
intention: in homework, 183; in instructional strategies, 180
intentionality, in backward design, 173
interdisciplinary team, 332–33, 335, 340, 353, 367; collaboration with, 331, 339, 344; in flexible block schedule, 338; flexible grouping relation to, 343; for middle grades curriculum, 167; PBL in, 342
interdisciplinary units, 168, 367
interest, 367; journals relation to, 212–13; in Layered Curriculum, 205; literature circles relation to, 210–11; varied questions relation to, 209
interests, 29, 37; differentiated instruction relation to, 193–94, 197–98; environments relation to, 198; flexible grouping relation to, 202
interpersonal skills, 330
interventions, 73, 285; data collection for, 172; for executive function, 68–71; in MTSS, 114–16; SEL in, 124–25, 127; word study, 263. *See also* multitiered system of supports; positive behavioral interventions and supports

interview grid, debrief circle and, 159
inventive plan, 117
Iowa, 52
IRE. *See* initiate, response, evaluate
Iris Center, 240

Jake (pseudonym), 63
Jennings, P. A., 122–23
journals, 367; in differentiated instruction, 212–13; self-reflection in, 68
junior high, 322, *323*, 330, 334, 367

Kaiser Family Foundation, 44–45
Kassel, Kayleigh, 13, *13*, 171
Khalil (pseudonym), 17, 24, 31, 33–34
King, Martin Luther, Jr., 249
King-Sears, M. E., 102
Know, Want to Know, Learn (KWL), 181
know-learn strategy, 248–49
knowledge bases, 25–27
Knowles, Malcolm, 66
know-want, 248–49
Kombe, D., 89
Krashen, Stephen, 156, 358
Krystal (pseudonym), 19, 76, 81–83
Kucan, L., 261
KWL. *See* Know, Want to Know, Learn

Ladson-Billings, Gloria, 138–39
language comprehension, 235
language structure, 157–58, 367
Larry (pseudonym), 18, 76, 78, 79–80
Layered Curriculum, 203, 205, *205*, *206*, *207*, 367. *See also* learning contracts
leaders, 327–28
learned behavior, culture as, 155
learner profile, 367
learning activities, in backward design, 174–75
learning approach, 205, 212–13, 327
learning contracts, 203–4, 367; differentiated instruction relation to, 197; tiered assignments and, 207
learning gaps, 248, 252
learning goals, 367; backward design relation to, 174; grade-level, 250; in lesson planning, 173
learning management systems, chosen names in, 91

learning needs, 193–94, 367
learning objectives, 176, 190
learning process, 4, 199
learning styles, 198, 250
least restrictive environment (LRE), 367; co-teaching relation to, 104; IDEA relation to, 101
Lee, C. D., 240
Lerner, R. M., 22
lesson planning, 165, 368; backward design in, 173; differentiated instruction relation to, 195; goals in, 190; instructional objectives in, 175–76, 177–78, 179–80; for science classes, *169–70*; student autonomy in, 168, 171–72
Letter from the Birmingham Jail (King), 249
LGBTQIA+, 76, 368; advocacy for, 91; body image relation to, 46; mental health and, 85, 86; young adult literature about, 155
LGBTQIA+ Organizations and Resources, *93*
libraries, high-interest texts in, 153
life experience: in culturally responsive teaching, 141; in early adolescence, 23
lifelong learners, 325
Lily (pseudonym), 63
limbic system, in Hand Model of the Brain, 126
linguistically responsive teaching, 157
Lipsitz, J., 2
listening, 242–43, 245
list-group-label, 267, *270*
literacy, 238, 242–46, 273–74; note-taking for, 271; in science classes, 324
literature: disciplinary literacy and, 244; young adult, 153–55
Literature Circle Calendar, *211*
Literature Circle Job Rubrics, *212*
literature circles, 171, 210–11, 368
Liza (pseudonym), 24, 76; anxiety of, 35–36; asexuality and, 87; executive function and, 61; long-term projects and, 27–28; OCPD and, 19, 25, 132
local health department, 53
"locker problem," 213
logical argument, in writing, 244

long-term memory, 6, 25, 368; effortful learning and, 251; nonexamples, 252; prior knowledge and, 248
long-term projects, 27–28
looping, 343, 368
low-level questions, 186
low-prep differentiation strategies, 201, *201*, 214, 215, 368
LRE. *See* least restrictive environment

mainstreaming, 101–2
mandatory reporter, 49
mantras, 68, 333
Marcia's theory, 29–30, 31, 76, 366
marginalized groups, 83, 138, 150; deficit-based labels for, 139; stereotypes and, 142; zero-tolerance policies relation to, 281, 282
marijuana, 53
Marzano, R. J., 183–84
Masten, A. S., 133
math classes, *222*; co-teaching in, 104, 105, 109–10, 114; culturally responsive teaching in, 145, 161; differentiated instruction in, 196–97; direct instruction relation to, 180; disciplinary literacy for, 242, 243–44; ESSA relation to, 218; exploration activities in, 188; journals in, 212–13; MTSS relation to, 117; relationship skills in, 125; scripted questions for, 189; specialized language in, 245; word sorts in, 264; yearly plan for, 168, 171–72, *172*
meaning processes, 237
media environments, 23
memory, 263, 363; autobiographical, 6, 26, 358; executive function relation to, 69, 73; long-term, 6, 25, 248, 251, 252, 368; procedural, 6, 9, 25, 370; sequential, 123, 373; vocabulary and, 70; working, 5–6, 26, 27, 60, 376
menstruation, 23, 42, 43
mental health, 25, 50, 122, 351–52; environments relation to, 49; focus relation to, 132; LGBTQIA+ and, 85, 86; resources for, *51*; trauma relation to, 129; young adult literature about, 154
mental health and wellness programs, 352, 368

mental processing, 25
mentors, 325; in advisory programs, 346
menus, 203–4, *204*
Mertens, S. B., 344
metacognition, 6, 368; homework relation to, 66; motivation relation to, 9; self-regulation relation to, 64; SQRR for, 261
Michael (pseudonym), 63
microaggressions, 83–84, 141
middle grades curriculum, 165, 166, 346, 353; differentiation in, 175; interdisciplinary team for, 167
middle school, 368. *See also specific topics*
middle school movement, 321–22, 326–27, 334–35
mile-wide, inch-deep content, 251
mindfulness, 69–70, 127, 368; environments relation to, 130; executive function relation to, 69; for focus, 65; growth mindset and, 129; trauma-informed practice and, 134
mind map, 272
minority students, 80–81
misinformation, 95
missing assignments, 225, 226
mixed-genre units, 171
mobility, 33
modeling, 181, 247, 266, 294, 368; consistency of, 67; of self-regulation, 65, 298; by special-education teacher, 105, 108
Model of the Mind, *4*, 4–5
moral compass, 41, 90, 97
moratorium identity status, 29–30
morphological analysis, 263
motivation, 3, 27, 34, 181, 368; culturally responsive teaching relation to, 140, 161; differentiated instruction relation to, 194; extrinsic, 60–61, 285; for growth mindset, 183; metacognition relation to, 9; resilience relation to, 133; safe spaces relation to, 127–28; self-regulation relation to, 64
MTSS. *See* multitiered system of supports
multiculturalism, 139
multimodal learning, 238
multiple intelligences, 198, 369
multiple languages, literacy in, 245–46
multisyllabic words, 263, 369

multitiered system of supports (MTSS), 99–100, 114–16, 128, 285, 368; behavior management and, 117–19; PBIS compared to, 345; restorative circles and, 286–87
music and dance classes, 152
mutuality, collaboration and, 128
myelination, 47, 369

narrative strategies, in writing, 244
National Association of Secondary School Principals, 351
National Council for Teaching English (NCTE), 144, 195
National Council for the Social Studies (NCSS), 143–44, 146, 161, 195
National Council of Teachers of Mathematics (NCTM), 145, 195
National Direct Instruction Institute, 180
National Forum to Accelerate Middle-Grades Reform, 334, 369
National Health and Nutrition Examination Survey, 45
National Middle School Association, 326
National Science Teachers Association (NSTA), 144, 195
national standards, 167, 369
Nation's Report Card, 218, 369
Natterson, C., 51–52
NCLB. *See* No Child Left Behind Act
NCSS. *See* National Council for the Social Studies
NCTE. *See* National Council for Teaching English
NCTM. *See* National Council of Teachers of Mathematics
negative attention, 289
nervous system, 133, 134, 369
Netherlands, 86
New America, 140–41
Nichols, Morgan, 16, *16*
No Child Left Behind Act (NCLB), 103, 218, 230, 357
nonbinary, 18–19, 76, 86, 87, 343, 369
nonexamples, 252–54, 265
nonfiction reading strategies, 171, 261
nonlinguistic representations, 183, 369
nonverbal communication, 295, 303
North Carolina, 150
note making, 272

note-taking, 271–72, *273*, 374; direct instruction relation to, 181; for retention, 183
novelty, 8, 28–29
NSTA. *See* National Science Teachers Association
Nunley, Kathy, 205
nutrition, 45, 56

obesity, 45; of adolescents, *45*; body image relation to, 46
objectives, 184, 190
observation, 221
obsessive-compulsive personality disorder (OCPD), 19, 25
Olivia (pseudonym), 19, 59–60, 61, 72, 73
omnibus grade, 226
one-minute papers, 220
one teach, one assist (co-teaching model), 105, 111–12
one teach, one observe (co-teaching model), 105, 112, 114, 369
1-3-6 protocol, 159
one-word-answer questions, 252
online instruction, 334
on your own questions, 262
open-ended questions, 188
operational thinking, 25
opinion continuum, 159
opioids, 53
oracy, 156, 369
oral language development, 158, 161
organization, 293, 294
organizational structures, 329, 337, 352–53
Organization of Time in Schools, 339
Organizations and Resources for Cultural, Ethnic, and Racial Identity, *96*
orienting attention, 5, 369
orthographic mapping, 237
orthographic processes, 236
Orton-Gillingham method, 238
outline frameworks, 272

pacing guide, 167, 172, 369
"parable of the polygons," 151
parallel teaching (co-teaching model), 105, 109, 370
parents, 31–32, 52, 349, 353; EAHCA relation to, 101; expectations of, 83; resilience relation to, 37, 132

Parents Bill of Rights, 87
Paris, Django, 139
Parris, Salem, 16, *16*, 171
partial alphabetic phase, 237
partner quizzes, 221
part-time jobs, 77
passion projects, 333
PBIS. *See* positive behavioral interventions and supports
PBL. *See* Project-Based Learning
peer feedback, 221
peer groups, 3
peer pressure, 63, 78, 370
peer relationships, 59, 71, 79–80, 370; identity development relation to, 76, 78, 82; well-being relation to, 55
peers, 33–34, 37
peer support, 128, 199
Pep rally, *18*
performances, 223–24
performance tasks/assessments, 370; differentiated instruction relation to, 199–200; for enduring understanding, 174
permissive parenting, 32
personal bias, 141
phonological processes, 236
physical activity, 3, 44, 46
physical appearance, 30
physical development, 22, 41, 42; psychological development relation to, 23–24; social development relation to, 75
physical disorders, 50
physical-education class, 46
physical instructional space, 298
Piaget, J., 25
plasticity, 194
PLCs. *See* professional learning communities
Poe, Edgar Allen, 109
police, 305–6
policymakers, 223
political climate, 87
political movements, LGBTQIA+ relation to, 86
popularity, 33, 37
pornography, 52
positive affirmation, 24
positive behavioral interventions and supports (PBIS), 115, 280, 282, *283*, *284*, 370; behavior management and, 116, 311; data-based decision-making

and, 283; expectations and, 285; MTSS compared to, 345; universal screening in, 375
Positive Youth Development orientation, 22, 122
posted reminders, 68–69
postsecondary education, 242
power struggles, 299
prealphabetic phase, 237
pre-assessment, 196, 370
preschool years, 24, 26
presentations, 223–24, 254
preventative measures, 300–301
prior knowledge: long-term memory and, 248; reading comprehension relation to, 240–41
privacy, 89
privilege, awareness of, 167
probes, 255
problem-and-solution outline, 267, *271*
problem-based learning, 27–28, 370; indirect instruction relation to, 181; NCTM relation to, 195
problem context, 151
problem-solving: amygdala relation to, 61; frontal cortex relation to, 47; high-level questions for, 186
procedural memory, 6, 9, 25, 370
procedures, 291–94, 299, 311, 370
product, *200*; for assessment, 224; differentiated instruction relation to, 199–200; tiered assignments and, 207
productive struggle, 9
professional development, 325, 329, 350
professional learning communities (PLCs), 172, 286
proficiency, 226
progress monitoring, 114, 115, 116
project-based learning (PBL), 182, *182*, 190, 195, 370; in flexible block schedule, 337–38; indirect instruction relation to, 181; in interdisciplinary team, 342
project rubric, 227–28
prompts, 255
pronouns, 86, 88–89, 91
pronunciation, 263
propinquity, 33
propositional knowledge, 6
protocols for discussing, 370
protocols for responding, 370

proximal development, 35
psychological development, 22; environments relation to, 95, 97; physical development relation to, 23–24
psychology, developmental, 21
psychomotor objectives, 176, 370
puberty, *42*, 48, 370; body image relation to, 43–44; emotions and, 128; hormones and, 45; self-esteem relation to, 55; transgender and nongender-conforming youth relation to, 42
public academic standards, 325
punishment, 9, 370; exclusionary, 280–81; trauma relation to, 123
punishment-based discipline, 282, *282*, 370

QAR. *See* question-answer relationship model
QtA. *See* Questioning the Author
question-answer relationship model (QAR), 262
questioning the author (QtA), 261–62
questions, 252, 255–56, *256–60*; checking-the-box, 251; divergent, 254, *255*; scripted, 186, 188, 189–90; text-dependent, 247, 262; varied, 209, 376
Question Stems for Bloom's Taxonomy, *187*
quizzes. *See* assessment

racial identity, 371; development of, 80; Organizations and Resources for, *96*
racial inequities, 94
RAFT (role, audience, format, and topic) assignments, 209–10, *210*, 371
Ramdass, D., 65–66
REACH program, 67
read-alouds, 246
readiness, 371; differentiated instruction relation to, 193–94, 196–97, 199; flexible grouping relation to, 202; journals relation to, 212–13; in Layered Curriculum, 205; literature circles relation to, 210; varied questions relation to, 209
reading, 171, 273–74; close, 247; as communication, 239; direct instruction for, 180; disciplinary literacy and, 242–43; Ehri's Phases of Word, 237; self-regulation relation to, 236; shared, 246
reading comprehension, 234–35, 273; discipline-specific strategies for, 241;

vocabulary relation to, 233, 239, 240, 264, 274; word recognition and, 263; writing relation to, 238
Rector, Meghan, 15, *15*, 171–72
redirecting question, 255
reflective assessments, 224
reflective practices, 301, 303
refugees, young adult literature about, 154
rehearsal, 5
reinforcing effort and providing recognition, 371
reinforcing language, 297–98, 371
relationships, 22, 122, 145, 350; in advisory programs, 131, 346; in community, 288, 324, 325–26; in co-teaching, 112–13; with families, 343; trust in, 155, 288–90. *See also* peer relationships
relationship skills, 125, 134, 371
reminding language, 298, 371
remote learning, 334
repetition, 5, 9
ReQuest, 262
research, 22, 330; on adolescent brain, 47–48; cultural differences in, 23; on differentiated instruction, 193; in English language arts, 171; on marginalized groups, 138–39; on peer relationships, 78; on writing, 244
resilience, 133, 371; parents relation to, 37, 132; safe spaces relation to, 127; SEL relation to, 132; stress relation to, 121, 134
resilience zone, 133, *133*, 134–35, 371
resources, for mental health, *51*
responding, protocols for, 370
responsible decision-making, 125, 134, 371
Responsive Classroom, 67, 131, 297, 371
responsive discipline, 282, *282*, 371
responsiveness, 193, 371
restitution, 281, 309, 371
restorative circles, 286–87, 311, 372
restorative discipline, 280, 287–88, 311, 372; communication in, 285–86; for fighting, 351
restorative practices, 128, 372
restrictive environments, 101
retellings for situational appropriateness, 372
retention, 6; Bloom's taxonomy for, 184; note-taking for, 183

right there questions, 262
risky behaviors, 53, 372; decision-making relation to, 26–27; environments relation to, 49; Generation Alpha relation to, 48; as hyperarousal, 123; peer pressure and, 78; social media and, 54
Robinson, J. P., 86
Rock, Paper, Scissors, 130–31
role-playing for situational appropriateness, 372
role reciprocity, 103
routines, 372; ELs and, 160; procedures and, 291–94, 299, 311
rubric, *229*, 366, 372; for accountability, 215; feedback and, 224, 229, 230; for literature circles, 211; project, 227–28; tiered assignments and, 207
Russell, S. T., 138

Safe Schools Act, 281
safe spaces, 129, 301, 326, 372; for identity development, 97; motivation relation to, 127–28; trauma-informed practice and, 121, 134. *See also* environments
same-sex marriages, 86
SAMHSA. *See* Substance Abuse and Mental Health Services Administration
Sample Schedule One, *340*
Sample Schedule Two, *341*
Sarah (pseudonym), 62
Say Something, 50
SBG. *See* standards-based grading
scaffolded approach: in journals, 213; for questions, 188; to tiered assignments, 207–8; for word learning, 266
Scarborough's Reading Rope, 235, *235*
schema, 248, 252–54, 372
schizophrenia, 351
school climate, 283, 349, 372
school codes of conduct, 308–11
School Discipline K-12, *281*
school governance, 324–25
school improvement plan, 326
school nurse, 53
school resource officers (SRO), 351
school shootings, anxiety from, 35–36
school-to-prison pipeline, 281
science classes: content standards in, 168; culturally responsive teaching in,

144–45, 161; disciplinary literacy for, 242, 243–44; ESSA relation to, 218; experiential learning in, 180; exploration activities in, 149–50; interdisciplinary team in, 332; lesson planning for, *169–70*; literacy in, 324; PBL in, 181, 182; RAFT (role, audience, format, and topic) assignments, 210; scripted questions for, 189
scientific reasoning, 26
scope and sequence, 168, 372
screen time, 44–45; healthy habits and, 46; well-being relation to, 56
scripted questions, 186, 188, 189–90
SDI. *See* specially designed instruction
second languages, in early adolescence, 8
Second Step, 131
secular effects, 23
SED. *See* significant emotional disability
sedentary lifestyle behaviors, 44, 56
Sedita, Joan, 238
segregation, bias and, 151
SEL. *See* social and emotional learning
selective attention, 5, 372
self-assessments, 30–31, 372; for executive function, 73; rubric relation to, 227
self-awareness, 125, 134, 372
self-confidence, 44
self-contained classroom, 339, 373
self-control, 301
self-correction, 9
self-directed learning, 66, 373
self-discovery, 18–19
self-efficacy, 373; resilience relation to, 133; SEL relation to, 125
self-esteem, 63; culturally responsive teaching relation to, 161; ethnic identity relation to, 80; exploratory curriculum relation to, 348; looping relation to, 343; puberty relation to, 55
self-evaluations, 221
self-exploration, 3
self-expression, experiments in, 77, 97
self-management, 373; emotions relation to, 126; resilience relation to, 133; SEL relation to, 134; of stress, 125
self-perception, 37, 122
self-questioning, 272
self-reflection, 9–10, 47, 68

self-regulation, 32, 49, 59, 72–73, 300, 373; compacting relation to, 207; executive function and, 19, 65, 67, 73; goals relation to, 64, 73; homework relation to, 65–66; interventions for, 68; modeling of, 65, 298; MTSS relation to, 117; parents relation to, 37; reading relation to, 236
self-worth, body neutrality relation to, 46
semantic map, 267, *268–69*, 373
semantic memory, 6, 373
sensory needs, autism and, 129
sentence frames, 156, 160, 373
separation anxiety, 50
sequential memory, 123, 373
service-learning opportunities, 309
setting objectives and providing feedback, 373
7th grade physics menu, *204*
sex education, 46, 51, 52, *53*
sex hormones, 45
sexual activity, 51–52
sexual fluidity, 52, 373
sexual identity. *See* sexual orientation
sexual maturation, 24, 55. *See also* puberty
sexual orientation, 84–85, *85*, 86, 373; experiments with, 88
shared authority, equity and, 150
shared goals, 34
shared reading, 246
shared vision, 327, 373
short-term memory, 5
Siegel, Dan, 126
sight words, 237
signals, 294–95, 373
significant emotional disability (SED), 304–6
sign language, 294–95
silent signal, 295, 373
situational appropriateness, role-playing for, 372
situational interests, 29
Six Models for Co-Teaching, *104*
sleep, 46; attention relation to, 10; mindfulness relation to, 130; puberty relation to, 45
SLOs. *See* student learning outcomes
Smith, Rick, 291, 299
Snap and Wink, 130

social and emotional learning (SEL), 1, 80, 121–22, 134, 297, 373; in advisory programs, 49, 117, 127, 131; identity development and, 90; in interventions, 124–25, 127; middle grades curriculum for, 166; MTSS and, 116; resilience relation to, 132; trauma-informed practice and, 127–28
social awareness, 374; SEL relation to, 134; in social studies classes, 125–26
social belonging, 77, 374
social development, 23; in advisory programs, 90, 91; physical development relation to, 75
social identity, 41, 55
social injustice, young adult literature about, 154
socialization, 32, 33
social justice, 90, 143, 374; culturally responsive teaching relation to, 140; culturally sustaining pedagogy and, 161
social media, 97; body positivity on, 46; risky behaviors and, 54
social norms, 59
social-personality development, 32
social phobia, 50
social sensitivity skills, 27
social skills, 33; peer relationships relation to, 78; in workforce, 77
social studies classes: content standards in, 168; culturally responsive teaching in, 143–44, 146, 161; disciplinary literacy for, 242; experiential learning in, 180; interdisciplinary team in, 332; scripted questions for, 190; social awareness in, 125–26; writing in, 245
speaking, 242–43, 245
special-education teacher, 374; EAHCA relation to, 101; modeling by, 105, 108; SDI and, 118
specialized language, 245
specially designed instruction (SDI), 101–3, 374; co-teaching relation to, 105; special-education teacher and, 118
Spratley, A., 240
SQRR. *See* survey-question-read-reasoning technique
SRO. *See* school resource officers

standards, 374; in lesson planning, 190; middle grades curriculum relation to, 166; national, 167; public academic, 325; in yearly plan, 173
standards-based grading (SBG), 147, 225, 226–27, 374
station teaching (co-teaching model), 105, 110–11, 114, 203, 374
Steinberg, L., 47, 48, 49
stereotypes, 141; awareness of, 167; marginalized groups and, 142
stigma: differentiated instruction relation to, 197; LGBTQIA+ relation to, 86
story mapping, 267, *271*
straight-gay-alliance club, 89, 90
stress, 135; coping strategies for, 126; mindfulness relation to, 130; NCLB and, 218; resilience relation to, 121, 134; self-management of, 125
structured literacy, 238
student autonomy, 32, 297, 374; de-escalation and, 301; environments relation to, 65; in Layered Curriculum, 205; in lesson planning, 168, 171–72; station teaching and, 203
Student Averages, *225*
student-centered, 338, 374
student-centered classrooms, 331
student code of conduct, 310–11
student-government association, 19
student learning outcomes (SLOs), 374; instructional strategies for, 190; in lesson planning, 175
students collaborating, *61, 81*
students getting feedback in ELA, *62*
"students will be able to . . ." (SWBAT), 178
Students Working, *17*
Substance Abuse and Mental Health Services Administration (SAMHSA), 122
The Successful Middle School: This We Believe (AMLE), 46, 87, 326–27, 375
Successful Schools for Young Adolescents (Lipsitz), 2–3, *327*
suicide, 49, 50, 351–52
suicide and crisis lifeline (988), 50
summarizing and note-taking, 374
summative assessment, 224, 374; for evaluation, 222–23; formative assessments compared to, 219

superficial learning, 251
superficial skim, 249
supplemental interventions, 114
support networks, 132
surface-level knowledge, 249
survey-question-read-reasoning technique (SQRR), 261
SWBAT. See "students will be able to . . ."
systemic bias, 141
systemic racism, 80, 374

"take-five" strategy, 117
taking hands, 249
tangential personal connections, 249
task-avoidant behaviors, 19
teacher bowtie, 252
teacher identity, 279
teacher persona, 295–96
teacher preparation, 331, 332
teacher retention, 349
teachers. See specific topics
teacher-to-student conferences, 202–3
teaming, 331. See also co-teaching
team rubric, 228
team teaching (co-teaching model), 105, 344, 375
technological tools, 220; ed-tech games, 222
teen birth rate, 51
"Tell-Tale Heart" (Poe), 109
Template for an Advisory Program, 347
tests. See assessment
text-dependent questions, 247, 262
text selection, 246
theory of mind, 27, 37
think-alouds, 246, 247–48, 266
think and search questions, 262
think-pair-share exercises, 220–21
Think Tac-Toe, 203
Third-Quarter Seventh-Grade Science Planning, 169–70
"3 S strategy," 70
tiered assignments, 197, 207–8, 375
time management, 69, 70
timers, 70
tobacco, 52, 53, 54
to-do lists, 72
Tomlinson, Carol Ann, 193–94, 198, 207
tone, of communication, 297
total physical response (TPR), 375

tracking, 338, 375
traditional scheduling, 337, 375
transgender and nongender-conforming youth, 375; harassment of, 86; puberty relation to, 42; well-being of, 87
transparency: of goals, 184; in SBG, 225, 226; trust relation to, 128
trauma, 18, 82, 127, 134, 212, 306; culturally responsive teaching relation to, 142; executive function relation to, 60; mental health relation to, 129; resilience relation to, 132; SEL relation to, 121; triggers for, 123–24; well-being relation to, 122
trauma-informed practice, 122, 375; in advisory programs, 131, 134; safe spaces and, 121, 134; SEL and, 127–28
triggers, for trauma, 123–24
truancy, LGBTQIA+ relation to, 86
trust: in relationships, 155, 288–90; transparency relation to, 128
Tunmer, W. E., 234–35
Turning Points, 324–26, 375
Twice Exceptional (2E), 101, 375

UDL. See universal design for learning
unambitious content, 250–51
unit plan, 165, 375
universal design for learning (UDL), 99–100, *100*, 101, 375; co-teaching relation to, 105; general-education teacher relation to, 103
universal screening, 283, 375
unplanned examples, 253
USA national phenology network, 8
US Department of Education, 281, 282

Vanderbilt Teaching Center, 184
vapes, 53, 54, *54*
varied and ongoing assessment, 218, 376
varied questions, 209, 376
Vatterott, Cathy, 66
vocabulary, 182, 262–63, 267; in Ehri's Phases of Word Reading, 237; memory and, 70; reading comprehension relation to, 233, 239, 240, 264, 274
voice and choice, 376; homework relation to, 66; in journals, 212; station teaching and, 203

Vomvoridi-Ivanovic, E., 151
Vygotsky, Lev, 35

Ward, J. V., 80
Webb's depth of knowledge (DOK), 184, *185*, 186, 376
weighted blankets, 129
Welcoming Schools, 91, *94*, *95*
well-being, 121, 300, 309, 330; collaboration for, 350; culturally responsive teaching relation to, 161; environments relation to, 56; middle grades curriculum for, 166; peer relationships relation to, 55; in resilience zone, 134; of transgender and nongender-conforming youth, 87; trauma relation to, 122
What Works Clearinghouse, 239
"white saviors," 145
whole-class discussion, 159; facilitation of, 190; varied questions relation to, 209
whole-class reviews, 70
whole-group instruction, 202, 203
William, D., 219–20
Willingham, D. T., 45, 46
Wilt, Amy, 16, *16*, 286
WINDOW mnemonic device, 108
Wing Su, Derald, 83
Winter, Kim K., 13, *13*
word identification, 240
word learning, 265, 266–67. *See also* vocabulary

word map, 267, 376
word recognition, 235–37, 263
Words for Each Level of Bloom's Taxonomy, *179*
word sorts, 263, 264, *264*
word study interventions, 263
workforce, social skills in, 77
working memory, 5–6, 27, 376; executive function relation to, 60; knowledge base relation to, 26
Wormeli, Rick, 226
worrying, 50
writer's workshop, 221
writing, 273–74; as communication, 239; disciplinary literacy and, 242–43; fluency in, 244–45; reading comprehension relation to, 238
writing assessments, 223
writing rope model, 238, *239*

yearly plan, 165, 167, 376; for math classes, 168, 171–72, *172*; standards in, 173
yearly planning for 6th grade mathematics, *172*
young adult literature, 153–55
Youth Risk Behavior Survey (YRBS), 44, 51, 376

zero-tolerance policies, 281, 282, 308, 376
Zimmerman, B. J., 64, 65–66
Zoe (pseudonym), 81–82